Leadership
and
Team Building

UDAY KUMAR HALDAR

Ex-Principal
Swami Vivekananda Institute of Management
and Computer Science
Kolkata

OXFORD

UNIVERSITY PRESS

OXFORD

UNIVERSITY PRESS

Oxford University Press is a department of the University of Oxford.
It furthers the University's objective of excellence in research, scholarship,
and education by publishing worldwide in

Oxford   New York
Auckland   Cape Town   Dar es Salaam   Hong Kong   Karachi
Kuala Lumpur   Madrid   Melbourne   Mexico City   Nairobi
New Delhi   Shanghai   Taipei   Toronto

With offices in
Argentina   Austria   Brazil   Chile   Czech Republic   France   Greece
Guatemala   Hungary   Italy   Japan   Poland   Portugal   Singapore
South Korea   Switzerland   Thailand   Turkey   Ukraine   Vietnam

Oxford is a registered trade mark of Oxford University Press
in the UK and in certain other countries.

Published in India
by Oxford University Press

ISBN-13: 978-0-19-806257-8
ISBN-10: 0-19-806257-5

Typeset in Baskerville
by Jojy Philip
Printed at Manipal Technologies Limited, Manipal
and published by Oxford University Press
22 Workspace, 2nd Floor, 1/22 Asaf Ali Road, New Delhi 110002, India

In the loving memory of

My parents, Durga Rani and Dr L.K. Haldar
My brothers, Pravat Kumar and Krishnendu
My brother-in-law and friend, Mridul Kanti Das

For their sacrifices and love

Foreword

In India, the concept of achieving organizational goals and promoting business through leadership development and team work has gained tremendous momentum. Following liberalization, business houses are now operating in a global village. Competitions are now more acute than ever before. Realizing that people are at the core of any development, organizations are paying sharper attention to enhancing teamwork, removing individual differences, rendering guidance, leading people to work in an orchestral manner, and thus to achieving business objectives and goals. The scope of human resource development includes leadership, in addition to training, organizational development and research, employee feedback and counselling, and career development.

The success of an organization very much depends on the competent leadership at all organizational levels. Leadership is essential for organizational excellence in the global economy. Human resource development and leadership potential development are intertwined, since leadership competence helps a person undertake challenging assignments, encourages and energizes the people, builds effective networks, and ultimately takes the organization to a greater height. Organizations need young leaders too to face the variety of challenges. Moreover, organizations also need to look for candidates with potential for leadership, who can be developed to take leadership roles. Academic courses are increasingly including leadership and team building in their curricula.

I am glad that Dr Haldar, receiving steady help from Ms Juthika, has come out with this book. He has rightly included leadership and team building in one volume. He has developed the book on two themes, considering current organizational and student needs. The author has first focused on theoretical fundamentals and applications of organizational leadership useful to graduate and postgraduate management students. Next, he has dealt with the various aspects of team building. The two appendices are of immense importance. The pedagogical features of the book are unique and appropriate in the selection and sequencing of topics.

All units of the book are interrelated, synchronized, and rhythmic. Two chapters, however, require special mention. Chapter 11, on research and training, would be useful for students who would get adequate guidelines from the chapter contents. To motivate students to participate in such research survey, the author has included the survey findings of his students used in their dissertations and projects. In Chapter 12, on team building activities and outcomes, Dr Haldar has drawn on his long experience in the industry. For each activity he has stated the organizational need, then sequentially arrived at the outcome, and, most importantly, discussed after-activity review, approval seeking, and documentation. Usually most team-building activities remain undocumented, and so people cannot benefit from them. I am sure that organizations would be greatly benefited from this chapter. Moreover, they can adopt the stated sequence.

After discussing all topics on leadership and team building, the author has included an essay on followership in Appendix A, as focusing only on leaders and leadership cannot make teams function effectively. Appendix B, which contains sketches of the biographies of seven renowned leader-achievers, is useful in understanding the steps initiated by them and is motivating. In various chapters of this book, the author has discussed in detail the principles, practices, and other aspects of leaders and leadership development, supported by case studies.

Another interesting aspect of the book is that in each chapter, the opening case is picked up at the chapter-end and discussed further as the closing case. This will enhance the interest of the students and other readers in the subject. Almost all the chapters furnish glimpses of practices in various organizations.

The author has shown originality in developing the entire book. I am sure that Dr Haldar will continue to contribute to the student community and HR fraternity by writing books. I wish him the best.

Udai Pareek
Distinguished Visiting Professor
Indian Institute of Health Management Research
Jaipur

4 June 2009

Preface

Business organizations today are witnessing a phenomenon that urges them to question their underlying assumptions and practices. The global markets are volatile and hence, competition is more acute than ever before. Added to this, the struggle for limited resources at the global level is another perennial business concern.

It is rightly said that the longest journey is the journey inwards and today organizational heads are compelled to search for leaders and leadership potential among their managers to achieve business goals and excellence. Each employee should have a vision about the future with respect to his/her role in organizational excellence. The need for developing potential leaders has never been felt so much before.

This collective awakening has brought a paradigm shift in the thought process of organizational heads, who are instrumental in developing leaders and encouraging people to work in teams. Gradually, affiliation to departmental structures in organizations is giving way to working in teams, wherein each member brings his/her skills, assumptions, and competencies. Today, there are even virtual teams, distinctive in the geographical dispersion of its members, that work to achieve common goals. With transformations in business processes, decision making, and communication strategies, building and managing teams have given rise to a different breed of leaders possessing a wide array of skills.

Effectiveness is the ultimate consideration for any team or organization. Due to the diversification of the workforce, the needs of team members have significantly increased. Achieving organizational goals and promoting business, through leadership development and team building, have gained a tremendous momentum as well. Also, various researches are being undertaken to explore the causal relationships between different organizational variables. Understanding leaders and leadership development, thus, has become an important area of study. Also, it has introduced an all-new perspective in the art of managing teams.

ABOUT THE BOOK

This comprehensive textbook is designed to meet the needs of graduate and postgraduate management students. It will help students understand and appreciate the various attributes, styles, theories, and dimensions of leadership behaviour, as well as identify with the different dimensions of teams and team effectiveness. Written in a student-friendly manner, the book focuses on theoretical fundamentals and concepts, which are explained through case studies and exhibits.

The book has a unique feature—each chapter opens and closes with an organization-specific case study to focus the topic and broaden the reader's understanding of business practices. The opening case explores a problem related to the topic of the chapter, thus setting the tone for what is to come. After a comprehensive discussion on the topic, the closing case resolves the problem, thereby adding depth to the concepts learnt. This also makes the topics more interesting and, thereby, augments the process of learning.

Few assignments and critical thinking questions are also given at the end of each chapter. These will enable the students to gain an insight into the concepts. The book will also prove to be highly useful for research scholars as it presents a wide variety of research activities along with their outcomes.

PEDAGOGY

The book facilitates the students to gain an insight and clarity through in-depth case studies, exhibits, and examples drawn mainly from the Indian context. Following are the various pedagogical features of this book.

- Chapters contain glimpses of practices in reputed organizations, which will aid readers to bridge the gap between theories and practice.
- Each chapter includes a summary followed by a glossary of key terms, which will help readers revise the important topics in the chapter.
- Chapter-end concept review and critical thinking questions will enable students to recollect the principal concepts learnt therein. In addition, the critical thinking questions will facilitate the application of theory in real-life situations.
- The assignments and questionnaires will assist students to pursue field survey in their dissertation work.
- Select references and web resources provided at the end of each chapter will encourage the acquisition of further knowledge inputs.

CONTENTS AND STRUCTURE

This textbook contains two parts: leaders and leadership covered in Chapters 1 to 8, and team building and activities covered in Chapters 9 to 12. The book also includes two appendices titled Followership and Biographies of Leaders.

Chapter 1, Leadership—A Conceptual Background, gives an introduction to leadership and discusses the difference between managers and leaders. It also focuses on the prerequisites of organizational leaders, the attributes of effective leaders, and other aspects of leadership.

Chapter 2, Attributes of Leaders, talks about the concept of power and authority, types and sources of power, leadership skills and traits, intelligence and leadership, and influence tactics.

Chapter 3, Perspectives on Effective Leadership Behaviour, describes the two dimensional leadership styles and leadership taxonomy.

Chapter 4, Theories of Effective Leadership, explains contingency leadership theories in detail.

Chapter 5, Contemporary Leadership Styles, discusses transactional, transformational, and charismatic leadership, value-based leadership, spiritual and servant leadership, boundary spanning and team leadership, and the latest theory—Level 5 leadership.

Chapter 6, Motivation, Satisfaction, and Performance, covers briefly the theories of motivation, significance and measurement of job satisfaction, and their contribution to performance. It also includes causes of demotivation. The chapter annexure contains an internationally acclaimed multifaceted scale to measure job satisfaction.

Chapter 7, Leadership Behaviour—Dimensions and Assessment, highlights leader behaviour, assesses leadership potential, managerial derailment, self-defeating behaviour, and development pipeline and planning.

Chapter 8, Leadership Development, describes various facets of leader development, need for leadership, and leadership pipeline. This chapter contains two flowcharts on leadership development for better elucidation.

Chapter 9, Essentials of Building and Managing Teams, talks about various facets of teams, theoretical approaches to groups, types of teams (including virtual teams), shaping team behaviour, fostering team creativity, collective wisdom, and team-building skills.

Chapter 10, Team Effectiveness, discusses the determinants of group processes and team performance, leaders' skills and behaviours in teams, interpersonal competence, and team effectiveness. It includes the team effectiveness leadership model (TELM) propounded by Ginnett.

Chapter 11, Research Findings and Training, starts with a discussion on two researches—one on leadership and the other on team building. Snapshots of few researches, including leadership styles in small businesses, have also been discussed, followed by research questions. The chapter ends with the impact of training on leadership.

Chapter 12, Team Building—Activities and Outcomes, presents ten team-building activities. Each activity starts with organizational need, purpose, materials used, team composition, duration of each session, tools used, physical settings, group size, procedure used, after-activity reviews, approval seeking, and documentation.

Appendix A, Followership, underscores the significance of followers in accomplishing team goals, roles and responsibilities of followers, importance of trust along with an equation, and strategies for promoting followership.

Appendix B, Leader Achievers, sketches the biographies of some well-known business tycoons.

I would appreciate all suggestions towards the improvement of the book. Readers may contact me at ukhaldar@rediffmail.com.

Uday Kumar Haldar

Acknowledgements

I am extremely grateful to the late Prof. Udai Pareek for writing the foreword, without which the book would have remained incomplete.

I am indebted to Dr Sushant Tharappan, Associate Vice President, Infosys Technologies, Bangalore, for sharing information on the leadership development practices at Infosys. Dr Tharappan further advised me to include a topic on leadership passages, as propounded by management thinker Ram Charan, Steve Drodder, and Jim L. Noel.

Prof. Dr S.N. Roy, Director, Indian Institute of Social Welfare and Business Management (IISWBM), has always been a source of motivation and a role model to me. I do express my sincere thanks to him.

I am extremely grateful to Prof. Ashoke K. Dutta, Director, Rajib Gandhi Indian Institute of Management, Shillong, and former Director, IISWBM, who has always motivated and encouraged me.

Prof. P.K. Misra, Prof. D.K. Sanyal, and Prof. P. Purokayastha of IISWBM have always extended various types of academic supports to me in all my educational endeavours. I am grateful to all of them.

Mr Indranil Bhattacharya, Regional HR East, TITAN Industries Limited, helped me by providing inputs on 360-degree feedback practices along with other knowledge inputs.

I do acknowledge the contributions of Ms Juthika Sarkar (logistics coordinator in a multinational telecom organization in Kolkata) for sharing academic information while developing the book, especially for the chapters on effective leadership theories, contemporary leadership styles, and leadership development and an appendix on leader-achievers.

I extend my sincere thanks to Mr P.K. Chatterjee, Senior Vice President (HR), Duncans Group of Companies, for allowing me to use the contents from his lecture material at the ISTD monthly lecture meeting organized by the Kolkata chapter.

Mr Sanjay Das, Associate Vice President, Tata Tele Service (former General Manager, Reliance Communication, Kolkata), has always helped in enriching the content, providing knowledge inputs at all stages of developing the book.

Saurabhi Chaturvadi of Shri Vaishnav Institute of Technology and Science, Indore, has helped me by sending a questionnaire on identifying factors affecting team effectiveness, which she used in a research conducted along with Pallavi Bhatnagar and Dr Rishu Roy.

Dr Tania Das (Shaw) helped me in framing the table of contents of this book at the initial stage. I do express my profound gratitude to her.

I am indebted to my colleagues Prof. Dr Kum Kum Mukherjee, and Prof. Buddhadeep Mukherjee and Prof. Dr Sumati Roy of IISWBM, for helping me broaden my knowledge spectrum. They have always extended emotional support throughout my journey.

I acknowledge the contributions of my students Ms Lipi Ghosh and Ms Sureeta Sen of IISWBM for sharing their dissertation findings, and Ms Satarupa Sarkar (TCS, Bangalore) for sharing information of her project findings.

Mr Sushanta Das and Mr Sujay Chakraborty have helped me in structuring and enriching the activities section in the book.

My daughter Sonali, son Amlan, and daughter-in-law Mitil have always been my source of motivation.

This book has become a reality because of the extreme love and continuous encouragement of my wife Sikha, who has transformed my life, inspired me to author books, and has led me from distress to de-stress in many instances.

I am indebted to the editorial team of Oxford University Press in bringing out this book.

While preparing the manuscript I have referred to many books, websites, and other knowledge resources. Mentioning each of them would be close to impossible, and hence, I have mentioned only a few here. But I do extend my thanks to all the scholars, writers, and managers who have helped me directly and indirectly.

I would appreciate all suggestions towards the improvement of this book. Readers may contact me at ukhaldar@rediffmail.com.

Uday Kumar Haldar

Contents

Part 1 Leadership

Appendices

Part 1

LEADERSHIP

CHAPTER 1

Leadership—A Conceptual Background

Learning Objectives

After studying this chapter, you will be able to

▶ Understand the changing nature of managerial work
▶ Explain the importance of leaders in a globalized environment
▶ State the difference between leaders and managers
▶ Define the changing paradigm of leadership in organizations
▶ Identify the various dimensions of leadership
▶ Understand leadership effectiveness and the need for developing leaders
▶ Define leadership in different cultures
▶ State the universal inner structure of effective leaders

In Search of Self-management Dimensions

Modern Caterers (MC),* headquartered in Kolkata, had been in business for more than three decades and acquired a good reputation. In the initial years, word-of-mouth publicity helped MC to get new business, even from distant places. Accordingly, MC had expanded its business to nearby cities, with a focus on adding industrial clients. The systematic upgradation and marketing of its services through various media channels added to its popularity. MC, owned by Mr Barin Ganguly, was one of the most admired organizations in social and corporate circles.

Till very recently, the business had witnessed an exponential growth and

---

* The case is based on a reputed caterer who gained huge popularity in the 1980s, expanded his business, but could not sustain it and so lost substantial market share. The name of the caterer has been changed.

the organization's human resources had grown manifold. MC had expanded its operations to Chennai, Mumbai, and Ahmedabad. It had recruited many chefs, waiters, supervisory personnel, and servers from the region, deploying the existing supervisory persons to take over the new offices as managers. But it was in 2006 that Mr Ganguly started feeling the need for a relook into the business processes. During an international seminar, organized by a nationally acclaimed professional institute, MC could not deliver the services on time. The institute strongly criticized the matter and took it up with the caterer's manager-in-charge, Mr Chaudhuri. It pointed out a series of lapses and also the unprofessional way of handling of the situation by Mr Chaudhuri, who got impatient and reacted to these allegations in an unacceptable manner. The institute, in its meeting, decided to look for a new caterer. When Mr Ganguly came to know about all this, he decided to pacify and renegotiate, but the discussion turned ineffective, what with Mr Chaudhuri reacting vehemently to the comments made by the organizers. Mr Ganguly failed to control the situation.

In another instance, a client wanted MC to undertake the interior decoration of the ceremony venue in addition to the catering. But Mr Chaudhuri expressed his inability to fulfil this requirement. Further discussions were futile and the client did not conclude the contract with MC. There were some other cases where waiters entered into arguments with clients/invitees, which led to serious issues later. One such case turned nasty because neither Mr Ganguly nor the manager was present at the venue. The host could not manage the situation and lodged a legal complaint against MC.

With business growing, the desired skill set of most of the employees was an attention area. The employees failed to understand the impact of their role in relation to the other people at MC. Interpersonal sensitivity and communication skills were low and resulted in MC losing many corporate customers and reputed social clubs. Mr Ganguly tried to analyse the various possible reasons behind these losses, with a view to rejuvenate the business. He felt that most of the disputes were a result of people having different beliefs, choices, attitudes, etc.

Learning points

1. Organizations need to develop a positive work culture.
2. A manager must have the ability to arbitrate.
3. Networking is essential for growth in business.
4. A manager should be able to assign responsibilities to people with the right attributes.
5. People at the helm of affairs should have a vision.

INTRODUCTION

The Indian economy continues to grow at a rapid pace, led by information technology-based services and the business process outsourcing (BPO) industry. Attracting and retaining talent is the key issue for companies. Organizations continually strive to improve the multi-skilling and multi-tasking abilities of employees, outsource several business processes, control production costs, reduce overheads, and undertake similar measures. Thereafter, the strategic challenge for companies is to develop leaders fast enough to keep up with the growth of the business and cope with the changes in the environment.

A leader needs to have certain characteristics—a positive attitude, honesty, consistency in behaviour, perseverance, and love for people. Moreover, a leader must be a good person; must have distinctive leadership characteristics—patience, kindness, goodness, faithfulness, gentleness, and self-control. He/she has to exhibit these characteristics in the course of working with others and leading team-mates, group members, and others.

In this chapter, you will be introduced to concepts regarding the nature of managerial work, leaders and leadership, distinction between managers and leaders, the changing paradigm of leadership, the prerequisites of organizational leaders, and, at the end, the universal inner structure of effective leaders.

THE BUSINESS SCENARIO

Business organizations are now operating in a dwindling business environment—domestic and international—and in a global village. Most of the modern industrialized world is unable to extract the best from the available human resources. The paradox is that to a large degree, we are constrained by the level of employee productivity. Huge investments are made in technology upgradation, process improvement, structuring system, and so forth. Collaterally, improving human productivity must be a never-ending effort.

Most of the modern industrialized world is focusing on the available human inventory. This organizational phenomenon permeates every aspect of business. Performance excellence leads to business excellence which is 'doing the simple things perfectly so that more time and money can be spent on the more complex issues'.

Any seminar information brochure on leadership will emphasize that as a result of globalization, we are witnessing integration or commonality in the context of businesses, economies, and societies across the world. It is an era of numerous social, economic, and cultural convergences, notwithstanding divergent consumer preferences, varied business perspectives, and atypical geopolitical conditions among nations. We all are required to look at the business scenario, particularly from a down-to-earth perspective, and initiate steps to survive. Let us take a brief look at the prevailing business scenario.

A Few Instances

In this section, examples of businesses like Shoppers Stop and the Future Group and of sectors and industries such as aviation, information technology, outsourcing services, and academia are highlighted (Majumdar and Dmonte 2008).

Till a few months back, Shoppers Stop, a leading chain of retail stores in India, was busy chasing headhunters to find candidates 'willing to join'. However, the company has decided to be very selective in filling up new vacancies and will recruit only when new stores come up. The Future Group says that its companies owning large retail chains, such as Pantaloons and Big Bazaar, have cut people cost by 1 per cent by linking salaries with performance and further emphasizes that 'human capability is infinite and multi-tasking is the order of the day'.

In the aviation sector, Jet Airways laid off 800 employees and announced a further lay-off of 1150 employees. But, the laid-off employees were reinstated within 24 hours after a public and political outcry. The company is still reeling under the pressure and is experimenting. In the same sector, Kingfisher Airlines has slashed the salaries of its co-pilots by 90 per cent.

Wipro Technologies has put 4–5 per cent employees under the scanner for non-performance though it says that 'this is a regular annual exercise'. Bangalore-based IT service provider MphasiS (part of Electronic Data Systems, commonly known as EDS) has reduced hiring plans by almost 50 per cent. It had earlier announced that it would recruit 8000 people, but now the company plans to recruit only 4000 people. TeamLease, the largest staffing solution company of India, was earlier recruiting people without much emphasis on job specifications. Now TeamLease has changed its recruitment strategy. It is obvious that we have moved from 'plenty' to 'paltry'. Just a few years back, McKinsey, the global management consulting firm, estimated that India's factories would need 73 million workers by 2015 (50 per cent more than the existing strength today).

All the above facts are posing threats and challenges to organizations, which are now finding ways and means to get more from people and encourage team work. Thus, they are looking for leaders capable of uniting, motivating, and driving the workforce and producing results. Let us now understand the activities of managers and their roles.

MANAGERIAL ACTIVITIES AND ROLES

Managers are organizational leaders who perform a variety of roles. A particular 'behaviour pattern' is expected of them. In order to perform their roles, managers need certain skills, that is, the ability to perform the roles effectively. To gain these skills, managers must have appropriate traits, a variety of individual attributes. Let us now focus on understanding the roles, skills, and traits of organizational leaders.

Roles

Role comprises the behaviour pattern expected of a person. The well-known strategic management guru Henry Mintzberg (1973), in one of his most authoritative studies, proposed the approaches used by managers. According to Mintzberg, broadly, the three types of roles are interpersonal, informational, and decision making.

The interpersonal role encompasses figurehead, leadership, and liaison roles. In order to discharge the interpersonal role, a manager has to represent his/her organization as a figurehead and perform ceremonial duties (greet visitors, attend weddings, entertain customers and certification bodies, attend invitations to social events conducted by civil authorities). As a figurehead, he/she also links the organization with the environment. As an organizational leader, he/she gets things done through people. He is also responsible and accountable for the actions and performance of his/her subordinates. He/she must keep in mind that a manager's performance is the sum of the performances of the junior colleagues, and he/she has to accomplish more than other junior members. Moreover, the liaison role, he/she works with everyone (insiders and outsiders), develops networks and partners, builds and joins alliances and coalitions, and constructs relationships.

While discharging the informational role, a manager has to monitor the inflow of information, disseminate information, and act as a spokesperson. To monitor, he/she has to constantly look for useful information, search both inside and outside the organization, talk to junior colleagues, and develop a network for collecting information from all possible sources.

The disseminator role includes conveying factual information in meetings, analysing and interpreting data, and providing the required information to subordinates. As a spokesperson, he/she transmits information to people outside and keeps the external agencies well informed, and hence, he/she must speak diplomatically.

A leader has to take decisions with regard to entrepreneurship, handling disturbances, allocating resources, and negotiating. He/she needs entrepreneurial zeal to improve the departments or cost centres, consider technological upgradation, and launch innovative products. He/she is required to make difficult decisions, think analytically, undertake problem-solving, and ultimately arrive at solutions. The leader has to assess resource requirements and provide the right resources in order to achieve the business goals. He/she has to negotiate, whenever required, between the employees and outsiders (in the turbulent business scenario of today) using knowledge, experience, maturity, pragmatism, wisdom, and authority.

Managers have to undertake challenges, accepting a variety of new types of assignments, and deal with improvement projects. Mintzberg (1973) explains in a very lucid manner how a manager should handle and deal with the improvement projects: 'The manager as supervisor of improvement project may be likened to the juggler. At any one point in time he has a number of balls in the air. Periodically, one comes down, receives a short burst of energy, and goes up again. Meanwhile, new balls wait on the sideline and, at random intervals, old balls are discarded and new ones added.' This excerpt is meaningful with regard to resource utilization, leading to the successful achievement of team goals.

The role of senior managers includes identity-creating, enabling, synergizing, balancing, networking, futuristic thinking, impact-making, and superordinating.

- **Identity-creating** is producing a special place or image by launching employee welfare measures, installing technological innovations, and initiating an optimal method.
- **Enabling** includes developing resources, providing an improved environment, empowering junior colleagues, and giving them challenging tasks.
- **Synergizing** refers to motivating people to work in teams, getting more and more from people, matching human resource with other resources, and maximizing the output from the workforce.
- **Balancing** encompasses encouraging subordinates to comply with rules, expectations, procedures, and norms, considering failure to

conformance, using the creative potential of subordinates, maintaining a balance between conformance and creativity, and achieving results using innovation.

- **Networking** means realizing social obligations, sharing technical know-how, and establishing linkages with technical and financial organizations and educational institutes.
- **Futuristic thinking** means discharging duties for the survival and growth of the organization, meeting emerging needs, withstanding market pressures, and foreseeing and preparing for changes.
- **Impact-making** refers to distinctly visible contribution, value addition to the product that influences customers, converting customers to ambassadors of the product and the company, and developing products that have competitive advantage.
- **Superordinating** is inculcating a sense of pride in the employees, ensuring a sense of fulfilment in the workforce, constantly motivating the workforce, and making the members feel that their contribution to the society organisation organisation is valued.

Major research findings about the nature of managerial work reveal that a manager's pace of work is hectic and unrelenting, the content of work is varied and fragmented, and many managerial activities are reactive (Yukl 2007). Typical managers work for long hours and take work home to keep their desk clear. Their content of work varies widely and is never of routine type. Added to this, they go ahead with a certain consideration; but actually, in view of changing situations, they are required to follow an alternative course of action. Thus, they become reactive though they desire to be proactive.

Managers Take Responsibilities

A company is a social institution. Its existence depends upon its harmonious relationship with the multiple segments of society. The harmonious relationship originates and emanates from positive responsiveness of the firm to society. The responsibilities of a manager arise out of the social interactions during the pursuit of business. A manager interacts with the employees, shareholders, distributors and retailers, customers (end-users), suppliers, regulatory bodies, etc. The interactions may be direct or indirect. In any case, the firm has to uphold a positive image. Upholding the firm's image is primarily the responsibility of managers.

The responsibilities of managers pervade many segments in an organization. Managers bear the responsibility towards employees, customers, shareholders, suppliers, retailers, unions, industry and competition, society, and the government.

A manager's responsibility towards customers (end-users) includes understanding and finding their stated and implied needs, providing the desired quality at a reasonable price, and ensuring on-time delivery in addition to considering the safety, purity, hygiene, and aesthetic appeal of the product.

Responsibility towards shareholders encompasses distributing dividends on a regular basis.

Developing suitable wage and salary structure and compensation packages, ensuring a safe and healthy work environment, providing facilities as stated in regulatory frameworks, such as the Factory Act and Safety Act, are the responsibilities towards employees.

Responsibility towards suppliers includes developing contacts with them, maintaining a two-way relationship, and helping to keep their wheel of production moving.

Organizations should bear the responsibility towards distributors and retailers suitably.

Unions and associations represent the collective strength of the work-force. Helping them to register with the competent authority, recognizing them, and involving and encouraging them in the decision-making process are some of the responsibilities of managers.

Responsibilities towards the government include fulfilling all the regulatory obligations, paying all taxes, dues, and duties regularly and fairly, and registering the company with the registrar of companies. An organization operates in a society. Therefore, it has to discharge its responsibility towards the surroundings and society by not polluting the environment and by ensuring that people can breathe fresh air and drink pure water.

In order to discharge the stated responsibilities, managers or the organizational leaders need a variety of skills. The skills definitely include technological skills; but what a manager needs more is to get along with people, unite various persons from diverse cultures and dissimilar academic backgrounds, and divergent views to achieve a common goal. A leader has to execute multiple responsibilities including dealing with individual differences. Changes in the nature of managerial work are discussed in the next section. The nature of managerial work is continuously changing.

Changes in the Nature of Managerial Work

Societal and cultural issues are now influencing the management of organizational personnel. In India, following globalization and economic liberalization, foreign companies are setting up their businesses individually in India or collaborating with Indian companies. Thus, people from widely different cultures and philosophies are changing the business environment, more so in the case of people of dissimilar and diverse cultures collaborating and working together. Depending on their level in the organizational hierarchy, diverse people are formulating the policy in multiple functional areas. People from different countries are impacting society as well. The cultural diversity of the workforce within the organization is increasing.

Computer and telecommunication technology is enabling storing of huge amounts of data and providing information in the desired format to anyone located anywhere in the world at any time. The scope of information technology has broadened. As a consequence, the demands from responsible persons have increased. Yukl (2007) emphasizes that as electronic communication becomes more important, leaders will need to adjust their behaviour to align with the new technologies.

Many organizations are decentralizing their activities, eliminating departments by switching over to self-managed groups, implementing a semi-autonomous work culture by splitting the organization into smaller units, flattening by removing middle levels to the extent required, introducing concepts of work levels, and restructuring around product teams that cut across functional or geographical domains. In team-based organizations, the persons responsible for heading the teams rely heavily on coaching and facilitating rather than directing and controlling.

These are some instances of change in the present organizational scenario. In order to cope with the changes in the socio-cultural, economic, and political spheres, the nature of managerial work is constantly changing and so too is the work content of a manager. The above changes need more 'leading' and less 'managing' in the context of the theory of demand, constraint, and choices.

Theory of demand, constraint, and choices

The 10 managerial roles identified by Mintzberg (1973) describe the behaviour commonly used while executing the tasks assigned to or identified by a manager. However, descriptive research indicates that managers also have unique role requirements that are specific to a particular type of managerial position in a particular type of organization (Yukl 2007). Yukl (2007) emphasizes that demands, constraints, and choices define the job of a manager and are strong influencers of the behaviour of everyone who occupies the managerial position.

Demands   Managers have to perform several activities to discharge the responsibilities assigned to them. They have to achieve quantitative targets within a scheduled time-frame, as well as meet the qualitative requirements. They have to conform to the set company standards, comply with the norms, and adhere to the code of conduct.

In quality system-certified organizations, a manager has to ensure compliance with the documented system, procedures, and instructions. He/she also has to maintain records in the prescribed formats.

A purchase manager has to consider the budget, a quality manager has to ensure compliance with the quality standards, a maintenance manager has to undertake certain preventive maintenance to reduce machine downtime, a material manager has to guarantee the availability of the right material of right quality at the right time, and a production manager has to keep the wheel of production rolling.

These are some examples of demands on managers in their respective functional areas. Some demands can be generic, being identical for all managers of an organization, and some demands specific to a functional area, encompassing operational requirements.

Constraints   Organizational rules, procedures, standing instructions, and the environment limit managers' way of working. But these are essential for a consistent response against the same stimuli. Under identical situations, different managers may initiate different actions based on their perceptions, which may lead to disparity and disproportionate treatments. If for the same grievance two persons receive different treatment in the form of benefits, it may lead to labour unrest. Thus, constraints like bureaucratic rules and regulations ensure consistent managerial responses.

Legal constraints include labour laws, environmental legislations, safety regulations, etc. Upgraded technology creates constraints for the segment of people not acquainted with that particular technology. Customer orientations and market considerations are constraints on the type of products and services—constraints on the product designers and production persons.

Choices   Managers are left with choices of certain activities that one may do though not required to do. In a particular managerial position, one may have the opportunity of applying discretion with regard to what to do and how to do it. Demands and constraints limit choices in the short run, but over a longer time period, a manager has some opportunities to modify demands and remove or circumvent constraints and thereby expand choices (Yukl 2007).

A manager can set the priorities of objectives, select strategies to pursue the objectives, consider complexities of the tasks where he/she has to be deeply involved, build bridges of relationships, decide upon what responsibilities to delegate and to whom, and finally the ways to exercise authority and influence followers.

The wide variations in managerial tasks, in addition to the demands and constraints, make managers flexible in their execution. They may not be successful if they are rigid. But, the flexibility does not permit them to compromise with the demands and constraints; they can only be so in implementing organizational policies. For being flexibly rigid, managers need leadership skills.

UNDERSTANDING LEADERS AND LEADERSHIP

Let us recall what Mahatma Gandhi said in his time that is valid even today. He said, 'I suppose that leadership at one time meant muscle; but today it means getting along with people.'

The term leader refers to any person at any level of an organization, in any field, who significantly influences others, for good or bad, to achieve the organization's mission or the mission of the people of the organization. The term is broad enough, having questionable utility.

Modern leadership studies view leadership as one of the most observed and least understood phenomena on earth. A leader creates things, innovates ways of accomplishment, mobilizes resources, aligns people, sets directions, generates mandates, bears responsibility for the overall outcome and impacts, and gets followers to achieve the organizational mission. Good and effective leaders are scarce. Particularly when it comes to finalizing a plan, we find serious shortcomings among decision-makers, and while implementing any plan or project, we find serious shortcomings among executives.

A leader must be able to plan considering all inputs and constraints, and have a vision as it provides direction, for without direction, there is no real benefit in undertaking planning. He/she has to take charge of a workgroup and share the vision with his/her people. He/she has to constantly motivate and inspire people and this should be done through personal example. Recall that the behaviour that wins is 'practice what you preach'.

You also can become a good leader if you make a conscious commitment and put consistent effort to develop leadership skills. But on the positive side, anyone who is willing to make the effort can become a good leader. It is needless to mention that good leadership is critical to business success;

your efforts to improve your leadership skills will be amply rewarded. By working on the five key aspects of leadership—planning, developing a vision, and sharing the vision, taking charge and accepting challenges, and motivating people through personal examples—you can become a good leader of your small business or the organization you are working for.

Leadership, a process adopted by a leader, refers to an extremely wide range of roles that have profound influence on the world. The range is so wide that sometimes the term 'leadership' seems to include almost everyone. In fact, some corporations believe that all organizational managers are leaders. The need for leaders at every level and in every domain has always been felt.

In the present day, organizations are in desperate need of good and effective leaders capable of producing results. The predominant role of leaders in the context of organizational success can hardly be overstated. It is the leaders who can transform an organization, and their capabilities can make or break an organization. The need for leadership was never felt so acutely before as in the present time. Leadership in organizations or managerial leadership occurs in all groups of people, regardless of caste, region, culture, geography, or nationality.

Leadership is a fascinating phenomenon gaining increasing importance in business organizations, particularly in today's highly complex and fast-changing situations. Leadership is an ongoing process. It is both a science and an art; it is a science because it is a field of scholarly enquiry and an art because it develops through cultivation and practice. Managers get work done by their subordinates while leaders work with their followers. Leaders involve themselves in the work as they prefer to work in teams.

Leadership characteristics include insight, initiative, inspiration, involvement, improvisation, individuality, and implementation. To survive and grow in a competitive business environment, organizations develop leadership potential. Leadership development is about supporting, propping up, buoying up, and developing an employee through experience sharing to enhance his/her problem-solving skills.

The concept and process of leadership are not new; yet homegrown companies and multinationals operating in the country are not only stepping up the pace of activity but are also virtually reinventing the development of leadership. The developmental efforts, if successfully implemented, help to get 'more from people' both individually and collectively. Those who have been good at leadership development are getting better, while those who had not put so much emphasis on it in the past are now focusing a lot more on this crucial issue. The disheartening side of the leadership development effort is that it puts the spotlight on those who are not so good, though the best talents get recognized. Leadership is the capacity to frame plans that will succeed and the faculty to persuade others to carry them out in the face of all difficulties.

In daily parlance and in an organizational situation, leadership is about what to do and getting that done. In management terminology, leadership can be expressed as capability and effectiveness. Some definitions of leadership are given in Chapter 3.

Need for Leadership

Renowned management consultants, organizational stalwarts, and academicians are of the opinion that leadership must be practised at all levels of an organization. More recently, organizations have realized that strengthening the connection between and alignment of the efforts of individual leaders and the systems through which they influence organizational operations can develop leadership. This has led to a differentiation between 'leader development' and 'leadership development' (Day 2000).

Leader development focuses on the personal development of the leader, such as the personal attributes desired in a leader, and the desired ways of behaving, and ways of thinking or feeling. On the contrary, leadership development focuses on the development of leadership as a process. This will include the interpersonal relationships, the social influence process, and the team dynamics between the leader and his/her team at the dyad level, the contextual factors surrounding the team such as the perception of organizational climate, and the social network linkages between the team and other groups in the organization.

Contextually, it is to be mentioned that Bhargava (2003) has provided a definition of organizational climate coined by Tagiuri and Litwin in 1968: 'internal environment of an organization that is experienced by its members, which influences their behaviour'. Organizational climate arises from and is sustained by the systematized and customary practices of the organization and its members. It influences members' behaviours and attitudes. It helps the leaders unify people, create bonds between them, remove individual differences, creatively build trust between team-mates and self, discharge their roles to achieve business goals. Summarily, leadership helps to

• Promote synergy
• Collect people and unify them

- Grow interpersonal bonds
- Remove individual differences
- Restore team cohesiveness
- Build trust between team-mates and self
- Discharge roles effectively and efficiently
- Promote dynamics within team-mates and with self
- Impact members' behavioural modification
- Recognize team efforts, resulting in effective team performance

In view of the foregoing discussions, we need to understand the differences between leaders and managers. Organizations need leaders. Multinational companies need global leaders who are required to consider cross-cultural issues and act accordingly. The Aditya Birla Group considers cross-cultural diversity as a major issue (see Box 1.1).

Box 1.1   Why the Aditya Birla Group needs global leaders

At the micro level, the Aditya Birla Group (ABG) is constantly forming communities and relationships in new ways. Across the world, more than 2 billion people use cell-phones and 1 trillion e-mails are sent every year. ABG works not only globally but also instantaneously. In the context of ABG, Aditya Vikram Birla set his sights outside India, making significant on-the-ground investments across South East Asia. Today, 60 per cent of ABG's revenue comes from outside the country as compared to 30 per cent in 2000, and 35 per cent of ABG's capital employed is outside India.

Globalization is a necessity, not a choice. The natural corollary to that is the need to create global leaders who have the ability to be effective across geographies, nationalities, and cultures and excel at collaboration, innovation, and managing change. An individual's hard-wiring can greatly impact how a leader operates globally.

Source: Based on a speech delivered by Kumar Mangalam Birla at the All India Management Association on 21 February 2009.

LEADERS AND MANAGERS

Leaders differ from managers. Managers exercise control, while leaders create systems. Managers endeavour for the survival of the business, but leaders endeavour for its survival as well as its growth. Some managers can definitely be viewed as organizational leaders, but not all. In any organization, all leaders are managers but all managers are not the leaders. Table 1.1 contains a comprehensive listing that brings out the distinction between a leader and a manager.

TABLE 1.1 **Manager vs leader (dimension-wise)**

Dimension	Manager	Leader
Task performance	Controls activities, processes, systems, etc.	Creates activities, processes, systems, etc.
Performing repetitive tasks	Keeps track of activities, processes, systems, etc.	Finds new ways of performing; changes activities, processes, systems, etc.
Resource utilization	Prepares and uses resources	Finds resources
Developmental inclination	Plans and executes policy	Defines the mission or gets the mission fulfilled
Activities	Runs the business	Develops the business
Business development	Organizes actions	Creates an environment
Product and service creation	Solves problems	'Shakes things up'
New customers and clients	Is conservative and cautious	Aligns people; takes calculated risks
Customer relationship	Copes with complexity	Sets directions
Rules and regulations	Complies with rules and follows systems	Is imagination based
Locus of control	External	Internal (and external)
Interaction with outsiders	Interacts internally; keeps people in line with systems	Interacts with outsiders; inspires people
Responsibility	Is responsible for specific production, planning, sales performance	Is responsible for overall outcome and impact
Work independence	Deductive process	Inductive process
Major viewpoint	Creates structures; avoids risks	Creates mandates; takes risk
Monitoring arena	Monitors organizational culture	Monitors outside culture
The people below/ around	Subordinates	Followers

Managers focus on day-to-day activities and maintain the business so that it runs smoothly. Leaders, on the other hand, look and think ahead. An effective leader needs to anticipate the future, set a vision, and prepare the organization to achieve future goals. Thus, leaders require a high degree of emotional intelligence (EI)—a strong 'people sense' to understand how to motivate individuals and teams to drive the organization forward. Having understood the differences between managers and leaders, you should know the essence of leadership, that is, the characteristics of a leader.

A manager working in a functional area plans to accomplish the tasks assigned to him/her and strives to comply with the set standards. He/she conforms to the rules and regulations and discharges his/her responsibilities by way of allocating and optimizing resources. The general public agrees with the business press and academic literature that management and leadership are different. Field (2002) captured from the Internet 187 leadership images and 186 management images. He pursued an interpretive and modest study of the differences between management and leadership (Table 1.2). Leadership was found to be about taking action and communicating values in the context of a relationship. It was not about reinforcing the status quo and the reliance on hierarchy (Field 2002).

TABLE **1.2**   **Manager vs leader (subject-wise)**

Subject	Manager	Leader
Essence	Stability	Change
Focus	Managing work	Leading people
Deals	Subordinates	Followers
Methods	Inspirational and motivational	Problem-solving
Acts as	Builder/producer	Architect/designer
Objectives	Ends	Means
Aims	Change	Status quo
Actions	Do the right thing	Do things right
Horizon	Short term	Long term
Seeks	Objectives	Vision

Contd

Table 1.2 contd

Subject	Manager	Leader
Approach	Plans detail	Sets direction
Decision	Makes	Facilitates
Power	Formal authority	Personal charisma
Appeals to	Head	Heart
Energy	Control	Passion
Dynamic	Reactive	Proactive
Persuasion	Tell	Sell
Style	Transactional	Transformational
Exchange	Money for work	Excitement for work
Likes	Action	Striving
Wants	Results	Achievement
Risk	Minimizes	Takes
Rules	Makes	Breaks
Conflict	Avoids	Uses
Direction	Existing roads	New roads
Truth	Establishes	Seeks
Concern	Being right	What is right
Credit	Takes	Gives
Blame	Gives	Takes

Source: www.limkokwingmba.wordpress.com/management-mco101-unit-8a-motivation-leadership-groups-and-teams/ (accessed on 21 December 2008).

Studying the conspicuous effects of leadership on organizational functioning and realizing the most important needs of leaders, business leaders are concentrating on leadership development in the present-day business environment to succeed.

LEADERSHIP—THE CHANGING PARADIGM

In view of the changing business scenario, growing complexities, acute competitions, government policies, the model of leadership is also changing. Humility is essential to be an effective leader. In the present scenario, a person needs to be creative. A leader must be tenacious; what is required at present is that he/she executes everything. The leadership paradigm is changing as the business environment is changing. Table 1.3 compares conventional and emerging leaders and brings out the leadership requirements that have emerged.

TABLE 1.3   Changing paradigm of leaders

Conventional	Emerging
Humility	Creativity
Tenacity	Execution is everything
Ability to go against the flow	Vision and innovation
Facilitate	Planned abandonment
Negotiate	Create simultaneously
Articulate	Create content
Understand business issues	Work with more competent people
Detachment/Egolessness	Ability to engage
Tough expectations	Recognize, create, and address larger constituents
Personal discipline	Balanced EQ/IQ
Scalability	Networks
Ability to take difficult decisions with speed	Ability to seek help

Source: www.cii-iq.in/Sectors/Quality per cent20in per cent20Education/events/NSQE08/ppts/ GVILI.pdf (accessed on 1 February 2009).

PREREQUISITES OF ORGANIZATIONAL LEADERS

Leaders need certain prerequisites. Leaders must have certain core competencies like self-management, leading others, task management, innovation, and social responsibility (Bapat et al. online paper). We will now discuss the first three competencies—self-management, leading people, and task management.

Self-management Dimensions

The self-management dimensions a leader must develop include work habits, work attitudes, stress management, self-insight, and learning.

Work habits

The work habits of a leader include time management, goal orientation, organization skills, work ethics, and follow-through. Time management is making good use of time by organizing, prioritizing, and scheduling tasks. Setting and attaining specific and challenging goals for oneself is goal orientation. Organization skills refer to organizing one's responsibilities and performing them in an efficient and effective manner. Work ethic involves being diligent to ensure the successful completion of tasks related to one's job as a leader. Follow-through is ensuring that one's promises are realized in behaviour and doing what one said one would do.

Work attitudes

Work attitudes include initiative, effort, persistence, energy, and optimism. Initiative of a leader means the enterprise has to be a self-starter, initiating tasks and taking on new challenges. Effort is exerting oneself to complete tasks successfully and achieve goals. Enduring in one's tasks despite challenges or difficulties is persistence. A leader must maintain progress and enthusiasm throughout the completion of a task for which he/she needs energy. Further, he/she has to energize his/her followers, develop an edge, and execute the tasks. A leader needs to be optimistic, having a positive outlook about oneself and others.

Stress management

Stress management demands self-control, stress tolerance, personal resilience, work–life balance, and adaptability. Self-control means emotional stability and controlling one's emotions even in difficult or challenging situations. Stress tolerance implies remaining cool and effective even if situations become stressful. Personal resilience refers to withstanding and overcoming stressful situations. Work–life balance is controlling the influence of stresses of one's non-work life on one's work life, and vice versa. Adaptability is by far the best stress management tool, which means adapting to changing or dynamic situations.

Self-insight

The insight of a leader helps to foresee something that may impede and obstruct the smooth working of a team or any other progress. Insight enhances self-confidence, self-awareness, self-reliance, humility, and suspending judgment. Self-confidence is the belief in oneself and in one's ability to perform a job successfully as a leader and act accordingly.

Self-awareness increases through introspection and assessing one's success in learning or working activities and being honest about judgments made. It is about knowledge of one's strengths and weaknesses, and knowledge of one's boundaries and limits.

Self-reliance refers to being able to work and think without the guidance or supervision of others. Humility, humbleness, or modesty is being able to have a realistic perspective of one's worth and the ability to admit to one's mistakes. Suspending judgment implies keeping one's personal beliefs and biases from influencing one's decisions which must be made through realistic analysis.

Learning

Learning for any person starts at birth and continues till death. This self-management skill incorporates learning strategies, intellectual curiosity, seeking feedback, and needs continuous learning. To learn and let others learn, a leader must devise strategies: learning new techniques for developing oneself through the use of multiple approaches.

Intellectual curiosity refers to valuing learning and seeking situations to increase one's knowledge. In order to gain total knowledge, a leader must seek feedback about his/her activities from the team members and others he/she is dealing with. Collecting feedback, formally or informally, helps one to learn and grow as a leader. Unless one does so, he/she remains unaware of many weaknesses. Thus, feedback results in behavioural modification, which in turn helps to be effective. Continuous learning is essential for keeping oneself informed and updated in one's profession and leadership in general.

Leader's action to self-management

Goal-setting for oneself and group members is of paramount importance. The set goals must be realistic so that group members are neither overloaded nor remain underutilized. An organization requires its members to periodically set their own goals. The leader has to be careful while setting team goals and member goals. The leader particularly needs organizational skills, time management, and self-awareness.

Role conflicts may develop in any work situation. A person has to often perform a variety of roles. When an individual has to deal with conflicting roles or duties as part of the job as a leader, a variety of self-management competencies emerge as essential. He/she can cope with the stress, be tolerant, maintain resilience, and prioritize demands.

Role overload means that there should not be any inconsistency between the expectations of a leader and member's ability to fulfil those expectations. To ensure this, the leader needs to have persistence, adopt learning strategies, and periodically review and monitor the progress. These work attitudes are important self-management competencies for a leader.

Errors or mistakes cannot be totally avoided. In fact, they often give an opportunity to learn. When an error results in extreme and extensive negative outcomes, leaders must be aware of their own performance to avoid mistakes.

Changes are part and parcel of organizational life. Changes always affect the working of all functional areas, departments, and teams. Leaders must be alert to the direction and speed of changes. If they cannot keep themselves on track and know how they must adapt to deal with a new situation, then it would be difficult to achieve the team goals.

Leading People

Leading people and maximizing team output has always been a complex task. Members often misunderstand instructions; the leader fails to realize the needs and deficiencies of the members; the leader does not appreciate the dynamics of motivation and the influence of relevant agencies. A leader must be an active listener, communicate using a language and style acceptable to others, be able to win trust, and create a healthy work environment. Thus, leading people effectively demands effective communication, interpersonal awareness, commitment and motivation, and the capacity to influence.

Communication

A leader communicates with his/her followers, peers, seniors, and many others. Team members need to know the team goals and tasks assigned. Unless they are clear about what is expected from them, goal accomplishment becomes difficult. Information is communicated using face-to-face discussion, in writing, through telephone, or through electronic devices. In any sort of communication other than face-to-face communication, the recipients of messages cannot interpret body language. Moreover, obtaining clarification needs time.

Leaders must be good listeners. Listening is a vital component of communication. While performing the role of coach, mentor, counsellor, or a family member, one has to be an active listener. Active listening makes communication meaningful, telepathic, motivational, and inspirational. Listening and its discrete skills will be discussed in leadership skills in team building in Chapter 9.

Involving people in discussion, encouraging their comments and inputs, discarding unacceptable submissions assertively without hurting them, and a norm of openness and collegiality during group discussions are the principal ingredients of communication.

Furthermore, public speaking is an art of vocalizing clearly, maintaining a comfortable pace, and using appropriate non-verbal behaviour during formal presentations. The use of visual aids for a mass audience enhances the quality and effectiveness of the presentations. Engaging the audience and responding to their interrogations promotes communication. Building bridges of relationship, developing a portfolio of external contacts within the professional community, and networking and partnering are essential for survival and growth. Building strong and lasting personal relationships is the ultimate organizational need (Haldar and Chatterjee 2007). Information sharing with others outside the organization (like customers, suppliers, regulating bodies, other stakeholders, and even competitors as benchmarking partners) is essential for an organization.

Interpersonal awareness

A leader has to expand interpersonal awareness by gaining knowledge of the following:

Psychological knowledge—knowledge of human behaviour, mental processes, and individual and group performance
Social orientation—being comfortable while interacting and working with others
Social perceptiveness—awareness and understanding of how and why others are reacting the way they are
Service orientation—actively seeking out ways to assist people in their duties
Nurturing relationships—building positive and cooperative working relationships with others and maintaining lasting relationships

Developing commitment and motivation

Organizational commitment, interwoven with job involvement, is the emotional reaction of employees towards the organization and its policies. Commitment depends on a number of factors like job security, loyalty, trust in management, self-identity, alienation, helplessness, etc. Motivation makes people work more and better and is the unifying concept of human relations that depends on the emotional connection with their manager and team members. The seven essentials of motivation are a sense of mission, compelling role, personal coaching, high probability of winning, professional growth, financial incentives, and emotional connection.

Managers face three challenges while dealing with the workforce— the wealthy employee, the burnt-out employee, and the emotionally disconnected employee. Organizations must organize trust-building workshops and create and maintain a motivational climate to get the best from the workforce to achieve the business goals. Motivating is not always associated with financial incentives; there are several non-monetary motivational drives. Employees turn negative due to depression, chronic problems, anxiety, some medication or medical condition, and inadequate personality development, which can be managed through the UAR (understand, apologize, resolve) process.

To motivate others, the leader must take charge, exhibiting willingness to initiate the activities of groups and lead others towards achieving common goals. He/she has to orient others, providing an overview of the team or department or the whole organization and its policies, work rules, and job responsibilities. He/she must set challenging but attainable goals for individuals and groups and specify actions, strategies, and timelines necessary for goal attainment. Further, he/she has to measure and track progress towards goals to evaluate individual and group performance and provide feedback and reward positive work behaviour to reinforce activities that are aligned with the team goals, leading to the organization goals. Organizations must accept the shifts from 'hard assets' to 'soft assets', and develop commitment and motivation to enhance productivity (Haldar 2009).

Developing others

It is an organizational and moral responsibility to develop the members as their efforts and outputs ultimately determine the team achievement. Developing others needs knowledge of learning theories and design of individual and group teaching plans, translating or explaining information in a way that can be understood and used to support responses or feedback to others, evaluating the strengths and weaknesses, and grasping capacities of the learners.

Professional development is also ensured through coaching, teaching, mentoring, and advising to help people develop their knowledge and skills. A person can contribute best to the organization if he/she is getting the opportunity of working in an environment where much role stress does not hinder his/her freedom at work. But stress cannot be totally avoided and stress impacts different persons differently. Counselling is an employee development mechanism that helps cope in stressful situations and in turn enhances performance.

Influencing

Influence is the change in a target agent's attitudes, values, beliefs, or behaviours as the result of influence tactics. It refers to one person's actual behaviours designed to change another person's attitudes, values, beliefs, or behaviours (Hughes et al. 2008). In order to influence, a person has to cooperate, persuade, resolve conflicts, negotiate, empower, and inspire the target person or group of persons.

Cooperating is working well with others to jointly achieve goals. Persuading refers to communicating with others to convince them to perform a task or approach something in a different manner. As a leader, you have to deal with complaints to resolve the conflicts and grievances of others. You have to encourage others to come together and reconcile differences through negotiation. More information and discussion about conflict resolution and negotiation is provided in the chapter on leadership skills in team building (Chapter 9). The leader must empower his/her followers by delegating authority and providing power to them, and inspiring them to believe in the organization's values and to act in accordance with those values. The leader must gain knowledge to understand the political climate and anticipate how decisions will be affected by the organization culture.

In order to lead people effectively, the leader has to encourage employee participation, consider the type of team, socialize, supervise the group, use multiple modes of communication, and finally, sell and market concepts. Employees will contribute their best if they are involved in the decision-making process. They will also cooperate and coordinate. Naturally, conflict resolution will not be an easy task. Depending on the type of team being led, the leader has to take into account whether the members are new or experienced as also the extent of interdependence (high interdependence versus low interdependence), and accordingly find how should he/she would be able to adapt and how to guide, direct, interact with, and motivate group members. After the joining of a new member in the group, the leader has to acclimatize the member to the group, teach and coach the member, and thereafter mentor and counsel the member whenever required.

Leaders are expected to train, coach, and supervise team members or other related persons, understanding and honouring their beliefs, abilities, and perspectives. While communicating with different types of groups and individuals, leaders must be able to recognize and adapt to the necessary modes of communication that will fit their needs. Leaders must realize that good communication helps persuade or influence people easily, and to market any concept they need to have negotiation skills and must be emphatic listeners. These steps or actions would further strengthen the communication process, interpersonal awareness, development of commitment and motivation, and capacity to influence.

Task Management

A leader has to execute tasks, undertake problem-solving, manage information and material resources, manage human resources, and concurrently enhance their performance.

Executing tasks

Task execution needs knowledge of standard practices and procedures necessary to accomplish tasks. It has already been discussed that knowledge of the job is essential for an effective leader. Assigning tasks to the appropriate people based on the knowledge and ability of individuals about the work processes, organizational planning, and work group flow is important. The leader must keep in sharp focus on the details of the task to be accomplished. The leader has to coordinate the work-related activities necessary for task completion of all relevant constituents (both inside and outside the team, department, or organization) and review to adjust the plans in light of how others are acting or how the environment is changing.

Feedback mechanism, both positive and negative, in a timely and constructive manner helps to unearth weaknesses and reveals whether a task is being performed in conformance to the plan. The concept of multitasking allows the absorbing of the sudden absence of key personnel in the team and shifting one's resources between multiple systems when needed.

Solving problems

Analytic thinking, data analysis, and interpretation of the data and decision-making help to design and redesign the work system. Analytic thinking enables using existing information to logically evaluate situations and solve problems and utilizing inductive and deductive logic to make inferences. Data analysis and interpretation refer to summarizing and making inferences from information through the application of statistical tools and/or qualitative analyses. Interpretation and proper judgment need adequate concentration, avoiding all distractions.

Managing information and material resources

Management of materials, facilities, and utilities needs close monitoring along with the delivery, inventory, and flow of materials, using tracking systems. It also demands identifying and designing the facility location/layout to maximize productivity. Any decision needs information in a particular structure for which we are required to get hold of the relevant database. If some data required for the information are not available, we have to collect them. Thus, information for decision-making needs prior analysis. Management of both information and material resources needs administrative activities accompanied by maintaining of documents and records. Therefore, management system also needs traceability to maintain and track quality.

Managing human resources

Human resource management deals with changing business scenario and emerging issues, job analysis and job design, human resource planning, succession planning, attracting and retaining talent, outsourcing human resource functions, socialization, mobility and separation management, human resource measurement and audit, managing personnel policies, human resource development system, balanced score card, and many more human resource functions. A leader must develop the human resource management system, review it periodically, and revise it to suit the changing needs.

Enhancing member performance

It includes enhancing job knowledge, eliminating hurdles to performance, adopting benchmarking, and strategic task management. Involving team members should be the primary concern in discovering methods to enhance task performance and redirecting the group to achieve better task completion. Identifying roadblocks and redundancies in work processes and promoting improvements in task performance also assume importance in this context. Benchmarking—an endeavour to know the best practices—and facilitating communication outside the organization to identify and integrate the best practices in task design and performance is vital to succeed against competition. Strategic task management refers to matching the appropriate people and resources in the organization to maximize task performance.

Sometimes, and in certain situations, a leader is required to lay more emphasis on task management. When an organization adopts quality management system, develops systems, procedures, instructions, and administrative rules, and documents these for compliance, then the leader must communicate these to his/her followers.

In some groups, tasks are characterized by autonomy. While leading such groups, the leader is required to discharge a variety of responsibilities and get extensive feedback, and therefore needs competence in many areas of task management. When a leader is expected to assign tasks and goals for the group, he/she has to provide the ideas for implementation and must give attention to detail.

Leaders are often made accountable for the output and judged based on the team performance. Obviously, in such cases, leaders should be extremely careful that everything happens according to plan so as not to adversely affect the end result. Formalization, job enrichment, task assignment, and accountability are vital considerations for task management. Task management further needs time management skills, particularly when stringent deadlines are set.

LEADERSHIP DEVELOPMENT DRIVES BY ORGANIZATIONS

Today organizations need leaders, not merely persons possessing managerial skills. Organizations are keen to impart leadership potential and develop leaders in many ways. Leaders might be born, but the majority of leaders are made.

Lakshmi et al. (2008) submit that some multinationals including their Indian subsidiaries like General Electric (GE), IBM India, and Hindustan Unilever Limited (HUL) have been at the cutting edge of leadership development for many years. They further say that Indian growth companies like Infosys Technologies, Tata Consultancy Services (TCS), Bharti Airtel, and Wipro have also been pioneers in the field of leadership development and have also focused on leadership in the last few years.

Eureka Forbes Limited (EFL) has established its leadership development centre. A recent global survey by consultancy firms Hewitt and RBS International along with *Fortune* magazine has placed two Indian companies, HUL and Infosys, in the top 10 on leadership development. ICICI, Wipro, and TCS are in the top 20.

Further, the Indian subcontinent has been classified as one of the global hotspots. Indian companies have grown in scale and global exposures require new mindset. Leadership development, proactively and innovatively, has emerged as a readymade solution to address the issue of an acute talent crunch. The drives of HUL, Infosys, TCS, IBM, and EFL are presented in brief here. Organizational drives to develop leadership will be discussed in detail in Chapter 8 on leadership development.

LEADERSHIP EFFECTIVENESS

Different authors view leadership effectiveness from their individual perspectives. To evaluate leadership effectiveness, researchers select the criteria based on the explicit or implicit conception of leadership. Leaders get along with followers and endeavour to achieve team goals. As such, leadership effectiveness can obviously be measured or evaluated in terms of the consequences of the leader's actions vis-à-vis the followers. That team performance affects the organization and therefore impacts organizational stakeholders is also considered by many researchers while evaluating leadership effectiveness.

The most commonly used measure of leader effectiveness is the extent to which the leader's organizational unit performs its task successfully and achieves its goals (Yukl 2007). Various parameters of success may be decided based on the task assignment and the nature of the group. Net profit, profit margin, increase in sales, market share, return on investment, return on assets, output and productivity, cost per unit of output, costs in relation to budgeted expenditure, and absenteeism of team members are some of the objective measures of team performance or goal attainments.

Besides the objective measures, there are subjective indicators also of leadership effectiveness. Effective leaders demonstrate strong abilities in nine basic leader skill dimensions, which are goal setting, delegation, motivation, communication, decision making, stress management, conflict resolution, performance coaching and counselling, and team development.

Furthermore, it is the moral responsibility of any leader to satisfy the needs and expectations of the followers, improve the quality of work life, ensure psychological growth and career advancements, develop group cohesiveness, and so forth. There must not be frequent incidence of complaints against any team-mate and/or grievances about the functioning of the team. Every member should be willing to cooperate and assist other members and work together to achieve team goals. In fact, the attitudes toward the leader should be positive and they should exhibit team belongingness.

Summarily, some of the subjective indicators are

- Satisfying followers' needs and expectations
- Improving the quality of work life
- Contributing to followers' psychological growth
- Inculcating group cohesiveness
- Complaining against team members and the leader
- Grievances against team functioning
- Not cooperating to achieve team goals

- Quality of group processes as perceived by followers
- Attitude of followers towards the leader
- Team belongingness

It is thus obvious that the evaluation of leader effectiveness needs considerations of multiple factors, both objective and subjective, that render the task difficult. It is also not clear as to which measure is most relevant. This poses problems to researchers to formulate hypothesis. Therefore, they combine several measures into a single, composite criterion, but this approach requires subjective judgment about how to assign a weight to each measure (Yukl 2007).

Multiple factors chosen to measure leadership effectiveness pose problems if any two of them are negatively correlated. Let us consider two subjective factors: (a) satisfying followers' needs and expectations and (b) complaints against team members and the leader. An investment of time and efforts in the first factor is likely to reduce the second factor. A company may decide to reduce the profit margin as a policy matter to bring down the price. This venture will result in the enhancement of sales. Thus, these two factors are negatively correlated. If a number of objective factors, along with these two, are considered to assess the effective leadership, then the result may be misleading due to trade-offs between the factors. If a company introduces multi-skilling and multi-tasking for interchangeability of task assignments, then quality and precision may be affected, at least initially. Keeping in view efficiency and customer satisfaction, the same company may opt for specialization and that would lead to reduced flexibility.

LEADERSHIP PIPELINE

Hiring an executive from outside is merely a short-term option and temporary solution of a problem. For survival and growth, an organization needs to develop a pool of successors to keep the wheel of excellence moving. Managers at each level of the organization take responsibilities to achieve business goals. In order to accomplish the objectives and goals, an organization must use a model of leadership development termed as 'leadership pipeline'.

GE developed such a leadership model and has been using that for many years. GE's model supports the company's approach to leadership succession (DuBrin 2008). The model comprises six levels, each with unique management challenges: (1) managing individual contributors, (2) managing managers, (3) managing functional managers, (4) being a business manager,

(5) being a group manager, and (6) being an enterprise manager. It is obvious that managing individuals is easier than managing managers.

For example, the first level needs coaching, while the sixth level needs intensive inputs on strategic planning. Skill development of persons at each stage is essentially required to make the transition easier, faster, and effective. While moving from one level to the next higher level, the leaders must learn to value different types of work and have fewer quantitative measures to evaluate the results of their direct reports (DuBrin 2008). As such, the model greatly contributes to succession planning. The leadership pipeline model applies primarily to a large hierarchical organization, but can be adopted by medium-sized organizations as well.

Benefits of Leadership Pipeline

Leadership pipeline, if meticulously designed, provides many benefits such as

- Helps to understand the distinct differences between managerial roles and leader roles
- Helps to organize structured coaching and mentoring programmes
- Facilitates objective decision-making for promotion
- Saves an organization when employees superannuate
- Identifies knowledge and skill gaps of an individual before moving him/her to a higher level
- Makes performing easier for a person at the next higher level in the organizational hierarchy
- Reduces wastage of time in developing an employee after assigning higher responsibilities

Limitations

Leadership pipeline approach has certain limitations too:

- It is primarily targeted at large organizations, though medium-sized organizations can also use this concept.
- The lead time required to adopt the approach is considerably high.
- The approach needs top management commitment.
- It needs consideration of organizational culture, which must be healthy.

MYTHS AND REALITIES OF LEADERSHIP

The maxim—nothing can be achieved without effort—applies to leadership also. Leadership development is accompanied by certain obstacles. Before examining what leadership and leadership development are in more detail, one needs to consider what they are not (Hughes et al. 2008). There exist several beliefs, termed as myths, that stand in the way of fully understanding and developing leadership. The three myths mentioned by Hughes et al. (2008) are as follows:

Myth 1: *Good leadership is all common sense.* This implies that a person needs only common sense to be a good leader. Studies of leadership reported in scholarly journals and books only confirm what anyone with common sense already knows. Now, we are all acquainted with the saying that 'common sense is very uncommon'. In many instances, we use this statement since the term 'common sense' is ambiguous.

Common sense generally refers to the body of knowledge acquired by a reasonable person about life through experience and what the person has learned from various incidents, observations, and the consequences of applications of thoughts in the workplace. The interpretations drawn by a number of persons from the same experiment and same observation differ widely based on their perceptions. The common sense they apply is guided by multiple factors including perception. Thus, common sense, it seems, can very often play tricks on us.

A leader has to lead confidently, know the theories and apply them judiciously. He/she has to be humble enough to recognize the viewpoints of others, and has to produce results. Leaders have to anticipate changes and set new directions for followers, which may not be structured at all. He/she has to energize and drive the followers with minimal problem in the workplace. Effective leaders must be something more than just 'common sense' holders.

Myth 2: *Leaders are born, not made.* We are familiar with many family-owned organizations. This observation prompts some of us to believe that leadership is in one's genes. On the contrary, the majority of people do not subscribe to this view and believe that leaders are made. Both the views are right in the sense that instinctive as well as formative experiences influence many sorts of behaviours, including those required in leading a team.

Hughes et al. (2008) emphasize that both the views are wrong to the extent they imply leadership is either innate or acquired; what matters more is how these factors interact. At this juncture, we need not consider who is a leader and who is a non-leader. It is more useful to consider and address the ways in which each person can make the most of the leadership qualities he/she is endowed with.

More specifically, research findings indicate that cognitive abilities and personality traits are at least partly innate. Of course, natural talent or characteristics may offer certain advantages or disadvantages while leading. Contextually, it needs to be mentioned that someone who had displayed leadership during childhood and succeeded may not be a good leader in the workplace, as the environment is different.

Myth 3: *The only school you learn leadership from is the school of hard work.* Formal study and learning are not mutually exclusive or antagonistic. Rather, they are complementary to each other. Certain kinds of study and training can improve a person's ability to learn critical lessons about leadership from experience. Knowledge disseminated through formal training helps accelerate the process of learning from experience.

The advantage of formally studying leadership is that it provides the participants with a variety of ways of examining a particular leadership situation. A participant gains the ability of selecting a theory to apply in the situation prevailing in the organization. It must be kept in mind that a theory chosen at random cannot be applicable in all work environments. There is no single theory that has universal application.

LEADERSHIP IN DIFFERENT CULTURES

In the era of globalization, India has experienced both continuity and change and has responded to the forces that have arisen from globalization. In the current phase, globalization is experienced as a two-way scheme: while multinational companies are entering India, many Indian companies have a clear ambition to 'take India to the world'.

Foreign companies are 'intruding' with their value system and culture including work culture. Some of the 'intruders' are collaborating with Indian companies to make their culture blend with that of the Indian counterpart. But the process of blending is not at all an easy task. Some academicians and business leaders opine that globalization is the most significant trend affecting business today.

Large-scale organizations cannot ignore the production and marketing of products and services in other countries. Microsoft now operates in 100 countries, in contrast to some 70 countries in 2000. In 2002, Toyota initiated the Innovative International Multi-Purpose Vehicle (IMV) project to optimize global manufacturing and supply systems for pick-up trucks and multi-purpose vehicles and to satisfy market demand in more than 140 countries worldwide. The Motorola A830 mobile phone with 2G, 2.5G, and 3G technologies combined in one device, operates in most major cities in more than 170 countries.

To be effective, leaders must adapt their leadership behaviour to the culture of the country they are working in and the societal institutions where they are situated. Unless they can cope with the prevailing culture, it would be extremely difficult for them to gain the spontaneous support of people of all strata and get along with the followers. Ultimately, it is the leaders' job to handle individual differences and bring people together to achieve team goals. Culture plays a predominant role in any organization.

Cross-functional leadership researchers began to address issues regarding the cultural values, norms, and beliefs that are most important for leadership, and effective leaders adjust their styles to fit into these cultural characteristics. Considering the immense importance of cross-cultural leadership, the Global Leadership and Organizational Behaviour Effectiveness (GLOBE) research project has identified nine cultural dimensions that are most important for effective leadership and is carrying out a cross-functional leadership research project throughout the world.

GLOBE was initiated by the world-class leadership researcher and writer Robert J. House, who also directs the GLOBE project. The project started in the early 1990s. About 200 social scientists and management scholars from more than 60 cultures/countries representing all major regions of the world are engaged in this long-term programmatic series of cross-cultural leadership studies. It is believed that the GLOBE project is the largest cross-functional leadership research project ever conducted. The dimensions on which the scholars are researching are power distance, uncertainty avoidance, humane orientation, institutional collectivism, in-group collectivism, assertiveness, gender egalitarianism, future orientation, and performance orientation (Howell and Costley 2006).

Leaders are putting enormous efforts to achieve the conglomeration of distinctly different cultures. Given the number and diversity of Indian organizations, all approaches and interventions of organization development have already been used. Family enterprises and the government have played a central role in shaping the Indian response to globalization. Developing a global mindset is India's major challenge for the future.

ATTRIBUTES OF EFFECTIVE LEADERS

The various attributes of any effective leader are the ability to adapt quickly to changes, administer efficiently, meet unpleasant situations, spot opportunities, and take decisions. He/she should have specific ambition, willingness to work hard, enterprise, astuteness, capacity for lucid writing, imagination, analytical ability, capacity for abstract thoughts, capacity to speak lucidly, curiosity, enthusiasm, integrity, open-mindedness, single-mindedness, understanding of others, willingness to take risks, and willingness to work long hours. A leader can never be successful without these attributes. You will learn more about attributes of leaders in Chapter 2.

CURRENT ISSUES IN LEADERSHIP

Howell and Costley (2006) discuss some current issues in leadership including ethics and fairness, diversity, leadership development, leadership paradigm, leading organizational change, and transformational leadership.

Ethics and Fairness

Ethics is encompassing the right conduct and good life. It is significantly broader than the common conception of analysing what's right and wrong. Ethics help create competitive advantage in business. Fairness concerns the equality of opportunity for members of every caste, creed, colour, origin, ethnicity, etc. while applying any sort of organizational processes like personnel selection, aptitude measurement, performance appraisal, promotion, applying diagnostic processes, and the like. Goal achievement needs interaction with followers and others, with the implicit assumption that both parties will behave ethically.

Ethical behaviours lead to trust building between people, mutual cooperation, improved interpersonal relations, and a healthy organizational climate. Unethical behaviour with employees and external parties simply leads to disaster. At this point of time, the world is witnessing the result of gross unethical behaviour by the top management of a renowned software company and its financial auditors. Being unethical, one can achieve short-term goals but in the long run, he/she cannot gain. On the other hand, an ethical leader becomes a role model to his/her followers and everyone in the organization, gains their love and respect, can help others to learn ethics and fairness, and ensures leadership development and organizational change, produces other leaders, and, ultimately, benefits the organization.

Diversity

Diversity refers to multiplicity, assortment, and miscellany with regard to many aspects including culture. At present, organizations operate in various parts of the world, where they employ people with different cultural beliefs and practices. A leader integrates the diverse groups of individuals into an orchestrated organizational effort to facilitate the achievement of business mission and organizational goals. Integrating people from diverse cultures is not easy at all and requires understanding of how culture affects us including the operation of human bias and prejudice (Howell and Costley 2006).

Leadership Development

In view of the differences between managers and leaders regarding the various dimensions, subjects, and the changing paradigm of leadership— conventional to emerging—leadership development has gained greater importance in today's context. Let us recall that all leaders are managers but all managers are not leaders.

Leadership development focuses on increasing the ability of a leader or an aspiring leader to carry out effective leadership behaviours, to drive a collection of people to work together for higher productivity. A leadership development programme typically emphasizes one or more of the three processes: assessment, challenge, and support (Howell and Costley 2006). Through the assessment process, people come to know about their strengths and weaknesses, which helps in building on strengths and improving on weaknesses. Challenge causes people to see the need for capabilities to help their followers adapt to the changing organization with least resistance. Support provides leaders with encouragement and reassurance as they move on to enhance their skills and the ability to lead. It is needless to mention that these three processes help them to initiate and maintain their continuous development in their journey. The issues have emerged as critical in the changing leadership paradigm.

Leadership Paradigm

Leadership paradigms are changing. Corporations across the world are bringing about major transformation. Michael Useem (Director, Center for Leadership and Change Management, and Professor of Management, Wharton) emphasizes that ideas must be taken upstairs; it takes courage to take ideas upstairs. Taking ideas upstairs by anyone at any level is referred to as 'upward leadership'.

Upward leadership is the ability to offer superiors or leaders a set of ideas that will help them and formulate strategies that will serve them and give a sense of better structuring of their operation. Useem argues that this will be the way corporations across the world can bring about major changes. In the US Marine Corps, it is obligatory for every officer to give ideas, identify what is going wrong, and where the gaps are identified and ideas implemented, the rest of the team simply salutes and follows the order. Upward leadership requires an ability to articulate and be persuasive.

Deccan Airways, a south-west equivalent of Jet Airways, has a business model characterized by low cost and high quality, and has depended upon many managers at the bottom of the hierarchy to come up with great ideas (Narayan 2006). This endeavour is encouraging upward leadership.

In a research conducted by US-based Citigroup, the bank found that the rate of growth for assets under management was highest in those departments where the bosses took up coaching and mentoring with younger people in the organization. In upward leadership, candour is important so that subordinates are not under the fear that the boss will fire them for being critical. You have to create a culture where upward leadership is rewarded like that of the US Navy.

Thus, in view of the issues and concepts talked about, organizations need effective leaders. It is of immense importance to appreciate the inner beauty or structure of effective leaders.

Leading Organizational Change

Globalization is multi-directional. One of the exciting things about the world today is that it cannot and does not stand still. In the last few decades, technological innovations have multiplied. Products and know-hows are fast becoming obsolete, competition is sharp, natural resources are depleting, and basic resources are becoming expensive. On the other hand, the drive for social equity and justice has gained momentum, and customers today are cost sensitive and quality conscious.

Changes are inevitable during the life of any organization. Introducing and implementing total quality management is also a change. An organization must cope with changes and, more importantly, decide on the correct change points so that it sustains and grows, else it will perish and go extinct. The direction and the speed of change are the key success factors.

A change does not just happen. It is driven by a reason, a thought, or an idea. The cause comes either from 'without' (the business environment) or from 'within'. Over the past 25 years, we have seen successful changes in health care and other service sectors, manufacturing technology, and financial industries. No organization can survive if it remains static. Besides, with its competitors and customers changing, organizations must also change.

A leader must realize the growth of an organization, appreciate the need for changes in the organization to cope with the environment, identify the forces behind the conditions of change, be acquainted with the phases in the process of change, and understand the phases of organizational growth. Moreover, he/she must be able to differentiate among changes at the individual, group, and organizational levels. A leader has to identify the changes essential for survival and growth, the applicable process of change, the organizational culture, and, most importantly, the people. (How is the current workforce? Does it have the knowledge to perform its tasks effectively? What HRD mechanisms may be used for organizational development?) Understanding the people is of paramount importance to successfully lead a change process. They must have the requisite competencies to successfully accomplish a task. Suitable HRD mechanisms need to be identified and applied to develop them for the ultimate benefit of the organization, to achieve its objectives and goals.

Leaders need to see the gap between the current state (where we are today) and the desired state (where we want to be tomorrow). This gap is also called the delta state. We all react to the delta state in different ways. A leader finds change challenging and energizing, whereas a manager finds it stressful and confusing. Resistance to change may come from those who find it stressful and confusing. In order to effect the change in a very smooth manner and make it successful, the leader must be proactive. He/she has to ascertain the volume, the direction, and the speed of change and anticipate the possible sources of resistance. The leader must unfreeze, move, and refreeze the change.

The leader must bear in mind the following to overcome resistance to change:

1. Resistance is natural and inevitable—Expect it.
2. Resistance does not always show its face—Find it.
3. Resistance has many reasons—Understand it.
4. Deal with people's concerns rather than their arguments—Confront it.
5. There is only one way to deal with resistance—Manage it.

Transformational Leadership

Transformational leaders focus sharper attention on essential changes and innovations, apply discretion, and possess entrepreneurial zeal. This variety of leadership is a behavioural process capable of being learned and managed. Transformational themes include recognizing the need to change, creating a new vision, and institutionalizing the change. Transformational leadership is a discipline with a set of predictable steps, where the themes are revitalization, creating a new vision, and institutionalizing the change. (This leadership style has discussed in depth in Chapter 5, Contemporary Leadership Style.)

UNIVERSAL INNER STRUCTURE OF EFFECTIVE LEADERS

We remember the leaders who have made their mark by doing lasting good to the humankind, a nation, an organization, or a cause. They come in all shapes and shades; they depart the earthly world but remain immortal. They are flamboyant because of their knowledge, contribution, scholarly behaviour, sense of art, and similar other qualities.

We remember Ramakrishna Paramahamsa Dev, Swami Vivekananda, and Mother Teresa for their deeds and service to humanity. It is difficult to define a gentleman. But, *sthithaprajnya*, a man of ready wisdom as described in the Gita, can be called a gentleman. A gentleman can be an effective leader, successful in accomplishing what he wants to achieve, both individually and collectively.

Certain universal virtues form the inner hard core of every outstanding leader. Broadly, selflessness, or an ideal or vision, and knowledge (of the job, of handling people, and of self) and character (courage to decide, will power to persist, and initiative to be a self-starter) form this core.

Selflessness

Selflessness is a relative virtue; total selflessness is rather a rare phenomenon. Prophet Muhammad, Guru Nanak, Ramakrishna Paramahamsa Dev, Swami Vivekananda, and Mahatma Gandhi are among the most exemplary personalities who are known for their selflessness or self-sacrifice. A character without knowledge puts a ceiling on a leader's potential. Again, knowledge without character makes one indecisive.

Furthermore, character and knowledge together also cannot elevate a person unless he/she is selfless. Thus, the three broad components of a successful leader are knowledge, character, and selflessness. These components determine a leader's effectiveness.

Unselfishness or selflessness is the fountainhead of all that is noble in human beings. Vision and ideology help one to be selfless. The higher the ideal, the higher would be his/her extent of selflessness, and hence, the higher would be the potential to be an effective leader. This is a universal truth. In the words of Swami Vivekananda, 'I cannot expect anybody to be totally selfless; it is not possible. But if you cannot think of humanity at large at least think of your country. If you cannot think of your country, think of your community. If you cannot think of your community, think of your family. If you cannot think of your family, think of your wife. For heaven's sake do not think merely of yourself' (Vaghal 1988). In this manner, Vivekananda explained the method to learn selflessness and how being selfless is essential to being an effective leader.

Selflessness vs organizational culture

Organizational culture values leadership, uses tools and techniques to create environments to produce executive leaders and empowers them, helps them to rise above their self-interest, and allows them to learn to make sacrifices. A good organizational culture is 'the regard for the honour and interest of the body one belongs to'. A major goal of strategic management must be to ensure that everyone in an organization is imbued with the feeling that 'no sacrifice is big enough to uphold its [organization's] honour and reputation'.

Such an organizational culture helps to promote selflessness. Purity of the mind, integrity, loyalty, honesty, and faith in the Almighty are the components of selflessness. Hindus purify their minds on Shivratri, Navratri, and the 41-day fasting prior to visiting the Sree Ayyappa Swami temple at Sabarimala. Muslims purify their minds through the fasting called *roza* in the month of Ramzan. In fact, there are many such examples.

Character

Character has always been an indicator of a person's potential for leadership. Character is the aggregate of features and traits that form the individual nature of someone and it comprises a bundle of virtues and weaknesses of the mental and moral qualities of a person.

If a balance sheet is prepared considering the mental and moral qualities of a person, it would reflect the character of the person. Character, excluding selflessness, is the single most important factor that makes for an effective leader. It stands for core values, self-discipline, loyalty, readiness to accept responsibility, and willingness to admit to mistakes.

Ash (2001) mentions about the core values of the US army where people are often required to work jointly. Joint operations are the rule rather than the exception. But joint operations pose problems. An editorial abstract in the *Aerospace Power Journal* raises a question, 'why then do interservice rivalries seem to work against becoming "more joint"?' Colonel Ash (2001) proposes that lack of a recognized set of common 'core virtues' is the root of the problem. The core values of the US army are provided in Table 1.4.

TABLE **1.4**   Core values of the US military services

Air Force	Army	Marine Corps	Navy
· Integrity first · Service before self · Excellence in all that the air force does	· Integrity · Selfless service · Duty · Honour · Courage · Loyalty · Respect	· Commitment · Honour · Courage	· Commitment · Honour · Courage

With regard to virtues and ethics, Bennett (1993) observes that people are not born with virtues; virtues must be learned. Arguably, they can also be unlearned. Therefore, the educational process must never let up but continually reinforce ethical fitness.

Courage

In all societies, courage or bravery is a much-admired human virtue. Many managers hesitate to take decisions though they are authorized and empowered to do so. Even if a decision is taken, it is forwarded to a higher authority for formal approval, delaying its implementation. Managers fumble due to lack of confidence.

A cowardly person does not hesitate to suppress the truth. A courageous person will never tell a lie. Courage gives distinctive direction to the entire approach of a leader's work by displaying which he/she gains distinctive competence and can perform to high standards. A courageous person can say no if the situation demands a negative response or where a positive response may be unethical. The most potent source of courage, both physical as well as mental, arises from knowledge. Knowledge makes one not only *nirbhaya* (fearless) but indeed *abhaya*—who knows no fear.

Will power

Outstanding leaders are characterized by their 'will power to persist'. They have obtained distinctive competence differentiable from others for having this vital virtue. Project management needs meticulous planning. Yet, hundreds of problems arise, or failures occur on the part of the people, technology, system, and for many other reasons. Sometimes, we cannot assign a reason and call it natural or chance occurrence. Strong determination of a leader drives to persist in spite of setbacks and the hurdles that emerge as roadblocks during execution of the plan. Will power is an inner beauty that prompts a leader to persevere, which is behind the famous saying 'try and try again till you succeed' or 'never, never, never, never give up'.

The fast food chain of McDonald's succeeded in spreading its supply chain due to the will power of the management. Will power significantly contributed to its gaining worldwide popularity. The orchestrated efforts of everyone in the organization backed by their will power helped the company achieve success.

Initiative

Initiative to be a self-starter An American company displayed a notice at its entrance stating, 'If you are a wheelbarrow moving no further than you are pushed, then you need not apply for any position in this company.' A leader with initiative looks for opportunities and makes the best use of them. He/she always jumps ahead of others. He/she creates his/her own information-gathering sources to identify and overcome the difficulties that impede the progress of a task.

The abilities of creating sources of information gathering, identifying hurdles and taking steps to overcome them, and smoothly marching towards goal accomplishment all taken together are signs of initiative that makes one dynamic. Organizational culture puts the initiative of leaders into full play, which is a vital consideration in strategic management. A person who thinks, introspects, and has the habit of forethought can develop initiative. The likely snags need to be visualized and that demands mental preparedness. This is possible if one has initiative.

Knowledge

Knowledge of the job, handling people, and self is essential to be effective. Knowledge and the experience gained in course of time do not have substitutes. Learning, as we know, is a lifelong process and should be a continuous endeavour of any leader. Learning from other people's experience, the indirect one, has always been a hallmark of success. The indirect experience is varied as it comes from multiple sources.

Knowledge of the job This is work-related knowledge and gives the leader competency. Knowledge broadens the outlook by virtue of which one sees everything related to the work clearly, enhancing his/her expertise.

Let us recall the well-known maxim 'knowledge is power'. The attitudes towards work in conjunction with aptitude help build one's altitude. A person with knowledge collects feedback from associates. When his/her mind is inquisitive and open, he/she collects criticism, does realistic analysis, identifies the root causes behind any lapse, and ultimately rectifies them. Thus, his/her spectrum gradually increases. He/she becomes wise and never ignores comments. At this point, remember that 'wisdom begins at the point of understanding that there is nothing shameful about ignorance.' Also recall the maxim: 'If you ask a question for clarification, you express your ignorance once; if you do not ask then you carry your ignorance for ever.' Knowledge of the job generates work leadership, helps to influence colleagues, enables problem-solving, gives intrinsic satisfaction out of the mastery, and the like.

Knowledge of handling people People management is and has always been a matter of interest and is different from management of other resources. It is the quality of handling people that determines leadership capacity and handling people is the essence of leadership. Effective handling needs conceptual, human relations, and technical skills. Managerial effectiveness is the management terminology for leadership. Understanding human nature is useful for a leader to deal with people. Remember that 'a good leader knows his people better than their mothers do and cares even more'. This is the *mantra* for handling people.

Knowledge of self This is the most important knowledge and is absolutely vital. Leadership mainly refers to interaction between the leader and the followers. A leader has to focus on the people he/she is working with to understand them. He/she has to be thorough in behavioural dynamics to improve the quality of interpersonal relations and group dynamics. As such, he/she needs knowledge about his/her own strengths and weaknesses.

If a leader feels that he/she is the epitome of perfection and refuses to look at himself/herself objectively as in a mirror, he/she will commit a blunder. What is needed is introspection. It is believed that quiet introspection and examining one's real motives are the ways to know oneself. A leader has to ask certain questions such as: have I been truthful, honest, selfless, courageous, tenacious, helpful, and objective? A leader has further to verify whether any action resulted from greed, anger, selfishness, jealousy, or envy has impaired the collective outcome. Deep silence helps our conscience to the truth and to tell us very clearly when we are less than ethical and moral. Knowing the identified strengths and weaknesses, we can put in effort to fully develop our potential as a leader.

Effective and successful leaders transform their organizations. Transformational leadership is a discipline with a set of predictable steps wherein the themes are revitalization, creating a new vision, and institutionalizing change. Transformational leadership has been discussed in detail in Chapter 5.

SUMMARY

Managers as organizational leaders perform a variety of roles to discharge responsibilities. The nature of managerial work is changing. Managers perform tasks whereas leaders can transform. Organizations need leaders, regardless of whether the environment is orderly or turbulent. Leaders differ from managers in many dimensions and areas. Leaders find new ways of performing, unearth resources, define the mission, create an environment for developing the business, align people, take calculated risks, rely on imagination, interact with outsiders, inspire people, create mandates, observe the outside culture, and consider cross-cultural issues. Demands, constraints, and choices define the job of a manager, being strong influencers on the person's behaviour.

In the changing business scenario and growing complexities, the leadership paradigm is also changing. Leaders need certain self-management dimensions. A leader must develop proper work habits, work attitudes, stress management, self-insight, and learning.

Organizations are keen to develop leaders through leadership development drives. To evaluate leadership effectiveness, researchers select the criteria based on the explicit or implicit conception of leadership and attempt to measure the extent to which a leader's organizational unit performs its task successfully to achieve its goals. Leadership pipeline helps to develop a pool of able successors and to keep the wheel of excellence moving. Leadership is associated with certain myths and realities. Leadership in cross-cultural teams needs adequate attention. Universal inner structures of effective leaders are analogous.

KEY TERMS

Leadership pipeline refers to developing a pool of able successors at each level to keep the wheel of excellence moving.

Selflessness or altruism is a relative virtue, indicating selflessness and unselfishness, that a leader needs to possess to be effective, though it is a rare phenomenon.

Self-management dimensions mean the core competencies any leader must have, which include work habits and attitudes, stress management, self-insight, and learning.

Upward leadership is the ability to offer superiors or leaders a set of ideas that will help them and strategies that will serve them and pave the way for better structuring of their operation.

Will power is an 'inner beauty' that prompts a leader to persevere.

EXERCISES

Concept Review Questions

1. Discuss the various roles managers perform and responsibilities they discharge.
2. Discuss the responsibilities a manager commonly discharges.
3. What are the arguments for and against the leadership–management distinction?
4. Discuss the universal inner structure of effective leaders.
5. Discuss the prerequisites of organizational leaders vis-à-vis self-management.

Critical Thinking Questions

1. Consider the job of a manager in an organization you are familiar with. Critically analyse the theories of demand, constraint, and choices in an organizational context.
2. The nature of managerial activities is changing. Attempt to assess the direction and speed of change. How should a leader handle the changes?
3. Should an organization invest in developing leadership potential among its managers? Critically discuss the statement, citing examples.

Assignments

1. Design a table to collect views on the functions of managers and leaders. Let the respondents decide the points of differences. Compare the responses with the information provided in Tables 1.1 and 1.2. Draw a conclusion and discuss with your professor.
2. Develop a questionnaire of 15 subjective indicators to measure leadership effectiveness. Use the Likert Scale to express the opinions. Contact at least 20 managers and administer the questionnaire. Analyse to find the indicators that would receive maximum weightage. Draw a conclusion from your findings.

REFERENCES

Ash, Lt. Col. Eric (2001), Purple Virtues—A Leadership Cure for Unhealthy Rivalry, *Aerospace Power Journal,* Summer 2001, Document created on 16 May 2001 (www.airpower.maxwell.af.mil/airchronicles/apj/apj01/sum01/ash.html, accessed on 17 February 2009).

Bennett, William J. ed. (1993), *The Book of Virtues: A Treasury of Great Moral Stories,* Simon & Schuster, New York.

Bhargava, Shibganesh (2003), *Transformational Leadership,* Response Books (A division of Sage Publications), New Delhi.

Birla, Kumar Mangalam (2009), J.R.D. Tata Memorial Award Lecture delivered at the All India Management Association on 21 February. *AIMA News,* Newsletter of the All India Management Association, New Delhi.

Day, David V. (2000), Leadership Development: A Review in Context, *The Leadership Quarterly,* 11, 581–614.

Dubrin, Andrew J. (2008), *Research Findings Practice and Skills, bizfantra* (Houghton Mifflin Company, Boston), Delhi.

Field, Richard H.G. (2002), 'Web Images Reveal the Differences between Leadership and Management', University of Alberta. (apps.business.ualberta. ca/rfield/papers/leadershipDefined.htm accessed on 20 November 2008)

Haldar, U.K. (2009), *Human Resource Development,* Oxford University Press, New Delhi.

Haldar, U.K. and Ankhi Chatterjee (2007), Building Bridges of Relationship, *Manav,* a journal published by the Indian Institute of Social Welfare and Business Management (IISWBM), Master of Human Resource Management (MHRM) during 'Genesis 2007'.

Howell, Jon P. and Dan L. Costley (2006), *Understanding Behaviours for Effective Leadership,* Prentice-Hall India, New Delhi.

Hughes, Richard L., Robert C. Ginnett, and Gordon J. Curphy (2008), *Leadership Enhancing the Lessons of Experience,* Tata McGraw-Hill Publishing, New Delhi.

Krishnan, Sandeep K. and Varkkey Biju (2004), Nurturing Fast Track Leaders—A Concept Paper, IIM, Ahmedabad.

Lakshmi, S., Shyamal Mazumdar, and George Skaria (2008), Building Future Leaders, *Indian Management,* January, Vol. 47, No. 1.

Majumdar, Shyamal and Lesliy Dmonte (2008), Down to Earth, *Indian Management,* November, Vol. 47, No. 11, pp. 22–30.

Mintzberg, Henry (1973), *The Nature of Managerial Work,* Harper & Row, New York.

Mukherjee, Kum Kum (2004), Effect of Leadership Styles on Followers' Satisfaction and Perceived Effectiveness, *South Asian Journal of Management* (ISSN 0971 5428), Vol. 11, No. 1, January–March, p. 7.

Narayan, Tarun (2006), It Takes Courage to Take Ideas Upstairs, *Indian Management*, February, Vol. 45, No. 2.

Vaghal, N. (1988), Raja Ramdeo Anandital Podar Sixteenth Memorial Lecture, delivered at Jaipur on 10 December 1988.

www.chsbs.cmich.edu/leader_model/CompModel/OnlineModel.doc, accessed on 25 July 2008 (A Leadership Competency Model: Describing the Capacity to Lead).

Yukl, Gary (2007), *Leadership in Organizations*, Pearson Education, Delhi.

Web Source

Bapat, Ashwini et al., A Leadership Competency Model: Describing the Capacity to Lead, at www.chsbs.cmich.edu/leader_model/CompModel/OnlineModel. doc, accessed on 25 July 2008.

Fostering Young Leaders

Mr Ganguly, an excellent entrepreneur, discussed the issues regarding his business with one of his friends. His friend, a professional, advised him to consult an HR consultant Mr Singh who was also a reputed leadership expert.

Mr Singh and Mr Ganguly had a series of discussions and came up with an action plan. A tailor-made training programme for MC was designed and developed. Various probable outcomes were discussed, and a contract was finalized. The series of sessions were customized for all the four major centres where MC had substantial manpower and business. This 12-day training programme was conducted in batches with minimal disruption to the work schedules of MC: sometime sessions were conducted in the mornings or in the evenings, just after the day's work was over. Sometimes these sessions were held during breaks and spread over the weekend also. The course coverage included customer orientation modules, interpersonal relations, sensitization modules, communication skills, and stress management. The need for coordination with peers and subordinates, honouring their viewpoints, and learning from experience were an essential part of the supervisory-level training. Management games emphasizing on these areas along with some leadership cases made the training sessions more effective. Most of the knowledge-sharing sessions were informal. Participants freely shared their problems and subsequent sessions tried to incorporate some of the suggestions as well.

Mr Ganguly made it a point to attend all the sessions. The first programme was organized in Mumbai. It was initially decided that the second programme would be organized after about six months. The deliberations in the first programme appeared extremely convincing and Mr Ganguly decided to organize the second programme in Ahmedabad at the earliest. A separate training programme for the lower levels of employees was also designed. This time also he attended the sessions and addressed the participants to further elucidate the knowledge transferred by Mr Singh.

The vision and leadership abilities of Mr Ganguly gradually started to become evident and his contributions to the training sessions were full of insights. In one instance, Mr Singh jokingly asked Mr Ganguly if he had decided to terminate Mr Singh in the third training programme at Chennai. Mr Ganguly laughingly responded that the problems at Chennai were huge and asked Mr Singh to continue.

The outcomes of this training endeavour were immensely useful for Mr Ganguly and Mr Singh to deliberate further. The data generated clearly showed the areas that needed urgent attention and a long-term action plan was devised.

Discussion Questions

1. Identify and elaborate the aspects that might have motivated Mr Ganguly to hire the HR expert.
2. Comment on the course content used by the HR consultant.
3. Do you think Mr Ganguly was a leader? Explain.
4. Assess the gains of the consultant apart from the consultancy charges he received from Mr Ganguly.
5. What are your derived learnings from this case?

CHAPTER 2

Attributes of Leaders

Learning Objectives

After studying this chapter, you will be able to

▸ Understand and differentiate between power and authority

▸ Define and differentiate between leadership skills and traits

▸ State the value of the components of intelligence

▸ Appreciate the need for emotional intelligence in leaders

▸ Comprehend influence tactics and influence processes

OPENING CASE

Misappropriation of Power

Magna Hospital is a nationally acclaimed hospital, rendering its services to patients for more than sixty years. The hospital celebrated its golden jubilee a decade back. It has all the modern facilities and is now an 1800-bed hospital with multiple departments, diagnostic centres, and guest houses for the accompanying relatives of patients. Patients from Nepal, Bangladesh, Sri Lanka, Bhutan, Myanmar, and other nearby countries visit the hospital for treatment.

The hospital is professionally managed. A dynamic medical superintendent heads the hospital. He expects performance of a high order at every level. It is more so at the managerial and supervisory levels. Normally, people of high calibre are selected through open advertisements to meet the human resource requirements at all levels, specifically higher levels. However, the hospital fills junior-level vacancies by recruiting local people and then provides them in-house training. The hospital with its team of 10 specialist doctors in each department in addition to senior doctors provides personal attention to patients. Gradually, the reputation of the hospital has been growing. It claims to be a world-class hospital. It has a public relations cell. About eleven years back, the hospital received quality system certification

(ISO 9001) from an international certification agency. A senior doctor (Dr Raman) who obtained his MBA (with specialization in HR) is responsible for performing the duties of an HRD manager, which also includes designing training programmes for junior doctors and nurses.

The hospital has developed a system of refresher courses, professional development courses, and leadership courses for doctors at all levels. Magna invites expert faculties from both within the country and from outside. The hospital has its own training schemes; it offers two-year training for fresh science graduates/entrants. During the first year of training, the trainee nurses are offered theoretical knowledge, which is considered to be the core of the training programme for this category of trainees. In the second year, the trainee nurses are posted in various departments on a rotational basis. They receive on-the-job training during this time. The hospital records the attributes of the trainees and places them in a suitable department.

In the programme of nursing, the performance of trainees is normally appraised once annually at the beginning of the year. Dr Raman personally talks to the trainees about their progress, identifies strengths and weaknesses, and advises them on how to overcome the shortcomings and develop a professional career. Dr Raman further encourages the doctors in charge to periodically examine the performance of the trainee nurses. The hospital has developed a system of continuous evaluation of trainees against selected parameters that carries 50 per cent weightage in the final assessment. The hospital conducts a 'gradation test' after two years and absorbs excellent performers based on continuous evaluation and gradation test results as senior nurses.

Miss Rosni Sharma joined the hospital as a trainee in the year 1997 after graduating in science with zoology, physiology, and chemistry. She also did a one-year certificate course in health care and hospital management in which she obtained a distinction. Her grasping capacity was high, care for patients was noteworthy, accompanied by many other qualities that nurses require in a hospital. Furthermore, Rosni never hesitated or objected to working in night shifts whenever the situation demanded. At the end of the second quarter of the second year, the HRD manager called Rosni to provide feedback about her performance in the preceding quarter. He appreciated her exceptionally good performance. The HRD manager also said that the hospital has got a 'gem' and concluded with 'keep it up'. The medical superintendent also called and praised her. A month later, Miss Sharma met the HRD manager and requested him to curtail her training period and to absorb her as a senior nurse. Dr Raman was so impressed with her performance that he declared early completion of her training period and put her on the rolls of the hospital as a regular nurse.

Soon after this, other three trainee nurses approached the HRD manager with a similar request. When Dr Raman turned down their requests, problems erupted. They argued in their favour stating that they had been working in the respective departments as regular nurses, assisting the matron, and detailed on night duties in emergency situations. The hospital had no system of detailing trainee nurses in night duty. But the HRD manager was not convinced.

A series of problems started. The nurses collectively approached the medical superintendent. On getting a negative reply, they approached the only registered union. All the nurses declared a one-day strike. The management warned and cautioned them. But ultimately the strike took place. The nurses who took a leading role in the strike faced disciplinary action like stoppage of increment. This led to further problems. The majority of the nurses received the sympathy of the doctors who requested the higher authority to withdraw the punishment. But, based on the recommendation of the HRD manager, the medical superintendent did not relent.

The employees union of Magna Hospital complained in writing and declared a strike for an indefinite period of time. In the absence of nurses, all the activities of the hospital came to a standstill. Each member of the collective bargaining forum was reminded of the particular incidence of premature termination of the training period for Miss Rosni and her induction as a regular staff. But neither anyone hurt Rosni in the hospital personally nor disturbed her in the nurses' hostel. The strike continued for three days. The situation further worsened, and the management convened an emergency meeting to decide upon the future course of action.

Rosni was a silent observer of all these incidents. She was getting isolated from all other nurses and trainees, and had started feeling guilty. One day, she approached the HRD manager to narrate her psychological suffering. But immediately after entering his office, she received a lambasting. Where before her promotion she had received affection and sympathy from all the matrons, doctors, and specialists, today she received only criticism.

Learning points

1. Violating rules may hinder the smooth functioning of an organization.
2. A senior manager must understand the sentiments of juniors and consider the consequences during decision-making.
3. Before overruling a request from employees, a senior manager must try to anticipate the consequences.
4. Power derived from association with influential persons lasts only till they are in the influential person's favour.

INTRODUCTION

The characteristics of an effective leader are the ability to adapt quickly to changes, administer efficiently, meet unpleasant situations, spot opportunities and take decisions. They should have ambition, willingness to work hard, enterprise, astuteness, capacity for lucid writing, imagination, analytical ability, capacity for abstract thoughts, capacity to speak lucidly, curiosity, enthusiasm, integrity, open-mindedness, single-mindedness, understanding of others, willingness to take risks, and work for long hours. A leader can never be successful without these characteristics.

Leaders also have power and authority. Leaders gain and enhance their skills to drive their team members. Power as potential to influence individuals and groups, as well as organizational outcomes, is a worthy concept for discussion. Influence can be both covert and overt. Covert or hidden influence includes attitudes, values, and thought processes of persons. Overt or explicit influence embraces behaviour and actions.

An organizational leader bears the responsibility of driving his/her people, whatever be the nature of the group, to achieve the objectives and goals of the organization. Leaders need to have skills, requisite traits, and intelligence in their possession. At present, amid complexities, leaders need emotional intelligence as well.

CONCEPTS OF POWER AND AUTHORITY

Power is required to establish supremacy while interacting with people. Some synonyms of power are control, influence, command, dominance, and sway. The concept of power is essential to interpret and understand the way people influence others in the organization. When two parties or groups interact, each of them needs power to influence the other.

Influence refers to use of power. A leader needs power to convince the followers. The collective bargaining forum needs power to win over the management. The management, on the other hand, tries to negate the demands of the forum and refused to not accede to their claim by putting forth facts and figures. However, either party exercises power in different ways. The party or agent can also be a department, group, union, association, or organization depending on the type of negotiation.

Sometimes the term power refers to one's potential influence over things or events as well as attitudes and behaviour. Defining power in certain instances often becomes difficult when it needs to be done in relative terms. The power of a party cannot be described without specifying the target party and specific purpose. One party appears to have more power than the other party while it appears to be having lesser power than yet another party. The relative power between parties also depends on the issue. From this standpoint, power is a dynamic variable that changes according to the change in condition.

Authority involves the rights, prerogatives, obligations, and duties associated with particular positions in an organization or the social system (Yukl 2007). Leaders are either assigned the tasks or they themselves choose the tasks to achieve the business goals of the organization. In either case, the leaders have authority to decide the course of actions, draw resources, deploy members, instruct them to conform to rules and standing instructions, etc. Thus authority is a source of power. Yukl (2007) states that the scope of authority for the occupant of a managerial position is the range of requests that can properly be made and the range of actions that can properly be taken. Managers need a variety of powers to execute the tasks and drive the people to perform.

Power is defined by Kotler (1979) as 'a measure of a person's potential to get others to do what he or she wants them to do, as well as to avoid being forced to do what he or she does not want to do?' This definition captures the spirit of most definitions of power.

Power is the ability of one person to cause another person to perform and accomplish something. Authority is a specific kind of power that a person uses in an organization for task accomplishment.

Types of Power

In organizations, people utilize power to influence each other; an organizational leader uses his/her power to drive the team members to achieve the team goal. One needs to know the types and sources of power. French and Raven (1960) identified five bases of power. This laid the groundwork for most discussions on power and authority in the latter half of the twentieth century. These five main types of power are coercive, legitimate, reward, referent, and expert. Power can be manifested through one or more of these bases.

Coercive power   This is the ability of a manager, as an organizational leader, to threaten, punish, or initiate punitive action against a delinquent employee. Based on the manager's initiation the employee can ultimately be tangibly punished. The punishment can be a less satisfying work assignment, low rating, stoppage of increment, a demotion or a discharge, or even dismissal. Intangible or psychological punishments include criticism, avoidance, disapproval, and withdrawal of work assignments. He/she may also receive sarcastic remarks by colleagues.

Coercion is not always negative. For example, teachers coerce students to accept what they (the teachers) want them (the students) to do or think. Teachers can influence students and this may give the students the freedom to think, do, and experiment. Influencing behaviour encourages, compliments, makes students ask open questions and come up with alternative answers, facilitates sensing and voicing that develops group feelings, and so forth (Flander 1970). Followers comply with the instructions given to avoid any sort of punitive actions.

Legitimate or position power   By virtue of the position of a manager in the organizational hierarchy and on accepting the responsibilities, the person gains and enjoys this power. The police, regulatory authorities like pollution control boards, environmental protection bodies, directorate of factories for safety in industries, and many other forums have legitimate power. Thus, this power is assigned. At home, parents use this power; similarly in educational institutions, teachers acquire this power by virtue of their superior position. The followers comply with instructions because they admire or identify with the leader and desire to gain the approval of the leader.

Reward power   A person possesses the intrinsic desire to be recognized for any notable contribution to the organization. Anyone may be recognized through financial or non-financial rewards, time off, better space in the office, attractive work assignments, or even promotion. A manager is said to have reward power if he/she has the potential ability to reward worthy behaviour.

Reward further includes offering psychological rewards or positive sensory gratification like praise, appreciation, approval, and recognition. This power inculcates the belief in the subordinate that he/she has access to the higher authorities who value him/her. Obviously, this reward power helps the superior to gain charismatic and legitimate power.

Referent power   In organizations, few managers get adequate respect from employees, who become their followers and desire to emulate them. Such managers become leaders and lead by example. Employees unconsciously follow them. Referent power rests heavily on trust. It often influences followers who may not be particularly aware that they are modelling their behaviour on that of the manager. They do what the managers do in similar situations. This power may take considerable time to develop and thus may not prove particularly effective in a workforce with a rapid turnover of personnel.

Referent power reduces the psychological distance between a manager and his/her follower. French and Raven (1960) caution against applying referent power in cross-cultural situations. In the United States, employees are likely to identify with managers by personally liking them and feeling liked in return, whereas Argentine and Mexican employees are likely to identify with managers by respecting them and feeling respected in return.

Expert power A person gains this power by virtue of his knowledge, skills, experiences, ability, pragmatism, and anything else that enhances his/her credibility. These intangibles are of a special kind—essential in executing a job and getting it done well. Professional competencies and knowledge give a person this power. He/she can gain the confidence of his/her associates and lead them to achieve a common goal. They trust their leader's judgment, decisions, and directives. Multiple skills are required to perform a job, which a single person may not possess and for which he/she can take the help of experts in that particular field. Thus, experts need the knowledge to identify persons with a knowledge base in particular fields.

French and Raven (1960) highlight that expert power rests on the belief of employees that the individual has a particularly high level of knowledge or a highly specialized skill set. Managers may be accorded authority based on the perception of their greater knowledge of the tasks at hand than their employees.

Knowledge power This power stems from one's technical skills and academic achievements. Knowledge power helps to perform the role better, faster, and with perfection. Knowledge of the job, knowledge of handling people, and most importantly knowledge of self are essential to be effective. The knowledge and experience gained in course of time do not have a substitute. The need for knowledge in these areas was discussed in Chapter 1. In a constantly changing global economy, leaders are being challenged to find new methods for performance improvement. Knowledge helps to gain authority, establish credibility, accept responsibilities, make decisions, and facilitate skills. The present millennium is truly knowledge driven. Effective leaders need to improve performance through knowledge of self and team members and by relying on knowledge management.

Many authors have also included reflected power, charismatic power, and emotional power to the above list.

Reflected power   A person gains this power by virtue of his/her closeness to a power source. For example, if a supervisor is very close to the general manager, he/she is viewed differently by the organizational members. Even a supervisor with reflected power is approached and requested by many seniors for getting some sort of favour, legitimate or illegitimate, from the general manager. You will find examples of reflected power in abundance in organizations. For example, the power of the general manager is reflected to the employees through the supervisor. As soon as the object (the general manager) changes, others can no longer see the image of power through the supervisor. Personal secretaries or assistants of senior officers, as well as confidential secretaries of ministers, possess this power in abundance.

Charismatic power   Charisma refers to magnetism, allure, and it is a type of authority or influence based on exceptional characteristics of an individual, which is also an important social influence that attracts people. By virtue of this power of positive attraction or devotion, one gets admiration from others. This power helps the subordinate understand and value the leader. The leader, in turn, on account of increased credibility can lead other persons to trust what he/she says, and his/her judgments and decisions. Just consider the case of a renowned legal practitioner or a doctor. These professionals receive enormous trust from their respective clients. A subordinate identifies himself/herself with the leader, feels a positive attraction towards him/her, and ultimately accepts him/her as a role model.

Emotional power   Often, personal relationships can also act as a source of power for a person. Mothers possess this relationship with their children. A mother gives a toffee to her child for doing the homework. An elder sister gives something in kind to her younger brother just to run an errand for her. In organizations also, the influencing person needs to maintain a personal relationship to influence others in getting them to accept the tasks assigned to them. The influencers manipulate the relationship to get things done.

Summarily, knowledge power contributes to developing work leadership. Legitimate or position power facilitates discharge of duties in some specific areas. Reflected power is volatile in nature. Reward power establishes credibility. Charismatic power facilitates acquiring followers. Expert power resembles knowledge power. Pursuing research on one multinational, one public sector, and one private sector company, Pareek and Purohit (2010) quotes Keshote who observed in 1991 that production managers need much more coercive power than service managers.

Sources of Power

A person may acquire power from various sources. One may derive power from his/her organizational position, being close to a power source as a result of charisma and a charming nature, the ability to punish, personal relationships and networking skills, the ability to withhold or deny information, having expertise, level of competency, role modelling, a capacity to reward, through help and a caring nature, and from access to vital and confidential information. Legitimate power is vital in performing the role and allocating resources. The legitimate power is utilized by persons in higher positions in the organisation. Conversely, higher positions are the base of legitimate power. The capacity of initiating disciplinary action and punishing subordinates for mistakes comes in the category of coercion, the base being the highest position in the organizational hierarchy.

In the organization, the power of a person can be derived from interpersonal, structural, and situational bases. Power bases and leadership effectiveness are intertwined. Whether leaders gain power or the followers give it to them is still a matter of debate. Again, it is true that a manager in isolation cannot exert his/her power. But, when two or more managers sit together, they can collectively exert more power on any agency—presumably in conformance to the maxim 'unity is strength'. Studies have found that task-oriented managers tend to do better in situations of good leader–member relationships, structured tasks, and position power (weak or strong). However, they do well when the task is unstructured but position power is strong.

Basically, interpersonal power is vested in a person as prescribed by the organization (that is, legitimate, reward, and coercive) and by the person's qualities (that is, expert and referent). While structural and situational powers (that is, resource, decision-making, and information) normally go by the hierarchy of the organization's structure, that is, the higher the position of a person in the organization, the greater is his/her power in accessing resources, making decisions, and having access to important information.

Most of the problems of effectiveness faced by organizations are created by improper use of power by managers. There are cases where managers made in charge of businesses lack the required knowledge and skills. Without sufficient capabilities, these managers would not be able to utilize their powers professionally, and thus they contribute to reduce the performance of the organization. There are also cases where managers intentionally seek power in the organization for their personal benefits. Similarly, these managers would not bring any benefit to the organization in the long term. They rather become 'pretenders' than be diligent workers.

Power is important to many people as it can enhance status and prestige. It is also responsible for promotion and opportunities to lead and rule. Anyhow, such intentions, if not properly associated with the organizational purposes and directed goals, will not benefit the organization. Thus, the reality of power should be wisely accepted that it is important to enable someone to contribute effectively to his/her organization. Wrong application of power such as corruption and other unethical actions are problems generated by improper attitude of people towards the usage of power.

The importance of power in an organization is that people need it for task accomplishment. All managers need it in varying degrees. The differences are in the degree and intention; whether someone has a high or low need for power, and whether the need for power is directed towards personal or organizational purposes. The issue of the reality of power in an organization is important enough to be closely studied.

Multidimensional power

Powers are derived from different bases. Authority depends on organizational culture. Managers influence, encourage, and motivate their employees in their own ways. They try to win over and transform subordinates into followers. Making followers productive depends on many variables like the personality of the leader, human resource management skills, skills of the group members, the complexity of the tasks, amount of interaction within the group, interpersonal relations, help required from other groups, etc.

Due to the multiple variables behind making followers productive and effective, there cannot be any single leadership style. Obviously then, each base of power in management can be effective in the right setting and right situation. Both power and leadership shape and mould the conception of authority within an organization.

Power and leadership are two facets of authority. Both these facets of authority differ drastically from culture to culture, because authority itself is conceived differently by different societies. Furthermore, no single dimension of authority and power is likely to hold equally for all managers and subordinates or followers in a multicultural domestic setting or in the multicultural milieu of the multinational corporation. Power and authority are multidimensional because relationships are by nature multidimensional. A single power cannot make a group productive; rather a combination of powers is needed. The multidimensional nature has become more distinct in the changing leadership paradigm.

LEADERSHIP SKILLS

Many people view leadership expertise as a distinguishing trait of the leader. Some call it charisma and style. Any person can become a leader and be able to meet the needs of the team in a manner appropriate to his/her own needs, style, and strength. Leaders need skills to set goals, conduct meetings, manage conflict, negotiate, solve problems, improve creativity, identify strengths and weaknesses, review performance, and many more activities.

Leaders are required to analyse various types of problems, carry out problem-solving exercises, develop creative ideas, generate and evaluate alternatives, undertake feasibility analyses, identify patterns and trends, segregate and store useful information, differentiate relevant and irrelevant information, and interpret complex relationships for which they need technical and cognitive skills. They further need to understand and influence people, get their willing participation, facilitate teamwork and resolve conflicts, besides building and maintaining personal networks to develop coordination, cooperation, and collaboration. The skills required vary from situation to situation.

A leader needs multifaceted skills of which technical, conceptual, and interpersonal skills are worth mentioning for most leadership roles and functions.

Technical skills refer to knowledge about systems, processes, procedures or methods, and techniques for conducting a specialized activity as done by engineers, doctors, musicians, players, and accounts. Technical skill also involves the ability to select and use equipment, a procedure, standing instructions, technique, and knowledge. The professionals mentioned above possess these skills in their respective fields.

Conceptual skills encompass rational thinking, concept formulation, interpreting and conceptualizing complex and uncertain relationships, problem-solving ability, analysing the speed and direction of change in a business scenario, ability to accept change and meet challenges, ability to anticipate threats and initiate balancing actions, recognize opportunities and make the best use of those, and finally, the ability to coordinate and integrate all activities of an organization to achieve business objectives and goals. A manager striving to procure and retain talent in the organization needs conceptual skills.

Interpersonal skills or human relation skills include the ability to interact and work with, and understand and motivate people at any level. The interaction may be with an individual or a group. This skill needs profound knowledge about human behaviour and interpersonal processes. The ability to understand others, their sentiments, feelings, attitudes, motives, occupational values, JOHARI window (named after its inventors, Joseph Luft and Harry Ingham, is a schematic presentation to view the extent of self-disclosure and feedback one uses while interacting with others), personality traits, level of satisfaction, and so forth. People having this skill communicate assertively and effectively, extend empathy to others and honour their sensitivity, develop relationships, leading to networking. As such, they can form a team and successfully drive the team to achieve its goals. They are tactful, diplomatic, knowledgeable, listen attentively, and accept social behaviour.

Top-level managers commonly need skills to build strong teams of people, understand middle management, create a learning environment, monitor and review periodically, ensure that team members are open to feedback, enhance their problem-solving skill, identify and resolve conflict, attract and retain talent to prevent attrition, share ideas regarding organizational growth, recognize innovative work done, make the middle level involved in the decision-making process, and comprehend and practise OCTAPACE (openness, collaboration, trust, authenticity, proactivity, autonomy, confrontation, and experimentation) (Pareek 2007).

Managers also need planning skills, organizing skills, leading skills, controlling skills, and decision-making skills.

LEADERSHIP TRAITS

To discharge the responsibilities, in addition to having certain skills, managers need to have certain personality traits. The term 'trait' refers to a variety of individual attributes, including aspects of personality, temperament, needs, motives, and values (Yukl 2007). Qualities such as self-confidence, emotional maturity, energy level, etc. constitute the personality traits. These are relatively stable behavioural dispositions.

A leadership trait is a relatively permanent characteristic that does not change as the individual moves from one situation to another (Howell and Costley 2006). Howell and Costley also mention three broad categories of leadership traits: physical or background traits, personality or ability traits, and task or social traits. The physical or background traits include the level of activity or energy, education, and social status. Assertiveness, dominance, originality or creativity, self-confidence, administrative ability, fluency of speech, social perceptiveness, and adaptability belong to the category of personality or ability traits. The various tasks or social traits comprise willingness to take initiatives and responsibilities besides being motivated, persistent-task-oriented, cooperative, and social.

People differ in their characteristics. Some people are shy, trustworthy, serious, thorough, meticulous, painstaking, anxious, and good communicators. Again, some are outgoing, corrupt, indifferent, careless, and cannot communicate lucidly. These characteristics are inherent and natural, and express the personality type.

Traits for Effectiveness

In order to be effective, a leader must have the ability to see, communicate, interpret, and verbalize. The leader must have concern and respect for people, appreciate their needs, and inspire them. He/she should be able to provide direction to the team and sustain their enthusiasm. He must also have a keenness for change management and the ability to energise people. Leaders need to get along with people, make sound and timely decisions, and achieve team objectives by getting things done through people. Weiss (2007) identifies eleven traits essential for a person to be an effective leader.

1. The ability to see the big picture
2. The ability to communicate the big picture to other people
3. The ability to interpret and articulate the group's needs, aspirations, and feelings
4. Concern and respect for individual needs, aspirations, feelings, and abilities within the group
5. The ability to communicate the group's needs, aspirations, and feelings to people outside the group
6. A grasp of what people need or want for themselves
7. The ability to inspire people to do what they otherwise might not do for themselves or for others
8. The ability to provide people with direction and to focus people's energies on specific goals while maintaining high group morale
9. Enthusiasm for the group's mission, objectives, and standards
10. An avid desire for change, growth, and improvement
11. The energy necessary for conducting the business of the group

It is evident from the observation of Weiss (2007) that seeing or visualizing the big picture is not the end; exchanges with the team members and other relevant persons are also essential. To be effective, a leader is required to possess the capacity of interpreting and expressing the group's needs, aspirations, and feelings, and in addition must have concern and respect for individuals' needs, aspirations, feelings, and their abilities within the group.

A leader needs to inspire and provide people with direction, and constantly enthuse them. Jack Welch also very strongly emphasizes that energy, energization, edge, and execution are important for a leader's mission. Krames's (2005) book entitled *Jack Welch and the 4 E's of Leadership* says individuals with energy love to 'go, go, and go'. Such people possess boundless energy and get up every day ready to attack the job at hand. High-energy people work very fast. Energizers must know how to spark others to perform. They outline a vision and get people to carry it out. Energizers know how to get people excited about a cause or a crusade or movement. They are selfless in giving others the credit when things go right, but quick to accept responsibility when things go awry. Those with edge are competitive, challenging, contending, and risk-taking. They know how to make the really difficult decisions, such as hiring, firing, and promoting, never allowing the degree of difficulty to stand in their way. The fourth and final 'E' is the key to the entire model.

Without measurable results, the other 'Es' are of little use. Executers recognize that activity and productivity are not the same and are capable of converting energy and edge into action and results. Executers convert dreams into reality.

Leaders need certain personality traits like being adaptable, authoritative, energetic, diplomatic, dramatic, dutiful, empathetic, enterprising, frank, gamesmanship, inquisitive, moralistic, persuasive, philosophical, systematic, a thought leader, tenacious, tolerant, unbiased, optimistic, and wise. They should be initiators, negotiators, trendsetters, and visionaries. Different job categories need different sets of traits. The personality traits required by leaders have been described. Personality traits and the situations, as described by Prashant Brahmane, are elaborated in Annexure 2.1.

Three Traits of a Tough Leader

Baldoni (2008) identifies three traits of a tough leader. He does not refer to what's on the outside (gruff and ready), but rather what is inside the individual (character and resilience). Toughness matters because you need a leader who has the resources to stand up for what he/she believes in, as well as stand up with others to achieve team and organizational goals. More important, toughness matters when things are not going well, when the economy is tanking, the market is shaky, and a new competitor has appeared on the horizon. Also, toughness matters when heads are being counted and everyone is wondering if the next head to roll may be theirs. Tough times demand tough leadership.

Baldoni talks about some of the ways leaders demonstrate toughness: they defuse tension, get up off the floor, and let off some steam.

They defuse tension   Leaders must be able to perform under pressure. Performing under pressure is a prerequisite for leadership. Of course, too much pressure can produce stress syndrome, resulting in a disaster. Effective leaders must maintain a sense of urgency and momentum; manage time, restrain themselves from putting members under too much pressure by giving them some time to breath. This does not necessarily mean slacking off; it is an indication to be careful and deliberate. Also, you should keep in mind that tension that comes from interpersonal conflicts is seldom positive; leaders need to eradicate it by taking some hard decisions about who works with whom and why.

They get up off the floor   A person can strive for success, but one may not always be recognized for it. One can always be knocked down but one must understand that there's no shame in getting knocked down. Coaches in every field teach this lesson very well. What matters is what you do next. One has to undertake realistic analysis and learn from experience.

In an organizational scenario, one of the reasons behind failure of some strategies may be due to changes in the environment. A strategy can always miss the mark due to inadequate skills or application of wrong skills. Obviously, the project will fail. Such is life in an organization. It is a leader's job to get back into the game and keep slogging. This requires resilience, an ability to flex with adversity as well as persevere when the going gets tough.

They let off some steam   Committing mistakes is a part and parcel of work life. If a team member makes a big mistake, a leader will naturally be annoyed. The leader must now focus some heat on the person who made the mistake and warn him/her. The erring person needs to be aware of the leader's displeasure; it may help him/her pay more attention the next time. A leader should always remember to criticize the action and not the person.

Humility   A leader must possess the courage to admit his/her mistake. Disclosing or declaring a failure is not a weakness, rather it is a strength. This is humility that indicates the leader has the right kind of inner toughness. First, it directly demonstrates a willingness to accept consequences. Second, it demonstrates humanness. It also creates an opportunity to move forward. Toughness gives the backbone to a leader's purpose and gives one the strength to continue. But one should also remember that boundary spanning and team leadership (discussed in detail in Chapter 5) in excess is a failure.

INTELLIGENCE AND LEADERSHIP

Intelligence means the brainpower of a person, and aptitude, cleverness, acumen, and astuteness are its synonyms. Intelligence is the ability to comprehend, to understand and gain from experience, and the capacity for gathering and interpreting information. An intelligent person possesses the ability to learn about, learn from, understand, and interact with one's environment. This general ability consists of a number of specific abilities, including adaptability to a new environment or to changes in the current environment, capacity for acquiring knowledge, capacity for reason and abstract thought, and also the ability to comprehend relationships. Intelligence is a collection of some mental abilities.

Hughes et al. (2008) mention that the first formal relationship between leadership and intelligence was established in 1115 BC in China, where the dynasties used standardized tests to determine which citizens would fit the key leadership roles in the institutions set up to run the country. Hughes (2008) emphasizes Sternberg's 'triarchic theory on intelligence' that offers some of the most significant implications for a leader. This theory focuses on what a leader does when solving complex mental problems, such as how information is combined and synthesized and errors are made, and the like.

The triarchic theory on intelligence mentions three components of intelligence: analytic intelligence, practical intelligence, and creative intelligence.

Analytic intelligence is similar to the standard psychometric definition of intelligence as measured by academic problem-solving, analogies, and puzzles, and corresponds to one's earlier componential intelligence, and reflects how an individual relates to his/her internal world.

Practical intelligence involves the ability to grasp, grapple, understand, and deal with everyday tasks. This is the contextual or relative aspect of intelligence and reflects how an individual relates to the external world around him/her.

Creative intelligence is the ability to produce work that is both novel and useful and involves insights and synthesis. It is the ability to react to situations and stimuli. This component considers the experiential or empirical aspect of intelligence and reflects how an individual connects the internal world to external reality.

These three components together help a leader to solve complex mental problems.

Emotional Intelligence and Leadership

Emotional intelligence (EI) refers to the intrinsic abilities that help a person perform well under pressure. It involves setting very high standards for oneself and the team even in tough situations, making the most of one's ability. Besides, it calls for always putting in hundred per cent effort, and being a good team player or performer or achiever. The concept of EI was developed about two decades ago. As such, EI does not fit the classic historical models of leadership. Autocratic styles are usually associated with great figures of military history. When people often use the same language for leadership today, they fail. In order to meet the changing demands, leaders of today need to develop and apply EI.

Goleman et al. (2001) describe a model of EI comprising four domains and twenty competencies. The four domains are self-awareness, self-management, social awareness, and relationship management. The first two of these domains are personal. Self-awareness is characterized by a deep understanding of one's emotions, strength and weaknesses, and an ability to accurately and honestly self-assess. A leader's self-management is about the control and regulation of his/her emotions, the ability to stay calm, clear, and focused when things do not go as planned, and the ability for self-motivation and initiative. The other two domains are social, and concern a person's ability to manage relationships with others. Social awareness covers empathy. For example, in the ability to consider employees' feelings in the process of making intelligent decisions either on a one-to-one basis or as a group.

EI enhances relationship management. It covers the ability to communicate, collaborate, and work with colleagues and to influence them. EI helps today's leaders to meet the significant challenges they come across in an ever more difficult leadership role when the 'talent war' is in progress (Childs 2004). EI has become a vital consideration for leaders to meet today's significant challenges. It helps leaders to extend leadership in ever more difficult situations.

In 1980, Reuven Bar researched on the qualities that lead to success. He showed that there was much more than traditional intelligence or IQ and developed the concept of emotional quotient (EQ). Psychologist Howard Gardener in 1985 challenged the current view of intelligence and proposed seven multiple intelligences, which included social intelligence (Childs 2004).

Demands from Leaders

Today's workforce does not accept an autocratic leadership style, and leadership needs to match the growing sense of democracy and independence in the workforce. The workforce of the present day is knowledgeable and has far more options and choices than the earlier times. As such, demands from present-day leaders have significantly changed as they need to manage and lead an 'empowered' workforce and go beyond the domain of consultative, cooperative, and democratic styles (Childs 2004). The new demands include

- Consultation and involvement—but leaders are still getting criticized for not having and communicating a compelling vision and purpose
- Autonomy and freedom—but leaders are still expected to take full responsibility when things go wrong whatever the reasons may be
- Opportunities for growth, challenge, and glory—but leaders must take on the task of coaching (develop in role) and mentoring (develop work leadership) to enhance workforce potential
- Inclusion and team spirit—but we still want our leaders to give us individual reward, recognition, and acknowledgement.

Thus, the task is to get persons with enough talent capable of meeting all these demands. See Box 2.1.

Box 2.1 Competencies common to global leaders

The Aditya Birla Group has identified the competencies that are common to global leaders. In the words of Dr Kumar Mangalam Birla:

'As the world has shrunk, thanks to technology, a global leader has to have the ability to make sense of changes in the competitive environment of his industry, his customer's industry and twice removed, his customer's competitive landscape.

'The onus to keep the organization's core values from getting diluted is a critical task for our global leaders.

'Global leaders invariably have true spirit of adventure in large doses and also great ability to handle failures.

'Our workforce today is fairly diversified with 100,000 employees of 30 nationalities dispersed over hundred locations in India and abroad, 30,000 of whom are women.

'Over the last 10 years, we have made 15 acquisitions worldwide of total value of nearly $10 billion.'

Source: Based on a speech delivered by Kumar Mangalam Birla at the All India Management Association on 21 February 2009.

Use of Emotional Intelligence

There are now a number of models and questionnaires aimed at measuring EI. The measurement is often based on self-report questionnaires. However, this approach has obvious limitations in identifying levels of self-awareness because a person cannot be aware of what he/she is not aware of. So, while questionnaires play a part, better approaches also involve (a) experiential learning through exercises, and (b) 360-degree feedback processes.

These are much more effective and comprehensive ways of identifying possible strengths and weaknesses in EI terms. When the self-assessment and 360-degree feedback system is undertaken online, and results are processed by someone independent, it ensures confidentiality and thus achieves a much higher level of honesty in the feedback and assessment. This approach challenges complacency and can enable people to grow and develop. The concept of EI allows individuals to go beyond their existing knowledge and comfort zones, thus producing real impact, growth, and change essentially for leaders.

INFLUENCING TACTICS

Influencing people is a primary need in organizational life. We need to influence finance persons and senior management for getting the budget, junior colleagues to get the work done, purchase people to get the right material at the right time, the store and dispatch people to send consignments to customers on time, and so forth. All endeavours to influence people are accompanied by certain consequences. An endeavour needs evaluation. One person, say, the manager, tries to influence the other person, say, the member. The manager may achieve the intended effect in totality or partially. The endeavour may have one of three distinct outcomes (Yukl 2006): commitment, compliance, or resistance.

Commitment Commitment is an outcome of the endeavour to influence a person in which he/she concurs with a decision or request from the person trying to influence. Organizational commitment is a state in which an employee identifies with a particular organization, its mission, policies, objectives, goals, and wishes to remain a member of the organization.

There are three separate dimensions of organizational commitment: affective commitment (an emotional attachment), continuance commitment (refers to perceived economic value), and normative commitment (the employee wants to remain with the organization for moral or ethical value). Organizational commitments are emotional reactions of employees towards an organization and its policies. Recent workforce trends, such as downsizing and re-engineering, have jeopardized employee commitment and morale in organizations. How an organization sustains commitment in these tumultuous times depends on a number of factors such as job security, loyalty, and trust in management. Feelings of alienation and helplessness influence the commitment of a workforce.

Organizational commitment affects the organizational climate that is bound by perception. The perception may not always correspond to organizational facts, but nonetheless comprise reality in the eyes of the employees. Numerous climates can exist depending on what facet of an organization is being described. There are, however, certain climate types that are common across a number of different organizations and industries. Examples include climates of fairness, safety, support, communication, tolerance for risk, flexibility, and continuous learning. Climate is related to employee behaviour, organizational outcomes, and management leadership styles, and as such, is an important factor to be considered.

Organizational commitment is the extent to which an employee feels a sense of allegiance to his/her employer.

Compliance Compliance categorically means that you follow the recommendations made by your team. The leader has to influence the followers to endeavour achieving team targets in compliance with the policies, standing instructions, procedures, norms, ethics, and other parameters. For simple and routine tasks, compliance is all that is necessary for the followers to accomplish the proposed target. But for challenging, complex, difficult, innovative assignments, compliance may lead to less successful outcomes. These assignments need commitment more than compliance.

Resistance Resistance is an organizational phenomenon we all come across. Wherein a larger mass of organizational persons oppose a target person or a group, rather than remaining passive while attempting to impose a change. The change may be incorporating a new system or policy, or imposing a disciplinary measure. The target person may act in various ways to pacify and reduce the resisting forces. He/she may like to (a) explain the benefits of the change, (b) disregard the request of the larger mass, (c) approach the higher authority to intervene and to overrule the requests, (d) delay taking action, (e) make a show of complying but doing otherwise, or using a combination of the above as he/she finds suitable in that organizational environment.

Influence Processes

Being influential is a unique capacity of any person whether he/she is a leader or not. One needs to influence to achieve what one wants from the target person. The influencing process involves the motives and perceptions of the target person in relation to the actions of the influencer and the context in which the interaction occurs.

Yukl (2007) mentions three different types of influencing processes: instrumental compliance, internalization, and personal identification. The processes are qualitatively different from each other, but more than one process can occur simultaneously. Let us take an example: getting quality system certification (ISO 9001). The person responsible (the management representative [MR]) for establishing, implementing, and maintaining the system has to work to achieve the defined goal. But he/she needs the involvement of many organizational persons to develop the documentation system and perform the associated tasks. In this case, the MR is the influencer and others involved are the targets.

Instrumental compliance The MR distributes tasks and a target person carries out the tasks, that is, the requested actions for the purpose of receiving a reward. He/she might do the tasks assigned to avoid any sort of punishment for non-compliance. He/she complies and the motivation for the behaviour is instrumental. The level of effort may be just enough to gain what he/she deserves.

Internalization Quite possibly the target may like quality management system as he/she knows the benefits that can be derived from the system. Thus, the assigned tasks are intrinsically desirable with regard to values, beliefs, and self-image. Thus, he/she performs and the effort put in by the MR is minimal. Commitment occurs regardless of any expectation of reward. The target is loyal to the system being introduced.

Personal identification In this case, the target neither desires any reward nor has any interest in the assignment. But, the target wants to please the MR and be liked by him/her. The motivation behind this behaviour is 'need for acceptance and esteem'. A close interpersonal relationship develops from the personal identification process. It is true that the target does not desire or get any immediate benefit. But on account of enhanced self-image, he/she may definitely get some benefit at a later stage.

From the explanations of the above three influencing processes, namely, instrumental compliance, internalization, and personal identification, with examples, it is clear that more than one process may occur for the same target for the same task assigned by the same leader.

DEVELOPING LEADERSHIP SKILLS

Leadership competencies can be developed through a number of ways like formal training, self-help activities, and developmental activities. Formal leadership training programmes are organized by leadership development centres. Self-help activities include reading success stories, listening to audio tapes, viewing video clippings, etc. Developmental activities may take many forms like coaching to develop in roles and mentoring to develop work leadership. Organizational practices have been discussed in Chapter 8 on leadership development.

SUMMARY

Power and influencing capacity establish a person's supremacy in the organization. A leader needs power to convince the followers. The collective bargaining forum needs power to win over the management, which, in turn, needs the capacity to convince them.

The most common types of power are charismatic, coercive, expert, reward, knowledge, reflected, legitimate, and position power. A person acquires power from various sources.

Organizational leaders need skills to set goals, conduct meetings, manage conflict, negotiate, solve problems, attempt to improve creativity, identify strengths and weaknesses, review performance, and many more activities. Leaders need to have traits like ability to see, communicate, interpret and verbalize, concern and respect for people, ability to appreciate people's needs, inspire and provide followers with direction, imbue enthusiasm, etc. Certain personality traits become useful in specific situations. Tough leaders defuse tension, get up off the floor, and let off some steam.

Leaders need intelligence, especially EI, to function under pressure. They must apply influence tactics that may have three distinct outcomes: commitment, compliance, and resistance. Organizations today are keen to develop leadership skills.

KEY TERMS

Analytic intelligence is the ability to solve problems and puzzles, and it reflects how an individual relates to his/her internal world.

Authority is specific power a person uses in the organization for task accomplishment.

Creative intelligence is the ability to produce work that is both novel and useful and it reflects how an individual connects the internal world to the external reality.

Emotional intelligence is the intrinsic ability that helps an individual to perform well under pressure, setting very high standards for himself/herself and the team even in tough situations.

Expert power is gained by a person by virtue of his knowledge, skills, experiences, ability, pragmatism, and established credibility.

Influence refers to use of power to get things done without resistance.

Power is the ability of one person to cause another person to perform and accomplish something.

Practical intelligence refers to the ability of grasping, grappling, understanding, and dealing with everyday tasks. It reflects how an individual relates to the external world.

EXERCISES

Concept Review Questions

1. Distinguish between power and authority. What dominant type of power does the chairman and managing director of a multinational company possess? What are the other powers he/she might have? Discuss the power possessed by his/her personal secretary.

2. Discuss the broad categories of traits. Specify the elements of personality of people. Discuss each element with example.

3. Identify the various contributors to the effectiveness of leaders. How do these help to achieve the stated or self-decided goals?

4. Enumerate the differences between skills and traits. Why should a successful leader have traits in addition to skills?

5. Assume that a company has been engaged in manufacturing and selling the same products for the last twenty years. It has neither changed its product range nor is interested to do that. Of the various types of powers which, in your opinion, are needed to run the business? Justify your answer.

Critical Thinking Questions

1. What type of intelligence does a leader mostly need to pacify a team member when he/she expresses grievances by citing examples of incentives provided by another organization?

2. Prepare an exhaustive list of demands from the top management of a multinational company in the era of economic recession.

3. A company is planning to implement a major change wherein more than 80 per cent of its employees would be affected. What type of intelligence does the change agent need to ensure minimal resistance?

Assignments

1. Collect or develop a questionnaire to identify personality traits. Approach any ten managers, administer the questionnaire, and find their traits. Prepare a list of the top five personality traits.

2. Consider ten politicians, their activities, contributions to society, and portfolio. Insert other parameters you feel are necessary. Attempt to rank the importance of the components of intelligence and emotional intelligence. Extend your survey to the professors of the college/university you are or were studying in. Compare and contrast your findings.

REFERENCES

Baldoni, John (2008), *Leadership at Work* (Voice of John Baldoni), Harvard Business Publishing (discussionleader.hbsp.com/baldoni/2008/09/.html, accessed on 21 February 2008).

Birla, Kumar Mangalam (2009), J.R.D. Tata Memorial Award Lecture delivered at the All India Management Association on 21 February, *AIMA News*, Newsletter of the All India Management Association, New Delhi.

Brahmane, Prashant, Director, Manscan Psychological Clinic, Mumbai. Total Personal Intelligence, Reading Material.

Childs, Roy (2004), *Emotional Intelligence* (www.teamtechnology.co.uk/emotional-intelligence.html, accessed on 28 February 2009).

Flander, Ned A. (1970), *Analyzing Teaching Behaviour*, Addison-Wesley, New York.

French, J.P.R., Jr., and B. Raven (1960), 'The Bases of Social Power'. In *Studies in Social Power*. Dorwin Cartwright, ed., University of Michigan Press, Ann Arbor, MI.

Goleman, Daniel P., Cary Cherniss, and Wareen G. Bennis (2001), *The Emotionally Intelligent Workplace: How to Select for, Measure and Improve Emotional Intelligence in Individuals, Groups.* Jossey-Bass, London (www.firstandsecond.com/store/books, accessed on 28 February 2009).

Howell, Jon. P. and Dan. L. Costley (2006), *Understanding Behaviours for Effective Leadership*, Prentice-Hall India, New Delhi.

Hughes, Richard L., Ropert C. Ginnett, and Gordon J. Curphy (2008), *Leadership Enhancing the Lessons of Experience*, Tata McGraw-Hill Publishing, New Delhi.

Kotler, John P. (1979), *Power in Management*, American Management Association, New York.

Krames, Jeffrey A. (2005), *Jack Welch and the 4 E's of Leadership*, McGraw-Hill, New York.

Pareek, Udai (2007), *Understanding Organisational Behaviour*, Oxford Higher Education, Oxford University Press, New Delhi.

Pareek, Udai and Surabhi Purohit (2010), *Treaining Instructions in HRD and OD*, Tata McGraw-Hill, Third Edition, New Delhi.

Victor, David A. and Monica Turner C., Multidimensional Power (www.enotes. com/management-encyclopedia/leadership-styles-bases-power, accessed on 17 April 2009).

Weiss, Donald H. (2007), Becoming an Effective Leader, Goyal Publishers, Delhi.

Weiss, Donald H. (2007), Becoming an Effective Leader, American Management Association, Goyal Publishers, Delhi, India.

Yukl, Gary (2007), *Leadership in Organisation*, Pearson Education, Delhi.

CLOSING CASE

Crisis Management

The chairman of Magna Hospital invited the medical superintendent, HRD manager, and a few senior doctors. He also invited some external persons like a legal expert, experienced medical superintendents of two more hospitals, a Member of Parliament, and a Member of Legislative Assembly of the constituency in which Magna Hospital is situated. The persons present in the meeting saw two unknown faces. The chairman introduced them as his personal friends.

In the beginning, the chairman narrated the incidents along with the background though it was known to all, as news dailies had extensively reported the incident. Even the name of Miss Rosni Sharma had appeared in the media.

The chairman sought the advice of all present at the meeting. In fact, the discussion was in the form of a brainstorming session. Each person could express his/her opinion. At last, the invited friends of the chairman, after having a little mutual consultation, expressed their consolidated views with confidence and clarity. What they expressed is briefly given below:

1. To refer to and review the performance review reports of Miss Rosni
2. To review the performance review reports of all the trainee nurses
3. To separate the reports of those having some sort of negative remarks
4. To organize an 'early gradation test' for all trainees
5. To assess further requirements and initiate actions accordingly

At the end, they requested the chairman to offer his comments on their submission.

The chairman added:

1. We will definitely organize the gradation test before completion of the training period.

2. 'In view of increased patients and urgency of fresh nurses, early gradation has emerged as a prime requirement.
3. To make the decision taken at the meeting known to all through the Intranet, electronic display board at the main entrance, and other places.
4. To inform all union office bearers and nurses through hostel display board.

The chairman introduced the invited friends stating their identities and thanked them and all others present at the meeting.

The chairman advised the HRD manager to engage in self-development in addition to developing others. The chairman further advised the medical superintendent and the HRD manager to strengthen their skills of foreseeing and anticipating what is going to happen, and highlighted the utmost need to adhere to the rules of the organization. However, he temporarily stripped some powers from the medical superintendent.

Discussion Questions

1. What do you think was the professional background of the two friends of the chairman?
2. Why did the chairman not initially disclose the identity of the invited friends?
3. Which power specifically was active that compelled the HRD manager to recommend early completion of the training of Miss Rosni?
4. Identify the intelligences based on which the medical superintendent ordered early completion of the training of Miss Rosni.
5. Do you feel that the chairman's actions were appropriate to the situation? Can you identify the power he used?

ANNEXURE 2.1

Personality Traits and Situations

Adaptable: You normally adjust very well and perform as usual in different playing conditions, with different captains or different forms of games, easily.

Argumentative: You are the first person to be seen contesting a point about anything on and off the field.

Authoritative: Whatever you do in the game, it has a stamp of the extraordinary on it.

Energetic: You are a tireless horse, which keeps galloping, whether it is the sun or the moon up in the skies.

Calculative: You normally set the field in a way that the ball goes where the fielder is placed.

Gentleman: If cricket is called a gentleman's game, then your game is an ideal personification of the same.

Definitive: You never move your feet unless you have prepared for an intended act.

Democratic: Your action always follows from a general opinion of the other members of the team.

Diplomatic: You have the capacity to communicate ideas in a most subtle form.

Dramatic: You are most likely to bring showmanship to everything you do.

Dutiful: You love responsibilities and you perform them diligently.

Egoist: Your sense of self-pride always affects your acceptance by others.

Empathetic: Your usual priority to understand others' feelings goes beyond team members and extends to the all.

Enterprising: Your purchase of listener's time and the effect you create is businesslike.

Esteemed: Irrespective of many compulsions, you never sacrifice your sense of self-esteem in any situation.

Experimentative: You try varied combinations to reach targets as a matter of habit.

Extrovert: You are always in an expressive mood and successfully draw the attention of others to whatever you are doing.

Finisher: You always finish the task you have in hand before starting another one.

Follower: You follow a school of thought and stick to it.

Frank: Nobody needs to take the trouble to find out what you think.

Gamesman: You can use many soft means to derive an advantage.

Initiator: You are always at the forefront of initiating an action.

Inquisitive: You have an enormous ability to ask questions in any given situation.

Innovative: In any given situation, you can find stunning ways to make good of the situation.

Just: Your sense of justice remains undeterred even in the most testing situations.

Loyal: Your loyalty to the team is undisputed.

Man-leader: Your ability to bring people together and make them perform to the fullest is remarkable.

Materialistic: Your commitment to an act is in proportion to the rewards.

Mature: You speak and understand things beyond your age.

Moralist: Your adherence to the values is strict and unwavering.

Negotiator: You seldom give up anything unless you see a larger gain in doing so, at present or in the future.

Opportunistic: You see and identify opportunities from miles away.

Open: You are always a person who looks forward to suggestions from one and all.

Optimistic: You always imagine your future to be a bed of roses.

Original: In your most natural form, you are one who cannot be compared to anyone.

Parent: You love to nurture children.

Patient: You seldom mind waiting irrespective of how long you have done that already.

Peace-loving: You avoid confrontation, quarrels, and conflicts at all costs.

Perfectionist: You always strive for meeting the results in a purist way.

Persuasive: You keep trying as long as it takes to produce results.

Philosophical: You are capable of amalgamating many truths and making greater, wider, and larger sense.

Positive: You are always committed to accepting the brighter side of life.

Qualitative: Your class is apparent through every mannerism and action.

Rational: You are unstoppable when it comes to the use of logic to understand the most mundane things.

Realistic: You accept only that which you see and experience.

Risk-taker: You love to explore even against heavy odds.

Romantic: You have an uncurbed tendency to possess, feel, touch, and think about something all the time.

Salesman: You love to explore possibilities to do business with everyone at every moment.

Sensitive: You are very easily affected by the smallest of changes in your surroundings.

Social: You always think of benefits for the masses in all your plans.

Sophisticated: You care a lot about maintaining an upmarket look and lifestyle.

Spiritual: You have a firm belief that the hands are yours but the wishes are His.

Sporting: You appreciate your opponents even when you are losing.

Systematic: Before you attempt to undertake any work you create a system of work.

Teacher: You love to help people understand the subject in totality.

Thought leader: You love ideas and strive to popularize them.

Team member: You always exist as a part of the whole you belong to and never focus on your personal presence.

Tenacious: When the going gets tough, you get going even stronger.

Tolerant: You have an incredible capacity to stand up to something much against your own taste.

Trendy: You are always on the lookout for something new and quick to follow trends.

Trendsetter: You have an innate desire to start a new system, culture, or trend.

Truthful: You always chase the truth and use it all the time.

Unbiased: You rarely have an extreme feeling for anything.

Visionary: You are capable of seeing far into the future.

Wise: You always look at the long-term repercussions of every event that takes place.

CHAPTER 3

Perspectives on Effective Leadership Behaviour

OPENING CASE

Searching for a Leadership Style

Unique Refrigeration Company (URC) is a small-scale company. It is owned by Mr Rakesh Mishra who is also the chairman. He completed MTech. (production engineering) twenty years ago, followed by an MBA (with specialization in finance) from a reputed institute. The company's business has grown steadily in the sixteen years since it came into existence. At present, Mr Sharma (public relations officer), Mr Gandhi (production manager), Mr Vidyut (materials manager), Mr Biswal (HR manager), and Mr Mazumdar (quality control manager) are the other people holding key positions in URC and have been working in the company since it was formed in 1990. They all report to Mr Mishra. Mr Sanat, assistant manager (production), reports to Mr Gandhi.

Mr Gandhi, by nature, always looks after the welfare of the employees, listens to the workers, and tries to solve their problems. He frequently enquires about the problems they are facing while performing the tasks assigned. He collects facts and figures regarding production, machine breakdowns, availability of material, queuing for inspection, conformance to customer requirements, liaison with related departments, interacting with the research and development division, and other production-related activities.

Mr Sanat is a dynamic and enthusiastic person of about twenty-five years of age with a very good academic background. He also coordinates the production departments. He mainly collects production figures, that is, the target vis-à-vis quantity produced; seldom does he enquire about the well-being of the people working in his department. Whenever someone approaches him to share something, his stereotyped answer is 'concentrate on your work, you are paid for that'. His people do not like him.

One day a worker received a message that his son had met with an accident while returning from school. He approached Mr Sanat and sought his permission to leave some three hours before the scheduled time. Mr Sanat did not hear him carefully and, as usual, advised the worker to go back and continue with his work. On behalf of the worker, the foreman also requested Mr Sanat to allow the worker to go, but his effort was also in vain. Unable to take this, the worker fell down in the shop floor. He was taken to the factory dispensary. In fact, nothing serious happened and he recovered just after getting a little medical attention. The office bearers of the workers union came to know about the refusal of Mr Sanat to allow the worker to leave early. They organized a 'tool-down' in the work area of the concerned worker. Mr Gandhi came to know about the incident and granted permission for the worker to leave the office to attend to his son. He also asked whether the worker needed any more help.

Despite the timely intervention of Mr Gandhi, the matter did not end there. The next day, the representatives of the workers union met the labour welfare officer and then Mr Gandhi. They vehemently protested the behaviour of Mr Sanat towards the worker. Mr Gandhi made an effort to explain the situation to the representatives and assured them that this sort of incident would not occur in future. But the union representatives argued that it may happen in other functional areas. Ultimately, the chairman, Mr Rakesh Mishra, had to intervene to settle the dispute.

Learning outcomes

1. A supervisor should be an empathetic listener.
2. Understanding the problems of subordinates makes the work environment healthy.
3. The characteristics of key people in an organization should be conducive to achieving the business goals.

INTRODUCTION

Viewpoints and perceptions regarding leadership differ from person to person. Developing leadership traits follows many courses of action including acquisition of knowledge and skills that enhance the ability of a person to attain effectiveness.

Effective leaders perform various activities that we assume to be leadership behaviours. Some researchers have attempted to study the behaviours of leaders and have developed models to facilitate our understanding of these leadership behaviours. These models are often referred to as leadership style. There are many ideas about leadership styles that have been presented over the years. But most leadership theories are centred on the key idea that leaders have styles which are a conglomeration of two types of basic styles.

In one style, the leader adopts a managerial style and helps subordinates figure out what is expected of them and manages the daily activities of a group to accomplish a task. This is task-oriented behaviour of the leader. In the other style, organizational leaders play a more supportive role in providing a positive work environment in which workers can maximize their productivity. This set of behaviours is referred to as people-oriented style. Hughes et al. (2008) have provided the definitions of leadership of some researchers, which are as follows:

- The process by which an agent induces a subordinate to behave in a desired manner (Bennis 1959).
- Directing and coordinating the work of a group of members (Fiedler 1967).
- An interpersonal relation in which others do because they want to, not because they have to do (Merton 1969).
- Transforming followers, creating visions of the goal that may be attained, and articulating for the followers the ways to attain those goals (Bass 1985; Tichy and Devanna 1986).
- The process of influencing an organized group towards accomplishing its goals (Roach and Behling 1984).
- Actions that focus on resources to create desirable opportunities (Campbell 1991).
- The leader's job is to create conditions for the team to be effective (Ginnett 1996).
- The ends of leadership involve getting results through others, and the means of leadership involve the ability to build cohesive, goal-oriented

teams. Good leaders are those who build teams to get results across a variety of situations (Hogan and Curphy 1974).

The study of leadership styles has received significant attention in management literature. The findings of these studies suggest that an effective leadership style may not depend on whether an organization is not-for-profit or not. The findings further indicate that even in a not-for-profit context, effective leadership is defined not only by task and people orientations but also by the interaction between them.

Therefore, in developing the psychological profile of effective not-for-profit leaders, as is the case with profit sector leaders, management researchers should explore both their task and people orientations. Knowledge of the early works on leadership styles is also necessary.

LEADERSHIP STYLE—TWO-DIMENSIONAL

Researchers on leadership styles strive to explore the relationship between the interests of managers and leaders of organizations towards the welfare and psychological well-being of the workforce. They also study the specific efforts required to achieve business goals alongside. Some of the studies on leadership styles are presented below.

Ohio State Leadership Style

At Ohio State University, researchers studied the effectiveness of what they called 'initiating structure' (task-oriented) and 'consideration' (employee-oriented) in leadership behaviour.

Initiating structure, a task-oriented leadership style, is the degree to which a leader defines and organizes his/her role and the roles of followers. It is oriented towards goal attainment, and establishes well-defined patterns and channels of communication (Bass 1990).

Consideration is defined as the degree to which a leader shows concern and respect for followers, ensures their welfare, and expresses appreciation and support (Bass 1990). Both these styles are closely linked to the ideas of people-oriented and task-oriented behaviours.

The Ohio State researchers found, as might be expected, that employee turnover rate was lowest and employee satisfaction rate highest under leaders who were rated high in consideration (Stoner and Gilbert 2006). Conversely, leaders who rated low in consideration and high in initiating structure had high grievance and turnover rates among their employees. The leadership styles studied at Ohio State University is presented in Figure 3.1.

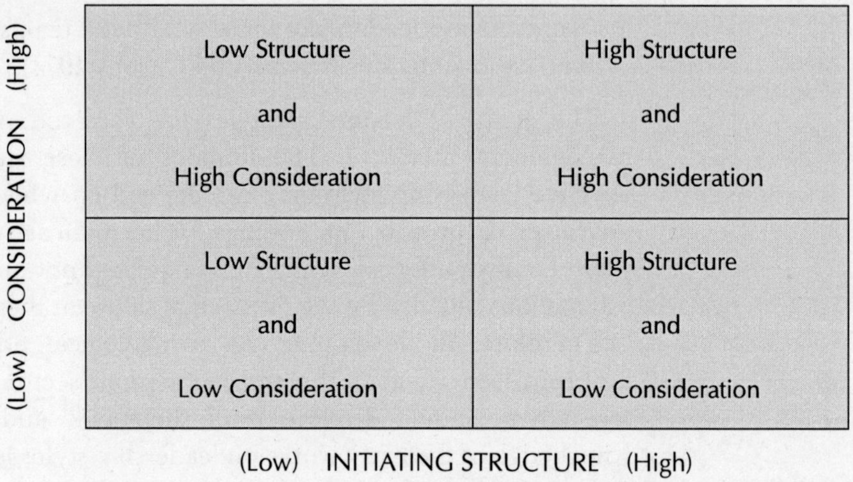

(High)	Low Structure and High Consideration	High Structure and High Consideration
CONSIDERATION	Low Structure and Low Consideration	High Structure and Low Consideration
(Low)		

(Low)   INITIATING STRUCTURE   (High)

FIGURE **3.1   Initiating vs consideration structure**

In the Ohio State University study, most interestingly, the researchers found that employees' ratings of their leaders' effectiveness depended less on the particular style of the leaders and more on the situation in which leaders used one of the styles. In fact, people do not hesitate to exert to accomplish the tasks when the leader at the workplace adopts a task-oriented style in emergency situations. For example, a medical team is engaged in giving first aid and treatment where an accident has taken place. The team or workforce spontaneously accepts and responds to task-oriented leadership.

Task-oriented leadership in military operations is a common feature. Soldiers are accustomed to fight following that style. When the enemy invades the country, the Indian army functions in this style to save the country and to achieve the superordinate goal of victory.

Initiating structure

The initiating structure style is about the extent to which a leader structures his/her role and the roles of his/her followers or subordinates to achieve the goals of the organization. Structuring includes organizing the work, work relationship (organization structure), and goals.

Managers possessing this style are goal oriented, distribute specific tasks, expect preset quality standards, fix accountability, emphasize meeting deadlines, etc. The style of leadership can be inferred from the behavioural disposition of a leader. A group member cannot work if he/she does not know his/her role, the procedure or process of working, performance standards, etc. Some behaviours of leaders who are strong in the initiating structure style are:

- letting group members know their role, and what is expected of them;
- encouraging them to conform to company procedures;
- allowing members to innovate, try out ideas in the group;
- making his/her attitudes clear to the members and others having regular work relationships;
- deciding the course of action and the means of achieving the goals;
- assigning responsibilities to group members relating to particular tasks;
- ensuring that his/her part in the group is understood by group members to avoid role conflict;
- scheduling the task/activities/work to be accomplished;
- defining and measuring performance standards; and
- questioning and ensuring that group members stick to standard rules and regulations.

Initiating structure relates to many of the competencies in the 'task management' dimension (discussed later), as well as 'leading others' dimension. These competencies include the following:

From task management dimension

While managing a project, a manager may study the details in depth as against superficial supervision. During execution, he/she may like to be involved and coordinate with the team, provide opinions wherever and whenever sought, design or redesign the work system, help the team to overcome barriers, discharge administrative activities, set and maintain the standard of qualitative requirements, institute and ensure safety measures, gather and provide information, organize resources, deploy personnel, and manage tasks strategically. These are some of the examples of the task management dimension of the initiating structure. To sum up, the initiating structure entails

- attention to detail;
- coordinating work activities;
- decision-making;
- designing work systems;
- eliminating barriers to performance;
- executing administrative activities;
- maintaining quality standards;
- maintaining safety;
- managing information resources;
- managing materials, facilities, and utilities;

- personnel decision-making; and
- strategic task management.

From leading others dimension

To lead, a supervisor needs to concentrate on and perform a few more activities. For example, he must interpret the information collected from various sources. He/she must consider tacit and explicit knowledge. He has to learn about the people and orient them to the task, develop the capacity to adjust with others, set realistic goals, take responsibility, share success to enthuse others, and so forth. These are some of the examples of the leading others dimension. To sum up, leading others involves

- interpreting the meaning of information for others;
- orienting others;
- setting goals for others; and
- taking charge.

Consideration

The consideration style refers to the extent to which an organizational leader is likely to have job relationships characterized by mutual trust, respect for colleagues and followers, and also respect for their viewpoints, sentiments, and feelings. A leader shows concern for the followers' well-being, comfort, development, status, satisfaction, and their intrinsic motivation. A highly considerate leader develops a more human touch approach and shows keen interest in his/her people. Such leaders are also concerned about the personal problems of their followers. They create a work environment characterized by friendliness, warmth, and approachability, and most importantly they treat their followers as equals. Some behaviours of leaders who are strong in consideration style are:

- being accessible, friendly, and cooperative;
- acting and reacting in a way that attracts followers;
- engaging in an effort to make the work environment pleasant for the group members;
- encouraging suggestions from members and implementing them after scrutiny;
- restoring equity, treating all group members with fairness and justice;
- inculcating the feeling that in dynamic environment, changes are inevitable;
- keeping people aware of organizational changes, even if the group is not affected by the change;
- making oneself accessible to all group members;

- looking after the personal well-being, welfare, and benefits of group members;
- being willing to welcome changes for the ultimate benefit of the group or the organization as a whole;
- explaining actions that are being planned; and
- consulting the group, with facts and figures, while planning changes.

These competencies, which relate to the consideration style of leadership, can mostly be found in the 'leading others' dimension of the Leadership Competency Model (that comprises leading others, task management, self-management, innovation, and social responsibility), and the following:

- Communicating with co-workers
- Active and emphatic listening
- Facilitating group discussion
- Social orientation
- Social perceptiveness
- Nurturing relationships
- Reinforcing success
- Developing and building teams
- Assessing others
- Coaching, developing, and instructing
- Cooperating
- Persuading
- Resolving conflicts
- Negotiating
- Empowering
- Inspiring

Task management and leading others are primary needs, but to be successful, consideration is a vital factor. A manager has to be involved and get along with people. For example, welcoming suggestions, restoring equity, looking after the personal well-being of employees, making oneself accessible, cooperating, motivating and inspiring, resolving interpersonal misunderstandings, recognizing agony, negotiating, etc. indicate the considerate dimension of a manager.

The better style

In today's business scenario, it is established that both initiating structure and consideration are important for leading teams to successfully achieve business goals. This is so because without the initiating structure behaviours of the leader, subordinates would not know what is expected of them, how to coordinate their work with others, or how their work relates to other groups or to the organizational goals. Lack of this behaviour among leaders would result in frustration among employees, which in turn would ultimately affect productivity negatively. Likewise, lack of considerate behaviour in the leader may lead to employees feeling insecure, unsupported, unrecognized, or confused as they would have to navigate conflicts and issues in their roles without feedback on how they are doing.

Developing these styles

It is obvious that leadership style theory measures behaviours of leaders, and these are among the easiest competencies to develop. Focus on the specific competency behaviours related to the style of initiating structure improves this competency. In order to develop these styles, one has to look into the specific ideas of each competency, identify specific behaviours that one can try that will increase his/her competence in this area.

You should obtain regular feedback from subordinates and others about how you are improving your 'initiating structure' behaviours. You have to take a similar approach for developing the behaviours in the consideration style. First, look at the list of competencies that are most closely aligned with the people-oriented behaviours of the consideration style. You have to utilize the resource guide to specifically understand what it takes to develop your skills in these areas. You need good information about how to improve your people-oriented behaviour. People around you should be able to notice the changes in your behaviour, and you should encourage and welcome their feedback as you develop these skills.

Michigan Leadership Style

Leadership studies were undertaken at the University of Michigan in its Survey Research Center. Studying the leadership style at the University of Michigan, the researchers found a different result. They distinguished between production-centred and employee-centred managers. People who emphasize on interpersonal relations and show a personal interest in the welfare of employees were termed as employee-centred managers. On the contrary, production-centred leaders tended to emphasize on business goals and highlighted the technical and task aspects of a job. These types of leaders used the members as a tool for achieving the group target. Employee-centred managers encouraged employee participation in decision-making, goal-setting, and other managerial processes by inspiring trust and respect. It resulted in the increased involvement and improved performance of the workforce.

The Michigan studies further found that productive work groups tended to have leaders who were employee centred rather than production centred. The researchers also found that most effective leaders had supportive relationship with their employees, tended to depend on group rather than individual decision-making, and encouraged employees to set and achieve high performance goals (Stoner and Gilbert 2006).

Managerial Grid

Mouton and Blake in the year 1964 propounded the two-dimensional view of leadership. It is also referred to as the 'leadership grid' (Figure 3.2). The dimensions proposed in the managerial grid are 'concern for production' and 'concern for people'. These dimensions represent the Ohio State dimensions of 'initiating structure' and 'consideration'.

In the managerial grid, five different types of leadership based on concern for production (task) and concern for people (relationships) are located in the four quadrants.

The five leadership styles of the managerial grid are impoverished, country club, task, middle of the road, and team.

1. The *impoverished style* is located at the lower left-hand corner of the grid, point (1-1). Low concern for both people and production characterizes the impoverished style. Impoverished style managers avoid conflicts.

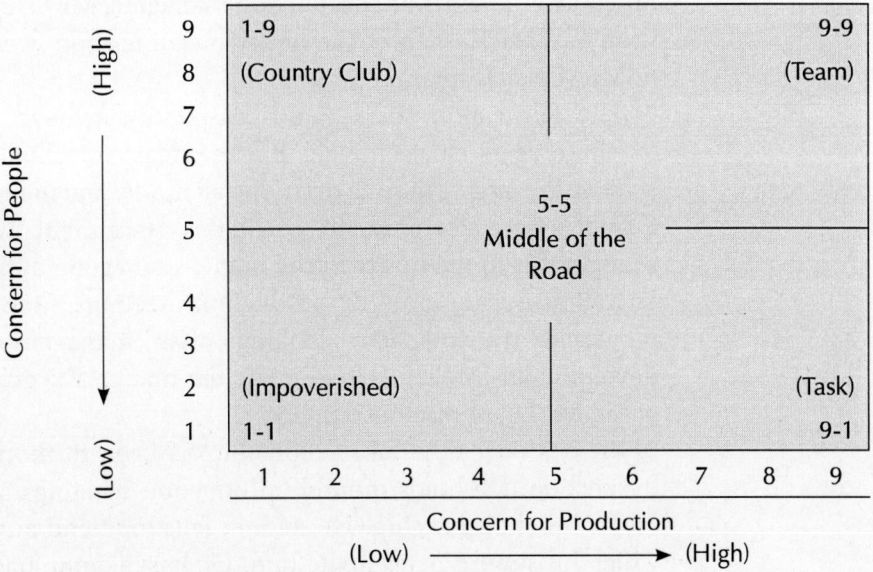

FIGURE 3.2 **Managerial grid of leadership styles**

2. High concern for people and a low concern for production characterizes the country club style; it is located at the upper left-hand corner of the grid, point (1-9). The primary objective of the country club style is to create a secure and comfortable atmosphere and trust that subordinates will respond to it positively.

3. The *task style* or the *produce-or-perish style* is located at the lower right-hand corner of the grid, point (9-1). A high concern for production and a low concern for people characterizes this style. The primary objective of the produce-or-perish style is to achieve the organization's goals. To accomplish them, employees' needs are not considered as important.

4. The *middle-of-the-road style* is located at the middle of the grid, point (5-5). A balance between workers' needs and the organization's productivity goals characterizes this style. The primary objective of the middle-of-the-road style is to maintain employee morale at a level sufficient to get the organization's work done.

5. The *team style* is located at the upper right-hand corner of the grid, point (9-9). It is characterized by a high concern for people and production. The primary objective of the team style is to establish cohesion and foster a feeling of commitment among workers.

Example

Mr Venkataraman, production manager of ABC Manufacturing Limited, was keen to achieve the production targets in all the departments under his control. The deputy production managers, Mr Sekhar of the fabrication shop and Mr Keshab of the heavy machine shop, were directly reporting to Mr Venkataraman.

The fabrication shop could reasonably achieve the sectional target for three years consecutively. But the heavy machine shop could seldom achieve the targets in spite of having all modern-generation CNC machines. Conflicts were a common feature in this department. Mr Keshab frequently brought this to the notice of the higher management through official notes as well as during monthly production meetings. Once Mr Venkataraman requested the manager looking after management and leadership development (MLD) to investigate the matter. Excerpts from the findings of the MLD are discussed below.

Mr Sekhar of the fabrication shop is keen to monitor the progress of the section. He holds monthly production meetings at the sectional level under his chairmanship. He seldom fails to attend any social gathering to which his subordinates invite him. He has taken initiative to form a group to organize picnics in winter. While walking around the production floor daily, he enquires from employees about their welfare. Once an employee in Mr Sekhar's department met with an accident and was hospitalized. Mr Sekhar visited the hospital, discussed the injured employee's condition with the doctor, and asked if all required resources were available. Mrs Sekhar was constantly in touch with the wife of the injured employee. During year endings, Mr Sekhar worked overtime and surprisingly, many workers also did the same to achieve the target. The MLD remarked: 'The fabrication shop appears to be Mr Sekhar's family.'

Mr Keshab is keen to monitor the progress and generally does not consider the difficulties of his subordinates. Once an employee, on receiving a message from his wife, approached Mr Keshab and sought his permission to leave early. Mr Keshab did not give any opportunity to the employee to explain his situation but rather ordered him to go back and resume his work. Of course, Mr Keshab's team was far behind the target.

In another instance, a female employee, on receiving a harsh comment on her performance, started crying in the office of Mr Keshab. In both cases, all the three registered and recognized unions initiated labour unrest. The MLD remarked: 'The heavy machine shop appears to be Mr Keshab's kingdom.'

Analysis from the standpoint of the managerial grid

Mr Sekhar is a task-oriented as well as people-oriented manager. His position in the grid may be (8, 7) or even (8, 8). As such, he gets the willing support of his people in his drive to meet the organizational goals. His subordinates are his followers.

Mr Keshab is a manager with high task orientation and low people orientation. This leads to frequent union intervention, complaints, and labour unrest. His position in the grid may be (6, 2) or (7, 2), or (6, 1).

Managerial Style

Reddin (1987) emphasizes two dimensions, namely, task orientation and relationships orientation, of the managers to assess their managerial styles (Figure 3.3 and Table 3.1).

TABLE 3.1 Task vs relationships orientation

Behaviour	Task Orientation	Relationships Orientation
Integrated	High	High
Related	Low	High
Dedicated	High	Low
Separated	Low	Low

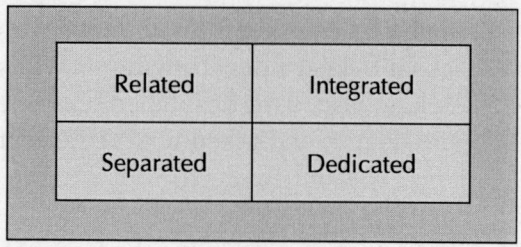

Related | Integrated

Separated | Dedicated

Relationships Orientation

Task Orientation

FIGURE **3.3** **Tasks vs relationships orientation**

Basic situation demand indicators

Work situations vary from one organization to another and also within the same organization; and from time to time. Some situations, often in the production department, require dedicated behaviour to be effective. Managing professionals, like research and development scientists, who are generally not working as a team, demands related behaviour. In situations where one has to monitor without any bias needs separated behaviour. Similarly, some situations may demand more task orientation but less relationships orientation when the target must be met at any cost. In this case, the dedicated style emerges as indispensable. Reddin (1987) discusses the situation demand indicators for the four types of situations (Figure 3.4).

Related	Integrated
1. To trust	1. To participate
2. To listen	2. To interact
3. To accept	3. To motivate
4. To advise	4. To integrate
5. To encourage	5. To innovate
Separated	**Dedicated**
1. To examine	1. To organize
2. To measure	2. To initiate
3. To administer	3. To direct
4. To control	4. To complete
5. To maintain	5. To evaluate

Relationships Orientation

Task Orientation

FIGURE **3.4** **Basic situation demand indicators**

The manager has to identify the style applicable in a particular situation.

TABLE 3.2   Theories and their dimensions

	Propounded by	Dimension 1	Dimension 2
Ohio State Study (1950s)	Group of researchers	Initiating structure	Consideration
Michigan Study (1950s)	Group of researchers	Production centred	Employee centred
Managerial Grid (1964)	Mouton and Blake (*)	Concern for production	Concern for people
Management Style (1987)	W.J. Reddin (**)	Task orientation	Relationships orientation

(*) Mouton and Blake (1964) identified five leadership styles.
(**) Reddin identified managerial styles in 1960s in the North America. He published his book in 1987.

Studies conducted at the Ohio State University and the University of Michigan identified two leadership styles and two types of leader behaviours. The Ohio State study identified two leadership styles—consideration and initiating structure—whereas the study at University of Michigan classifies behaviours of leaders as production centred and employee centred. Table 3.2 gives a comparison of the theories.

The primary concern of leaders with consideration and employee-centred style is employee welfare. The primary concern of leaders with initiating structure and production-centred styles is achieving organizational goals. However, employee-oriented leaders appear to be associated with high group productivity and job satisfaction. In a similar way managerial grid includes concern for people whereas management style emphasizes on relationship orientation.

LEADERSHIP TAXONOMY

Leaders perform multiple roles to achieve the objectives of the organization through the employees. Taxonomy is a method of categorizing and linking related information; it stimulates parsimony in complex fields and provides a helpful and necessary framework to researchers. The leadership taxonomy is often confused with just a list of effective leadership characteristics though taxonomy is much more than a list. Taxonomy identifies the key behavioural components of team leadership and thus establishes the theoretical foundation for examining the role of leaders in teams. Identifying the behaviour categories that are relevant and meaningful for leaders continues to be a major problem in researches on leadership behaviour.

Yukl (2007) quotes that in the past half century, researchers have produced a bewildering variety of behaviour concepts pertaining to managers and leaders. What one theorist treats as a general behaviour, another theorist may view in two or three distinct categories.

Developing Leadership Taxonomy

Leadership taxonomy is developed for describing the primary purpose of a leader using the primary method. The purpose may be to 'describe effective behaviour' or 'describe job requirements', and 'classify observed activities'. The researcher-theorist may use a method like 'factor analysis' or 'theoretical deductive' or 'judgemental classification'. Yukl (2007) has provided a list of several behaviour taxonomies proposed during the past half century (Table 3.3).

Table 3.3   Behaviour taxonomies

Author (Year)	Categories	Primary Purpose	Primary Method
Fleishman (1953)	2	Describe effective behaviour	Factor analysis
Stogdill (1963)	12	Describe effective behaviour	Theoretical deductive
Mahoney et al. (1963)	8	Describe job requirements	Theoretical deductive
Bowers and Seashore (1966)	4	Describe effective behaviour	Theoretical deductive
Mintzberg (1973)	10	Classify observed activities	Judgemental classification
House and Mitchell (1974)	4	Describe effective behaviour	Theoretical deductive
Morse & Wagner (1978)	6	Describe effective behaviour	Factor analysis
Yukl and Nemeroff (1979)	13	Describe effective behaviour	Factor analysis
Luthans and Lockwood (1984)	12	Classify observed activities	Judgemental classification

Contd

Table 3.3 contd

Author (Year)	Categories	Primary Purpose	Primary Method
Page (1985)	10	Describe job requirements	Factor analysis
Yukl et al. (1990)	14	Describe effective behaviour	Factor analysis
Bass and Avolio (1990)	7	Describe effective behaviour	Factor analysis
Wilson et al. (1990)	15	Describe effective behaviour	Factor analysis
Podsakoff et al. (1990)	6	Describe effective behaviour	Factor analysis
Fleishman et al. (1991)	13	Describe effective behaviour	Theoretical deductive
Conger and Kanungo (1994)	6	Describe effective behaviour	Factor analysis
Yukl, Gordon, and Taber (2002)	12	Describe effective behaviour	Factor analysis

Source: Yukl (2007), Table 3–1, page 80.

From Table 3.3 you can observe that the majority of the researchers have sought to 'describe effective behaviour' and have chosen either the 'factor analysis' or 'theoretical deductive' method for their analysis. Again, to 'classify observed activities', Luthans and Lockwood (1984) and Mintzberg (1973) used the 'judgemental classification' method. Table 3.3 clarifies that 2 to 15 categories were made when the primary purpose was to 'describe effective behaviour'. In order to 'describe job requirements', Mahoney et al. (1963) used the 'theoretical deductive' method whereas Page (1985) used factor analysis as the primary method. You can also observe that the behaviour categories vary from 2 to 15.

Answers to the following questions can be of help in developing the leadership taxonomy.

- What jobs are required to be done?
- What are the activities to be performed?
- What are the various associated roles?
- Who is meant to play what role?
- Who are the members assigned or detailed to achieve the goals?
- Is the size of the team adequate, just enough, or inadequate?
- Are there too many team members in one role?

- What type of knowledge and skills are required to perform the roles?
- How could you develop team members to perform those roles?
- How could you engage new members to perform the role if existing members do not have the expertise to perform it?
- Does the team have the ability in terms of knowledge and skills to do the job correctly the first time?
- Has the team done this type of work earlier?
- Is your team missing some key roles? What could you do about that?

The Advocacy and Leadership Center (ALC) has worked on effective social justice and aims to identify the distinct, yet complementary leadership roles that are almost always present in a successful campaign. The ALC has identified the right combination of leadership roles that can result in a coalition that responds faster, more flexibly, and more strategically to challenges, increasing the chances of success. The current version of this evolving 'taxonomy', or set of leadership roles, includes the following:

- Visionaries dream and raise achievement levels.
- Strategists chart and plan the vision and achieve whatever is attainable.
- Statespersons influence the minds of both the public and the decision-makers.
- Experts wave around knowledge to back up the organizational growth.
- Outside sparkplugs provoke and energize, fiercely holding those in power to account.
- Inside advocates understand, analyse, and decide on actions to turn power structures and established rules and procedures to advantage.
- Strategic communicators use rhetoric and oratory to intensify and direct public passion towards the objectives of the movement.
- Movement builders generate optimism and goodwill, motivating others with dedication to the common good.
- Generalists anchor a movement, based on and grounded in years of experience.
- Historians uphold a movement's memory, and collect and convey its stories.
- Cultural activists team up movements with powerful cultural forces.

You are now familiar with leadership styles and leadership taxonomy. Now you should understand leadership, and the leader, the follower, and the situation.

LEADERSHIP

Leadership is a dynamic responsibility that rests on a leader, the capacity to influence subordinates, followers, and colleagues. Leaders and collaborators come together for a common purpose in which both move to higher levels of motivation and moral development; in the process, the morale of both them is enhanced. Three important parts of this definition are the terms relationship, mutual, and collaborators. Relationship refers to the connection between people, mutual means sharing a common goal, and the term collaborators implies cooperation, working together, and a sense of interdependence. Some definitions of leadership by known researchers are as follows:

- Leadership is a relationship between those who aspire to lead and those who choose to follow (Kouzes and Posner 2002).
- Leadership is a process whereby an individual influences a group of individuals to achieve a common goal (Northouse 2004).
- Leadership is the influencing process of leaders and followers to achieve organizational objectives through changes (Lussier and Achua 2004).
- Leadership is the ability to step outside the culture… to start evolutionary change processes that are more adaptive (Schein 1992).
- Leadership is the process of making sense of what people are doing together so that people will understand and be committed (Drath and Palus 1994).
- Leadership is about articulating visions, embodying values, and creating the environment within which things can be accomplished (Richards and Engle 1986).
- Leadership is the ability of an individual to influence, motivate, and enable others to contribute toward the effectiveness and success of the organization… (House et al. 1999).
- Leadership is the ability of developing and communicating a vision to a group of people that will make that vision true (Valenzuela 2007).

Leadership is a basic equation; it is a function of the leader, follower, and situation.

The Leader

A leader drives his group. The group may be small or big, doing simple or complex functions, working in favourable or unfavourable work environment. The success of a group of people to a great extent depends on their leader's ability to mobilize resources, be constantly in touch with people and getting them to do their best, interact with all those who can directly or indirectly contribute to the functioning of the group, keep everybody in the group informed, collect feedback, making the roles of subordinates clear, and such similar activities.

To perform all these activities, the leader must have a unique track record, proven ability, interest to achieve, commendable personal history, leadership traits, motivation, and an urge to motivate others. In short, leaders' effectiveness is largely due to a unique and exceptional combination of personal qualities and talent. Leaders must aspire, articulate vision, embody values, and create a positive environment. All leaders, though not alike, tend to share many common characteristics. Hughes et al. (2008) have mentioned, based on research studies, that leaders differ from their followers, and effective leaders differ from ineffective leaders. A leader's personality depends on his/her temperament, by which he/she either remains calm or is prone to emotional outbursts.

A leader can be nominated or selected by group members. If one achieves the leadership status following appointment by superiors, he/she may have less credibility with his/her members of the group and naturally may get less loyalty from them. Members of a group may not become followers and rather continue as members only. On the other hand, if one member is elected or emerges through consensus, he/she can better influence the members, who are converted to followers. Such leaders gain more credibility, get willing support from the followers, and become effective in achieving goals. The group, then, in the true sense, becomes a team.

The Followers

All the members of a group or a team have to play their own roles, as the combination of their roles determine their success or otherwise. Although they happen to be a critical part of the leadership equation, their roles may not always be appreciated. Furthermore, major reviews of the leadership research show that researchers have paid relatively little attention to the roles followers play in the leadership process (Hughes et al. 2008). They have further explained the findings regarding followers' expectations, personality traits, maturity levels, levels of competence, and motivation that affect the leadership process.

While in a group, followers must derive intrinsic motivation, in which the leader and the leadership play a predominant role. When the team gets success, small or big, members should be made to feel intrinsically rewarded for the good work done by them. If they are rewarded by the organization, that would be an extrinsic reward, the short-lasting one.

Intrinsic satisfaction is long-lasting, remembered for a long time, very often described to others, and gives pleasure whenever the member is in a solitary mood. Thus, this reward acts as a health tonic.

Changing role of followers

The business environment is continuously changing; managing and leading people is becoming more and more complex. As such, leadership must be understood in the context of a particular group of followers as well as in the context of a particular leader. Ginnett et al. (2008) have observed that the leader–follower relationship is in a constant flux of change. At present, understanding followers is central to understanding leadership.

The changing relationship between the leader and the followers is imposing pressure on the group, and also on organizations of all kinds, particularly, when the resources are scarce. Company policy on downsizing, attrition of knowledge workers, reduced number of managers, increased span of control are compelling followers to share many of the functions hitherto done by their leaders. Companies are doing business in a global village. This has led organizations towards greater power sharing and decentralizing authority. This, in turn, has created a greater degree of interdependence among departments, strategic business units, and functions. The overall situation is forcing followers to take up new roles— the roles of leadership.

Ginnett et al. (2008) emphasize that leadership must be understood in terms of leader variables and follower variables, and also by the interaction between them.

The Situation

The leader and his/her followers work in a particular work environment that is organization-specific. In the leadership equation, situation is the third critical part. If the same group of followers work with the same leader, but in different situations, then the outcomes are quite likely to be different. If it is similar, we will treat that as an 'act of god'. Truly, leadership makes sense if the leader as well as the followers are able to coordinate in different situations.

Human beings differ widely in their perceptions. For the same experiment and the same observation, two experimenters may draw different inferences. See Box 3.1.

Hughes et al. (2008) have developed certain statements about the triangle constituted by the leader, followers, and the situation. These statements systematically clarify and bring out the interactions among the three:

Box 3.1 Perception—A virtual experiment

The experiment

In a management development programme, a faculty member performed an experiment. He took an empty glass and half-filled the glass with whisky. Then, the faculty member carefully picked up an insect with a piece of paper and dropped it in the glass half-filled with whisky.

The observation

The insect took some three rounds inside the glass (half-filled with whisky) and stopped to death.

About inference

The faculty member now distributed blank sheets to all the 44 attending participants (junior managers) and requested them to write their inferences individually. He gave them five minutes for this purpose. After about ten minutes, he could collect only 17 responses.

He studied all the 17 inferences and selected only two from the lot. He selected two participants sitting in the front desk, gave one response to each, and requested them to read the responses.

Reader 1—A small insect has died in a small quantity of whisky. If we consume whisky every day, then the effect will be like that of the insect. We should not consume whisky.

Reader 2—Our stomach contains many worms. If we consume whisky, they (the worms) will die. As a result, we will not suffer from any disease. We should consume whisky.

The lesson

An individual interprets everything from his/her perspective. The response comes based on his/her perception. That is why for the same experiment and same observation, the two inferences varied.

- A leader may need to respond to various followers differently in the same situation.
- A leader may need to respond to the same follower differently in the same situation.
- Followers may respond to various leaders quite differently.
- Followers may respond to each other differently and differently with different leaders.
- Two leaders may have different perceptions of the followers or situation.

LEADERSHIP AND MANAGEMENT

A leader can be a manager, but a manager is not necessarily a leader. The leader of a work group may emerge informally as the choice of the group. If a manager is able to influence people to achieve the goals of the organization, without using his/her formal authority to do so, then the manager is demonstrating leadership. The website www.teamtechnology. co.uk differentiates between leadership and management and then discusses the consequence of leadership without management and vice versa.

The difference between leadership and management is defined as follows:

- Leadership is setting a new direction or vision for a group to follow, that is, a leader is the spearhead for that new direction.
- Management controls or directs resources including human resources in a group according to the principles or values that have already been established.

The difference between leadership and management is best illustrated from a consideration of what happens when you have one without the other. Leadership without management, management without leadership, and leadership combined with management are discussed below.

Leadership without Management

Leaders set a direction or vision that others follow. They may not be very meticulous regarding the procedural approach and the implementation details required to achieve the new direction. Other people then have to work hard on the path that has been envisioned, identify the shortfalls, pick up the pieces and make things work. The leadership function provides a vision that identifies a unique goal, but the ways and means to reach the goal is a management function.

Management without Leadership

Managers control resources, manage events to maintain the status quo, and ensure execution according to established plans, rules, and regulations. For example, two umpires manage a cricket tournament and take help from the third umpire when needed. Any dispute is settled by the match referee. But neither the umpires nor the referee provide leadership. Similarly in a football match, a referee manages a match without having any scope to provide 'leadership' because that is not his job. In the match, the referee is controls the resources (the teams) to ensure that the laws of the game are followed.

Leadership Combined with Management

The key point in differentiating between leadership and management is the idea that employees willingly follow leaders because they want to, not because they have to. Leaders attract people by virtue of their charisma. They do not always possess formal power to reward or sanction performance. However, employees give power to their leader by complying with what he/she requests. On the other hand, managers may have to rely on formal authority to get employees to accomplish goals.

An organization must survive and grow. To ensure that, managers must know how to lead as well as manage. Today, without leading as well as managing, organizations face the threat of extinction. Management is the process of setting and achieving the goals of the organization through the basic functions of management—planning, organizing, directing (or leading), and controlling. A manager is hired by the organization and is given formal authority to direct the activity of others in fulfilling the organization's goals. Thus, leading the workforce is a major part of the manager's job. Yet, a manager must also plan, organize, and control.

Generally speaking, leaders deal with the interpersonal aspects of a manager's job, whereas planning, organizing, and controlling are the administrative aspects. Leaders deal with change, inspiration, motivation, and influence. Management deals more with achieving of the organization's goals and maintaining equilibrium.

The differences are outlined in Table 3.4.

TABLE 3.4 Leader vs manager

The Leader	The Manager
A leader does the right things.	A manager does things right.
Leadership is about effectiveness.	Management is about efficiency.
Leadership is about what and why.	Management is about how to do things.
Leadership is about trust and about people.	Management is about systems, controls, procedures, policies, and structure.
Leadership is about innovating and initiating.	Management is about copying, about managing the status quo.
Leadership looks at the horizon, not just the bottom line.	Management is about the bottom line.

Note: Adapted from W. Bennis and J. Goldsmith (1994), *Learning to Lead: A Workbook on Becoming a Leader*, Addison-Wesley, New York.

SPECIFIC BEHAVIOURS

In an organization, people organize work activities to improve organizational effectiveness, develop rules and procedures, plan and monitor activities, undertake operation management, provide guidelines and support to employees, allow people to think and develop the best way of doing work, determine employee shortcomings and provide training, and encourage people to do something innovative. They are also involved in scanning the business environment, assessing emerging threats, finding business opportunities, and multiple activities of different latitudes. To be effective, leaders need specific task-oriented and relation-oriented behaviours.

Specific Task Behaviours

Three specific types of task-oriented behaviours are: (a) short-term planning, (b) clarifying roles and objectives, and (c) monitoring operations and performance (Yukl 2007).

Short-term planning

Short-term or short-range planning is focused on deciding what to do, how to do, and when to do a specific activity. The primary purpose of planning is ensuring achievement of organizational goals by utilizing the right resources, incurring minimum costs, maximizing profit without compromising on quality, and ensuring on-time delivery. Moreover, in case of any customer, a complaint, a meeting etc. also come within the purview of short-term planning. The purposes and features of short-term plans are the following:

- They cover a specific functional area or department.
- They are made to achieve short-term goals.
- They generally cover a short-term perspective, say, one year.
- They contain greater detail and are more specific.
- They are executed by middle- and lower-level management staff.
- They act as a step-by-step approach to medium-range planning.
- They relate to product design, training of workforce, production budget, etc.
- They are directed towards efficient and effective utilization of resources.
- They are action-oriented.
- They focus on the internal environment.

Operational planning, action planning, and contingency planning are sub-varieties of work activity planning. Operational planning is the scheduling of daily routine work including determination of human resource deployment for a following few days or a week or so. Action planning is the development of step-by-step actions and schedules for implementing a new policy or managing a project. Contingency planning is developing procedures, deciding alternatives for avoiding or coping with unprecedented events, potential problems, or disasters. For example, a marriage house in a posh urban area hires a generator just to avoid hassles in case of a power failure. Arranging a generator is contingency planning.

Planning is a predominant function of leaders and its importance for effectively driving a collection of people has been highlighted by many researchers and organizational stalwarts.

Clarifying roles and objectives

The leader and the members of his/her group must be clear about the roles and objectives. The goal, plans, policies, and role expectations must be communicated for overall effectiveness. Broadly, the leader has to discharge interpersonal, informational, and decision-making roles. Major functions to clarify roles and objectives include

- Defining job responsibilities and requirements
- Setting performance goals for each member
- Assigning specific tasks to each member without any overlaps

The basic purpose of clarifying behaviours is to guide and coordinate activities and ensure that people know their task content (what to do, how to do, when to do, whom to give feedback, etc.). Clarifying behaviour reduces role ambiguity and restores role clarity. In an organization in which the work system is structured with elaborate rules, procedures, quality management system, quality plan, work instructions, there is less need for clarifying behaviours. The structured system dictates what is to be done, who is to do it, and what grade of people are to be utilized for what type of work. Clarifying is a core component of the initiating structure dimension in the Ohio State leadership style model.

Yukl (2007) gives guidelines for clarifying roles and objectives— (a) defining job responsibilities, (b) assigning work, and (c) setting performance goals.

Defining job responsibilities Explain the importance of a job, the consequence if it is not accomplished. Also important is to clarify the extent of authority that one can exercise, the contribution of the work to achieve the mission of the unit, and, finally, important policies, rules and requirements, and the relevant systems associated with the work.

Assigning work   Specifying the reasons and mentioning the deadline.

Setting performance goals   With specificity, measurability, attainability, relevance, and time-bound (SMART).

Monitoring operations and performance

Decision-making is an essential aspect of monitoring, which calls for data collection, and information gathering pertaining to the department and the associated persons. The information you would need may include progress of the work, quality of the products, availability of resources, supply of utilities and facilities, and anything essential for the continuance of an operation.

Monitoring may be done through many means like direct observation, scrutinizing feedback sheets, production reports, inspection reports, and machine breakdown history, and organizing review meetings periodically. In case of any deviation of any nature, you may require brainstorming, problem-solving tools, cause–effect diagrams, force field analysis, nominal group technique, or any other suitable tools to facilitate decision-making. Monitoring is also required to obtain information needed for performance evaluation, recognizing achievements, locating deficiency in performance, identifying training needs, providing need-based training, evaluating the training, and so forth.

As a leader, you have to decide the extent of monitoring. A competent, skilled, and self-propelled person needs less monitoring, prefers to work without supervision, and rather dislikes excess interference of the supervisor. However, people of this category approach the supervisor to obtain clarification in case of any ambiguity. Frequent disruptions retard their output both in qualitative and quantitative terms.

Specific Relation Behaviours

There are a number of behaviours that promote interpersonal relations. Yukl (2007) mentions three specific types of relation-oriented behaviours that are especially relevant for effective leadership: (a) supporting, (b) developing, and (c) recognizing. Yukl (2007) explains the behaviours.

Supporting

In management, the function 'control' is probabilistic, particularly when this function is related to human resources. But by the act of supporting we can easily control human beings. Supporting encompasses a wide variety of human behaviours that includes consideration, acceptance, and concern for others including their well-being, advancement, development, and many other things. Yukl (2007) explains that 'supporting' is the core component of 'supportive leadership', and has given guidelines for supporting. The guidelines are simple but strong. According to Yukl,

- show acceptance and positive regard;
- be polite and considerate, not arrogant and rude;
- treat each subordinate as an individual;
- remember important details about the person;
- be patient and helpful when giving instructions and explanations;
- provide sympathy and support when the person is anxious and upset;
- express confidence in the person when a difficult task is to be executed by that person;
- provide assistance with the work when it is needed; and
- be willing to help with personal problems.

On a careful study and conceptualization of these statements, it is evident that an assertive approach and communication is vital to create a supporting and healthy work environment.

Developing

Human beings need development in multiple directions and as such developing incorporates several managerial practices like enriching knowledge, enhancing skills, modifying behaviours, bringing attitudinal changes, facilitating job adjustment, and, career advancements. It also includes developing in the profession through coaching, mentoring, and counselling, and in many other facets. Coaching is mainly for developing in the role, mentoring is for developing leadership at work, and counselling for helping people cope with situations (Haldar 2008).

Coaching

Coaching is arguably the primary method for remedying deficiencies in management style and also a tool for diverse professional development. Coaching, a collaborative style, has now become a key tool both in developing talent and adapting to new cultures, particularly for the strategic needs of top organizations. The concept of coaching in organizations is not new. But structured coaching is a part of the new performance-led culture of employment. It is a process and a solution that suits the function of an organization and facilitates its survival and growth.

Coaching systematically is an effective human resource development (HRD) mechanism for enabling an organization to meet competitive pressures, plan for succession, and bring about changes. Coaching benefits the organization, the individual, and also the coach. Focusing on goals rather than on problems, listening with empathy, giving advice or instructions instead of interrogating, and giving observational feedback instead of passing a verdict are some of the prerequisites of coaching.

A coach must have the knowledge and skills relating to interpersonal relation maintenance, knowledge of content and curriculum, knowledge of pedagogy and andragogy, awareness of coaching resources, and knowledge of the practice of coaching. Coaching needs management support. Effective coaching yields greater self-awareness, enhanced self-belief, added ability to set and achieve goals, increased fulfilment in work and life, augmented leadership skills, boosted self-confidence, and developed balance, and enjoyment of life and work. Like any other system, coaching needs top management support. Coaching is about creating buy-in and shared goals and needs building of loyalty and trust. You must remember that coaching is not a magic formula and does not present any easy answers. Techniques of coaching have been proven to work, and some of the techniques stand scientifically tested. Coaching will work provided you work.

Guidelines for coaching
* Ask questions and identify weaknesses
* Provide feedback in a non-threatening way
* Provide specific knowledge to enable him/her to improve performance
* Show him/her the way to work better and faster, and maintain quality
* Express confidence that he/she can learn and do
* Provide opportunities to him/her to gradually undertake difficult works
* Upgrade his/her problem-solving skills

Mentoring

Mentoring is an old concept of developing leadership skills. Mentored employees discharge their duties and responsibilities effectively, performing better in the workplace. Leadership is different from managerial tasks. All organizational leaders are managers but all managers are not necessarily leaders. Managers get the work done by their subordinates while leaders work with their followers. Leaders involve themselves with the work as they prefer to work in teams. Leadership characteristics include insight, initiative, inspiration, involvement, improvisation, individuality, and implementation.

To survive and grow in the competitive business environment, organizations develop leadership potential for which they arrange mentoring programmes. Mentoring can be both natural mentoring and planned or structured mentoring. Mentors and mentees possess different views about the quality that mentors should have.

In the process of mentoring, a mentor performs a variety of roles—sponsoring, teaching, advocating, coaching, advising, counselling, negotiating, and whatever else is required to develop the mentees. Mentoring is about supporting, propping up, buoying up, and developing an employee through experience-sharing to enhance his/her problem-solving skills. As such, the benefits of mentoring are multiple. Both mentoring and coaching are professional development tools. Mentoring is a useful adjunct to coaching; yet these two tools have certain differences. Organizations must implement mentoring practices methodically taking steps like specifying objectives, building a mentoring support structure, training mentoring coordinators, identifying mentors and mentees, training them, matching mentors and mentees, implementing, and setting guidelines for evaluation.

Guidelines for mentoring
- Help the employee to discover his/her strengths
- Help the employee to identify and realize his/her weaknesses
- Express and inculcate confidence in the employee, that he/she has the ability to accomplish the given task
- Supply the tools and techniques for developing quality plan of activities
- Practise what you preach
- Elevate yourself to serve as a role model

Counselling

Counselling is assisting, developing, and helping employees, that is, workers, staff, and managers, in their professional development. Counselling reduces work role stress and improves the quality of work life and, in turn, the quality of life as a whole. A counsellor needs to build a trusting relationship with the counsellee, be warm and friendly, contribute to the thought process of the counsellee, and hold discussions, leading to the solution of the problem. The process should be undertaken with the ultimate aim of simply helping the person. Active listening, interest, compassion, acceptance, etc., are essential for making the sessions fruitful and the counselling process effective.

An employee should not be selected randomly for counselling. Supervisors should look for the symptoms that determine the need for counselling. Stress management interventions, that includes coping strategies, and self-imposed behaviour modification methods are essential in order to prevent employees from deteriorating mentally and physically.

Counselling can go a long way in helping employees to have a better control over their lives, take decisions wisely, and better discharge their responsibilities, and reduce the level of stress and anxiety. Counselling of employees can have desirable consequences for the organization. The organization benefits when employees know that it cares for them. It restores a sense of commitment among the employees for their organization. In other words, coping with stress promotes job satisfaction, job involvement, and employee commitment. Counselling can be of significant help in modifying the behaviour of employees and, thereby, enhance the achievement of organizational goals.

Guidelines for counselling
- Identify the source of work role stress
- Build a trusting relationship with the counsellee
- Schedule counselling sessions in advance
- During counselling, listen attentively
- Identify similarities of likes and dislikes, personalities, extracurricular and co-curricular activities with the counsellee
- Explain the harmful effects of persisting stress
- Advise him/her to adjust to the environment on which he/she has no control

Recognizing

A person needs his/her contribution to be acknowledged on successful accomplishment of an activity. People high on this need work hard but lose their motivation, sometimes completely, if their work is not recognized immediately. They strive to have their presence felt, and endeavour to be in the limelight and get attention. This need is basic in nature and is present in all of us but in varying degrees.

Recognition motivates people; motivation is 'the psychological processes that cause the arousal, direction, and persistence of voluntary actions that are goal directed'.

There are four phases in the process of motivated behaviour—a need is aroused in the organism, behaviour is directed towards satisfying the need, the need is satisfied, and the organism relaxes (Pestonjee 1991). During the period between arousal and satisfaction of the need, the organism is in a state of tension, a condition of unrest or uneasiness. The organism can relax only after the need is satisfied because the equilibrium has been restored. Equilibrium is the state or condition in which no pressure (needs) is compelling the organism to be active. From this standpoint, he/she needs to be recognized as soon as possible after evaluating what he/she has done.

The primary purpose of recognizing is to strengthen the desirable behaviours among people. Recognition gives the employee an impetus and momentum for exerting more. At this stage you can recall that 'success breeds success'. Positive sensory gratification is a unique way of recognizing. You must remember the management mantra 'praise in public, but criticize privately'. If you praise someone in the presence of colleagues, that is also an exclusive and distinctive way of recognizing. But you need to justify such recognition. Otherwise, others who have contributed more might get demotivated. The impact of the contribution of some person or a group may be significantly high. In such a case, you can think of recognizing such an effort in a ceremonial manner. For instance, our country gives awards to noteworthy achievers on Republic Day.

Certain guidelines for recognizing are

- Maintain records of contributions by members
- Search for variety of contributions and grade them
- Identify significant contributions that can have further impact
- Recognize contributions that produced great impact
- Recognize commendable efforts even if they are not successful
- Recognize those who are sincere, devoted, and goal directed, and contribute to the team
- Decide the mode of recognizing by considering the person, situation, and impact
- Be prompt in recognizing

EVALUATION OF BEHAVIOUR APPROACH—A DISCUSSION

You are now familiar with the Ohio State study, Michigan leadership style, managerial grid (Mouton and Blake 1964), and management style (Reddin 1987). Each of the four styles discusses two dimensions. The first dimension comprises initiating structure, production centred, concern for production, and task orientation. The dimensions convey the same meaning of structured procedure. The second dimension comprises consideration, employee centred, concern for people, and relation orientation, which again convey the same sense of respect and sympathy for people.

Admired leaders must be honest, forward-looking, competent, inspiring, intelligent, fair- and broad-minded, supportive, straightforward, dependable, cooperative, determined, imaginative, ambitious, courageous, caring, mature, loyal, self-controlled, and independent. These qualities are essential components with both the dimensions.

Yukl (2007) has reviewed research studies on leadership behaviours and emphasizes on the weaknesses in most of them. He speaks about the proliferation of leadership taxonomies and lack of agreement about what behaviours were considered in the studies. Yukl further points out that the selection of behaviours made the studies more difficult to integrate with the research on leader behaviour.

Moreover, research on leadership effectiveness has examined behaviours individually rather than examining how effective leaders use patterns of specific behaviours to achieve their agendas; the specific behaviours interact in complex ways, and leadership effectiveness cannot be understood unless these interactions are studied (Yukl 2007).

Monitoring is essential to discover the problems at the origin, and then use problem-solving techniques. A plan will work only if it is based on facts and figures, and on the quality and extent of data collection. When a leader clarifies issues like new responsibilities assigned, roles to be performed, and extent of authority one can use, it further ensures that the subordinate has understood and has willingly accepted his/her responsibilities; and when the leader details the system of monitoring, then delegating will also be effective. Next the leader can focus his/her attention on empowerment, the person who can be empowered and in which direction. The leader must meticulously apply his/her skills to select people and adopt appropriate behaviours as these are related to the success of the group outcomes. However, the selected set of behaviours may differ, because different patterns of behaviour may be used to accomplish a given task.

SUMMARY

Leadership is a process in which the leader and the followers interact dynamically in a particular situation or work environment. Leadership is a dynamic relationship that rests on the capacity to influence subordinates, followers, and colleagues. A study of leadership styles enables us to understand the behaviour one should use in a given situation to get results.

Early studies of leadership styles have brought forward two dimensions, one of which emphasizes sympathy, kindness, and inclination towards people. The other dimension underlines the need for concentrating on a structured system of working. Both dimensions are essential in varying degrees in different situations to be effective.

Leadership taxonomy helps us understand and select behaviours to effectively manage a group of people. Leadership is a complex function of the leader, the followers, and the situation in which leadership is applied. In the changing business environment, we have to take into consideration the changing role of followers.

Both leadership and management are simultaneously required for task accomplishment. We have to take into account specific task behaviours and specific relation behaviours to improve organizational effectiveness. Evaluation of behaviour approach and qualities of admired leaders and their implementation may help organizations to achieve excellence.

KEY TERMS

Action planning is the development of step-by-step actions and schedules for implementing a new policy or managing a project.

Contingency planning is developing procedures, deciding alternatives for avoiding or coping with unprecedented events, potential problems, or disasters.

Leadership is a dynamic relationship that rests on the capacity to influence subordinates, followers, and colleagues.

Leadership taxonomy refers to categorization of leadership behaviours for a primary purpose (describing effective behaviour, describing job requirements, or classifying observed activities) using a primary method (factor analysis, theoretical deduction or judgemental classification).

Operational planning is the scheduling of daily routine work including determination of human resource deployment for the following few days or a week or so.

EXERCISES

Concept Review Questions

1. Discuss the need for studying leadership styles. Discuss briefly the findings of early research on leadership styles.
2. What is meant by dimensions in research on leadership styles? Choose one of the research studies mentioned in the chapter and discuss the dimensions.
3. Consider today's business environment and discuss the roles of followers in the leadership equation. Cite examples.
4. What are the various features of short-term planning? Discuss them in an organizational context.

5. Suggest a suitable road map to enhance specific relation behaviours in the organization you are working in or are familiar with. Briefly describe the organization you are referring to.

Critical Thinking Questions

1. 'Leadership is a dynamic relationship that rests on the capacity to influence subordinates, followers, colleagues.' Discuss with examples.
2. What do you understand by leadership taxonomy? How can it be developed? If two groups of researchers are working on the same research questions, can the findings be unique? Justify your answer.
3. In a company, the production manager (Mr ABC) was in the good books of the general manager (Mr PQR). Mr ABC always used to be instrumental in collecting information about the welfare of employees. He was fairly keen to achieve the production target though he was not very particular about reviewing the progress of work. As Mr ABC was close to the general manager, he was not facing much of a problem. Comment on the management style of Mr ABC. Justify your answer.

Assignments

1. Develop a questionnaire that you can use to identify the task orientation and the relation orientation of any leader.
2. Consider any five managers of your organization, record their behavioural pattern while getting work accomplished by the followers, identify their task orientation and the relation orientation, and place them in the managerial grid.

REFERENCES

Bass, B.M. (1990), *Bass and Stogdill's Handbook of Leadership.* Free Press, New York.

Fiedler, F.E., M.M. Chemers, and L. Mahar (1976), *Improving Leadership Effectiveness,* John Wiley & Sons, New York.

Haldar, U.K. (2008), *Human Resource Development,* Oxford University Press, New Delhi.

Hughes, Richard L., Robert C. Ginnett, and Gordon J. Curphy (2008), *Leadership Enhancing the Lessons of Experience,* Tata McGraw-Hill, New Delhi.

Judge, T.A., R.F. Piccolo, and R. Ilies (2004), The Forgotten Ones? The Validity of Consideration and Initiating Structure in Leadership Research, *Journal of Applied Psychology,* Vol. 89, No. 1, 36–51.

Kouzes, J. and B. Posner (2002), *The Leadership Challenge* (3rd edn), Jossey Bass, An Imprint of John Wiley & Sons, Hoboken, New Jersey.

Lussier, R.N. and C.F. Achua (2004), *Leadership: Theory, Application, Skill Development* (2nd edn), South-Western.

Mitchell, T.R. (1974), 'Expectancy Models of Job Satisfaction, Occupational Preference, and Effort: A Theoretical, Methodological, and Empirical Appraisal', *Psychological Bulletin*, 81, 1053–1077.

Northouse, P.G. (2004), *Leadership Theory and Practice* (3rd edn), Sage Publications.

Pestonjee, D.M. (1991), *Motivation and Job Satisfaction*, Macmillan India Limited, Delhi.

Reddin, W.J. (1987). *How to Make Your Management Style More Effective*, McGraw-Hill, Maideshead Berkshire, England.

Schreisheim, C.A. and R.M. Stogdill (1975), Differences in the Factor Structure Across Three Versions of the Ohio State Leadership Scales, *Personnel Psychology*, Vol. 28, No. 2, 189–206.

Stoner, A.F. and Gilbert Jr. (2006), *Management* (Eastern Economic Edition), Prentice-Hall India, New Delhi.

Valenzuela, K. (2007), *I Want to be a Leader* (ezinearticles.com/?I-Want-To-Be-A-Leader&id=630935, accessed on June 7, 2009).

Yukl, Gary (2007), *Leadership in Organizations*, Pearson Education, Inc. (Prentice-Hall India), New Delhi.

Web Resources

www.chsbs.cmich.edu/leader_model/Development/media/Targeted%20Lessons/leadership_style.htm (accessed on 25 July 2008).

www.teamtechnology.co.uk/leadership-basics.html (accessed on 3 September 2008).

tools.iscvt.org/advocacy/build_the_team/start (Advocacy and Leadership Center) (accessed on 22 July 2008).

www.bealeader.net/5/leadership_definitions (accessed on 22 March 2009).

CLOSING CASE

Specific Relation Behaviours by Leaders

URC had three more units in three different cities manufacturing different items. The dispute continued for three days and affected the entire lot of people involved in the production process across all these units. During this period, the management discussed the various issues with the union representatives several times to reach a consensus. A unique observation here was the fact that the intervention of a third party was neither sought nor was it deemed necessary.

An agreement was signed by the management and unions on behavioural patterns. However, the workers' union demand for the transfer of Mr Sanat to another unit was not accepted by the management.

Discussion Questions

1. What steps might Mr Mishra have taken to reach a consensus?
2. Had you been in the position of Mr Mishra, what would you have included in the agreement?
3. Which professional development tool would you suggest for Mr Sanat? Justify your response.

CHAPTER 4

Theories of Effective Leadership

Learning Objectives

After studying this chapter, you will be able to

▶ Understand the contingency theories of leadership
▶ Explain Fiedler's LPC model of leadership and its recommendation
▶ Compare the different contingency theories

Lesson on Leadership Style

A big software company employing about 2500 employees has four units in India and is now planning to open another unit in the US. The proprietor, Mr Advani, obtained his master's degree in computer technology from a US university, and also completed his Ph.D. in the US. After working in three world-class companies, he came back to India in 1996 and started a software company called Global Software Limited (GSL) in Hyderabad. The company is engaged in software development. In addition, GSL has a mechanical testing laboratory within the same premises. All the machines are program controlled. The major customers of software products are from the US, Canada, and the UK. However, the testing facilities are utilized by local medium and large industries.

The laboratory has modern testing equipments and a 3-D coordinate measuring machine as well. Moreover, the laboratory division is NABL (National Accreditation Board for Laboratories) accredited. Mr Advani recruited Mr Ramachandran, who is now the manager, product development. Mr Dwivedi is the marketing manager. Both Mr Ramachandran and Mr Dwivedi are dynamic enough and are doing their respective jobs well. Naturally the company is growing at a great pace. There are as many as twenty virtual teams in which the members are mainly from India, China, and Pakistan.

Mr Banerjee and Mr Taneja are deputy managers (product development) and report to Mr Ramachandran. Both the deputy managers are technically competent though they differ in their dealings with the team members. They have been assigned separate divisions to manage. Mr Taneja can get along with any type of member, accepts any person in his division, and does not face any problem in getting work done, and, finally, to meet the target of the division. On the other hand, Mr Banerjee is choosy, considers a person's characteristics before accepting him/her as a member in his division. He further finds it difficult to extract work from some people. In turn, Mr Ramachandran also finds it difficult to assign any new project to Mr Banerjee as he is selective in accepting members in his division. Things continued like this.

Once Mr Banerjee submitted a note sheet to Mr Ramachandran complaining about the behavioural patterns of some of his subordinates chosen by himself some time back. On receipt of the note, Mr Ramachandran gave an exercise to Mr Banerjee.

About the Exercise

1. The format contained some adjectives expressing behavioural attributes like pleasant, friendly, rejecting, helpful, unenthusiastic, tense, cooperative, supportive, boring, quarrelsome, efficient, gloomy along with their antonyms.
2. The format was in tabular form having the adjectives in the first column and the corresponding antonyms in the last column. In between, there were eight more columns numbered 1 to 8.
3. Mr Ramachandran requested Mr Banerjee to use one format for one colleague, write the name on top of the format, and express his feelings about him/her encircling or ticking the number against an adjective and its antonym.
4. Mr Banerjee was further told about the scoring system.
5. Mr Ramachandran advised him to prepare a tabulation sheet, depicting the name of the subordinate and his score. He also asked to submit the comments about each subordinate based on the overall scores.
6. Most astonishingly after preparing the tabulation sheet, Mr Banerjee found that all his subordinates were almost equally placed in the scores.

He did not approach Mr Ramachandran with the summary tabulation sheet until he was called. Mr Ramachandran minutely studied the scores and comments, and offered advice on a few points to Mr Banerjee.

The Advice

'You will get various types of persons in the organization. They may differ widely in their characteristics. Each person will have his/her own inherent styles, attributes, likes and dislikes, motivation, occupational values, lifestyle, personality traits, and so forth. All persons cannot be identical or equivalent. Moreover, their overall scores are almost equal. (In fact, seeing this Mr Banerjee did not approach Mr Ramachandran.) Therefore, you study them and develop your own way of dealing with them. Consider the situation of the company and your team members. First try to identify the good qualities in each and utilize those to meet the goals of your division to achieve the organizational objectives. I have total confidence in you. I am sure that you will be successful and be rewarded with success.'

Mr Banerjee learnt a very good lesson from this exercise and took the advice given by Mr Ramachandran sportingly. People noticed distinct behavioural changes in Mr Banerjee after the exercise.

In several meetings, Mr Advani admits the instinctive ability of Mr Ramachandran to predict changes in the business environment, both at the micro and macro levels, and to institutionalize any change smoothly in GSL. He can create a new vision and revitalize the company. His human management techniques are exemplary. Because Mr Ramachandran possessed such abilities, Mr Advani desired that Mr Ramachandran takes over the charge of another unit (a strategic business unit) of GSL as works manager. Mr Ramachandran also accepted the offer wholeheartedly. It was truly difficult to release him from this unit. Ultimately came the day when he was given a warm farewell. Mr Ramachandran left with a heavy heart as he was emotionally involved with all the people. He could not deliver his farewell address properly.

Learning points

1. A manager must be psychologically close to the people and understand them.
2. Human management skills are essential for success.
3. Career counselling leads to behavioural modification and develops ability to cope.

INTRODUCTION

Managers are responsible for getting work done by engaging the persons under their supervision. While discharging duties and performing their roles, managers use certain styles for work accomplishment.

Leadership is a fascinating social phenomenon that occurs in all groups: in society, organizations, academia, and in all other spheres of life. Each person has a leadership style that he/she feels comfortable with. There are different styles of leadership that have proved effective in different situations. What one must understand is that a leader may have to switch from one style of leadership to another to get the job accomplished smoothly. Managerial behaviour varies across situations.

The various theories of leadership provide useful insights. Theorists have researched and strived to discover the most effective leadership style in a given situation. This chapter discusses some contingency theories of effective leadership. One should understand them and be aware of their applications in specific organizational situations to be able to derive the best from the followers.

CONTINGENCY THEORIES

Contingency theories implicitly assume that leaders accurately diagnose the key aspects of followers and the situation in which leadership is applied. In all the contingency models, except in one model by Fiedler, leaders are assumed to perform in a flexible manner. With the change in situational and follower characteristics, leaders also change their behavioural pattern. A correct match between situational and follower characteristics and leaders' behaviours is assumed to positively impact the group and organizational outcomes.

In early approaches, researchers attempted to understand leadership with the ultimate objective of identifying leader traits or behaviours that effective leaders had in common. A common set of characteristics proved to be indescribable and elusive to them. As a result, researchers began to focus on the style of leadership that was most effective in a particular situation. Contingency or situational theories examine the fit between the leader and the situation, and provide guidelines for managers to achieve this effective fit.

Contingency theories describe key leadership behaviours observed by research and proposed in conjunction with the various leadership models. Successful leaders must be able to identify clues in an environment and adapt their behaviour to meet the needs of their followers and of the particular situation. Even with good diagnostic skills, leaders may not be effective unless they can adapt their leadership style to meet the demands of their environment.

Contingency theories are alternately called situational theories of leadership because a leader's impact on followers depends on or is contingent on both leader behaviour and the characteristics of the organizational situation. The contingency models focus on leaders' effect on individuals, their attitudes, and performances. Six theories, namely, Fiedler's least preferred co-worker (LPC) scale, cognitive resource theory, path-goal theory, situational leadership theory, leadership substitutes theory, and multiple linkage model, are discussed.

Fiedler's Contingency Theory

Fred E. Fiedler's contingency theory (Howell and Costley 2006) centres on the belief that there is no best way for managers to lead. Different situations create different leadership style requirements for managers. The style that works in one environment may not work in another. Fiedler looked at three elements that dictate a leader's situational control. These elements are:

Leader–member relations: How well do the manager and the employees get along to accomplish the task? This element applies to the amount of loyalty, dependability, and support that a leader receives from his/her employees. In a favourable relationship, a manager has a highly formed task structure and is able to reward and/or punish employees without any problems. In an unfavourable relationship, the task structure is usually poorly formed, and the leader possesses limited authority. The relationship may be either good or poor.

The task structure: The theory considers whether a job is structured or unstructured. In case the company has definite systems of working, the staff and workers know their job, and each complicated job has 'work instruction', then the tasks are structured. The job can be structured or unstructured when leader–member relations may be either good or bad.

Position power: How much authority does the manager possess to get work done by the subordinates? This power measures the amount of power or authority a manager perceives the organization has given him/her for the purpose of directing, rewarding, and punishing subordinates. Position powers of managers depend on the taking away or increasing of the decision-making power of employees. The position power can be high or low depending on whether the task is structured or unstructured.

Judging whether a leadership style is good or bad can be difficult. Each manager has his/her own preferences for leadership styles. Task-motivated leaders are at their best when their teams perform successfully, such as achieving new sales records or outperforming major competitors. Relationship-oriented leaders are at their best when greater customer satisfaction is gained and positive company image is established.

Fiedler's least preferred co-worker scale

Fiedler developed a least preferred co-worker (LPC) scale, an instrument to be used by a leader to identify the least preferred co-worker with whom he/she has worked. While leading a team, a leader experiences problems, particularly with a follower who poses difficulty. The postulate of Fiedler's contingency theory is that there is no one best way for managers to lead. Situations will create different leadership style requirements for managers. The solution to a managerial situation is contingent on the factors that impinge and encroach on the situation.

For example, in a highly routine or mechanistic environment, where repetitive tasks are a norm, a certain leadership style may result in the best performance. The same leadership style may be totally unsuccessful in an ever-changing dynamic environment.

Fiedler advises to pinpoint such a co-worker or group member with whom you faced the greatest difficulty and do not like to work with at all and use a questionnaire to identify his/her characteristics. The questionnaire contains several adjectives, bipolar in nature, that describe the individual. Some of the bipolar adjectives are friendly–unfriendly, sincere–insincere, boring–interesting/exciting, etc. All the bipolar adjectives are provided in Table 4.1.

TABLE 4.1 Fiedler's bipolar adjectives

Pleasant	8	7	6	5	4	3	2	1	Unpleasant
Friendly	8	7	6	5	4	3	2	1	Unfriendly
Rejecting	1	2	3	4	5	6	7	8	Accepting
Helpful	8	7	6	5	4	3	2	1	Frustrating
Unenthusiastic	1	2	3	4	5	6	7	8	Enthusiastic
Tense	1	2	3	4	5	6	7	8	Relaxed
Distant	1	2	3	4	5	6	7	8	Close
Cold	1	2	3	4	5	6	7	8	Warm
Cooperative	8	7	6	5	4	3	2	1	Uncooperative
Supportive	8	7	6	5	4	3	2	1	Hostile
Boring	1	2	3	4	5	6	7	8	Interesting
Quarrelsome	1	2	3	4	5	6	7	8	Harmonious
Self-assured	8	7	6	5	4	3	2	1	Hesitant
Efficient	8	7	6	5	4	3	2	1	Inefficient
Gloomy	1	2	3	4	5	6	7	8	Cheerful
Open	8	7	6	5	4	3	2	1	Guarded

Source: Howell and Costley (2006) quote these sixteen paired bipolar adjectives proposed by Fiedler, Chemers, and Mahar (1976).

Some more bipolar adjectives are provided in Table 4.2.

TABLE **4.2 Additional bipolar adjectives**

Backbiting	1	2	3	4	5	6	7	8	Loyal
Untrustworthy	1	2	3	4	5	6	7	8	Trustworthy
Considerate	8	7	6	5	4	3	2	1	Inconsiderate
Nasty	1	2	3	4	5	6	7	8	Nice
Agreeable	8	7	6	5	4	3	2	1	Disagreeable
Insincere	1	2	3	4	5	6	7	8	Sincere
Kind	8	7	6	5	4	3	2	1	Unkind

Source: www.msubillings.edu.

After scoring and interpretation of Fiedler's bipolar adjectives, a score greater that 76 indicates a relations orientation and a score less than 63 indicates a task orientation. The LPC score is a measure of the leader's emotional reaction to a person who obstructs goal attainment.

The LPC scale was proposed by Fiedler to identify a person's dominant leadership style. Fiedler believes that this style is a relatively fixed part of one's personality and therefore cannot be changed easily. This led Fiedler to his contingency views, which suggest that the key to leadership success is finding (or creating) good 'matches' between style and situation. The interpretation of the LPC score is given in Tables 4.3 and 4.4.

TABLE **4.3 LPC score**

LPC Score	Leader Style
76 or above	Relationship oriented
Between 63 and 75	Both task and relationship orientation
62 or below	Task oriented

TABLE **4.4 Orientations on the number line**

Relationship Oriented	Both	Task Oriented
128 76		62 16

It is important to understand that the score is thought to represent the leader, but not the specific individual the leader evaluates. Based on the scores, leaders are categorized into two groups: 'low LPC score' and 'high

LPC score' leaders. From the standpoint of motivation hierarchy, 'high LPC' leaders are primarily motivated by relationships and lay emphasis on establishing and maintaining interpersonal relationships, inclined to build bridges of relations and personal contacts.

Researchers rated managers to identify their extent of relationship orientation and task orientation. They found that task-oriented managers tend to do better in situations that have good leader–member relations, structured tasks, and position power (weak or strong). However, they do well when the task is unstructured but position power is strong.

Researchers also found that task-oriented managers did well when leader–member relations were moderate to poor and the task was unstructured. Relationship-oriented managers did better in all other situations. Thus, a given situation might call for a manager with a different style or a manager who can take on a different style for a different situation. The LPC score cannot accurately identify the motivation hierarchy of those with a certain intermediate score (Friedler 1976). Again, individuals within the intermediate range of the LPC score may more easily or readily switch between task oriented and relation-oriented styles than those individuals whose scores are at the extreme of the LPC scale. The situation and leadership style are correlated in Table 4.5.

The situation is characterized as most favourable when the leader–member relations are good, task is structured, and the leader's position power is high; and in that situation, the leader will have high control on the group. On the other hand, the situation will be most unfavourable when the leader–member relations are poor, task is unstructured, and the leader's position power is low.

TABLE **4.5** **Situation classification and model of leadership**

Octant	I	II	III	IV	V	VI	VII	VIII
Leader–member Relationship	Good				Poor			
Task structure	Structured		Unstructured		Structured		Unstructured	
Position power	High	Low	High	Low	High	Low	High	Low
Recommended leader type	· Task motivated (low LPC) · Socio-independent (medium LPC)				Relationship motivated (high LPC)			Task-motivated (low LPC)

Source: Model as proposed by Howell and Costley (2008).

The situational favourableness or situational control depends on:

(a) the quality of leader–member relations—high-quality relations indicate high cohesiveness and support for the leader by the group members, which is a favourable situation for the leader;

(b) the degree of task structure—the leader's task is highly structured if there is role clarity, and the goals and procedures are clear and unambiguous. This allows the leader to confidently guide the group, which is again a favourable situation;

(c) the amount of position power—this power is gained from the position a person occupies, his/her administrative authority, and control over rewards and punishment. All these are favourable to the leader's influence.

The model incorporates three characteristics: good or poor leader–member relations, high or low task structure, and high or low position power. The model classifies leadership situation as either high or low on each of the three characteristics. The model further recommends the following:

- Task-motivated (low LPC) leaders are expected to produce high group performance irrespective of whether the situation is favourable or unfavourable.
- Socio-independent leaders with medium LPC scores stay between task-oriented and relation-oriented leaders. These leaders will perform their best only if the situation is very favourable.
- Relation-oriented leaders will be successful in producing high group performance when the situation is only moderately favourable.

Another aspect of this contingency model is that leader–member relations, task structure, and position power dictate a leader's situational control. Leader–member relations are the amount of loyalty, dependability, and support that the leader receives from employees. It is a measure of how the manager perceives the employees and the extent to which a group of employees is getting along together.

The task-motivated style leader derives pride and satisfaction in the task accomplishment for the organization, while the relationship-motivated style seeks to build interpersonal relations and extend superfluous help for team development in the organization. There is no absolute good or bad leadership style.

Summarily, Fiedler's model considers this LPC as a leader trait; it does not mention any leader behaviour and the intervening variables. However, the model highlights situational variables like leader–member relations, position power, and task structure.

Cognitive Resource Theory

Intelligence helps one to perform, but there are times when intelligence may be a disadvantage. Recent research suggests that stress plays a key role in determining just how a leader's intelligence affects his/her effectiveness (Hughes et al. 2006). It is not surprising that stress affects leader behaviour in various ways. Fiedler and Garcia (1987) developed the cognitive resource theory (CRT) to explain the interesting relationships between leader intelligence and experience levels, and group performance in stressful and non-stressful work conditions. Fiedler also observed that people often act differently when stressed.

CRT is an approach to leadership that focuses on the interaction between the leader's cognitive resources (intelligence, technical competence, and job-related knowledge), job performance, and stress. The level of the leader's cognitive ability relates to the nature of the plans, decisions, and strategies that will guide the actions of a work group. The better the leader's abilities, the more effective the plans, decisions, and strategies. If the group supports the leader's goals and if the leader is not under immoderate stress, then the leader's programmes are likely to be implemented.

Stress refers to some stimulus resulting in a detectable strain that cannot be accommodated by the organism and which ultimately results in impaired health or behaviour (Pestonjee 1999). Interpersonal stress for the leader moderates the relation between leader intelligence and subordinate performance (Yukl 2007). Stresses may be induced by multiple sources like demands miracles, inadequate resources, frequent work crisis, serious conflicts with subordinates, and so forth.

At this stage, one should know the various stressors in organizational life. Srivastav (2006) mentions some role stresses–inter-role distance, role stagnation, role expectation conflict, role erosion, role overload, role isolation, personal inadequacy, self-role distance, role ambiguity, and resource inadequacy.

- *Inter-role distance:* Represents conflict between organizational and non-organizational roles.
- *Role stagnation:* The capabilities of persons performing identical activities and occupying the same position differ significantly. Role stagnation represents the inability to take over the new role and stagnation in the old role due to lack of competence for the new role,

and the accompanying feeling of insecurity in the new role together with comfort in the old role.

- *Role expectation conflict:* This role stress arises due to conflicting demands placed by the role senders or the significant people having expectations from the role occupant.
- *Role erosion:* This is generated when some of the important functions belonging to one's role are performed by others or when the credit for one's role performance is given to others.
- *Role overload:* The stress arises when there are too high or too many expectations from the role performer. In this situation, the role performers suffer from burst or burn out stress syndrome.
- *Role isolation:* This occurs when the role occupant feels isolated from the channel of communication, or for not being a part of what is happening.
- *Personal inadequacy:* A person may not have the competency required to perform the role.
- *Self-role distance:* Different roles demand different types of behavioural disposition. When the role a person occupies goes against his/her self-concept, then he/she feels self-role distance type of stress. This is essentially a conflict arising out of a mismatch between the person and his/her job.
- *Role ambiguity:* Role ambiguity refers to the lack of clarity about the expectations regarding the role, which may arise out of lack of information or understanding. It may exist in relation to activities, responsibilities, personal styles, and norms.
- *Resource inadequacy:* This arises when the role occupant perceives non-availability of any resource essential for his/her satisfactory role performance. An example of resource inadequacy is the manager's time required for obtaining any clarification or taking any decision.

Work role stress and interpersonal stress emotionally disturb and divert the leader and the role performer from problem-solving activities. On considering the stress factor, CRT makes two major predictions with regard to intelligence, experience, stress, and group performance. A leader's cognitive ability contributes to the performance of the team only when the leader's approach is directive.

CRT is based on the following assumptions:

1. When leaders are under stress, their cognitive abilities are diverted from the task and they pay attention to problems and activities that are less relevant. As a consequence, group performance suffers.

2. The cognitive abilities of directive leaders will exhibit a higher positive correlation with group performance in comparison with the cognitive abilities of non-directive leaders.

3. Plans and decisions can only be finalized and implemented when the group complies with the leader's directives. Therefore, the correlation between a leader's cognitive resources and group performance will be higher when the group spontaneously supports the leader than when it does not.

4. The cognitive abilities of the leader will augment performance only to the degree to which the task requires those abilities, that is, the degree to which the task is intellectually demanding.

5. The directive behaviour of the leader will also partly depend on the nature of the relationship between the leader and his/her followers, the degree of task structure, and the leader's control over the situation.

Propositions of CRT

Under low stress, high intelligence results in good plans and decisions. In this situation, a highly intelligent leader relies on his/her intellectual ability to analyse the problem and finds the best solutions. On the contrary, if the leader is highly stressed, there will be no relationship (or a negative relationship) between his intelligence and decision quality. Under high stress, a leader is likely to be more distracted and unable to focus on the task, and his/her intelligence will not be useful for the team in such situations. The leader may temporarily display behaviours not conducive to team functioning and disrupt team progress.

However, interpersonal stress for the leader moderates the relationship between leader experience and subordinate performance. CRT describes one aspect of leader behaviour that intervenes and mediates the relationship between a leader's cognitive resources and group performance. When a leader is directive, his/her intelligence and expertise contribute to group performance. He/she can also contribute when subordinates seek clarification and guidance to perform effectively.

Fiedler attempted to establish a link between CRT and the LPC contingency model by proposing that the LPC scores of leaders may be a primary determinant of directive behaviour in high-stress and low-stress situations.

A major source of stress for leaders arises from their own superiors in the organization. Through stress management techniques, the cognitive resources of leaders can be developed and applied more effectively. When managers have a stressful relationship with their superior, they tend to rely on responses or behaviours that worked for them in the past, rather than on their cognitive resources. When leaders are free of stress, they rely on their intelligence instead of being constrained by past experiences.

Summarily, the theory considers intelligence and experience as leader traits and directive leader behaviour, and does not mention any intervening variable. However, CRT considers stress and group ability as situational variables.

Path-Goal Model

Evans (1970) is credited with developing the first version of the path-goal theory. However, Ginnett et al. (2007) intended to focus on the later version of the theory developed by House and Dressler in 1974. Path-goal theory is a sophisticated and all-inclusive contingency model developed on the basis of the expectancy theory of motivation, which also deals with expectancy to understand motivation. Some people try to calculate effort-to-performance probabilities. This theory is based on the expectancy theory of motivation and views managers' job as coaching or guiding workers enabling them to choose the 'best' paths for reaching their goals. Since the term 'best' is relative, it is judged by the accompanying achievement of organizational goals.

The theory provides a cognitive approach to understanding motivation. It is based on the principles of goal-setting theory and emphasizes that leaders will have to engage in different types of leadership behaviour depending on the nature and demands of a particular situation. It is the leader's job to assist followers in attaining goals and to provide direction and support needed to ensure that their goals are congruent with the organizational goals. Leaders can increase their subordinates' motivation, satisfaction, and job performance by administering rewards for the achievement of particular goals. Effective leaders will help employees reach personal and organizational goals by pointing out the paths they should follow and by providing them with the means to do so.

Followers' characteristics, like traits and locus of control, influence the impact of the leader behaviours on their levels of satisfaction. People may have various traits like authoritative, energetic, calculative, dutiful, enterprising, inquisitive, innovative, initiator, negotiator, perfectionist, persuasive, systematic, truthful, visionary, wise, etc. From the standpoint of locus of control, people may be categorized as 'internals' and 'externals'.

- Internals believe that results are achieved through personal efforts, decision-making skills, and other driving forces. Napoleon belonged to this category. He said, 'I am the master of my fate and commander of my soul.'

- Externals believe that whatever happens to them is controlled by outside factors like fate, luck, and destiny. You must have seen people wearing several 'stones' in rings on their fingers just to save themselves either from the adverse effects or to gain the favour of the various planets. They are 'externals' as they depend on outside factors.

Researches have established that different followers like different styles of behavioural patterns from their leader, depending on their traits and locus of control.

Leaders can adopt four styles to facilitate employee attainment of goals. The styles are directive, supportive, participative, and achievement-oriented leadership.

- *Directive leadership:* This leader behaviour is very similar to task-oriented behaviours. The leader tells subordinates what they are expected to do, how they should do the work, and when they should do it. This behaviour includes developing systems and procedures, establishing norms, and expressing the need for conforming to the structured system and rules and regulations. The leader further schedules and coordinates the work.
- *Supportive leadership:* The leader shows genuine concern and support for subordinates, has courteous and friendly interactions with them, enquires about their well-being and individual needs, remains approachable to the followers, and discusses issues openly. As such, this behaviour is very similar to relation-oriented behaviour.
- *Participative leadership:* The leader creates an environment of trust, engages subordinates in consultations, and encourages their participation in decision-making processes that affect their work. Obviously, the leader shares their work problems with the team members, and seeks suggestions and recommendations. He/she evaluates the suggestions and then accepts or rejects them, taking the followers into confidence.
- *Achievement-oriented leadership:* The leader exhibits both demanding and supporting interactions, sets challenging goals for subordinates, involves them to improve performance, and drives them to give their best. The leader always tries to raise the confidence levels of the team-mates and emphasizes high levels of job performance.

Internal locus-of-control followers, who believe that outcomes are a result of their decisions, were much more satisfied with leaders who exhibited participative behaviours than they were with leaders who were directive (Hughes et al. 2006). Conversely, external locus-of-control followers were more satisfied with directive leaders than with participative leader behaviours.

Situation

With regard to situation, Hughes et al. (2006) mention that situational factors impact or moderate the effects of leader behaviour on follower attitudes and behaviours. These factors include the formal authority system and the primary work group. Each of these factors can influence the leadership situation in one of the three ways serving as (a) an independent motivational factor, (b) a constraint on the behaviour of followers, or (c) a reward.

For newly formed work teams, members need many instructions regarding what to do, how to do, and when to do, and obviously the leader will have to exhibit directive behaviours. On receiving directions from the leader, followers' role ambiguity will reduce, and they will be able to make efforts to enhance their role performance. The outcomes will be higher efforts and higher satisfaction. Rewards can be well linked with performance. If the performance of followers is above the set standard, then directive leader behaviour will make rewards commensurate with the performance. The leader will link rewards and other incentives directly with the followers' performance. The linking, in turn, will result in higher efforts and higher satisfaction.

Thus, the leadership style that will be most effective depends not only on the characteristics of the situation, but also on those of the subordinates. Leaders must be flexible, rather flexibly rigid, and adopt whichever style is called for in that particular situation.

Prescriptions of the Path-Goal Theory

The discussions above are diagrammatically represented (Figure 4.1) as examples of application of the path-goal theory. Hughes et al. (2008) refer to it as prescription of the theory.

Summarily, the path-goal theory considers four leader traits, namely, directive, supportive, participative, and achievement oriented. It does not mention any leader behaviour. As situational variables, it considers task, environment, and many others. As intervening variables, the theory considers expectancies, valences, and role ambiguity.

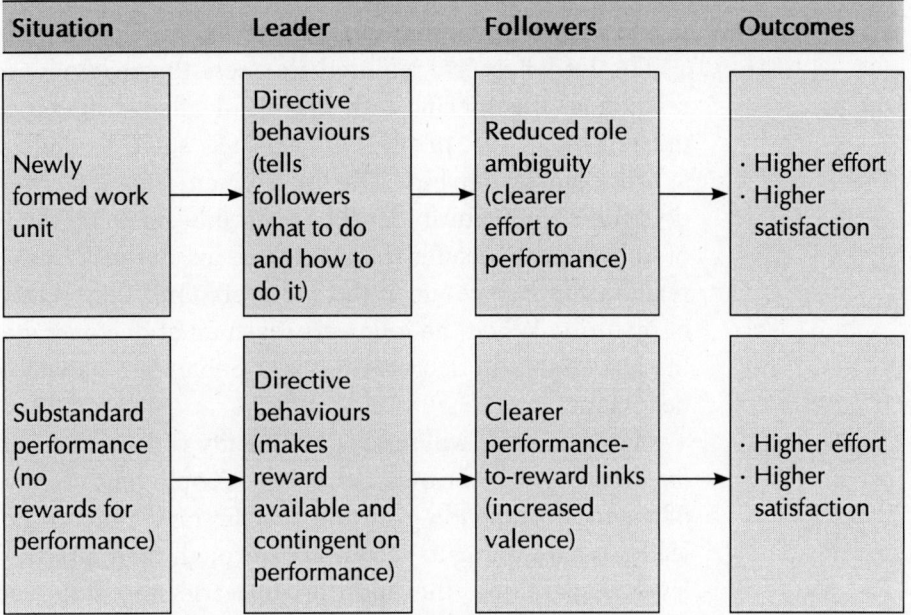

Situation	Leader	Followers	Outcomes
Newly formed work unit	Directive behaviours (tells followers what to do and how to do it)	Reduced role ambiguity (clearer effort to performance)	· Higher effort · Higher satisfaction
Substandard performance (no rewards for performance)	Directive behaviours (makes reward available and contingent on performance)	Clearer performance-to-reward links (increased valence)	· Higher effort · Higher satisfaction

FIGURE 4.1   Applying path-goal theory diagram based on Hughes et al. (2008)

Situational Leadership Theory

The situational leadership model has evolved over time. Hersey and Blanchard (1977) first prescribed its essential elements. The roots of this theory are in the Ohio State studies, in which the researchers initially identified two broad categories of leader behaviours, namely, initiating structure and consideration. Situational leadership theory is based on the amount of direction (task behaviour) and the amount of socio-emotional support (relationship behaviour) that a leader must provide given the situation and the level of maturity of the followers.

Task behaviour is defined as the extent to which the leader engages in spelling out the duties and responsibilities to an individual or a group. This behaviour includes telling people what to do, how to do it, when to do it, where to do it, and who should do it. In task behaviour, the leader engages in one-way communication. Relationship behaviour is defined as the extent to which the leader engages in two-way or multi-way communication. This includes listening, encouraging, sympathizing, facilitating, clarifying, explaining the importance of the task. While developing relationship behaviour, the leader engages the follower in two-way communication to provide socio-emotional support.

The leader is first required to assess the readiness of the followers in relation to the specific task that the leader is attempting to accomplish utilizing the effort of the followers. As such, to conclude, for using the appropriate leadership style in a given situation, the leader must first determine the maturity level of the followers. With the increased maturity of followers, the leader should reduce his/her task behaviour and increase relationship behaviour to the followers until they reach a moderate level of maturity. When the followers reach an above-average level of maturity, the leader should decrease the task behaviour, as well as his relationship behaviour.

Maturity is the willingness and ability of a person to take responsibility for directing his/her own behaviour. People tend to have varying degrees of maturity, depending on the specific task, function, or objective that a leader is attempting to accomplish through their efforts. Once the maturity level is identified, the appropriate leadership style can be determined. The four leadership styles are telling, selling, participating, and delegating (Figure 4.2 and Table 4.6).

- *Telling:* This style reflects high task and low relationship behaviour (S1). The leader provides clear instructions and specific direction. Telling style is best matched with a low follower readiness level.

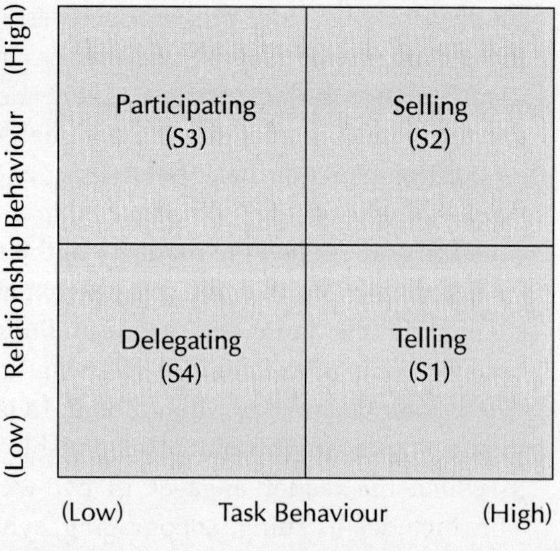

FIGURE 4.2 **Task vs relationship behaviour**

TABLE 4.6   Behaviour vs readiness and style

Task Behaviour	Relationship Behaviour	Follower Readiness Level	Style
High	Low	Low	Telling
High	High	Moderate	Selling
Low	High	Moderate	Participating
Low	Low	High	Delegating

- *Selling:* This style reflects high task and high relationship behaviour (S2). The leader encourages two-way communication and helps build confidence and motivation on the part of the employee, although the leader still has responsibility and controls decision-making. Selling style is best matched with a moderate follower readiness level.
- *Participating:* This style reflects high relationship and low task behaviour (S3). With this style, the leader and the followers share decision-making and no longer need or expect the relationship to be directive. Participating style is best matched with a moderate follower readiness level.
- *Delegating:* This style reflects low relationship and low task behaviour (S4). Delegating style is appropriate for leaders whose followers are ready to accomplish a particular task and are both competent and motivated to take full responsibility. This style is best matched with a high follower readiness level.

Summarily, situational leadership theory does not consider any leadership trait or intervening variable. Task and relationship are the leader behaviours that are taken into account. As a situational variable, this theory considers follower readiness or subordinate's maturity.

Leadership Substitutes Theory

In certain situations, the importance of leadership by managers and organizational leaders reduces. Kerr and Jermier (1978) wanted to identify aspects of such situations in which the importance reduces. Their theory draws a distinction between situational variables, namely, substitutes and neutralizers. In some cases, followers may be skilled, knowledgeable, sincere, dedicated, know their job and roles well, do not need guidance, are capable of achieving the team objectives, and in addition, they are involved, committed to, and satisfied with the tasks assigned to them. In such cases, leaders' roles become redundant. Substitute situational variable or simply 'substitutes' make leader behaviour unnecessary and redundant.

In some organizational set-up, a team leader may not have the authority to reward effective performance and also may not have the right to initiate any disciplinary action against a subordinate. 'Neutralizers' are any characteristics of the task or the organization that prohibits leaders in some ways or that nullify the effects of the leader's actions.

Role clarity and task motivation are implicit in the assumptions of the model though the theory does not explicitly identify other intervening variables. Certain groups of factors can provide important benefits to leaders. This is situational, and the follower characteristics in this case substitute for specific leader behaviours. Substitutes are ways in which the characteristics of organizations, teams, tasks, and individuals can provide substitutes for the task and social behaviours of leaders. Leadership neutralizers are situational or follower characteristics that can decrease the effectiveness of the leader's influence on followers (Howell and Costley 2008). Self-managed teams are a replacement for leaders.

They also mention certain examples of such situational factors:

- By a high degree of training and experience, followers can enable followers to perform well without the leader's direction and guidance.
- Work tasks that followers find intrinsically satisfying can result in improved follower attitudes and alleviate the need for the leader's supportive behaviours.
- Networked computer systems and computer-integrated manufacturing can make needed knowledge, information, and feedback available to followers and alleviate the need for much direction by the leader.

Kerr and Jermier (1978) were mostly concerned with identifying substitutes and neutralizers for supportive and instrumental leadership. Supportive leadership is similar to consideration whereas instrumental leadership is similar to the initiation structure of the Ohio State leadership style. Examples of substitutes and neutralizers include experience, ability, training and professional orientation. Yukl (2007), quoting Kerr and Jermier, has given a list of substitutes and neutralizers both for supportive leadership and instrumental leadership styles (Table 4.7).

From the information provided in the table, it is evident that if followers are experienced, trained, have professional attitudes, contribute to the team and the organization without looking for rewards in return, then from the standpoint of subordinate characteristics, the leader's role becomes unessential and superfluous.

Table 4.7 Leadership substitutes and neutralizers

Substitutes/ Neutralizers	Supportive Leadership	Instrumental Leadership
Subordinate Characteristics		
Experience, ability, and training		Substitute
Professional orientation	Substitute	Substitute
Indifference towards organizational rewards	Neutralizer	Neutralizer
Task Characteristics		
Structured, routine tasks		Substitute
Feedback provided by task		Substitute
Intrinsically challenging task	Substitute	
Organizational Characteristics		
Cohesive team	Substitute	Substitute
Low position power	Neutralizer	Neutralizer
Formalization (roles, procedures)		Substitute
Inflexibility (rules, policies)		Neutralizer
Dispersed subordinate work sites	Neutralizer	Neutralizer

Again, if we concentrate on task characteristics, then unambiguous tasks, direct feedback from the task, and a challenging task can well replace the leader. A cohesive and team leader's lack of position power, standardization and formalization, organizational rigidity can also replace the leader, Furthermore, physical distance between the leader and subordinates, as in the case of virtual teams as elements of organizational characteristics, can also result in the same.

Contextually, it is opined that in some situations the number of neutralizers may be massive. In such cases, it may be difficult, and rather impossible, for the leader to succeed (Howell and Costley 2008). Naturally, the need for providing training to the leader may arise. But it would be wiser to search for the root cause behind, say, indifference toward rewards and low position power. Kerr and Jermier (1978) suggest the interesting possibility that substitutes may be increased to the point where leadership is altogether superfluous (Yukl 2007).

Summarily, this model does not consider any leader trait, takes into account supportive and instrumental leader behaviours, emphasizes substitutes and neutralizers as main situational variables, and does not speak about any intervening variable.

Multiple Linkage Model

The multiple linkage model is developed by Yukl (1981), based on earlier leadership models and group effectiveness. The model mentions four variables, namely, managerial behaviours, intervening variables, criterion variables, and situational variables. The managerial behaviours and the situational variables interact on the intervening variables that determine the performance of a work team.

The situational variables exert influence on three points:

- They constrain leader (managerial) behaviour and moderate its effect and hence these are neutralizers.
- They directly influence the intervening variables.
- They determine the relative importance of the intervening variables.

Yukl (2007) emphasizes that to understand how a leader can influence the performance of a group or a sub-unit of an organization, it would be helpful to examine the intervening variables that determine group performance. The six intervening variables mentioned in the model, based on earlier research and theory of determinants of individual and group performance, are:

- Subordinate efforts
- Role clarity and task skills
- Organization of work
- Cohesiveness and cooperation
- Resource and support services
- External coordination

The definitions of the intervening variables in the language of Yukl (2007) are as follows:

Task commitment The extent to which unit members strive to attain a high level of performance and show a high degree of personal commitment to unit task objectives.

Ability and role clarity   The extent to which unit members understand their individual job responsibilities, know what to do, and have the skills to do it.

Organization of the work   The extent to which effective performance strategies are used to attain task objectives and the work is organized to ensure efficient utilization of personnel, equipment, and facilities.

Cooperation and mutual trust   The extent to which group members trust each other, share information and ideas, help each other, and identify with the work unit.

Resources and support   The extent to which the group has the budgetary funds, tools, equipment, supplies, personnel, and facilities needed to do the work, and the necessary information or assistance from other units.

External coordination   The extent to which activities of the work unit are synchronized with the interdependent activities in other parts of the organization and other organizations (like suppliers, clients, and joint venture partners).

Influencers of intervening variables

In any organization, good compensation management and reward systems intrinsically motivate the people in the organization. Job-involved, job-satisfied, and committed members contribute their best to the team and the organization and help achieve business goals. Intrinsic motivation will be high if employees get work requiring varied skills, and the work is interesting and challenging and requires creativity and originality.

Situational variables impact the abilities of group members. An organization may utilize the AIDA (attention, interest, desire, and action) model in its recruitment and selection process. In the advertisement itself, such companies highlight the company background, its growth, career progression of employees, advancing employees through training and development. Naturally, these companies get and can retain talent through attrition management techniques. Thus the recruitment and selection process is a situational variable that affects the intervening variable.

The nature of a group, its size, norm, cohesiveness, group dynamics, performance, etc., influence cooperation and teamwork. The cohesiveness, interpersonal relations, psychological bonds, and mutual cooperation of a small group are stronger than those of a large group. Team performance increases when the team functions under a seasoned leader. Obviously, situation and situational variables exert influence on the intervening variables. However, leader behaviour influences all situational variables. In Yukl's multiple linkage model (see Figure 4.3), Yukl (2007) suggests

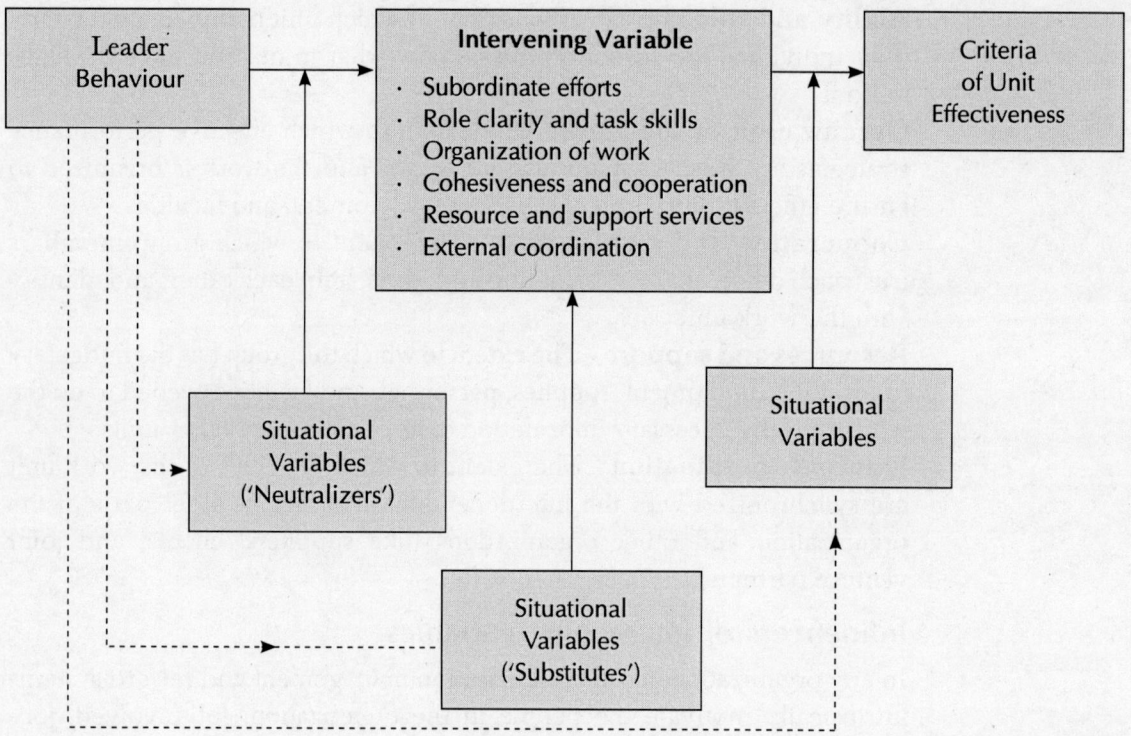

FIGURE 4.3   Yukl's Multiple Linkage Model: Causal relationships in multiple linkage the model

short-term actions to correct deficiencies in the intervening variables to ultimately improve group performance. He has identified certain common deficiencies and proposes corresponding leader actions. The deficiencies identified by Yukl include the following:

(a)   Subordinates are apathetic or discouraged about the work.
(b)   Subordinates are confused what work to do or how to do it.
(c)   The group is disorganized and/or it uses weak performance strategies.
(d)   Little cooperation and teamwork exist among members of the group.
(e)   The group has inadequate resources to do the work.
(f)   External coordination with other sub-units or outsiders is weak.

For each of the deficiencies, Yukl has prescribed leader actions. However, only the actions that suggest weak external coordination with other sub-units or outsiders are reproduced:

•   Network with peers and outsiders to develop more cooperative relationship.

- Consult more with peers and outsiders when devising a plan.
- Keep peers and outsiders informed about changes.
- Monitor closely to detect coordination problems quickly.
- Meet with peers and outsiders to resolve coordination problems.
- Negotiate favourable agreements with peers and outsiders for group output.

From the above suggestions, it is obvious that Yukl has emphasized the need for knowledge about environment as much as he has stressed upon the relationship with outsiders for networking, consulting, keeping informed, resolving problems, and for negotiation. Yukl (2007) has further discussed long-term effects on group performance and has given examples of possible actions a leader may take.

Summarily, the multiple linkage model does not mention any leader trait, discusses leader behaviours considering many aspects based on short-term and long-term performances, takes into account task commitment and reward systems as situational variables, and mentions many intervening variables as shown in the model.

CONTINGENCY THEORIES AT A GLANCE

Managerial behaviour varies across situations. The various theories provide useful insights. Theorists researched and strived to discover the effective leadership style in a given situation. While one theorist laid emphasis on leader traits, the other stressed on leader behaviours. Some other theorists emphasized on situational variables and a few others focused on the intervening variables. In fact, the leadership theorist considered some combination of leader traits, leader behaviours, situational variables, and intervening variables. The considerations of six theories that we discussed earlier are summarized in this section (Table 4.8).

Table 4.8 Comparing contingency theories

Theory	Leader Traits	Leader Behaviours	Situational Variables	Intervening Variables
LPC Contingency model	Least preferred co-worker	Nothing mentioned	· Leader–member relations · Position power · Task structure	Nothing mentioned

Contd

Table 4.8 contd

Theory	Leader Traits	Leader Behaviours	Situational Variables	Intervening Variables
Cognitive resource theory	· Intelligence · Experience	Directive	· Stress · Group ability	Nothing mentioned
Path-goal theory	· Directive · Supportive · Participative · Achievement oriented	Nothing mentioned	· Task · Environment · And many more	· Subordinate expectancies · Valences · Role ambiguity
Situational leadership theory	Nothing mentioned	· Task · Relationship	Follower readiness or subordinate's maturity	Nothing mentioned
Leadership substitutes theory	Nothing mentioned	· Supportive · Instrumental	· Substitutes · Neutralizers · And many more	Nothing mentioned
Multiple linkage model	Nothing mentioned	Many aspects based on short-term and long-term performance	· Task commitment · Reward system	· Efforts · Role clarity · Task skills · Organization of work · Teamwork · Cohesiveness · Cooperation · External coordination

Out of the six theories, three do not take into account leader traits and four are silent about the intervening variables. But all the theories do consider leader behaviours and situational variables. This clearly highlights the roles of these variables in effective leadership.

SUMMARY

Leadership theories incorporate various aspects of an organization and the characteristics of followers. Some theories concentrate on leaders' impact on followers. The impact results from the leader trait, leader behaviour, and also the characteristics of the organizational situation. The theories that consider these as inputs to the leadership process are contingency theories. Six contingency theories have been discussed. These theories emphasize aspects like leader traits, leader behaviours, situational variables, and intervening variables.

Fiedler's LPC theory considers leader traits and situational variables. Cognitive resource theory emphasizes on leader traits and behaviours, and situational variables. The path-goal theory takes into account leader traits, situational variables, and intervening variables. Situational leadership theory concentrates on leader behaviour and situational variables. The leadership substitutes theory also speaks about leader behaviours and situational variables. The multiple linkage model lays emphasis on leader behaviours, situational variables, and intervening variables.

Out of the six theories, three do not take into account leader traits and four are silent about the intervening variables. But all the theories consider leader behaviours and situational variables. This clearly highlights the roles of these variables in effective leadership. Transactional leaders adhere to rules, systems, and procedures and thus perform routine and repetitive works well. They rely on the concept that rewards and punishments influence performance.

KEY TERMS

Instrumental leadership is similar to the initiating structure, the leadership style that describes the extent to which a leader structures his/her role and the roles of followers or subordinates to achieve the organizational goal.

Neutralizers are any characteristics of the task or the organization that prohibit a leader in some ways or that nullify the effects of the leader's actions.

Substitutes or substitute situational variables are ways in which the characteristics of organizations, teams, tasks, and individuals can provide substitutes for the task and social behaviours of leaders.

Supportive leadership is similar to the consideration style; the extent to which an organizational leader is likely to have job relationships is characterized by the mutual trust, and respect for colleagues and followers, and also respect their viewpoints, sentiments, and feelings.

EXERCISES

Concept Review Questions

1. Which of the contingency models would be most useful to you to be as effective as a leader? Justify your choice. Describe briefly the organization you are referring to.

2. What do you mean by least preferred co-worker? How is the LPC score measured? What does it imply? Discuss the elements of a leader's situational control.
3. Define stress. What are the various stressors in organizational life? How does stress affect leadership style?

Critical Thinking Questions

1. How does the multiple linkage theory of leadership expand our understanding of the leadership process?
2. What do you understand by the term situational leadership? How is the readiness level of the followers linked with the leadership style? Discuss the styles taking into account leader behaviours.

Assignments

1. Carefully study the environment of the company you are working for. Identify some substitutes and neutralizers relevant to leadership. Classify them, explaining the basis for the classification.
2. Identify an organizational leader who has significantly contributed to the company he/she is working for. Mention some of his/her qualities.

REFERENCES

Howell, Jon P. and Dan L. Costley (2008), *Understanding Behaviours for Effective Leaders*, Prentice-Hall India, New Delhi.

Hughes, Richard L., Robert L. Ginnett, and Gordon L. Curphy (2008), *Leadership Enhancing the Lessons of Experience*, Tata McGraw-Hill, New Delhi.

Srivastav, Avinash Kumar (2006), Achieve in Quality Assurance–An Empirical Study on Relation with Stress, Coping, and Personal Variables, *Indian Journal on Training and Development*, Vol. 36, No. 1, January–March 2006, pp. 65–76.

Yukl, Gary (2007), *Leadership in Organizations*, Pearson Education, New Delhi.

Stoner, J.A.F., R.E. Freeman, and Jr. D.R. Gilbert (2006), *Management*, Prentice-Hall India, New Delhi.

Web Resources

www.msubillings.edu/BusinessFaculty/larsen/MGMT321/Leas%20Preferred CoworkerScale.pdf (accessed on 7 September 2008).

Leadership Style for Effectiveness

(*Note:* This case is a continuation of the opening case. You are provided with the following additional information about GSL.)

About a year had elapsed after the departure of Mr Ramachandran. During his stay, Mr Ramachandran developed his officers and staff members. He prepared manuals (administrative, quality management, environmental management, and safety management systems). He designed and implemented '5S'—*Seiri* (sorting out, organizing in order), *Seiton* (systematic arrangement, neatness), *Seiso* (spik and span, cleaning, inspection), *Seiketsu* (serene atmosphere, sanitizing, standardization), and *Shitsuke* (self-discipline) in all offices and shops. In fact, he created the track and, even in his absence, people are walking that track. His credit lies in the fact that his absence is not felt at all, except the physical distance.

In the last one year, the company has developed further. Both Mr Banerjee and Mr Taneja have contributed to the growth. Though both of them are successfully managing the company, there exist some differences in their approaches.

Mr Banerjee does not take any risks, not even calculated ones. He dedicatedly follows the system, standards, procedures, and rules and regulations. In other words, he does not apply any discretion. He only applies his chain of command but remains within the framework. He guides his subordinates and reminds them to follow the company's standing instructions. However, he honours juniors' ideas and innovations, but before implementing them for practical use, obtains approval of seniors.

Mr Taneja appears to be psychologically close to the people of GSL, whether they are from his division or not. He has a strong influence on them. The company organized a family get-together. Mr Taneja took the leading role. He mobilized resources, collected substantial funds, and received amazing support from one and all, both internal and external people. He invited Mr Ramachandran as a guest of honour, who attended the get-together with his family. People do what Mr Taneja wants. He does not need to make any effort to get something done by others. His influence on others is unparalleled. Of course, he is considering and mostly honouring the emotions, values, beliefs, attitudes, and behaviours of others. Presumably for all these characteristics, he could make such a colossal arrangement and successfully organized the get together.

Discussion Questions

1. Which contingency leadership type was used by Mr Ramachandran?
2. Identify the learning outcomes from the advice offered by Mr Ramachandran to Mr Banerjee.
3. Make out the leadership style of Mr Ramachandran.
4. What leadership styles are followed by Mr Banerjee and Mr Taneja?
5. Attempt to establish the links among the leadership styles of Mr Ramachandran, Mr Banerjee, and Mr Taneja with the help of contingency theories.

CHAPTER **5**

Contemporary Leadership Styles

Learning Objectives

After studying this chapter, you will be able to

▶ Describe the need for studying various leadership styles
▶ Define transactional, transformational, and charismatic leadership
▶ Understand the importance of value-based leadership
▶ Explain how to develop spiritual and servant leadership
▶ Understand the concept and utility of boundary spanning in work areas
▶ Conceptualize level 5 leadership

OPENING CASE

Leading Differs from Managing

A company recruits management trainees from reputed B-schools, and offers intensive induction for 26 weeks before confirming them as assistant managers and assigning them regular tasks. During the induction, the new recruits are given exposure to the profile of the organization, its product range, technology, principal customers, growth rate, and growth prospect of the organization, and career progression options available for employees. The induction also includes an introduction to company procedures and acquaintance with administrative, quality, environment, and safety manuals. The company has its headquarters at Pune and five units in Pune, Ahmedabad, Faridabad, Nashik, and Nagpur. The induction curriculum also includes an industrial and educational tour programme to all the units. In all the cities, they are accommodated in luxury hotels and guest houses to enhance self-esteem of the trainees.

In the preceding five years, the annual turnover of the company has doubled. An entrepreneur in 1975 started the company that has grown through diversification. It started its training and development department way back in

1988. At the initial stage, it was conducting supervisory development courses. Since 1990, the company started recruiting management trainees. Attrition is low in this company. In this case, the managerial reserves of trainees recruited in the year 1992 are discussed. A total of 15 trainees were selected and offered appointment. All the 15 joined and underwent the induction programme. One of the 15 assistant managers left the company three years ago and is now working in a senior position in a multinational company in New York. Of the remaining, 4 are deputy managers, 8 are managers, and 2 are senior managers. Of the 8 managers, 3 are likely to become senior managers shortly. Obviously, after recruitment in the same batch, different trainees have reached different levels in the organizational hierarchy. The objective of this case study is to make the reader understand this differential ascend of 15 recruits along the organizational hierarchy.

Mr Rajan and Mr Tilak graduated from the same B-school and are close friends. Almost every weekend they get together along with their families. Mr Rajan is now a manager whereas Mr Tilak is already a senior manager. The various differences are visible to all personnel in the organization. Mr Rajan is always inclined to adhere to rules and regulations, complying with the chain of command. He possesses capabilities and accepts challenging assignments, but faces difficulty in mobilizing human resources. On the contrary, Mr Tilak can easily get people to work willingly. Mr Tilak is also technically sound. Both Mr Rajan and Mr Tilak read business magazines and possess huge managerial reserves. It is understood that Mr Tilak reads the Bhagavad Gita every morning and shares some thoughts and teachings of Lord Krishna to Arjuna with staff, who listen with rapt attention. He believes that while working, he must serve humankind and do something for the next generation; he wants to plant seeds so that others can get the fruits. Furthermore, Mr Tilak believes in innovation, finding new ways of doing work, changing the work system, and creating a new vision.

The four deputy managers are academically brilliant like others recruited with them, but fumble in decision-making. Even if they make decisions, they submit the draft to their seniors 'for approval'. This process of obtaining approval happens in cases where they can implement the decision themselves. Approval seeking consumes unnecessary time.

Mr M.B.S. Sastry is director (HRD) and looks after human resource and leadership development of the company. He observes that Mr Rajan remains busy in directing, supervising, recording, preparing and issuing circulars, and other kinds of formal communication. On the contrary, Mr Tilak can achieve any task assigned to him or chosen by himself, with no or little hurdle. In fact, he can see things from another person's perspective. People are eager to be associated with him. Even people from other divisions or functional areas are ready to lend a hand to him. People willingly undertake to execute the tasks assigned by Mr Tilak. Mr Sastry discerns that Mr Tilak has something that others lack. Once Mr Sastry, during a discussion with the chief executive officer, brought to light that 'Mr Tilak gets excellent ideas and has the remarkable ability to distil complex ideas into simple messages', which the followers can understand and implement.

Learning points

1. A manager should have something to pull people towards him/her and get their willing support in development drives.
2. Sanctified knowledge helps one to manage and control oneself, and organize.
3. Self-confidence is an essential ingredient for managers.
4. A manager should build and maintain relationships.

INTRODUCTION

A leader has his/her own way of executing work and getting the work done by junior colleagues, style of interacting with peers, approach to interacting with seniors, and techniques for dealing with outsiders. Some leaders prefer to follow the organization's standing rules and regulations in minute detail and do not use their discretion. Some leaders are inclined to bring about changes in the organization and apply their discretion, whereas some leaders possess magnetic personality and people listen to them spellbound. Again, a few more leaders lay stress on human values and rely on the spirit of the employees. A few leaders believe in analogizing their activities to that of a servant.

In fact, leadership is a fascinating social phenomenon that occurs across all groups of people regardless of geography, culture, or nationality. In this chapter, some contemporary leadership styles in practice, such as transactional, transformational, charismatic, value-based, spiritual and servant, boundary spanning and team leadership, and level 5 leadership, are discussed.

FAMILIAR LEADERSHIP

In any organization, you will find various types of leaders. They all try to adhere to the organization's mission, policy, and objectives. The types of leaders are identified from their component behaviours, mostly or frequently used to influence subordinates or followers. As an influencer, each style impacts followers' response and determines their performance.

Transactional Leadership

Transactional leadership is based on contingency, that is, rewards or punishments are treated as determinants of performance. As contingents, these influence employee performance.

Transactional leaders conform to rules and regulations and structured systems and procedures, and they treat any deviation from them as non-conformity. When people have agreed to do a job, they concede all authority to their manager. Transactional leaders determine what employees' need to do to achieve their own and organizational objectives, classify those requirements, and help employees become confident to reach their objectives by expending the necessary efforts (Stoner et al. 2006). Transactional leaders work through creating clear structures whereby it is clear what is required of their subordinates, and the rewards that they get for following the orders. Punishments are not always mentioned, but formal systems of discipline are usually in place. This leadership style rests on the belief that social systems work best with a clear chain of command, that the prime job of subordinates is to do what their manager tells them to do, and that people are motivated by reward and punishment.

Transactional leadership begins with negotiating the contract whereby the subordinate is given a salary and other work-related benefits, and the company and the subordinate's manager get authority over the subordinate. This style assumes that (a) people are motivated by reward and punishment, (b) social systems work best with a clear chain of command, and (c) when people have agreed to undertake an assignment and responsibility, a part of the deal is that they give up all authority to their manager. Transactional leadership is based on contingency, in that reward or punishment is conditional upon performance. Northwestern University conducted a study with respect to transactional, transformational, and laissez-faire leadership styles. From the study, it was observed that while female leaders used the transactional leadership style, they were more likely to focus on the reward component of that style. On the other hand, when men utilized the transactional style, they were more likely to focus on the punishment aspects of that style.

Transformational Leadership

Transformational leadership is about change, innovation, and entrepreneurship. This type of leadership is a behavioural process capable of being learned and managed.

The leadership process is systematic, comprising purposeful and organized search for changes, methodical analysis, and has the capacity to utilize resources to enhance productivity. The underlying assumptions of transformational leadership are: (a) people will follow a person who inspires them; (b) a person with vision and passion can achieve great things; and (c) the way to get work done is by injecting enthusiasm and energy. Transformational leaders inspire followers, gain their trust, exhibit such behaviour that contributes to the achievement of organizational goals, and perform at a high level. Transformational leaders (a) increase awareness of subordinates of the importance of their tasks and the significance of performing them well, (b) alert subordinates of the need for personal growth, development, and accomplishment, and (c) inspire and stimulate subordinates to work for the good of the organization. They influence their followers by intellectually stimulating them to become aware of problems in their teams and organization and view their problems from a new perspective that is consistent with the leader's vision.

A transformational leader encourages the followers to view problems differently and feel some degree of responsibility in helping to solve them. In a study conducted by Northwestern University it was observed that women are more likely to use transformational methods than male leaders. This means most women were more interested in working with people holistically, not just making deals (money-zine). Transformational leadership is a discipline with a set of predictable steps. The transformational themes are revitalization (recognition of the need to change), creating a new vision, and institutionalizing the change.

Step 1: Revitalization—Recognition of the need to change

Organizations today are operating under various types of pressures from multiple directions. These pressures are triggering the need for changes. But not all organizations can sense this need. Among those that do, only a few respond. The key decision-makers in the organization must be made to feel dissatisfied with the status quo.

But a question may arise about who will inculcate this feeling. It is the transformational leaders in the organization who do this. It may not be possible for external experts due to their non-acquaintance with the organizational systems and procedures. The felt and appreciated need for change endows an organization with the impetus for transition. One must remember that the process of transition is seldom smooth. It will invariably be accompanied by resistance from employees. This resistance must be overcome.

Step 2: Creating a new vision

Vision is the overriding principle that guides an organization. It defines what the organization wants to be. It is often the dream of the strategic apex. The leader involved in transformation needs to create a vision that the critical mass of employees will accept and they must accept the vision willingly as a desirable change for the organization. The vision must correctly respond to the environmental pressures. The leader must communicate his/her vision to all the members of the organization to create transition. There is a need for the leader to tap a deeper sense of meaning for followers for smooth and successful transition.

Step 3: Institutionalizing the change

Vision is a dream that must be translated into reality. Revitalization will remain empty talk until the vision becomes reality. New realities, actions, practices, and norms must be shared to institutionalize change. The leader will be required to shape, mould, and reinforce a new culture that fits the revitalized organization. Any kind of change evokes feelings of fear and hope, anxiety and relief, pressure and stimulation, threats and opportunities in the minds of those likely to be affected by the change. Transformational leaders need to consider the individual psychodynamics to recognize these mixed feelings, act to help people to move from negative to positive emotion, and mobilize the energy needed for individual renewal.

Thus, it is obvious that transformational leaders must possess good visioning, rhetorical, and impression management skills, and use these skills to strengthen emotional bonds with their followers. Bass (1985, 1997) researched on transformational and transactional leadership. He used perceptions and reactions of followers to ascertain whether or not a leader was transformational.

A person with the transformational leadership style is a true leader who inspires his/her team constantly with a shared vision of the future. Transformational leaders are highly visible, spend a lot of time in communicating, and are result oriented. They do not necessarily lead from the front, as they tend to delegate responsibility among their team members. In many organizations, both transactional and transformational leadership are needed. Transactional leaders lay emphasis on routine work being done reliably, while transformational leaders bring in initiatives that add value.

Transformational leadership blends behavioural theories and trait theories. Transactional leaders, such as those identified in contingency theories, guide followers in the direction of established goals by clarifying role and task requirements. However, transformational leaders, who are charismatic and visionary, can inspire followers to transcend their own self-interest for the good of the organization and to achieve the organizational mission. These leaders appeal to followers' ideology and moral values, and inspire them to think about problems in new or different ways. The behaviours they use to influence followers include vision, self-esteem, personal example, and impression management. Visionary skill is the ability of the leader to foresee and foretell and bind people together with an idea. Transformational leaders define the purpose of their movement in highly meaningful terms. They assess themselves by getting feedback from others. Impression management is the leader's attempt to control the impression that others form about the leader by practising behaviours that make the leader more attractive and appealing to them.

A transformational leader positively contributes to productivity enhancement, humanpower retention, and higher employee satisfaction as it instils feelings of confidence, admiration, and commitment in the followers. He/she is charismatic, creating a special bond with followers, articulates a vision with which the followers identify and for which they are willing to work. The leaders coach, mentor, and counsel each of the followers, and delegate them some authority. See Box 5.1.

A transformational leader stimulates followers intellectually, arousing them to develop new ways of thinking about problems. Transformational leaders put their best efforts, use contingent rewards to positively reinforce performance that is consistent with their wishes. They prefer management by exception. They take initiative only when there are problems and are not actively involved when things are going well. They are people committed to actions and strive to convert followers into leaders.

Transformational leaders are flexible, flexibly rigid, and innovative, and today's changing business environment needs such leaders for overall growth. It is of utmost importance to have leaders with the appropriate orientation, defining tasks and managing interpersonal relationships. But it is even more important to have leaders who can convert an organization into a world-class one.

Box 5.1 Kumar Mangalam Birla on transformation

Transformation is about turning aspirations into reality and converting setbacks into opportunities. Kumar Mangalam opines that, 'Transformation is the end result of a highly energized process that combines human ingenuity with its indomitable spirit to make new things happen and create value.' His mantra is: 'The creation of new alchemists from ordinary people.' The transformational process can be so absorbing that often its lessons reveal themselves long after its implementation. Today, as I reflect on our group's journey over nearly a decade, I do believe that we have changed in some very fundamental ways. In fact the genetic coding of our group stands altered substantially. We have become a transnational, multi-cultural entity with more than 72,000 people, drawn from twenty different nationalities of whom more than 70 per cent are under the age of forty.

Under K.M. Birla, the Aditya Birla Group did not just acquire a new logo, it transformed itself from a commodity-based organization to an aggressively modern, multi-cultural transnational.

Source: Extract from K.M. Birla's nine important learnings on leadership.

Transformational leadership is the essence of creating and sustaining competitive advantage. 'Leaders are truly transformational when they increase awareness of what is right, good, important, and beautiful; when they help to elevate followers' needs for achievement and self-actualization; when they foster high moral maturity in followers; and when they move followers to go beyond their self-interests for the good of their group, organization, or society' (Bass 1997).

Paradoxes of transformational leadership

A leader strives to bring about a transformation through change in the organization that is characterized by the ability to manage uncertainty in the environment. The inconsistencies or paradoxes in the environment create dramatic tensions in the transformation, as discussed below.

A struggle between the forces of stability and the forces of change—Adaptation and stability often contradict each other. To be successful, an organization must find ways and means to balance the need for adaptation with the need for stability. Organizations that cling to tradition may fail to transform.

Tensions between denial and acceptance of reality—If an organization tries to transform without properly understanding transformations like revitalization (recognition of the need to change), creating a new vision, and institutionalizing the change, the effort may end up as tragedies particularly when the key players attempt to deny the reality.

A struggle between fear and hope—An organization should renew or regenerate itself periodically. The renewal process demands that an ageing organization must destroy its conventional form of working, thinking, system of working, and technology, and implement new-generation state-of-the-art way of working. Fear will definitely hinder the process but hope helps to eliminate the restraining forces that appear as barriers.

A struggle between manager and leader—Managers maintain the system whereas leaders have visionary skills. A leader takes the organization into the future by creating a positive view of what the organization can become. He/she can simultaneously provide emotional support to individuals during the transition process. Once the transition has occurred, a manager helps in maintaining the new system.

Transformational leadership and gunas

Indian philosophy provides a composite framework to aid the understanding of the mental make-up of a person (Agrawal 2008). It offers the *guna* theory, alternatively termed as three-dimensional personality theory. The three *gunas* are *sattva* (awareness), *rajas* (dynamism), and *tamas* (inertness or passivity). These are the fundamental constituents of every being. The transformational leader's personality is based on the leader's ability to inspire and raise the consciousness of the followers by appealing to their higher needs utilizing the *rajas guna*. In a study, Agrawal (2008) collected information from secondary sources and considered inspirational motivation, intellectual stimulation, idealized influence, and individualized consideration as factors of transformational leadership. The findings show that *sattva* and *sattva–rajas* enhance transformational leadership whereas *tamas* reduces it.

The study, however, did not reveal any support for the claim that *rajas* when combined with *sattva* would aid transformational leadership more than what *sattva* alone would do. Agrawal suggests that companies should organize training programmes around the *guna* framework to develop *sattva* and reduce *tamas*; it also suggests encouraging sattvic food like fruits and fresh juices, considering the subtle implications diet has on a person. Agrawal's suggestion also includes building corporate culture recognizing knowledge as the status mechanism and not power and wealth. The benefits of *sattva guna* will grow in leaps and bounds and will not only be helpful for the organization but for the entire society.

Charismatic Leadership

Charisma has synonyms like charm, appeal, magnetism, and allure. It is a divine and heavenly gift of grace. It is a type of authority or influence based on exceptional characteristics of an individual. Charisma is also an important social influence that pulls people, irrespective of caste, creed, or colour to a person.

Some leaders have exceptional qualities and appeal that inspire people to devote and commit to them. Followers of such a leader identify themselves with the leader, and become emotionally involved in the leader's mission, ideology, and thought process. Being associated with such a leader for some time, followers feel increased self-esteem. Such leaders are called charismatic leaders. A charismatic leader does not demand attention, rather he/she commands it.

Charisma matters for the success of a leader though it can also let one down. People are ready to tread the path of a charismatic leader even if the path is ridden with difficulties. These leaders do not demand attention, rather they command it. They have got something which many may not have with. Messages from these leaders inspire and motivate followers. The 'spinning wheel' that Mahatma Gandhi used symbolized self-reliance, the value of cottage industries, and the demand for Indian independence. The message 'Give me blood, I will give you freedom' by Netaji Subhash Chandra Bose produced tremendous impact on his followers. Messages of Mother Teresa attracted followers towards her voluntary efforts.

Howell and Costley (2008) define charismatic leadership as an attribution conceived by followers about leaders who exhibit certain personal traits, abilities, and behaviours, and who have unusually strong influences on followers' emotion, values, beliefs, attitudes, and behaviours. In all walks of organizational life, you would find gifted charismatic leaders who advocate radical solutions to critical problems. They are able to see things from another person's perspective. Charismatic people speak emotionally about putting themselves on the line. Obviously, followers are unquestioningly attracted to such leaders.

Naturally, a charismatic leader easily induces huge doses of enthusiasm into his/her team, and is very energetic in driving others forward. However, a charismatic leader tends to believe more in himself/herself than in the team. This can create a risk as a project, or even an entire organization, might collapse if the leader was to leave. In the eyes of his/her followers, success is tied up with the presence of the charismatic leader. As such, charismatic leadership carries great responsibility and needs long-term commitment from the leader. They model their own behaviours for followers to emulate by setting high performance standards for themselves, having high expectations from followers, showing confidence in their abilities to meet the standards, and exhibiting determination, optimism, and self-confidence. They demonstrate creativity, innovative behaviours, risk-taking propensity, self-sacrifice to project their courage, compassion, credibility, and convictions about achieving the mission. Charisma matters enormously in start-ups, turnaround contexts, or whenever a business is ripping through rapid and unpredictable change.

Howell and Costley (2008) identify certain leadership behaviours of a charismatic leader. According to them, a charismatic leader

- Makes inspirational speeches
- Builds ones own image in followers' eyes
- Uses and frames alignment to guide followers
- Distils complex ideas into simple messages
- Models behaviour for followers with high expectations and confidence
- Takes risks to achieve mission
- Advocates moral mission and vision

All the behaviours tend to generate loyalty, dedication, trust, devotion, and commitment to the leader, emotional involvement in the leader's mission, increased self-esteem, and belief in the leader's values. By distilling complex ideas into simple messages these leaders stimulate and challenge, prod, push, and poke their followers. Robert House, a Wharton School professor who has studied charisma for 20 years, says that when conditions are uncertain, charismatic bosses spur and stimulate subordinates to work above and beyond the call of duty.

Charismatic vs Transformational Leadership

Some theorists treat the two types of leadership as essentially equivalent. Again, some other theorists identify these styles as distinct but overlapping processes.

A transformational leader delegates significant authority to his/her followers, develops their skills, enables capacities and self-confidence, creates self-managed teams, provides sensitive information, while eliminating or reducing unnecessary control measures. He/she leads and in the process empowers his/her followers. On the contrary, a charismatic leader probably does more than just foster an image of extraordinary competence of himself/herself. He/she engages in impression management, information restriction, personal risk-taking, and so forth.

A transformational leader can be found in any organization and at any level. These leaders are universally found to be effective in all situations and are identified through results. By contrast, charismatic leaders are rare.

If a transformational leader is transferred elsewhere, his/her absence does not cause much hindrance in the team's progress. Followers move on the track created by him/her, and following the guidelines given to them. In the event of separation from a charismatic leader, followers feel helpless and the team may eventually become dysfunctional.

Contextually, the concept of transactional leadership emphasizes that effective leadership is the product of reciprocal exchange between leaders and followers.

VALUE-BASED LEADERSHIP

Value is indicative of worth, ethics, honour, and finally right and wrong actions. Values are stable and enduring. It is a 'ghostly' phenomenon and a strong force in people. The values that can be satisfied in one's work are creativity, independence, adventure, cordial personal relations, money, status, etc. These are occupational values since they guide a person in choosing his/her occupation. These values also play a dominant role in continuance in one's career, satisfaction, performance in the position held. When a person chooses his/her occupation, he/she believes there is something good in it. The concept of 'good' is a part of an internalized mental structure, which establishes priorities regarding what he/she wants out of life.

Liberalization, privatization, globalization, and dynamic market forces are compelling organizations to evaluate their strategies and also how material and human resources are managed. State-of-the-art technology is a dominant force for a successful organizational performance. But for organizational excellence, a positive mindset of the workforce including the top management is indispensable, as this leads to effective leadership. Organizations today are realizing the need for change in their management practices. Whatever be the leadership style of a manager, effectiveness is possible only if the leader's values emanate from the heart and not just from what he/she preaches. This is value-based leadership.

Value-based leaders do not use authority or exercise power over their people. This voluntary relationship of the leader with work becomes the guiding and driving force for the followers in pursuing their tasks and assignments. By virtue of the values, these leaders can foresee the direction and speed of changes, understand people, and gain the confidence of supporters. Value-based leadership goes beyond transformational and charismatic leadership.

In today's business environment characterized by acute competition, intrusion of foreign players, and increased customer demands, it is a major challenge for an organization to create and sustain high performance. In the days of growing global competition, excellence can be achieved through value-based leadership. Adopting value-based leadership is also an instance of transformation, where the role of a transformational leader is essential to bring about change and a paradigm shift in the organization.

Values, ethics, and trust are the keys to the growth of organizations and the societal capital in business. An organization carries out business in a society having its own culture, belief, and traditions. For sustainable growth, the business organization cannot ignore the social, cultural, global realities of the present times. There must be congruence between societal needs and organizational practices. For leaders, some skills are innate and some are learned.

Good management is a skill and leadership is an art. To be on top of the craft, an organization needs socially conscious organizational leaders. This consciousness integrates leadership skills in a value-based system. Obviously then, value-based leadership involves vision, motivation, organization, and action of the leader. All these inculcate a sense of power and hope, provide guidance, direction and inspiration, and empower people to realize their potential. See Box 5.2.

Information technology has created possibilities for communication that were unimaginable in the past. This tremendous change has altered the avenues to promote ideas and the path of doing business. The reality is that an artisan-driven organization has changed to a knowledge-driven one. It is being increasingly realized that to cope with the challenges, organizational leaders of the new economy need wider knowledge, a broader perspective and vision, newer skills, and greater understanding of people, processes, and technology. Leadership may prove to be a strategic tool to achieve organizational excellence. Value-based corporate leaders with human values, enhanced confidence, and professional commitment possess the ability to transform and revitalize an organization with vision and foresight, ensure a trusting environment and healthy organizational culture, and promote a human approach, which is essential for an organization to survive and grow in any economy including a downturn.

Box 5.2 Narayana Murthy on leadership and values

Ethics and values transcend the legal framework and as a society evolves, what is in the realm of ethics and values moves into legality. In India, before the Securities and Stock Exchange Board of India (SEBI) was established in 1990, a lot of good practices were part of ethics and values. Today, it is all part of legality. Similarly, in the United States, a lot of practices were part of ethics and values before the Blue Ribbon Committee report. John Hunstman, says in his book, that successful people never cheat. That is same as saying good people never cheat.

Ethics and values can be defined as anything that stands the test of golden behaviour. That is the rule, that you must do unto others what you would like to be done unto you. I define ethics and values in a more elaborate manner.

Ethics and values form the protocol for conduct and behaviour in a community for each of its members, enhancing the confidence, the enthusiasm, the energy, the joy of everyone else in the community. If I conduct myself as per that protocol of behaviour, it enhances confidence, enthusiasm, energy and joy of everyone else in the company.

A leader has to have followers to be a leader. That is why I stood by my controversial decision on CEO salaries being linked to company's earnings. If you want to enhance the trust of employees in the leader, then the leadership of the company has to conduct itself in a manner that enhances trust.

Source: www.managementparadise.com

Creation of Values

Both value creation and living the values are important for leaders to be successful. Inspiration, innovation, and communication and collaboration help create values. Inspired employees generate passion and commitment, resulting in them taking on leadership roles. Innovative employees generate competitiveness and sustainability. Communication and collaboration are about making large projects successful. They are the largest value creators in today's globalized and competitive business environment. Employee involvement and participation are critical to an organization's value creation, and for the subsequent generation of new values from the old ones.

The factors that affect employees' hearts and spirits are accelerating change, rewards and recognition, and emphasis on individualism and rationalism (Kalpa 2007). Accelerating change refers to meeting the escalated productivity and performance expectations periodically (say every quarter) without impairing the work–life balance. Management has to consider the extent of rewards and recognition for even the smallest of achievements. Laying emphasis on individualism and rationalism includes tapping into the collective intelligence of team members, the organization, and the society as a whole.

Values of Global Leaders

Let us get acquainted with the values of global leaders. Kalpa (2007) quotes the study by Laura Tyson, Dean of London Business School, and Nigel Andrews, Venture Capitalist, and discusses the interview results with over 100 corporate leaders in 2004 on what they looked for in the new generation of business leaders. Most astonishingly, functional and technical knowledge did not get much emphasis.

Global leaders, primarily, must have an unyielding integrity to remain consistently true to the expressed values. It is a most universal attribute and quality critical to business success. The other attributes are worldly awareness, thriving on change, judgement and intuition, perseverance and tenacity, passion and persuasion, curiosity and creativity, self-awareness, self-confidence, involving others, boundless energy to motivate and energize, judging performance and capacity, desire to learn, and being coachable. Prasad Kalpa (faculty member at the Centre for Executive Education, Indian School of Business [ISB], Hyderabad) also surveyed several executives from the UK, the US, Belgium, and India. The values identified to be important are honesty, empathy, gratitude, humility, and selflessness.

Creating Value Out of Values

In today's organizations, leadership crisis develops from the conflicting agendas between value creation and living the values (Kalpa 2007). You are required to concentrate on three domains—business, technology, and spirituality. Business provides clear measures to let us know how well we are doing in creating values. Technology provides tools and processes to be effective, gain distinctive competence and a competitive edge, and finally succeed in the marketplace. Spirituality is at the root of our passion and energy, which helps us uphold our values and feeds our capacity for innovation. We operate exclusively from one domain of the three domains discussed. Kalpa adds that this is our 'normal state of leadership' or normal zone.

SPIRITUAL AND SERVANT LEADERSHIP

We have so far studied various facets of leaders and leadership. But spiritual leadership is distinctly different from the categories already discussed. Leadership, in this millennium, needs a new style that motivates, inspires, and engages a critical mass of committed and capable people, whose concerted efforts would lead to business success smoothly. Of course, achieving success has always been both a criterion and a concern of business leaders. However, today's business environment, characterized by downsizing, has posed a threat to organizations restructuring, cost reduction, business process re-engineering, flat organization structuring, and de-layering.

Spiritual leadership comprises the values, attitudes, and behaviours required to intrinsically motivate self and others in order to have a sense of spiritual well-being (Indian Institute of Spiritual Leadership [IISL]). The purpose of spiritual leadership is to create vision and value congruence across the strategically empowered team, and individual levels and, ultimately, to foster higher levels of organizational commitment and productivity. Spiritual leadership deals with workplace spirituality and spiritual survival. It strongly aids organizational transformation to create an intrinsically motivated and learning organization.

Organizational leaders with spiritual values make a difference, and feel understood and appreciated. It stands established from the findings of many research reports that organizational commitment strengthens motivation and reduces turnover, and that organizational productivity is at the heart of the total quality movement. Obviously, technology is essential for progress as much of industrial change revolves around it.

Fry (2003) pursued a research to examine leadership as a motivation to change and review motivation-based leadership theories. He noted the accelerating call for spirituality in the workplace. He describes the universal human need for spiritual survival through calling and membership, and distinguishes between religion and spirituality. He also reviewed religion and ethics and values-based leadership theories and concluded that to motivate followers, leaders must get in touch with their core values and communicate them to followers through vision and personal actions to create a sense of spiritual survival through calling and membership. Fry (2003) argues that spiritual leadership theory is not only inclusive of other major extant motivation-based theories of leadership, but that it is also conceptually more distinct, parsimonious, prudent, and less confounded.

Effective human performance and success in the workplace need vision, efforts, hope and faith, whereas rewards are associated with altruistic love. Spiritual leadership contributes to performance, efforts, and altruistic or selfless love.

Leadership through Vision, Hope/Faith, and Selfless Love

We generally lay emphasis on physical, mental, and emotional elements of human interaction in organizations. But these elements alone cannot assure success of leadership. We need to go beyond the current leadership theories. History is littered with examples of organizational leaders with ethics and spirit who have taken their organizations to great heights. Spirituality, however, is concerned with those qualities of the human spirit that balance the individual and the organization. The bridge between spirituality and religion is altruistic, and philanthropic love is regard or devotion to the interests of others with selflessness. Contextually, it is advocated that spirituality and religion are distinctly different as religion is concerned with claims of a particular religious tradition, their teachings, dogma or rituals.

Transformation occurs within an individual, organization, and/or team is empowered through spiritual leadership. The IISL model on qualities of spiritual leadership are shown in Table 5.1.

TABLE 5.1   Qualities of spiritual leadership

Vision	Altruistic Love	Hope/Faith
· Broad appeal to key stakeholders · Defines the destination and journey · Reflects high ideals · Encourages hope/faith · Establishes standard of excellence	· Trust/Loyalty · Forgiveness/Acceptance/ Gratitude · Integrity · Honesty · Courage · Humility · Kindness · Compassion · Patience/Meekness/Endurance	· Endurance · Perseverance · Do what it takes · Stretch goals · Expectation of reward/victory · Excellence

Source: International institute of Spiritual Leadership (IISL); www.iispiritualleadership.com/ index_files/spiritual_leadership_theory.htm (accessed on 27 February 2009).

Inner Beauty of Spiritual Leaders

Virtue is the inner beauty of a person and any person. It makes a person lovely and unusual and shapes his/her personality. It is the way one does things; the way he/she moves, speaks, and dresses. One may not have money, but if he/she has virtue, he/she will always seem rich, for everything that is close to him/her will be filled with quality (Brahma

Kumaris 1996). A few thoughts on 'inner beauty' will be discussed to help the readers develop their workers and subordinates. Some of the important virtues are benevolence, cheerfulness, contentment, cooperation, courage, determination, humility, tolerance, truthfulness and wisdom. Spiritual practices help to develop all these virtues. These are briefly described.

Benevolence   Benevolence means kindness, compassion, and generosity, and is a state of being reliant on oneself alone. Benevolence is silent goodwill like the sun shining on the hard ground softening the earth, melting the ice, but with no design or intention to heal (Brahma Kumaris 1996).

Cheerfulness   Cheerfulness is exuberance, jollity, happiness, and a state of clarity and conviction. To be cheerful, you have to be able to see beyond the present and have vision for a good future. Cheerfulness in its true form is earned. You have to work for it, while clearing away the negativity inside. For this, you have to know how to cordon off weaknesses and refuse their entry into your life.

Contentment   It refers to pleasure, gratification, and happiness. It is like an underground river whose course just cannot be altered. On the surface, people are stamping, pushing, pulling; the ground is cracking or left derelict, but underneath the river is flowing.

Cooperation   Collaboration, support, teamwork, mutual aid are some synonyms of cooperation. Cooperation is perhaps the least recognized but most valuable of human virtue. It is to do with the process of achieving something and its greatness lies in the fact that it is expressed through ordinary everyday actions. If you extend cooperation to someone, you will get back cooperation when needed directly or indirectly.

Courage   Think only of the destination and nothing in between. Courage is the fruit of consistent effort to live life by the rules. Courage helps us to take a step forward into an area of difficulty without a solution in mind, but yet feeling that victory is ahead. It is like starting a venture empty-handed, but knowing that the 'will' will help to achieve success; the Almighty always assists courageous persons.

Determination   Determination means willpower and fortitude, and refers to the strength of mind. Determination makes one sit up straight and develop an inclination to love everything: the task, the team-mates, and the process, because determination is about moving forward. Determination develops from genuine involvement and intrinsic satisfaction. Silence brings the strength to go on, the steadiness to succeed, and the softness to slip past difficulties unnoticed. If determination breaks, it is best to stop for a few moments and be silent to regain determination.

Humility   Humility signifies modesty and humbleness. Humility dismisses nothing, rather it takes into account every small thing seriously. It teaches us to respect everything in front of us. Any creative task needs humility to appreciate it, for humility is plainness and on plainness, the colour and shape of the work become clearly visible. Humility adds strength to the mind. It is an attitude that encourages us to put others ahead of us and give them equal or more importance. Thinking too highly of oneself prevents one from genuinely caring for others. Humility enables you to serve others wholeheartedly and thereby set an example that others can follow.

Tolerance   Tolerance means broad-mindedness, acceptance, and patience. It develops from the feeling 'forgive and forget'. Tolerance prevents bouncing back even if you are thrown against the wall. When you treat everything that disturbs you as riddles and that all things work in cycles. Tolerance develops from loving the people around you in the true sense, not in a superficial way. A tolerant person can accept any challenge and work in any situation, however adverse and unpleasant the situation may be.

Truthfulness   Truthfulness is seeing, communicating everything as it is without distortions. A truthful life is one without distraction. In truth, there is steadiness, deftness, economy, and yet humour, because humour comes from the contrast between what the picture is and what it will be.

Wisdom   Wisdom is richness of knowledge, not suspicion or reserve. Knowledge is applied with intuition and experience. Wisdom requires 'deep insight' to explore and interpret the principles of 'something'. Wisdom is making the best of what you have.

There are many other elements of virtue like accuracy, cleanliness, introspection, lightness, mercy, obedience, etc. Developing inner beauty does not need money or much effort. You are required to observe your people closely, be psychologically close to them, involve yourself and 'know your people better'. You have to help your people develop their 'inner beauty' to achieve organizational effectiveness. By doing so, you will be able to enhance their inclination to work with little or no resistance. All leaders, regardless of their position or nature of duty, need contentment, courage, determination, tolerance, gentleness, truthfulness, cheerfulness, and wisdom to be rewarded with success.

Research Findings on Spiritual Leadership

- Core values are viewed as one important way that both private and public sector institutions can improve organizational effectiveness and enhance employee attitudes and behaviours. Despite the strong case for the importance of values, many organizations have not gained their full benefits. Jeffery (2008) reviews the business literature to define core organizational values, discusses their impact on employees and organizations, and presents the key reasons why most institutions have not developed effective values. Jeffery submits that core values poorly articulated and implemented can have a significant negative impact on both employees and organizations and suggest that a *spiritual leadership* philosophy is needed for organizational executives to articulate, communicate, and implement truly meaningful and authentic core values.

- Ten internationally renowned human rights leaders pioneered social innovations through their non-violent, spiritual engagement with challenging circumstances. The study by Parameshwar (2005) illuminates the spiritual generativity of ego-transcendental processes underlying the transformation of challenges into opportunities by the human rights leaders responding exceptionally to challenging circumstances. The method adapted procedures of transcendental phenomenology, phenomenography, and other qualitative approaches to carry out in-depth analysis of 504 events from the autobiographies of the ten leaders.

- Some people work for longer hours conforming to the 'ideal worker norm' or 'extended work hours cultures' (EWHC). But many people do not conform to EWHC. Fry and Cohen (2009) propose that the processes of employer recruitment and selection, cultural socialization, and reward systems help create EWHC that reinforce these trends. EWHC organizations are becoming more prevalent and that organizations in which long hours have become the norm may recruit for and reinforce workaholic tendencies. Several negative forces prevail that impede EWHC when organizations need transformation. Fry and Cohen (2009) offer spiritual leadership as a paradigm for organizational transformation and recovery from the negative aspects of EWHC to enhance employee well-being and corporate social responsibility without sacrificing profitability, revenue growth, and other indicators of financial performance.

Servant Leadership

Robert Greenleaf coined this term in the 1970s to describe a leader who does not formally recognize oneself as a leader. He/she is someone, at any level within an organization, who leads simply in order to meet the needs of the team.

Servant leadership is a form of democratic leadership, as the whole team tends to be involved in decision-making. In some organizations, values are valued. There, organizational leaders, as servant leaders, achieve power on the basis of their values and ideals. On the contrary, many persons believe that in competitive leadership situations, people practising servant leadership will often find themselves left behind by leaders using other leadership styles. They treat their key roles as those of developing, enabling, and supporting their team members, helping them fully develop their potential and deliver their best. The 'adjective' of this style emphasizes that one has to work, listen, search for opportunity to serve, give feedback, and provide service whenever desired.

By this analogy, a servant leader has to work with the members, search for better ways of doing work, give feedback of team activities, provide guidance to members, and so forth. A servant leader cannot have separate status from that of the members though a servant has to maintain a safe distance from his/her masters. As a servant leader, you need to listen carefully. You need to be attuned to people around you and empathetically understand what they are thinking. You need to tune into what inspires and motivates them. You need to help remove barriers and help people be the best they can be. Followers like the idea of servant leadership—there is something immediately attractive about the idea of having a boss who's a servant leader. And people without responsibility for results may like it for its obvious democratic and consensual approach.

Humility is the key characteristic and focus of servant leadership. By virtue of humility of the leader, followers stand for him/her. The depth of understanding between the leader and the followers is another key. However, the depth depends on the love, power, grace, faithfulness, mercy, compassion, patience, peace, and joy the team derives from the work assignments. Followers glorify the leader and exalt the servant leader above all else.

The recognized father of servant leadership Robert Greenleaf describes this style: 'It begins with the natural feeling that one wants to serve, to serve first. Then conscious choice brings one to aspire to lead... The difference manifests itself in the care taken by the servant—first to make sure that other people's highest priority needs are being served. The best test, and the one that is difficult to administer, is: do those served grow as persons, do they grow while being served, become healthier, wiser, freer, more autonomous, more likely themselves to become servants?' (Wikipedia). The motto of servant leadership is 'Serve to lead'. Greenleaf is dedicatedly popularizing the concept of servant leadership.

Of course, before Greenleaf, in the 1940s the Royal Military Academy, Sandhurst (RMAS) continued to build leaders on the basis of this approach. Larry Spears (2002), through extensive work with Greenleaf, identifies ten characteristics which describe the essence of a servant leader. The characteristics are listening, empathy, healing, awareness, persuasion, conceptualization, foresight, stewardship, commitment to the growth of others, and community building (Wikipedia).

BOUNDARY SPANNING AND TEAM LEADERSHIP

Boundary spanning leadership is defined as leader actions that establish and maintain a group's integrity through negotiation with non-group members, resolving disputes among followers and sub-groups, obtaining resources, establishing influential networks, and helping followers deal with the external environment (Howell and Costley 2008).

Boundary spanning incorporates performing representative functions and linking-pin functions of leaders. Discharging the role of spokesperson is an example of representative function where one's loyalties remain entirely with the group. On the contrary, linking-pin roles refer to interaction with two or more groups, with loyalties to both, for instance fulfilling liaison functions. Thus, intra-group functions are representative roles, and inter-group functions are linking-pin roles. In Chapter 1, you have studied ten roles of managers, of which seven roles involve some sort of boundary spanning. Howell and Costley (2008) identified these roles which are described in brief below.

Figurehead Performing symbolic acts, such as representing the organization in social gatherings

Liaison Building and maintaining networks with members of ones own group and other groups, developing new contacts, keeping touch with significant outsiders, reciprocating help

Monitoring Gathering relevant information that might be helpful to the whole organization

Disseminator Sharing information with units, sub-units, and other insiders helping decision-making

Spokesperson Transmitting information and expressing value statements to outsiders to promote company image

Disturbance handler Identifying conflicts of any nature that may lead to loss of organizational members, closure, strikes, or other industrial disputes

Negotiator Bargaining logically for the unit demanding resources, constraints, interfering problems; buffering the unit and its members from higher-ups and outsiders

Skills, Traits, and Power Bases of Boundary Spanners

In Chapter 2, you have been acquainted with attributes of leaders. Effective boundary spanners need some skills, traits, and power bases to successfully accomplish the stated and desired tasks. They should have high locus of control, effective communication skills, political and negotiation skills, conflict management skills, competency or expert power, referent power, and network building skills. They need two types of power to execute tasks and discharge responsibilities: (a) legitimate power and (b) reward and coercive power.

High locus of control They should believe in abilities to influence environmental factors, have confidence in self and members.

Effective communication skills This skill is critical in advocating for the group, and upholding achievements of the group to others. Communication includes telling success stories, methods followed by other teams, etc.

Political and negotiation skills This skill is crucial for boundary spanning to place the team in a favourable position (where it actually should be).

Conflict management skills This skill is indispensable to overcome and triumph over disputes, internal and external, that can threaten smooth working and progress. A leader can develop this skill through formal education and experience, or from the lessons of coach and mentor.

Network building skills Boundary spanners usually build bridges of relationship with important individuals, groups, and associations outside the organization for lobbying and reciprocating favours. The interaction with various parties may be sources of power.

Competency or expert power A leader gains these from his/her qualifications, experiences to his/her credit, specialization in some areas, and problem-solving abilities. This power causes others to listen to him/her attentively. Any insider or outsider hesitates to question or challenge any view expressed. This power enables a leader to arrange adequate resources, support, cooperative agreements, and favourable relationship.

Referent power This results from a leader's past experiences, unique accomplishments, high status, and magnetic personality. Sometimes it complements expert power in helping the leader represent the team effectively.

Legitimate power This power, obtained by virtue of a higher position in the organizational hierarchy, helps a leader to resolve disputes, and mobilize resources using positional influence.

Reward and coercive power This power is also gained from higher position in the organizational hierarchy. The leader can sanction reward and recognition for brilliant contribution to the team and the organization. At the same time, he/she can initiate and impose disciplinary action for behaviours or outcomes not conducive to team progress.

LEVEL 5 LEADERSHIP

The concept of Level 5 leadership is an offshoot of a research project that started in 1996 when Jim Collins with his research teams set out to get an answer for the following question: 'Can a good company become a great company and, if so, how?' They researched companies that had shifted from good performance to great performance and had sustained it. They also identified the ones that had failed to make that sustained shift. The team studied the performance of the two groups to distinguish those who made and sustained a shift from those who could have but did not. The survey included eleven most effective leaders. The description of the research is, 'One Question, Five Years, 11 Companies'. This is so because Collins and team endeavoured to get the answer to only one question, took five years, and surveyed eleven companies.

'Level 5' refers to the highest level in a hierarchy of executive capabilities that they identified during their research. Leaders at the other four levels in the hierarchy can produce high degrees of success but not enough to elevate companies from mediocrity to sustained excellence. However, Collins confirms that Level 5 leadership is not the only requirement for transforming a good company into a great one—other factors include getting the right people on the bus (and the wrong people off the bus) and creating a culture of discipline. Good-to-great transformations do not just happen without Level 5 leaders at the helm or control.

The essential ingredient for taking a company to greatness is having a Level 5 leader, an executive in whom extreme personal humility blends paradoxically with an intense professional will. In his article, Collins paints a compelling and counterintuitive portrait of the skills and personality traits necessary for effective leadership. Collins identifies the characteristics common to Level 5 leaders: humility, will, ferocious resolve, and the tendency to give credit to others while assigning blame to themselves. The levels and their descriptions are as follows:

Level 1 The leader is a highly capable individual and makes productive contributions through talent, knowledge, skills, and good work habits.

Level 2 The leader is a team member who contributes to the achievement of group objectives and works effectively with others in a group setting.

Level 3 The leader is a competent manager who organizes people and resources towards the effective and efficient pursuit of predetermined objectives.

Level 4 The leader is an effective leader. He catalyses commitment to and vigorous pursuit of a clear and compelling vision; stimulates the group to high performance standards.

Level 5 The leader is an executive and builds enduring greatness through a paradoxical combination of personal humility and professional will.

Each level is appropriate in its own right, but none has the power of Level 5. A leader need not necessarily move sequentially through all the levels. But a leader at any level must have all the capabilities of the lower levels. Collins quotes the example of Abraham Lincoln, as nation builder, as a Level 5 leader.

Pareek (2008) very rightly quotes the example of Mahatma Gandhi as nation builder, and Narayana Murthy of Infosys as a corporate Level 5 leader. From these standpoints Ratan Tata and Kumar Mangalam Birla are also Level 5 corporate leaders. These leaders work for the future. Collins quotes a Level 5 CEO who said, 'I want to look from my porch, see the company as one of the great companies in the world someday, and be able to say, "I used to work there".' As already described before, a Level 5 leader needs humility to paradoxically blend with an intense professional will. Pareek (2008) lucidly explains these two attributes.

Personal Humility

The features of a leader exhibiting personal humility are:

- Demonstrating a compelling modesty, shunning public adulation, never being boastful;
- Acting with quiet, calm determination; relying principally on inspired standards, not inspiring charisma, to motivate;

- Channellizing ambition in the company, not the self, setting up successors for even greater success in the next generation;
- Looking out of the window, not in the mirror, to apportion credit for the success of the company—to other people, external factors, and good luck.

Professional Will

The features of a leader exhibiting professional will are:

- Creating superb results, acting as a clear catalyst in the transition from good to great;
- Demonstrating an unwavering resolve to do whatever must be done to produce the best long-term result, no matter how difficult;
- Setting the standards of building an enduring great company and settling for nothing less;
- Looking in the mirror, not out the window, to apportion responsibility for poor results, never blaming other people, external factors, or bad luck.

Succession Planning

Succession planning in the context of Level 5 leaders needs discussion. These leaders have ambition; they dream and realize the dream not for themselves, but for their future generations. Through a structured method, they select a superb successor. They use the mirror to apportion responsibility to develop juniors, introspect to see what has gone wrong, always take the blame, and never divert blame. They share credit for any success to enthuse others and to bring them up. Once again, it is emphasized that a Level 5 manager must have humility and professional will. The question is, how can a manager be a Level 5 leader?

'There are two categories of people: those who don't have the Level 5 seed within them and those who do. The first category consists of people who never in a million years could bring themselves to subjugate their own needs to the greater ambition of something larger and more lasting than themselves. For those people, work will always be first and foremost about what they get—the fame, fortune, power, adulation, and so on. Work will never be about what they build, create, and contribute. The great irony is that the animus and personal ambition that often drives people to become a Level 4 leader stands at odds with the humility required for rising to Level 5. When you combine that irony with the fact that boards of directors frequently operate under the false belief that a larger-than-life, egocentric leader is required to make a company great, you can quickly see why Level 5 leaders rarely appear at the top of our institutions' (Collins 2005).

Pareek (2008) comments that more people are from the second category who have the potential of becoming Level 5 leader. However, they should be helped to move to Level 5 through self-reflection, conscious personal development, association with a mentor, by becoming a great teacher and a loving parent, and working with a Level 5 boss.

SUMMARY

Leaders adopt different styles or approaches to accomplish team goals. A leader adopts a style or a number of styles depending on the specific situation. The styles are summarized below.

Transactional leaders treat rewards or punishments as determinants of performance. Transformational leaders concentrate on changes, innovations, apply discretion, and possess entrepreneurial zeal. This brand of leadership is a behavioural process that can be learned and managed. Transformational themes include recognition of the need to change, creating a new vision, and institutionalizing the change. These leaders need *sattva* and *rajas gunas* for success. Charismatic leaders generate loyalty, dedication, trust, commitment, and emotional involvement; and distil complex ideas into simple messages to stimulate followers. Value-based leaders can foresee the direction and speed of changes; they rely heavily on their voluntary relationship with work and the workforce. They do not prefer to use authority and exercise power for task accomplishment, but followers do what is required of them.

Spiritual leaders possess inner beauty, lay emphasis on vision, altruistic or selfless love, hope and faith, and contribute to effective performance. Servant leaders treat their key roles as a developer, enabler, and supporter of the team members and achieve power on the basis of their values and ideals; they treat their key roles as those of developing, enabling, and supporting their team members, helping them fully develop their potential and deliver their best.

Boundary spanning leaders perform representative functions where their loyalties remain entirely to the group and linking-pin functions to interact with two or more groups when their loyalties remain with both groups.

A Level 5 leader is an executive who builds enduring greatness through a paradoxical combination of personal humility and professional will.

KEY TERMS

Charisma refers to magnetism, allure, and a heavenly gift of grace, a type of authority or influence based on exceptional characteristics of an individual. It is also an important social influence that pulls people.

Charismatic leadership is an attribution made by followers about leaders who exhibit certain personal traits, abilities, and behaviours, and who have unusually strong influences on followers' emotions, values, beliefs, attitudes, and behaviours.

Linking-pin functions of leaders refer to interacting with two or more groups, with loyalties to all the groups.

Locus of control is the belief that one has the abilities to influence environmental factors and can remove hurdles without any external help. Leaders with high locus of control become effective boundary spanners.

Representative functions of leaders are performing intra-group activities where their loyalties remain entirely to the group.

Transactional leaders conform to rules and regulations, structured systems and procedures, treat any deviation as non-conformity, and believe that performance is influenced by reward and punishment.

Transformational leadership is a discipline with a set of predictable steps where the themes are revitalization, creating a new vision, and institutionalizing the change.

EXERCISES

Concept Review Questions

1. Compare and contrast transformational and charismatic leadership styles. Identify the common characteristics in these styles.
2. Discuss the paradoxes of transformational leadership. Are they truly paradoxical? Justify your answer.
3. Sort out the qualities a leader should have to be termed a spiritual leader. Can you identify a spiritual leader in any organization? Comment why you have identified him/her as a spiritual leader.
4. What is boundary spanning in leading? Identify the activities performed by a boundary spanner. Comment on how these activities contribute to effective team leadership.
5. 'Value-based leaders do not use authority or exercise power with their people.' Can leaders be successful without using power? How do they succeed keeping power aside?

Critical Thinking Questions

1. Can a transformational leader succeed totally ignoring his/her transactional leadership behaviour? Discuss with an example.
2. Identify the skills and traits essentially required by a transformational leader in an information technology company.
3. Do you feel that in today's changing and competitive business scenario spiritual and servant leadership styles can be successful? Spell out the reasons both in favour of and against your argument.

Assignments

1. Select any five successful organizational leaders, record some anecdotes and characteristics, and identify the leadership styles. You may select the leaders from the organization you are working for or an organization you are familiar with.
2. Select any four organizational leaders who are striving to achieve team goals but achievement may not seem commensurate with the efforts. What might be the reasons? Do they lack in boundary spanning?

REFERENCES

Agrawal, Kalpana (2008), 'Effect of Gunas on Transformational Leadership', *Indian Journal for Training & Development*, Vol. 38, No. 4, October–December, pp. 65–79.

Bass, B.M. (1997), 'Does the Transactional–Transformational Paradigm Transcend Organizational and National Boundaries?', *American Psychologist*, Vol. 52, pp. 130–39.

Brahma Kumaris (1996), *Inner Beauty*, Brahma Kumaris Ishwariya Vishwa Vidyalaya, Pandav Bhavan, Mount Abu, Rajasthan.

Collins, Jim (2005), *Level 5 Leadership: The Triumph of Humility and Fierce Resolve*, *Harvard Business Review*, July/August 2005, Vol. 83, Nos. 7/8, pp. 136–46, in *Best of Harvard Business Review, 2005, The High-Performance Organization* (search.ebscohost.com/; Business Source Elite) (accessed on 10 February 2009).

Ferguson, Jeffery (2008), 'Creating Effective Core Organizational Values: A Spiritual Leadership Approach', *International Journal of Public Administration*, Vol. 31, No. 4, pp. 439–59 (browsed through search.ebscohost.com/ accessed on 10 February 2009).

Fry, Louis W. (2003), *Toward a Theory of Spiritual Leadership*, Tarleton State University, Central Texas. Killeen, USA (www.tarleton.edu/~fry/SLTTheory.pdf accessed on 27 February 2009).

Fry, Louis and Melanie Cohen (2009), 'Spiritual Leadership as a Paradigm for

Organizational Transformation and Recovery from Extended Work Hours Cultures', *Journal of Business Ethics,* January, Supplement 2, Vol. 84, pp. 265–78 (accessed through search.ebscohost.com on 10 February 2009).

Howell, Jon P. and Dan L. Costley (2008), *Understanding Behaviors for Effective Leadership,* Prentice-Hall India, New Delhi.

Parameshwar, Sangeeta (2005), 'Spiritual Leadership Through Ego-transcendence: Exceptional Responses to Challenging Circumstances', *Leadership Quarterly,* October, Vol. 16, No. 5, pp. 689–722 (browsed through search.ebscohost.com/ accessed on 10 February 2009).

Pareek, Udai (2008), *Understanding Organizational Behaviour* (2nd edn), Oxford Higher Education, Oxford University Press, New Delhi.

Prasad, Kalpa (2007), 'Creating Values out of Values', *Indian Management, the Journal of All India Management Association,* Vol. 46, No. 3, pp. 65–67, All India Management Association, New Delhi.

Stoner, James. A.F., R. Edward Freeman, and Daniel R. Gilbert, Jr. (2006), *Management,* Prentice-Hall India, New Delhi.

Web Sources

www.iispiritualleadership.com (International Institute of Spiritual Leadership [IISL], accessed on 27 February 2009).

en.wikipedia.org/wiki/Servant_leadership (accessed on 27 February 2009).

money-zine http://www.money-zine.com/Career-Development/Leadership-Skill/ Transactional-Leadership/ (accessed on 10 March 2009).

www.rediff.com/money/2007/jan/22murthy.htm (accessed on 10 March 2009). (Narayana Murthy on Leadership and Values)

www.citehr.com/46786-nine-important-learnings-kumar-mangalam-birla.html (accessed on 10 March 2009).

www.managementparadise.com/forum/articles11095-narayana-murthy (accessed on 10 March 2009).

www.greenleaf.org (accessed on 10 March 2009).

CLOSING CASE

Transforming Managers to Leaders

(*Note:* This is a continuation of the opening case.)

Mr Sastry studied in depth the activities, approaches, and various attributes of the persons in the managerial cadre in two phases—(1) initially managers and above and then (2) junior managers and deputy managers. He advised the managing director regarding the need for organizing leadership skill development programmes for all in the managerial cadre.

1. For managers and above—one-week programme every six months
2. For assistant and deputy managers—one-week programme every four months
3. To invite external faculty members who provide a fresh perspective to managers

On receiving consent from the managing director, Mr Sastry discussed various personalities and framed the two syllabi of the programmes. The chairman and managing director (CMD) consulted Mr Sastry, decided to host a day-long party in a resort, and invited the external faculty members. He also invited managers of all levels to the party. The experts got a unique opportunity of interacting with the managers.

Thereafter, the experts visited the head office and all the units. Then they finalized the syllabi that were drafted earlier. The curriculum included

1. Workplace leadership
   - Passionate performance—Engaging mind and heart
   - Communication—A leader's lifeline, the power of words
   - Filling the talent pipeline
   - Case study, solving problems of the company

2. Change leadership
   - Identifying and learning how to achieve targets
   - Formulating strategy, turning strategy into results
   - Leading change—A real life story
   - Sticking to target achievement
   - Leading in tough times
   - Failure stories—The causes behind failures

3. Growth leadership
   - Lesson of success from similar companies
   - Leading sustained growth—A balancing act
   - Managing top ten risk factors

Mr Sastry prepared the scheduled leadership development programmes.

Discussion Questions

1. Identify the leadership style of Mr Rajan and Mr Tilak.
2. Discuss how Mr Tilak's leadership style is superior to that of Mr Rajan's?
3. Do you feel the need for organizing leadership development programmes by experts? Justify your response.
4. State the leadership qualities of Mr Sastry.

CHAPTER 6

Motivation, Satisfaction, and Performance

Learning Objectives

After studying the chapter you should be able to

▶ Define motivation and its various facets

▶ Determine factors that cause demotivation and steps to overcome them

▶ Recognize the importance of follower satisfaction

▶ Understand the need for measuring job satisfaction

▶ Determine steps taken in leadership to boost productivity

▶ State how job satisfaction is related to job performance

An Aggrieved Intolerant Employee

Miss Angela is a bright, young, smart, and good-looking girl with an excellent academic background. She consistently scored high marks throughout her academic career. She passed out from a reputed management institute in 2005. Her specialization is in finance (major) and marketing (minor). She stood first in the final MBA examination. In her college, she participated in debates, business quizzes, impromptu actions, and other co-curricular activities.

In the campus interview, she got an offer with a moderately high remuneration package. That was a marketing job. She joined the company. She could please the seniors through her contribution. She also received a 'Commendation Letter' acknowledging her significant contribution to the company. Though she was doing well in the marketing job, she was always inclined to do a job in which she would be able to use her knowledge in finance. In fact, she also desired to pursue a PhD in financial management.

She was searching for a finance job. After working in the marketing domain for two and a half years, she got an offer in the financial domain in a different company with an almost equivalent salary package. Her present company insisted that she continue to work, but did not assure her of a position in finance. Angela left the company to join the new employer, Genius Financial Consultants (GFC).

GFC is a big organization, with its headquarters at Mumbai and as many as fourteen branch offices in major cities including metro cities. It has nearly 2100 employees on its rolls. As discussed during the interview, Angela was posted at the headquarters. The office at the headquarters was well furnished, and the finance department was equipped with all modern and useful financial software packages. All documents and records were systematically indexed. Angela's impression about the headquarters and the office was excellent. After about three months, she approached the section superintendent and requested for an intersectional transfer. But he turned down the request stating that 'You are creative and original, and doing well'. Her tolerance presumably was of a low order. Moreover, she was not sharing her personal matters with any colleague.

In the course of six months, she approached the section superintendent three times for a transfer to some other department; the third time she approached with a written request, in which she mentioned: 'on extremely personal grounds'. The section superintendent forwarded the request to the manager. The manager called her, expressed his annoyance, and asked, 'Have you joined the company to ask for transfer? Don't you have any work?' However, the manager asked for a specific reason. But she did not mention anything. She just said 'sorry for disturbing' and left the office. After another two months, she tendered her resignation. The company requested her to continue for three months as per the company rules.

Meanwhile, the HRD manager referred the matter of Angela to the counsellor of the company. He convened a counselling session when he conversed with Angela at length. Though she was not at all expressive, the counsellor probably could guess something.

An excerpt from his diary is reproduced here: 'Angela is intelligent, diligent, keeps herself updated on all work-related information, appears to be in command of her work and browsing the company website, and maintains records of work. She is reserved by nature. She is an asset to the company, possesses the ability to substantially contribute to it, her career is promising, and she may take up higher responsibility… But, she is facing some problem in the work area, which she is not willing to disclose. Psychometric tests are required to be administered.'

Learning points

1. One should not repeatedly approach seniors with requests.
2. One must have patience.
3. Hiding facts from seniors hinders problem-solving.
4. One ought to be frank in counselling sessions.

INTRODUCTION

Motivation is a term frequently used but least understood. Organizational leaders must know 'how to make people work more or work better'. A member of the strategic apex has to know how he/she should keep himself/ herself motivated. Motivation is the unifying concept for human relations. In case of working in a team, member *motivation* is based on emotional connection with the leader and team members. Satisfaction is an important aspect of work life.

Leaders have to follow the seven rules of motivation. Organizational leaders face challenges while dealing with the workforce. Motivational needs are closely linked with productivity. In organizations, people with negative attitude and tough character also work. A person may become negative for several reasons and such persons need to be identified. It is the manager's moral responsibility to create a motivational climate conducive to effective working and exerting the best towards achieving the business goals. Such a climate must be established, implemented, and maintained. Motivating the workforce is not always associated with expenditure; there are several non-monetary motivational drives.

Organizations today have to accept the shift from so-called 'hard assets' to so-called 'soft assets', which include organizational knowledge, skills, human attributes, and intellectual capital.

MOTIVATION

Human relations encompasses the important reactions of a person to other people's actions and behaviour in society, in a club, an organization, or anywhere else. The relations between individuals, between individuals and groups, and between groups constitute a critical phase of industrial psychology. Motivation transcends all topics in industrial psychology.

Employee motivation and attitudes to an event may be positive or negative. An employer wishes to hire positively motivated people who want to work and will continue to work hard throughout the years of employment. People work for various reasons: Some work for money, while some people like the power associated with the position, or for an attractive position in the organization, or for enhanced self-respect as a result of executing a useful or a difficult job.

There are four phases in the process of motivated behaviour: a need is aroused in the organism, behaviour is directed towards satisfying the need, the need is satisfied, and the organism relaxes (Pestonjee 1991). During the period between arousal and satisfaction of the need, the organism is in a state of tension, a condition of unrest or uneasiness. The organism can only relax after the need is satisfied because the equilibrium has been restored. Equilibrium is the state or condition in which no pressure (needs) is compelling the organism to become active. Motivating employees should be an ongoing activity though during good times when a company is growing and energy is high, this often seems unnecessary. Employees show up for work, work is done, activities progress, and business is good. But if people start suffering from complacency, then the results may be serious and invite disaster for the organization.

In times of uncertainty, however, employee motivation becomes not only more important as a general principle but is often critical to survival. In reality, employee *motivation* underlies success during all market cycles but problems with employee *motivation* become even more apparent in times of uncertainty and change (Kennedy 2001). Motivating employees should be a continuous process in an organization.

People come to work in an organization from different cultural, social, and economic backgrounds. They come with diverse aspirations and work because their needs differ and expectations from the organization vary. Some people work to support their family financially, while some people need power, social status, and prestige, while some people need self-respect for accomplishing work in an exemplary way. For the same person, the needs change from time to time. A person is considered to be an organism in this context. First, a need is aroused in the organism. Then the organism's behaviour turns towards satisfying the need. When the need is satisfied, the organism relaxes. Needs occur when there is a perceived discrepancy between an actual state and a desired state of being.

Motivation is an activated state within a person that leads to goal-directed behaviour. Motivation comes in many forms and what motivates one individual is not necessarily the same for other team members. Therefore, it is important to understand how motivation differs among individuals and how these differences affect the overall drive and determination of a team towards achieving a goal. Motive is a construct representing an unobservable force that stimulates and compels a behavioural response, and provides specific direction to that response.

People are the functional instruments of an organization. Unless their behaviour and elemental attributes are fully understood, it will become difficult to plan and execute any action. We may make gross mistakes if we desire a particular behaviour from a particular person for a particular cause, all the time. There is no better method of understanding human nature than by actually handling the person. However, it takes a long time to understand human behaviour.

The second method of acquiring knowledge about a person is through study, but one should know what to study, how to study it, and how much to study it. It is the moral responsibility of the organization to ensure a proper motivational climate. This can be done by

- creating an environment where the workforce can work freely, and apply their creativity and innovative skill;
- creating an organizational climate that facilitates interdependent work;
- establishing a competitive but healthy climate through reward systems;
- generating a productive climate through personal example;
- setting up an environment to encourage problem-solving rather than avoidance; and
- motivating individuals through coaching, counselling, and mentoring.

In an industrial set-up, motivation may be intrinsic as well extrinsic. Intrinsic motivation is related to the job the person is doing, that is, the job content. When a skilled person performs a job well, he/she derives a sense of satisfaction. This is intrinsic motivation that satisfies the creative instinct in that person. Thus intrinsic motivation has its relevance in performance improvement and productivity enhancement.

Extrinsic motivation is external to the job or task, that is, the job context. For example, financial incentives for doing a job well or higher production may motivate workers. Other external motivators are:

- Praise from the superior for good work
- Recognition of good performance by the company in the form of public citation or award
- Admiration of fellow workers
- Improved working conditions and other facilities.

Now, a few theories of motivation are briefly discussed to enable the reader to understand them.

Theory of Motivation

The most common theories of motivation are (a) Abraham H. Maslow's need hierarchy (or deficient theory of motivation, (b) Alderfer's ERG theory of motivation), (c) Herzberg's two-factor or hygiene or maintenance theory, and (d) McClelland's three needs theory.

Abraham H. Maslow's need hierarchy (or deficient theory of motivation)

The crux of Maslow's theory (1943) is that human needs are arranged in a hierarchy composed of five categories. The lowest level needs are physiological and the highest levels are the self-actualization needs. Maslow starts with the formulation that humans are wanting animals with a hierarchy of needs, of which some are lower in scale and some are in a higher scale or system of values. As the lower needs are satisfied, higher needs emerge. Higher needs cannot be satisfied unless lower needs are fulfilled. A satisfied need is not a motivator.

This resembles the standard economic theory of diminishing returns. The hierarchy of needs at work in the individual is a routine tool of the personnel trade, and when these needs are active they act as powerful conditioners of behaviour—as motivators. The needs, from the lowest to the highest level, are physiological or body needs, safety and security, social or affiliation needs, ego or esteem needs, and self-realization or self-actualization needs.

- Physiological or body needs—The individual moves up the ladder responding first to the physiological needs for nourishment, clothing, and shelter. These physical needs must be equated with pay rate, pay practices, and to an extent with the physical conditions of the job. To the hungry man, food is God.
- Safety and security—The next in order of needs is safety, the need to be free from danger, either from other people or from the environment. The individual wants to be assured that once bodily needs are satisfied, these are secure and will continue to be satisfied for the foreseeable future. The safety needs may take the form of job security, security against disease, misfortune, old age, etc. as also against industrial injury. Such needs are generally met by safety laws, measures of social security, protective labour laws and collective agreements.
- Social or affiliation needs—Going up the scale of needs, the individual feels the desire to work in a cohesive group and develop a sense of belonging and identification with a group. He feels the need to love

and be loved and the need to belong and be identified with a group. In a large organization, it is not easy to build up social relations. However, close relations can be built up with at least some fellow workers. Every employee wants to feel that he/she is wanted or accepted and that he/she is not an alien facing a hostile group.

- Ego or esteem needs—These needs are reflected in our desire for status and recognition, respect, and prestige in the workgroup or workplace, such as conferred by the recognition of one's merit by promotion, by participation in management, and by the fulfilment of one's urge for self-expression. Some of the needs relate to one's self-esteem, for example, need for achievement, self-confidence, knowledge, competence, etc. On the job, this means praise for a job well done. But more importantly, it means a feeling by the employee that at all times he/she has the respect of his/her supervisor as a person and as a contributor to the organization's goal.

- Self-realization or self-actualization needs—He/she becomes growth-oriented, self-directed, detached, and creative. This need reflects a state defined in terms of the extent to which an individual attains his/her personal goal. This is the need which lies totally within oneself and there is no demand from any external situation or person.

To quote Maslow, 'A musician must make music; an artist must paint, a poet must write, if he is to be ultimately happy. What a man can be he must be. This need we may call self-actualization.' He has 'the desire to be more and more what one is, to become everything what one is capable of becoming'.

In practical terms, in an organization, one seldom achieves self-realization. However, the creativity of a person in producing new and practical ideas, in bringing about productivity, innovation, and reducing costs might satisfy some of these needs. Level 5 leaders of organizations achieve self-realization.

Alderfer's ERG theory of motivation

Taking Maslow's theory (1943) as the starting point, Clayton Alderfer has built up a theory that he claims has realistic application to a work organization. According to him, Maslow's five levels of needs can be amalgamated into three, that is, 'existence, relatedness and growth', resulting in his approach being termed ERG theory. His 'existence needs' include all forms of physiological and safety needs or Maslow's first two level needs, 'related needs' include relationships' with other people (social needs of Maslow's third level) and that part of Maslow's fourth level (esteem needs), which is derived from other people. 'Growth needs', like Maslow's notion of self-actualization, are concerned with the desire to be creative and to achieve full potential in the existing environment.

The novelty of Alderfer's theory lies not in the regrouping of needs but in Maslow's hierarchy of human needs. He conceives of ERG needs along a continuum, thus avoiding the implication that the higher up an individual is in the hierarchy, the better it is. According to him, different types of needs can operate simultaneously, and if a particular path towards the satisfaction is blocked, the individual will both persist along that path and at the same time regress towards more easily satisfied needs. In this way, he/she distinguishes between chronic needs, which persist over a period, and the episode needs, which are situational and can change according to the environment.

Herzberg's two-factor or hygiene or maintenance theory

Herzberg propounded in 1954 that humans have two different categories of needs, which are essentially independent of each other and affect his/her behaviour in different ways. When people are dissatisfied about their jobs, they are concerned about the environment in which they are working. Whereas, when people feel good about their job, this has to do with the work itself. Herzberg calls the first category of needs hygiene factors because they describe man's environment and serve the primary purpose of presenting job dissatisfaction. He calls the second category of needs as motivators since they seem to be effective in motivating people to deliver superior performance.

Hygiene factors include company policies, administration, supervision, working conditions, interpersonal relations, wages and allowances, status, and security. Motivators or job content factors include achievement, recognition, and increased responsibility, challenging work, growth, and development. According to Herzberg, both sets of factors work in one direction only. Absence of hygiene factors may dissatisfy workers but will not demotivate them. Similarly, in the presence of demotivators, workers may be motivated, but their absence does not make them dissatisfied. Hardly any organization can offer unbounded opportunities for personal growth to its executives. So a middle way has to be found.

McClelland's three needs theory

McClelland (1961) posits that we are all motivated by a bundle of certain basic needs and that some of us are motivated more strongly by some of these needs than by others. Are you the sort of person who is happiest when you are able to develop lasting relationships within a group, or are you a more independent sort of person who feels happiest when you have been recognized as the best at something? Are you a 'mover and a shaker' who enjoys motivating other people to get a job done, or are you the type of person who avoids the aggravation of getting everyone else to pull their own weight?

In early studies that attempted to understand the qualities of leadership, one of the first types of personality traits to be observed was an apparent need by some people to excel without any external rewards. Asked to play a ring toss game without the imposition of any rules, some people will stand so close that they will never miss and some will stand so far away that winning or losing is greatly due to chance. Others, however, will be very calculating in their distance to ensure that winning or losing is due in large part to their own skill. If they miss the toss, they will move a little closer; if they make the toss, they will step back a bit.

The idea of these multiple needs theories is that we all have the drive to excel or achieve to some degree, but some people have a lesser amount of this drive and others have a greater amount. These theories propose that each of us has other needs, to a greater or lesser degree, as well. The needs that are proposed in McClelland's theory are as follows:

1. n_{ACH}:
The need for achievement—drive to excel or; drive to achieve in relation to a set of standards; to strive to succeed.

2. n_{POW}:
The need for power—the need to make others behave in a way that they would not have behaved otherwise.

3. n_{AFF}:
The need for affiliation—the desire for friendly and close interpersonal relationships.

Some Motives

Achievement, affiliation, power, extension, aggression, dependence, independence, security, status and prestige, recognition, and activity are some important motives.

Achievement means an inclination for excellence and to perform to a desired degree of excellence.

Activity is the desire to keep oneself engaged and constantly perform activity.

Affiliation implies concern for relationship building and relationships establishing relationships, and maintaining warm and affectionate relations with others.

Aggression implies a need to dominate others, demonstrate one's own strength, maybe even physically. Many persons inherit this motive.

Dependence is the need to unnecessarily rely on and consult others before making any decision. This need arises due to lack of confidence or self-reliance.

Extension is the desire to be helpful to others—to colleagues, to society, to the organization, and to the nation.

Independence is the desire to do things individually and to be one's own self. This need arises from one's level of confidence.

Power is the urge to influence others, gain control over them, and establish superiority over them.

Recognition is the need to be acknowledged for successful accomplishment. Probably everybody needs recognition.

Security is the need to secure one's own living and to be sure that one continues to get it. (For example, leaving a good job in the private sector and taking a job with a lower salary in the public sector.) This need arises due to lack of confidence or self-reliance.

Status and prestige are the desire to be respected and treated with deference by others, especially in social gatherings and environments.

Unless the motive of a person is satisfied and the organism relaxes, the person cannot contribute the best to the organization whatever be the extrinsic factors.

Determinants of Motivation

The traditional concept that workers need work only for monetary rewards has shifted. People work to fulfil a variety of needs. Individual factors, organizational components, external or exogenous variables, etc. determine a person's motivation.

Individual factors To know what can motivate employees, a leader must know their aims, objectives, and values. Human needs are both numerous and complex and often it is difficult to identify them. Motivation is not an easily observed phenomenon. A leader has to closely observe individual action and behaviour at work and interpret the same in terms of underlying motivation.

Organizational components Organization structure, organizational culture, technological system, physical facilities, and whatever constitutes the internal environment of an organization affects motivation.

External or exogenous variables A worker's life outside the factory is also an important factor affecting his/her motivation or willingness to work inside the factory. Life at work and life outside work are interdependent of each other. A strong motivational role is also played by culture, customs and norms, images, and attributes conferred by the society on particular jobs.

Characteristics of Motivation

Some important characteristics of motivation which may be inferred from the above discussion of its determinants are that individuals differ in their motivation, motivation is highly situational, motivation changes, motivation is expressed differently, individual's lack of awareness of own potential and motivation, and that motivation is complex.

Individuals differ in their motivation There is no single economic drive that determines behaviour. As the desire and goals of individuals differ, so do their motivations. One person may do a job because it is remunerative, while the other may do it because it gives a sense of achievement, and a third may do it because it enables him/her to serve a cause which he/she likes.

Motivation is highly situational In an organization, a person may work very well in one department and poorly in another in the same position or type of the job. Similarly, the performance of a person may be poor in one section whereas he/she can prove his/her worth when he/she is placed in another section.

Motivation changes The motivation of each individual changes even over time. For example, a temporary worker or a staff on contractual agreement may produce more in the beginning to become permanent. After he/she has been made permanent, he/she may follow two paths— he/she may continue to produce more to gain promotion or may not be as dutiful as before.

Motivation is expressed differently Needs and the way in which motivation is translated into action may vary considerably between one individual and another. Different persons may also react differently to successful or unsuccessful fulfilment of their needs—differently due to individual differences.

Individual's unawareness Sometimes an individual is not aware of his/her motivation. This can be better explained by an example. One girl worker complained to her counsellor about her foreman. Later on, it was found that the reason why she disliked her foreman was that she had a step-father whom she feared and whose physical appearance was very similar to the foreman's. The result was that she had unconsciously transferred to the foreman the unfavourable characteristics of her stepfather. The foreman was in the bad register of the girl for no fault of his.

Motivation is complex   It is difficult to explain and predict the behaviour of workers. Use of one motivational device may not produce the desired result. It may produce a positive impact on one group and a negative impact on some other group. In a factory when a blue-green device was introduced to reduce eye strain, the output of men workers increased while that of female workers decreased. It was found that the latter disliked this change as the new type of light falling on them made them look ghastly.

Indications of Motivation and Demotivation

A leader must have the innate and instinctive ability to read the indications of motivation or otherwise through certain sets of questions, for example,
    Who can be considered a motivated worker?

- One who wants to come to work and works willingly
- When at work he/she gives his best
- He/she has a definite sense of belonging and pride in the organization and in the improvement of management effectiveness

What can be considered demotivation at workplace?

- Increasing absenteeism among employees and excessive labour turnover
- Low output and productivity
- Increasing rate of accidents and wastage of raw material
- Rank indiscipline
- Frustration and unrest in the workforce
- Defiant and violent behaviour of workers at or outside the workplace, and frequent confrontations or arguments with supervisors and managers
- Non-cooperation, strikes, *gheraos*, abusive and violent demonstrations

Frustration is the most common manifestation of demotivation. It may be caused by erosion of real wages due to rising prices and unsatisfactory personnel administration. But whenever it develops, a worker will either seek a better job elsewhere if he/she can, or will develop a sense of apathy towards the organization and his/her work so that he/she would do as little as possible. There are many other demotivating consequences of frustration. It is the organizational and moral responsibility of leaders to observe the behaviours of the followers because they may not always willingly display it.

Causes of Demotivation

Some management practices affect the morale, motivation, or willingness of employees. Some of the demoralizing or demotivating management practices are underassignment, overassignment, buckmastership, coercive type of control, and manipulative behaviour of management. While leading a team, a responsible leader takes care of the demotivating aspects.

Underassignment If a skilled operator is assigned a routine job or series of simple tasks, it may cause frustration or job dissatisfaction and consequently demotivation.

Overassignment If a good worker is overloaded because his/her work is good, he/she may feel exploited. This feeling makes him/her lose interest in work gradually. In big organizations, it is rather a common practice to deploy good employees as others cannot be trusted or depended upon. He/she will suffer from burst/burnout stress syndrome (BOSS).

Buckmastership Buckmastership may be a tendency among persons at any level. This very often manifests as a demotivating factor. Superiors or leaders avoiding hard work themselves pass on the same to subordinates, that is, junior colleagues. Once the work is completed, the superiors or leaders find faults with the person who executed the job. This is a common management practice and erodes employee motivation. If the assignments are of an intellectual nature, then the erosion takes place at a much faster rate, which may even result in conflict. A leader should not be a buckmaster.

Coercive type of control Coercive type of control or supervision may give an employee a feeling that he/she is not being trusted. When this feeling persists for a long time, it is quite likely to cause demotivation and erode his/her interest in the work. No doubt, supervision is essential as a means of control but if it is too coercive, the morale of the employee may be affected. From this point, mistrust crops up.

Manipulative behaviour of management Manipulative behaviour of management may take the form of 'divide-and-rule' policy or tactics. Management may not fulfil its promises and may encourage groupism, but at the same time appeal for unity or patriotism in times of a national crisis. An appeal to a workforce having negative built-in image about the management may also have a demotivating effect. A leader must practice what he/she preaches.

Understanding and Influencing Follower Motivation

Leaders and managers must consider the motivation of their followers, determinants and characteristics of motivation, indications of motivation and demotivation, and causes behind demotivation for improved results. So the question is 'what leaders should do to motivate the followers to accomplish the team goal?' Leaders have to motivate the followers and at the same time also motivate themselves. The requirements from teams differ widely depending on the application area, purpose of the team, nature of activities, and other aspects.

To better understand the complexities of motivation, researchers over the years have developed a number of theories to try to explain why people behave in the ways they do and to try to predict what people actually will do, based on these theories. These theories, called motivational theories, are often split into two categories: *content* theories and *process* theories. Leaders who are knowledgeable about different motivational theories are more likely to choose the right theory for a particular follower and situation, and often have higher-performing and more satisfied employees as a result (Hughes et al. 2008).

Individual Differences in Motivation

Individual differences play a dominant role in assigning tasks to keep the performers of the task motivated. People differ in key personality traits, work values, and the task they love to perform. Various personality traits have been discussed in Chapter 2 under the topic 'Attributes of Leaders'. The different work values are recognition, power, hedonism or pleasure-seeking, altruistic or selfless, affiliation, tradition, security, commerce, aesthetic, and science. One unique way to motivate the workforce is by hiring and engaging those with the right traits, work values, and interests. If they get what they want, naturally they will invest more efforts. The need for supervision or control would be nil or negligible. Some people are better motivated than others. It is evidenced that some invest more efforts to accomplish the team goal simply because they enjoy what they do. The individual difference approach to motivation assumes that people vary significantly in their achievement orientation, work values, and intrinsic motivation.

For example, if the dominant motivation of someone is affiliation, then he/she is expected to contribute the best and perform well if tasks like marketing, sales, or public relations are assigned. Of course he/she should have other motivations like activity, achievement, and recognition.

Having studied the facets of motivation, we will now move on to satisfaction.

SATISFACTION—CONCEPTS AND MEANING

Satisfaction in the workplace or job satisfaction is just a constellation of attitudes about the job, that is, the extent to which people like or dislike the various aspects of the work and the fulfilment of the requirement of an individual by the work environment (Spector 1994). One can look at a person's attitudes about work in different ways. But researchers generally collect data on job satisfaction using some type of job satisfaction survey.

Spector (1994) proposes nine facets, namely, pay, promotion, supervision, fringe benefits, contingent rewards, operating procedure, co-workers, nature of work, and communication, as determining the global or total job satisfaction of a person. In fact, essential aspects of job satisfaction are very much ingrained in psychological attachment with the job and derivation of mental pleasure or happiness. Job satisfaction, stated otherwise, is the ultimate culmination of successful job accomplishment. Many academicians and research scholars have dealt with issues related to job satisfaction in their valuable works. Job satisfaction, according to Hopcock (1935), is the combination of psychological and environmental circumstances that cause a person truthfully to say, 'I am satisfied with my job'.

However, Smith (1955) stated that job satisfaction was the employee's judgement of 'how well he is on the whole or the whole is satisfying his vigorous needs'. Job satisfaction is an attitude, which results from the balancing and summation of many specific likes and dislikes experienced in connection with the job. The evaluation of the job might rest largely upon one's success or failure in the achievement of personal objectives and also upon the perceived combination of the job and company towards this end (Bullock 1952).

Blum and Naylor (1968) define job satisfaction as a 'general attitude, which is the result of many specific attitudes in three areas, namely (a) specific job factors, (b) individual characteristics, and (c) group relationships outside the job'.

Job satisfaction is 'the verbal expression of an incumbent's evaluation of his job'. However, Locke (1969) defined job satisfaction as a pleasurable or positive emotional state resulting from the appraisal of one's job or job experiences. Herzberg (1959) focused on the individual, and analysed the personality, range of expectations, and need of employees. He then concluded that job satisfaction is a function of the extent to which a worker felt his/her 'needs' were satisfied.

Cranny et al. (1992) observe that employees are most likely to be adaptable, cooperative, and productive if they are satisfied with their work. They further opine that top academic researchers working in the field of job satisfaction share state-of-the-art information on creating job satisfaction. The attempt to create job satisfaction brings benefits, but remains associated with the risks of having too many employees dissatisfied with their jobs. Job satisfaction is an indicator of the quality of work life in an organization and the importance of job satisfaction is worth understanding even if it does not relate to job performance (Lawler 1973).

On reviewing studies on job satisfaction, Herzberg et al. (1957) list various job aspects in ten different categories, each representing on-the-job components of job satisfaction. The ten categories comprise intrinsic aspects of the job, supervision, working conditions, wages, opportunity for advancement, security, company and management, social aspects of the job, communication, and benefits.

Vroom (1964) formulated a theory which attempts to explain what determines the willingness of an individual to contribute his personal efforts to achieve organizational tasks. Vroom further suggests that the attractiveness of the job for a person is (a) directly related to the extent to which it provides him/her with rewarding outcomes and (b) inversely related to the extent to which it provides him/her with aversive outcomes. Job satisfaction is the attractiveness of the job for a person, an attitude that results from the balancing and summation of specific 'likes' and 'dislikes', 'what is expected', and 'what is experienced'. The variables job performance and job satisfaction are highly correlated.

Whether a person will stay with an organization or leave depends on the level of satisfaction he/she derives from the workplace. Limited recognition and praise, compensation, limited authority, and personality conflicts are the assignable causes behind leaving an organization. On the contrary, people stay with an organization if they are committed to it, get support through training and development, experience congenial relationships, and receive encouragement for creativity and innovation. Hughes et al. (2008) quote two sets of factors behind a person leaving an organization or staying in it (Table 6.1).

TABLE **6.1** **Reasons behind leaving or staying in an organization**

Why do people leave an organization?	Why do people stay with an organization?
Limited recognition and praise	Promises of long-term employment
Compensation	Supports training and education
Limited authority	Hires/Keeps hard-working, smart people
Personality conflicts	Encourages fun, congenial relationships
Others	Bases job evaluation on innovation

Source: Hughes, et al. (2008), Table 9.3, page 322.

Empowerment

Empowerment is giving a person the freedom to perform activities on the basis of their own ideas and initiative. Empowering makes the empowered person more confident. It is a multi-dimensional social process that fosters power in people and helps them gain control over their own lives. Though it starts with giving authority, it runs much beyond that. Obviously, it is a top-down process encompassing delegation and making the empowered person accountable. The senior leaders articulate a vision and specific goals, and hold the empowered follower responsible for achieving them.

The other view is that empowerment is a bottom-up approach that focuses on intelligent risk-taking, growth, change, trust, and ownership; followers act as entrepreneurs and owners who question rules and make intelligent decisions (Hughes et al. 2008). Leaders tolerate mistakes and encourage cooperative behaviour in this approach.

Hughes et al. (2008) define empowerment as having two components: leaders truly empower employees when they delegate leadership and decision-making down to the lowest level possible. Empowering is a situational approach to motivation that, in turn, satisfies people with achievement motivation. Hughes et al. discuss the empowerment continuum differentiating empowered employees and unempowered employees (Table 6.2).

TABLE **6.2** **The empowerment continuum**

Empowered employees	Unempowered employees
Self-determined	Underdetermined
Sense of meaning	Not sure about what they do is important
High competence	Low competence
High influence	Low influence

Recognition, achievement, possibility of growth, advancement, salary, interpersonal relation, technical supervision, responsibility, company policy and administration, working conditions, work itself, factors in personal life, status, and job security are fourteen top level factors of job satisfaction (Pestonjee 1991). Leaders who allow a higher degree of discretion to their subordinates and seek their suggestions and advice concerning organizational strategies are strongly linked with the leadership dimension of followers' satisfaction (Mukherjee 2004). Mukherjee adds that a leader's willingness to take decisions on the basis of consultation with subordinates and to relinquish overly control on followers seems to motivate them and ensure participation and cooperation from them.

Understanding and Influencing Follower Satisfaction

Followers or subordinates perform a variety of tasks to achieve the team's objectives. Maintaining their satisfaction at a high level is of prime importance to the leaders. You have studied that job satisfaction concerns one's attitudes about work. Considering the job satisfaction of followers should be a vital consideration of the leader. It stands established from several research works that satisfied employees are more likely to continue in the organization, and so possibilities of attrition would be less. Satisfied employees are good organizational citizens and engage themselves in organizational citizenship behaviour.

A transformational leader consciously contributes to follower satisfaction which, in turn, causes productivity enhancement, human power retention, and higher employee morale instilling feelings of confidence, admiration, and commitment in the followers. He/she is charismatic, creates a special attachment with followers, and articulates a vision with which the followers identify themselves and for which they are willing to work. The leaders undertake professional development exercises like coaching, mentoring, and counselling for each follower and empower them when they are found fit to be empowered through which they derive satisfaction. The transformational leader stimulates followers intellectually, arousing them to develop new ways to think about problems. They put their best efforts and use contingent rewards to positively reinforce performance that is consistent with their wishes. They prefer management by exception. The leaders take initiative only when there are problems and are not actively involved when things are going well. Transformational leaders are people committed to actions and they strive to convert followers into leaders.

A leader has to understand the extent of satisfaction of his/her followers, identify the root cause if satisfaction is lower than expected, and initiate remedial measures. As such, job satisfaction needs to be measured periodically using psychometric instruments. Study of follower satisfaction is essential, as it develops the employees and enhances team performances.

In a survey on follower satisfaction in small business houses, Ghosh (2009) observes that followers prefer to work under 'supportive' leaders; do not hesitate to work under leaders exhibiting 'reward and punishment' behaviour; do not have aversion to work with leaders with 'participative style', rather dislike 'directive behaviour'. Leaders should encourage and allow selected subordinates to exercise their discretion and seek their opinion and advice concerning organizational strategies.

Measuring Satisfaction

Job satisfaction is just a constellation of attitudes about the job and the extent to which people like or dislike the various aspects of their work (Spector 1994); it refers to successful job accomplishment. Measurement of job satisfaction emphasizes two types of measures, namely, global measure and facet measure. The global satisfaction measure assesses the overall degree to which employees are satisfied, and highlights their attitude towards the job in general that is measured with multiple items. The facet measure includes measurement of various facets of satisfaction that may encompass the job itself, pay, promotion, colleagues, co-workers, operating procedures, and so on. Measuring employee job satisfaction is very essential for team development and organizational development. Unless you measure the level of satisfaction, how can you manage and initiate measures to enhance performance? The job satisfaction of every employee at any level and in any functional area is measured using some scales suggested by researchers.

The various scales generally used to measure job satisfaction are:

- Brayfield and Rothe (1951)
- Quinn and Staines (1978)
- Smith, Kendall, and Hulin (1969)
- Minnesota Satisfaction Questionnaire (MSQ) (1967)
- Job Satisfaction Survey (JSS) by Paul E. Spector (1994)

Of these, the scales frequently used are MSQ developed by the University of Minnesota, and the JSS by Paul Spector. (The JSS is reproduced in Annexure 6.1.)

Description of the scale

The JSS is a thirty-six item, nine-facet scale to assess employee attitude about the job and aspects of the job. Each facet is assessed with four items, and a total score is computed from all the items. A summated rating scale format is used, with six choices per item ranging from 'Strongly disagree' to 'Strongly agree'. Items are written in both directions, that is, the positive items and negative items, so about half the items must be reverse scored. The nine facets are pay, promotion, supervision, fringe benefits, contingent rewards (performance-based rewards), operating procedure (required rules and procedures), co-workers, nature of work, and communication. Although the scale was originally designed for human service organizations, it is applicable to all organizations.

Reliability of the scale   The internal consistency reliabilities (coefficient alpha), based on a sample of 2840 people, are given in Table 6.3.

TABLE **6.3   Internal consistency reliabilities**

Scale	Alpha	Description
Pay	0.75	Pay and remuneration
Promotion	0.73	Promotion opportunities
Supervision	0.82	Immediate supervisor
Fringe benefits	0.73	Monetary and non-monetary fringe benefits
Contingent rewards	0.76	Appreciation, recognition, and rewards for good work
Operating procedure	0.62	Operating policies and procedures
Co-workers	0.60	People you work with
Nature of work	0.78	Job tasks themselves
Communication	0.71	Communication within the organization
Total	0.91	Total of all facets

Scoring technique   The JSS has some of its items written in each direction: positive and negative. Scores on each of the nine-facet sub-scales, based on four items each, can range from 4 to 24, while scores for total job satisfaction, based on the sum of all 36 items, can range from 36 to 216. Each item is scored from 1 to 6 if the original response choices are used. High scores on the scale represent high level of job satisfaction, so the scores on the negatively worded items must be reversed before summing with the positively worded into facet or total scores. A score of 6 representing strongest agreement with a negatively worded item is considered equivalent to a score of 1, representing strongest disagreement on a positively worded item, allowing them to be combined meaningfully. Below is the step-by-step procedure for scoring.

Step 1: Responses to the items should be numbered from 1 representing strongest disagreement to 6 representing strongest agreement with each item. This assumes that the scale has not been modified and the original agree–disagree response choices are used.

Step 2: The negatively worded items should be reverse scored. Below are the reversals for the original item score in the left column and reversed item score in the right. The rightmost values should be substituted for the leftmost. This can alternatively be accomplished by subtracting the original values for the internal items from 7.

Reverse scoring for negative items	1 = 6	2 = 5	3 = 4	4 = 3	5 = 2	6 = 1

Step 3: Positive and negative items:

Positive items	1, 3, 5, 7, 9, 11, 13, 15, 17, 20, 22, 25, 27, 28, 30, 33, 35
Negative items	2, 4, 6, 8, 10, 12, 14, 16, 18, 19, 21, 23, 24, 26, 29, 31, 32, 34, 36

Step 4: First reverse the scores of the negative items. Calculate the sum of responses to four items for each facet score. Items go into the sub-scales as shown in Table 6.4. Finally, find the total score for overall job satisfaction.

TABLE **6.4** **Sub-scales in job satisfaction survey**

S. No.	Sub-scale	Item Numbers
1	Pay	1, 10, 19, 28
2	Promotion	2, 11, 20, 29
3	Supervision	3, 12, 21, 30
4	Fringe benefits	4, 13, 22, 31
5	Contingent rewards	5, 14, 23, 32
6	Operating procedure	6, 15, 24, 33
7	Co-workers	7, 16, 25, 34
8	Nature of work	8, 17, 26, 35
9	Communication	9, 18, 27, 36
10	Total job satisfaction	1 to 36

Step 5: If some items are missing, an adjustment is required to be made, otherwise the score will be too low. The best procedure as advised by Paul Spector is to compute the mean score per item for the individual, and substitute that mean for the missing items. For example, if a person does not make a response to one item, we are to take the total from step 4, divide by the number answered or 3 for a facet or 35 for total, and substitute this number for the missing item by adding it to the total from step 4. An easier but less accurate procedure is to substitute a middle response for each of the missing items. Since the centre of the scale is between 3 and 4, either number could be used. One should alternate between the two numbers as missing items occur.

Interpretation of the score: In Paul Spector's JSS, the minimum possible score is +36 and maximum possible score is +216. The higher the score, the higher will be the level of job satisfaction.

PERFORMANCE

Performance concerns the behaviours directed towards achieving the organization's missions and business goals, and manufacturing the products or services resulting from those behaviours. It refers only to behaviours related to production of goods or services by maintaining the qualitative requirements. Performance differs from effectiveness, which generally involves making judgements about the adequacy of behaviour with respect to certain criteria such as work group or organizational goal (Hughes et al. 2008). Performance is a multi-dimensional variable (MacKinney 1967) and is a conglomerate of several dimensions. Hence, people high on one dimension may not be high on another, and such standings may change over time.

Performance is 'effective and efficient work which also considers personal data such as measures of accidents, turnover, absence and tardiness' where the performance index is the 'measure to determine if an executive's salary is commensurate with the organization's performance'. Each employee of the organization is evaluated through a formal process.

The top individual strengths identified by Ramusson (1999) include ego strength, assertiveness, willingness to take risks, sociable and abstract reasoning, healthy sense of scepticism, creativity, and empathy. Psychologists and behavioural scientists are engaged in fundamental research studies to investigate the determinants of performance.

Pestonjee (1991) mentions the global acceptance of a high positive correlation between job satisfaction and performance. An organization cannot excel unless it focuses on actions and behaviours of the human resources rather than focusing on the results, rigidly applies single indoctrinate approach, and installs suitable support measures to ensure empowerment. Performance excellence is characterized by teamwork, group cohesiveness, the values and value system and these have to be considered for boosting productivity and attracting customers. Performance excellence is also the congruence of employee output with the organizational goal.

However, some behavioural scientists believe that quite different factors cause 'job satisfaction' and 'job performance'. 'Job satisfaction' is closely affected by the rewards that are derived from jobs and 'level of performance' is closely associated with the attainments of the rewards. In a study by Haldar (2003) the values of $F(= 36.62)$ and p (<0.0001) established significant association between job satisfaction and job performance. Pestonjee (1991) found a global acceptance of a high positive correlation between job satisfaction and performance.

Leadership versus Job Performance

Leadership plays an important role in job or employee performance; as such leaders have to understand the following statements and responses to the questions:

- When people work hard and why they sometimes don't.
- Know the ideal leadership action to take and when to take it.
- Manage performance and conduct at workplace.
- Follow procedures, rules such as discipline and grievance redressal.
- Apply disciplinary sanctions.
- Manage absence; improve regularity and timekeeping.
- Appreciate leadership role in management.
- The skills inherent for success in leading.
- Support needed from the organization: extent and time.
- Empowering staff: who, when, and how much.
- Provide support and development for the followers.

In fact, leaders are required to manage in a motivating and empowering way by consulting and communicating with the followers. Reviews of followers' performance are vital and should be done with dedication. Leaders must assess what kind of support, training, mentoring, or coaching has taken place over the course of a year. Managers, as organizational leaders, need to understand employees to help them develop their talent.

A leader must not lose sight of the fact that the most critical aspect of leadership lies in the actual understanding of followers' expectations.

An effective leader says, 'I have ten reviews to complete within this fortnight. I feel more pleasure, and not pressure, while completing the reviews. I do this keeping aside other work. I feel it an obligation to the followers to let them know how they are really doing. Otherwise, how can I help them? I remember the four compartments of JOHARI window that lays emphasis on the importance of giving feedback.'

Leaders have to understand and influence followers' performance. They have to create a climate to encourage follower participation as a tool for their own development. As such, leaders must seek to:

- Increase the availability of developmental activities.
- Augment follower awareness of the availability of the activities.
- Encourage followers to be committed to participate in developmental activities by way of (a) publicizing and advertising the activities for their awareness and (b) making participation desirable and voluntary.
- Focus on factors that make participation attractive to followers, and make them aware of these factors.
- Make clear what the likely outcomes and benefits of participation will be, for example to one's job, career, and personal as well as organizational development.
- Maintain a record of quality activities and a positive reputation among followers for good word-of-mouth advertising; ensure that they will not think it a waste of their valuable time.
- Ensure that followers feel they have control over participating in those activities by (a) giving them a choice of activities, (b) removing any barriers to participation, (c) facilitating options regarding if they want to participate.
- Facilitate feeling of responsibility (to self and the organization) to participate, and develop their job-related knowledge and skills.

SUMMARY

The terms motivation and satisfaction are intertwined. A person motivated to work derives intrinsic satisfaction from the job. Motivating employees should be an ongoing activity of an organization. As a moral responsibility, the leader must take care of the factors that demotivate employees by studying the indicators of demotivation. Leaders create a proper motivational climate where the workforce can work freely, and apply their creativity and innovative skill. Individual factors, organizational components, external or exogenous variables, etc. determine a person's motivation. Satisfaction in the workplace is just a constellation of attitudes about the job. A leader must realize and appreciate the causes behind a person leaving the organization. People need to be empowered and given freedom to perform on the basis of their own initiative and ideas.

Understanding motivation and satisfaction is vital, as these have distinct implications on the performance of team members. By understanding the factors of satisfaction a leader can influence team members. There are psychometric scales to measure facet-wise and total satisfaction. Thereafter, emphasis needs to be laid on the scores of each facet. Performance is a multi-dimensional variable and is a conglomerate of several dimensions—motivation, satisfaction, etc. In today's organization, leadership plays an imperative role in job performance.

KEY TERMS

Effectiveness is the extent to which planned activities are realized and planned results are achieved; it is measured in relation to the output and not the input.

Empowerment is giving a person the freedom to perform on the basis of his/her own ideas and initiative, thus making the person more confident, with intention to satisfy and develop him/her.

Performance relates to the behaviours directed towards achieving the organization's missions and business goals, and manufacturing the products or services resulting from those behaviours.

Satisfaction at the workplace or job satisfaction is just a constellation of attitudes about the job; the extent to which people like or dislike the various aspects of the job and fulfilment of the need of an individual by the work environment.

EXERCISES

Concept Review Questions

1. Some descriptions of the behaviour of some individuals are presented. Identify the motive.

   (a) Mr M.M. involves himself in very few activities. Whatever he does, he does exceedingly well. He is always the first to arrive at the office. At school too, he always strived to be first. The motive is ....

(b) Mr A.A. loves music. He works in a family planning organization. He brings his transistor radio to the office to listen to music during leisure hours and breaks. He has been insisting that the best way to disseminate family planning education is through audio-visual aids and particularly through movies. He has recently organized a series of dance programmes in his family planning campaigns. He is a very active person. He is always doing something for others. In the office he never relaxes. The motive is ....

(c) Miss S.S. completed her MBA and joined an organization. Her salary package was Rs 7.2 lakh per annum. She left the job after about two years to join a government organization with a salary of Rs 3.8 lakh per annum. The motive is ....

2. Distinguish between intrinsic and extrinsic motivation. Cite three examples of each type of motivation. Specify the determinants of motivation.
3. Suggest some mechanisms for creating a motivational climate conducive to effective working. Critically evaluate the mechanisms.
4. Discuss the reasons behind attrition of employees. How can attrition be eliminated or reduced? Do you feel that attrition may be reduced through empowering?
5. 'Motivation and satisfaction collectively enhance employee productivity.' Critically discuss the statement.

Critical Thinking Questions

1. As the HRD manager you intend to create an environment of trust, mutual feeling, sympathy, and empathy in the organization you are working for. Identify three factors that impede your drive. Search for the steps you would adopt to eliminate or reduce the impeding factors.
2. Consider the external environment to identify factors that influence employee motivation and satisfaction of the organization where you are working. These factors are offering resistance to boost employee morale. As the leadership development manager of the company, what actions would you prefer to take?
3. Identify some few factors that retard the level of motivation of a qualified knowledge worker. Suggest possible antidotes from the standpoint of leadership. Assume that you are the senior manager of the company responsible for leadership development.

Assignments

1. Contact ten persons who have left one organization to join another one. Prepare a checklist including about fifteen possible reasons behind their leaving the organization. Interrogate them to identify the reasons behind why they left. Categorize the reasons into financial and non-financial. Draw a conclusion based on your findings.

2. Visit five organizations, contact a competent person who can permit you to pursue a survey in the company, tell him/her that you intend to undertake a study of leadership behaviour and follower satisfaction. Further show him/her the scales to measure motivation and job satisfaction. On completion of the study, prepare a draft of your findings and clearly bring out the learning points. (Your sample should be 25 or more. (Remember that the larger the sample size, the better your conclusion.)

REFERENCES

Alderfer, C.P. (1969), A New Theory of Human Needs, *Organizational Behaviour and Human Performance*, Vol. 4, pp. 142–75.

Blum, M.L. and J.C. Naylor (1968), *Industrial Psychology: Its Theoretical and Social Foundations*, Weather Hill, Tokyo.

Bullock, R.P. (1952), *Social Factors to Job Satisfaction*, Columbus, Research Monograph No. 70, Bureau of Business Research, Ohio State University.

Cranny, J. Charles, Eugene F. Stone, and Patricia Cane Smith (1992), *Job Satisfaction: How People Feel about Their Jobs and How it Affects Their Performance*, Jossey-Bass, New York.

Ghosh, Lipi (2009), Leadership and Team Building, Dissertation Report, Master of Business Administration (Human Resources), Indian Institute of Social Welfare and Business Management (IISWBM) affiliated to University of Calcutta, Kolkata.

Haldar, U.K. (2003), Job Performance of the Operational Agents of L.I.C.I. in relation to some specific job behaviours: A study of 24 Parganas (North), West Bengal. Unpublished doctoral thesis submitted to University of Burdwan, West Bengal.

Herzberg, Frederick (2008), *One More Time: How Do You Motivate Employees*, (7th Edn), Harvard Business School Press, USA.

Herzberg, F., B. Mausner, R. Peterson, and D. Capwell (1957), *Job Attitudes: Review of Research and Opinion*, Psychological Services of Pittsburgh, Pittsburgh, PA.

Hoppock, R. (1935), *Job Satisfaction*, Harper & Bros, New York.

Hughes, Richard L., Robert C. Ginnett, and Gordon J. Curphy (2008), *Leadership Enhancing the Lessons of Experience*, Tata McGraw-Hill, New Delhi.

Kennedy, Kevin (2001), Manager as Motivator, *Executive Excellence*, Vol. 18, No. 6, June, p. 13.

Locke, E.A. (1969), What is Job Satisfaction? *Organizational Behaviour and Human Performance*, Vol. 4, pp. 309–36.

MacKinney, A. (1967), The Assessment of Performance Change: An Inductive Example, *Organizational Behaviour and Human Performance*, Vol. 2, pp. 56–72.

Maslow, Abraham H. (1943), A Theory of Human Motivation, *Psychological Review* Vol. 50, No. 4, pp. 370–96.

McClelland, David C. (1961), *The Achieving Society*, Free Press, USA.

Mukherjee, Kum Kum (2004), Effect of Leadership Styles on Followers' Satisfaction and Perceived Effectiveness, *South Asian Journal of Management* (ISSN 0971 5428), Vol. 11, No. 1, January–March, pp. 7–19.

Pestonjee, D.M. (1991), *Motivation and Job Satisfaction*, Macmillan, Delhi.

Ramusson, Erika (1999), The 10 Traits of Top Salespeople, *Sales and Marketing Management*, Vol. 152, August, pp. 34–37.

Smith, H.C. (1955), *Psychology of Industrial Behavior*, McGraw-Hill, New York.

Spector, P.E. (1997), *Job Satisfaction: Application, Assessment, Causes, and Consequences.* Sage, Thousand Oaks, CA.

Vroom, V.H. (1964), *Work and Motivation*, Wiley, New York.

Web Resources

http://chuma.cas.usf.edu/~spector (Job Satisfaction Survey, P.E. Spector), accessed January 23, 2009.

Restoring Job Satisfaction

(*Prelude:* In the opening case, 'An Aggrieved Intolerant Employee', the counsellor recommended the need for administering psychometric tests. GFC decided to use a few psychometric tests.)

The top management of GFC in consultation with the HRD manager and counsellor decided to administer a few psychometric tests, and study the leadership abilities of promising employees of the organization in phases. It was decided to use scales to measure assertiveness, job satisfaction, job involvement, and organizational commitment of about 400 employees in the headquarters. The management also decided to identify the leadership abilities of all 70 persons in the managerial cadre and about 12 employees likely to be upgraded to the managerial level. Angela, as a prospective manager, was also a respondent in all the tests.

In fact, GFC formed a cell to administer the questionnaires, score the sheets, and compile the scorings, and for other relevant activities. In phases, internationally acclaimed questionnaires of known validities and reliabilities were administered. Thereafter, the scorings were done. While compiling, the cell identified one respondent (RS-73) whose scores were highest in assertiveness, job involvement, and organizational commitment, but second highest in job satisfaction. The HRD manager and counsellor made note of the scores.

The cell had allotted a unique respondent number to everyone administered by the psychometric tests. There was no name column in any questionnaire. Seeing the scores, the cell matched the respondent number with the list of employees to identify the one who had scored the highest in the tests. The employee turned to be Angela. The HRD manager and the counsellor further went into the detail of the scoring sheets, in particular the job satisfaction sheet.

The measure they used for the job satisfaction survey was JSS developed by Paul E. Spector. This was a 36-item, six options per item, nine-facet scale. The range of scores of each facet was 4 to 24, and the range of total satisfaction was 36 to 216. The facets were pay, promotion, supervision, fringe benefits, contingent rewards, operating procedure, co-workers, nature of work, and communication. Total job satisfaction was the sum of the scores of all the nine facets. While they reviewed the scores, they noticed to their utter astonishment that scores in each facet were very near to the higher side of the range except that of the facet 'co-workers' in which the score was as low as 5. The total job satisfaction score was 205. This disparity prompted them to pursue further investigation.

Ultimately, it was found that a few young employees working in the same department were throwing paper balls at Angela. But, the paper balls did not carry any messages. The department had a total of twenty cubicles, four in each row. Two office superintendents were sitting facing the twenty cubicles. The balls were being thrown when the superintendents were not present.

The cubicles were reallocated and Angela was allotted a cubicle at the extreme rear row. Moreover, she was advised to mix with others, attend official parties, and share information with others.

Gradually, the position, work environment, and feeling about co-workers improved for Miss Angela. When the job satisfaction scale (periodicity twice in a year) was administered again, significant improvement was observed.

Discussion Questions

1. Why did GFC decide to use a multi-faceted tool to measure satisfaction?
2. What might be the use of assertiveness scores for the employees?
3. Do you feel that organizational commitment is reduced due to a low level of satisfaction?

ANNEXURE 6.1

Job Satisfaction Survey
Paul E. Spector

Department of Psychology, University of South Florida, Copyright 1994.
(website: http://chuma.cas.usf.edu/~spector)

(Circle the one number for each question that comes closest to reflecting your opinion about it)

1 = Disagree very much	**4** = Agree slightly
2 = Disagree moderately	**5** = Agree moderately
3 = Disagree slightly	**6** = Agree very much

1.	I feel I am being paid a fair amount for the work I do.	1	2	3	4	5	6
2.	There is really too little chance for promotion on my job.	1	2	3	4	5	6
3.	My supervisor is quite competent in doing his/her job.	1	2	3	4	5	6
4.	I am not satisfied with the benefits I receive.	1	2	3	4	5	6
5.	When I do a good job, I receive the recognition that I should receive.	1	2	3	4	5	6
6.	Many of the rules and procedures make doing a good job difficult.	1	2	3	4	5	6
7.	I like the people I work with.	1	2	3	4	5	6
8.	I sometimes feel my job is meaningless.	1	2	3	4	5	6
9.	Communication seems good within this organization.	1	2	3	4	5	6
10.	Raises are too few and far between.	1	2	3	4	5	6
11.	Those who do well in the job stand a fair chance of being promoted.	1	2	3	4	5	6
12.	My supervisor is unfair to me.	1	2	3	4	5	6
13.	The benefits I receive are as good as most other organizations offer.	1	2	3	4	5	6
14.	I do not feel that the work I do is appreciated.	1	2	3	4	5	6
15.	My efforts to do a good job are seldom blocked by red tape.	1	2	3	4	5	6

Contd

Table contd

16.	I find I have to work harder at my job because of the incompetence of the people I work with.	1	2	3	4	5	6
17.	I like doing the things I do at work.	1	2	3	4	5	6
18.	The goals of this organization are not clear to me.	1	2	3	4	5	6
19.	I feel unappreciated by the organization when I think about what they pay me.	1	2	3	4	5	6
20.	People get ahead as fast here as they do in other places.	1	2	3	4	5	6
21.	My supervisor shows too little interest in the feelings of subordinates.	1	2	3	4	5	6
22.	The benefit package we have is equitable.	1	2	3	4	5	6
23.	There are few rewards for those who work here.	1	2	3	4	5	6
24.	I have too much to do at work.	1	2	3	4	5	6
25.	I enjoy working with my co-workers.	1	2	3	4	5	6
26.	I often feel that I do not know what is going on within the organization.	1	2	3	4	5	6
27.	I feel a sense of pride in doing my job.	1	2	3	4	5	6
28.	I feel satisfied with my chances for salary increases.	1	2	3	4	5	6
29.	There are benefits I do not have which I should have.	1	2	3	4	5	6
30.	I like my supervisor.	1	2	3	4	5	6
31.	I have too much paperwork.	1	2	3	4	5	6
32.	I don't feel my efforts are rewarded the way they should be.	1	2	3	4	5	6
33.	I am satisfied with my chances for promotion.	1	2	3	4	5	6
34.	There is too much bickering and fighting at work.	1	2	3	4	5	6
35.	My job is enjoyable.	1	2	3	4	5	6
36.	Work assignments are not fully explained.	1	2	3	4	5	6

CHAPTER 7

Leadership Behaviour—Dimensions and Assessment

Learning Objectives

After studying this chapter, you will be able to

▶ Understand leadership behaviour

▶ State the importance of assessing leadership potential

▶ Explain managerial derailment

▶ Enumerate and describe the impact of harmful effects of self-defeating behaviour

▶ Discuss the importance of development pipeline

▶ Gain an understanding about the need for good leader–member relations

---

OPENING CASE

Identifying Leadership Potential in Elite Engineering

Mr Basudev and Mr Arindam, after obtaining their master's degree in business administration with specialization in operations management, joined Elite Engineering, a medium-scale company. They had previously completed their graduation in mechanical engineering. After a short and unstructured induction, they were posted in the production department as assistant managers (operation). As per the office order, they were to report to production manager Mr Chatterjee.

Mr Basudev was keen to gain knowledge about the company rules and regulations in order to conform to them. He meticulously kept track of and controls operations. He was somewhat conservative and cautious in his approach. But his people orientation was always very high; he interacted with all employees of his department and endeavoured to keep them in line with the policies and procedures of the company. He also gave directions to his people.

Whereas, Arindam was imaginative, following the work systems but also trying to find new ways of doing work by applying creativity. While keeping in touch with all employees, he was always included in discussions with visiting technicians. He seldom reported any machine fault to the maintenance department, but was rather guiding his operators to diagnose the fault and rectify it. Arindam identified one or two needs at a time and planned the progress. He also involved others in decision-making. His people are happy. On the contrary, Mr Basudev tried to fulfil many needs at a time, which lead to a crowding of tasks and ultimately nothing fruitful was achieved.

Mr Basudev once organized a brainstorming session as a problem-solving tool. The group generated many ideas, sorted them, and finally selected the ideas to be acted upon in phases. The members of the group reached a consensus with regard to required actions. At the end of the meeting, the leader (Mr Basudev) summarized the points discussed to initiate development actions. But nothing was recorded for reference.

Mr Chatterjee, a middle-aged person, was a dynamic and an inspirational figure and had the habit of getting involved and also involved others, thereby improvising on the existing systems. He could foresee what was going to happen while implementing Mr Basudev's brainstorming ideas. He was in a favourable position with the chairman and manager director, Mr Raman, who relied heavily on Mr Chatterjee in decision-making. Mr Raman had already identified many leadership characteristics in Mr Chatterjee. Mr Raman asked Mr Chatterjee to submit half-yearly reports about Mr Basudev and Mr Arindam. Mr Chatterjee, keeping in view other qualities, appointed Mr Basudev as a manager but Mr Arindam as a leader.

Mr Basudev was timid but had the urge to learn and was consulting Mr Chatterjee for operational issues and troubleshooting in the department. The company through an 'official note' engaged Mr Chatterjee to support, share experience, develop decision-making skills, and enhance the confidence of Mr Basudev to transform him into a good manager.

Mr Arindam earlier attended a three-month course on high technology machining at IIT Kharagpur and learned many aspects of modern production technology. Mr Chatterjee came to know about this development. Being a senior manager, he never hesitated to discuss issues with Mr Arindam to enhance his knowledge base. Being pleased with the competency of Mr Arindam, Mr Chatterjee requested him to computerize the production planning and control activities. As days moved, both Mr Basudev and Mr Arindam developed in their leadership roles, and emerged as indispensable people for Elite Engineering, a company which was marching towards excellence.

Mr Chatterjee formed a team to achieve an emergent need of the company. He drew members from different functional areas. There were a total of twelve members including Mr Arindam and Mr Basudev. Within a fortnight, four members discovered that their opinions were of lesser value to their leader, Mr Chatterjee. The psychological distance of the four members from Mr Chatterjee gradually increased.

Learning points

1. One must be able to distinguish a manager from a leader.
2. Top management should identify leadership characteristics.
3. A 'record of discussion' must be prepared and documented.
4. A manager should not develop plans to meet several needs at a time.
5. A leader should give balanced value to all members.

INTRODUCTION

We have already discussed the managerial activities, roles, and responsibilities, and also the changes in the nature of managerial work. We also discussed differences between leaders and managers, the changing paradigm, the prerequisites of organizational leaders, and their self-management dimensions. Leaders need to have certain skills, traits (including personality traits), intelligence (including emotional intelligence), and other attributes.

The attributes of effective leaders were also a part of our earlier discussions. You now know the two-dimensional leadership styles, and the leader–follower interactions in specific situations, and specific task and relation behaviours. Leadership behaviour plays a dominant role in the organization's success. In this chapter, you will study leader behaviour, need of assessing leadership potential and measuring the effects of leadership, the meaning and facets of managerial derailment, development pipeline and planning, and professional development tools. Thereafter, you will learn the importance of leader–members relations' for effective working.

EARLY STUDIES OF LEADER BEHAVIOUR

We studied some leadership styles in Chapter 5. Several studies have been undertaken on leadership behaviour in which the researchers identified five core leader behaviours: (a) supportive, (b) directive, (c) participative, (d) leader reward and punishment, and (e) charismatic. The leader behaviours are described in brief below.

Supportive Leadership Behaviour

Some leaders are deeply concerned about the comfort and well-being of followers. They demonstrate a considerate, kind, and understanding attitude while dealing with followers. They behave in a friendly manner with followers, provide them with information, and encourage open, two-way communication, facilitate followers in problem-solving for task accomplishment, and strive to develop them. They provide information about the organization's operation and achievements, disclose information about self, and also listen and provide support when needed. Supportive leadership is associated with consideration, relationship orientation, and concern for people leadership.

Directive Leadership Behaviour

Leaders of this category assign specific tasks to followers, explain procedures to be followed, declare the deadline of completion, and specify quantitative requirements and qualitative expectations with regard to performance. Such leaders set goals for followers, plan and coordinate followers' work, organize resources, communicate job priorities, check to see if work is done properly and in time, monitor closely, supervise, and evaluate performance to improve the followers. Five key directive leadership behaviour indicators are structuring, organizing, teaching, supervising and evaluating.

Directive leadership behaviour is also known as task behaviour where the leader's task orientation dominates his/her people orientation. Junior-level managers are generally more directive than upper-level managers. Directive behaviours lower the supportive behaviours. Some seasoned leaders change their behaviours considering the gravity of situation.

Participative Leadership Behaviour

In participative leadership, the leader involves followers in decision-making processes. He/she may organize one-on-one meetings with individuals or the team to gather data as inputs for decisions. It involves a group decision-making effort initiated by the leader or it may involve assigning a particular problem to a follower to resolve. Each of these options represents different degrees or types of participative leadership behaviour.

Participative leadership is sometimes referred to as consultative, democratic, or delegatory leadership. This leadership behaviour generates psychological empowerment, which in turn leads to organizational commitment among employees. Strong association is observed between participative leadership behaviour and psychological empowerment.

Leader Reward and Punishment Behaviour

Leaders exhibit this behaviour when followers provide service to the organization. The leader rewards them with tangible benefits (like advanced increments, promotion) or intangible benefits (like a commendation letter, photograph in the company journal, or providing opportunity of leading, etc.). Both types of benefits have a significant impact on followers. Research shows that organizational leaders use more intangible rewards than tangible ones to influence followers. This is probably because leaders can use intangible rewards such as praise, recognition, and appreciation at short notice. When a follower does something that a leader desires, an immediate compliment by the leader is very useful to assure the follower that the leader is pleased with the behaviour. A tangible reward follows several informal rewards when the follower is encouraged to repeat the desired behaviour in the future.

Charismatic Leadership Behaviour

Some leaders state a desirable mission or vision of the future with goals, opportunities, and roles, which have a moral dimension and appeal to followers' needs and values. They make inspirational speeches that are emotionally expressive and intolerant of the status quo, and motivational with regard to the mission. This behaviour is referred to as charismatic leadership behaviour. They use impression management techniques to present their competencies and trustworthiness. This approach of leadership tends to generate loyalty, dedication, trust, and commitment towards the leader, and emotional investment in the leader's efforts.

Measuring the Five Leader Behaviours

Howell and Costley (2006) developed a 15-item scale to measure the patterns of leadership behaviour. They instructed to circle the number on the 1 to 5 scale that best indicated how one normally behaved as a leader of a group responsible for completing some task. The direction of scores is as follows: If a person rated high on items 1, 2, and 3 (by giving a rating of 4 or 5), then he/she would normally tend to be directive with followers. If he/she is rated high on items 4, 5, and 6, he/she tends to be supportive. High ratings on items 7, 8, and 9 indicate participative leadership. High ratings on items 10, 11, and 12 indicate reward-and-punishment type of leadership behaviour. Similarly, high ratings on items 13, 14, and 15 indicate charismatic approach with followers.

Howell and Costley (2006) further emphasize the importance of these behaviour patterns during task accomplishment. According to them, effective leaders vary their behaviour patterns with different situations and different followers. The scale designed by Howell and Costley (2006) is reproduced below.

S. No.	Statements	Almost Never				Almost Always
1	I assign specific tasks to others	1	2	3	4	5
2	I explain methods and set goals for the group	1	2	3	4	5
3	I explain what each group member needs to accomplish	1	2	3	4	5
4	I show consideration and acceptance to others	1	2	3	4	5
5	I show concern for the feelings of others	1	2	3	4	5
6	I help develop the abilities of others to contribute to the task	1	2	3	4	5
7	I get others involved in making decisions	1	2	3	4	5
8	I consult others to get their ideas and suggestions	1	2	3	4	5
9	I encourage subgroups to handle certain aspects of the group	1	2	3	4	5
10	I provide others with benefits and rewards	1	2	3	4	5
11	I punish others for undesirable behaviour	1	2	3	4	5
12	I compliment those who do a good job	1	2	3	4	5
13	I display high expectation and confidence	1	2	3	4	5
14	I communicate a vision for the group	1	2	3	4	5
15	I attempt to inspire others by pointing out the importance the group's task and their part in accomplishing it	1	2	3	4	5

Sen (2008) and Ghosh (2009) have used the scale to identify leadership patterns with minor modifications. They arranged the items based on the indicative patterns. The scale they used in their dissertations with modifications is provided in Annexure 7.1. While Sen (2008) administered the scale in big industries, Ghosh (2009) used the scale to identify leadership pattern in small business houses.

ASSESSING LEADERSHIP POTENTIAL

The top management of an organization needs to be aware of leader behaviour and follower satisfaction, which is a strong determinant of its success. Hughes et al. (2008) view that assessing leadership potential is fundamentally concerned with predicting who will and who will not be an effective leader before they have been placed in a position. Right prediction of potential contributes to organizational success. But predicting behaviour, though critical and vital, is not straightforward. Hughes et al. (2008) warn not to guess leadership potential simply by judgement, and confirm that research shows that human judgement is fraught with errors. If anyone thinks that he/she is a good judge that would be a false belief.

The most important skills of leaders are their motivating and inspiring skills, and developing skills. In fact, they need many other skills that constitute their leadership potential. Assessing leadership potential includes assessment of principal traits, intelligence, confidence level, determination, integrity, and sociability. In order to assess one's leadership potential, the personal history of the prospective leader needs to be considered, adopting assessment centre method, conducting behavioural interview, and administering psychometric and written tests. The 360-degree report provides many inputs.

The assessment centre method incorporates situational interview, in-basket technique, job simulation, and leadership group discussion. A leader needs to drive a group of people and this demands integrity. To assess integrity, we need to ascertain whether the person is overt or covert, and to what extent. In addition, all personality factors need testing. As such, his/her cognitive ability needs consideration. Personality dimensions mainly include conscientiousness, agreeableness, neurological system, experimenting, and extroversion. Conscientiousness refers to how meticulous or precise a person is, and this factor needs one to be persistent, hardworking, dependable, thorough, and responsible. Agreeableness demands a person to be good-natured, courteous, likeable, forgiving, and obviously soft-hearted to accommodate followers' minor mistakes. But he/she must give feedback in such a manner that the mistake is not repeated.

Some persons frequently become anxious or depressed, get angry and worried, and feel insecure and this forms their neurological system. The experimenting dimension encompasses imaginative power, creativity, broad-mindedness, and intelligence. Extroversion of a person is exhibited through his/her sociability, talkativeness, and activity. Leadership ability measures self-report or leadership opinion questionnaire, supervisory behaviour description, multi-factor leadership questionnaire, etc. Leadership potential significantly depends on the style a leader generally applies.

Measuring Three Leadership Styles

Donald Clark (www.nwlink.com) developed a 30-item, 5-point questionnaire to measure leadership styles—authoritarian style (autocratic), participative style (democratic), and delegative style (free rein). Responses to 10 items bring out one style. The five points are 1, 2, 3, 4, or 5.

- 1 indicates 'Almost Never True' (ANT)
- 2 indicates 'Seldom True' (ST)
- 3 indicates 'Occasionally True' (OT)
- 4 indicates 'Frequently True' (FT)
- 5 indicates 'Almost Always True' (AAT)

This questionnaire helps you assess what leadership style a person normally uses. The lowest score possible for any stage is 10 (Almost Never) while the highest score possible for any stage is 50 (Almost Always).

The highest of the three scores indicates what style of leadership a person normally uses. If the highest score is 40 or more, it is a strong indicator of a normal style. The lowest of the three scores is an indicator of the style least used. If the lowest score is 20 or less, it strongly indicates that the leader normally does not operate out of this mode.

If two of the scores are close to the same, you might be going through a transition phase, either personally or at work, except if you score high in both participative and delegative, then you are probably a delegative leader. A small difference between the three scores indicates that you have no clear perception of the mode you operate out of, or you are a new leader and are searching for the style to be successful in leading the workforce.

Reliability and validity

This survey is a learning tool used in training programmes on leadership development, rather than a research tool. It has not been formally checked for reliability or validity. However, Donald has updated this tool many times and has received feedback from various sources on the accuracy of the tool.

The questionnaire on 'Leadership Style Survey' is given in Annexure 7.2.

MEASURING THE EFFECTS OF LEADERSHIP

Having studied the importance of assessing leadership potential, now we need to find the answer to a simple question: 'Does a leader achieve results?' Getting the answer is not so easy. We need to observe certain factors: (a) effects of the leader on followers or subordinates. One can use the term 'follower' if the impact is positive and conducive to achieving goals. Otherwise, if the impact is not positive, we call the people 'subordinates'. Leadership potential and effectiveness of leadership is best judged from: (a) quality of behavioural interaction with members, (b) quantifiable achievements of leaders, (c) exchange of information with other groups for the benefit of the organization as a whole. Of course, task achievement is a process and it includes dealing with followers.

On measuring leadership potential and the effects of leadership, very often a manager's failure comes to the fore. You have to know the means of measuring the effects of leadership. Leaders may be classified as successful and unsuccessful depending on their achievements. Hughes et al. (2008) furnish three methods: (1) superiors' ratings, (2) subordinates' ratings, and (3) unit performance indices. Of these, the superiors' ratings method is frequently used though this method has the disadvantages of superiors' biases, raters' unawareness of true performances, and the raters' unwillingness to provide tough feedback, if any. The advantages of subordinates' ratings are that they work with the leader and hence know the leader better, and multiple raters offer their opinions. However, some of the people working with a leader may be frustrated, lack motivation, have a grudge on personal grounds, and so forth. Their ratings would definitely be misleading.

MANAGERIAL DERAILMENT AND SELF-DEFEATING BEHAVIOUR

Some leaders can exhibit a good track record, while some others cannot. Leaders greatly differ in their behavioural disposition. Again, a leader successful in many situations may fail to achieve the target in a specific case. Behaviours of leaders, group members, and others are visible and hence we can draw a conclusion about success or failure on account of the behaviour. We need to consider many invisible aspects of leadership like traits, intelligence, emotional intelligence, values, and value system using psychometric tests.

A leader may be totally puzzled to decide what to do and what he/she need not do. Leaders may not be able to realize how they are impacting the followers. But it stands established that behaviour is a complex function of many invisible determinants. Over time, a leader learns and discriminates which behaviour is more appropriate and effective and will meet with success. Leader support, interaction facilitation, goal emphasis, and work facilitation are the four broad categories of leadership behaviour that bear a causal relation to effective group performance.

Senior managers need to be aware of community leadership—the process of building a team of members to accomplish some important organizational outcome. Community leaders need not have any position power and need not necessarily be discipline followers. They need three competencies: framing, building social capital, and capacity to mobilize resources to successfully drive any change effort. Framing means recognizing and defining opportunities (what, why, and how), building social capital refers to networking or building relationships to work together and getting along with others, while mobilization means utilizing resources for execution.

The characteristics of successful leaders are the ability to develop or adapt, build and lead a team, and establish collaborative relations, consistent exceptional performance, non-authoritarian behaviour, and ambitious nature.

Characteristics of Derailment

Derailed leaders suffer from some common shortcomings. A short list of the shortcomings is as follows:

- inability to develop or adapt
- inability to build and lead a team
- lack of networking and partnering skills
- lack of relation building skills
- failure to anticipate how the external environment is changing
- authoritarian style
- lack of ambition or overconfidence
- lack of emotional intelligence
- aggressive behaviour with colleagues
- fault-finding attitude
- lack of capacity to utilize opportunities

It is evidenced that almost half of the organizational leaders fail to build cohesive teams or achieve business results.

Four enduring themes in derailment research are problems with interpersonal relationships, failure to achieve business objectives, inability to build and lead teams, and inability to develop and adapt (Hughes et al. 2008). Now you should know about self-defeating behaviour.

SELF-DEFEATING BEHAVIOUR

Derailed managers may resort to self-defeating behaviours. Some common self-defeating behaviours are procrastination, suspiciousness, defensiveness, overcommitting, worrying, being overly critical, alienating, rigid, hostile, over-controlling, perfectionism, and inability to trust others. To get rid of self-defeating behaviours a leader should carry out a realistic analysis.

Leaders, once derailed, can be at their best by challenging, inspiring, enabling, benchmarking, and encouraging their followers. They have to challenge the process searching for opportunities and taking risks, inspire others to act by predicting the future, enable others to foster collaboration, and strengthen others. Furthermore, they have to encourage subordinates by recognizing individual contribution, celebrating accomplishments, and sharing minor successes to enthuse others. They must strive to identify the reasons and then use problem-solving tools to prevent recurrence. Pondering over failure simply aggravates frustration. This action or attitude might help a leader cope with stressful experiences. Pondering on failures might interfere with the individual's ability to cope in new situations. Both the behaviours are highly practised and often performed automatically with little conscious thought. But people need to adopt a behaviour considering the situation. Changing behaviour is not an easy task; it demands a strong will to change. Thus, behavioural modification must be done steadily and carefully. Changing behaviour, especially long-standing patterns of behaviour, can be quite difficult. Learning how to change your own and others' behaviours is a key leadership skill. Good leaders know how to change and modify the behaviours of their followers so that they can be more effective team members and better achieve team goals. Any leader can gain this skill if he/she has a strong will.

DEVELOPMENT PLANNING AND THE PIPELINE

Development planning is much more than a plan; rather it is a process. Good development plans are constantly revised as new skills are learned. Development planning is a tool to permanently change behaviour. The factors which contribute to permanent behaviour changes are: (a) having written development plan and (b) periodically reviewing the development plan with direct supervisor like that of periodic performance review. Research findings provide several suggestions that leaders can take to accelerate their own development skills. Hughes et al. (2008) quote a leadership 'development pipeline' categorizing the suggestions.

Development Pipeline Model

The development pipeline model (see Figure 7.1) describes five components: insight, motivation, new knowledge and skills, real-world applications, and accountability, to travel from initial capabilities to final capabilities. The five components correspond to five critical behavioural change questions. The leader willing to develop must have answers to all five questions.

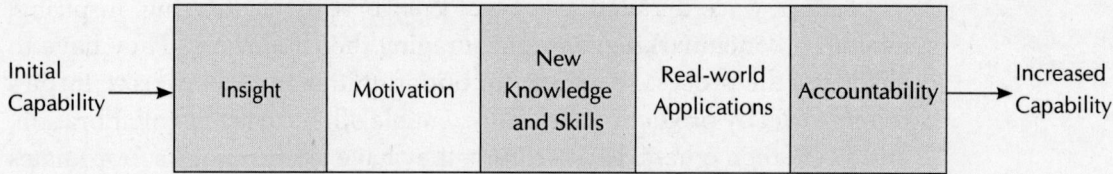

Initial Capability → | Insight | Motivation | New Knowledge and Skills | Real-world Applications | Accountability | → Increased Capability

FIGURE 7.1   Development pipeline

Five questions

Question 1   Do leaders know what behaviours need to change? The answer to this question helps to gain 'insight', the first component. In fact, a leader may have several behaviours to exhibit. But he/she knows the behaviours that should be dropped, needs to be started, and used to achieve the desired results. This component is concerned with providing accurate feedback to leaders on their strengths and weaknesses. Leaders need to have an insight about their development needs through the 360-degree feedback mechanism in which all parties interacting regularly participate.

Question 2   Is the leader motivated to change these behaviours? A leader should be willing and self-motivated to learn new skills that matter for a particular task. He/She has to determine the highest personal and organizational payoffs. Accordingly, he/she has to build development plans in conformance with the developmental needs. A plan should never address many needs; rather it should be designed based on only one or two needs. Planning multiple needs in a single plan may lead to disaster.

Question 3   Do leaders have plans in place for changing targeted behaviour? The answer to this question relates to new knowledge and skills and the changes required to fulfil a particular need. At this stage of the pipeline, leaders need to create a 'written development plan'. The developmental needs may comprise remaining calm in stressful situations or networking and relation building. The leader must design a matrix depicting action plan, time-frame, person responsible, criteria for success, etc. for each and every need. The written development plan helps the leader and followers to keep track of the progress, take actions to learn new skills, review the progress periodically, and apply corrections whenever needed.

Question 4 Do leaders have opportunities to practise new skills? Responses to this question correspond to 'real-world application'. The learned skills need application in the work area. The new skills get validated only after application and comparing the actual results with the planned achievement. Hughes et al. (2008) say that 'good development plans capitalize upon on-the-job experiences to hone needed leadership skills'. The skills get sharpened while applying; otherwise they get blunted.

Question 5 Are leaders held accountable for changing targeted behaviour? Accountability is the ultimate requirement and leaders must be held responsible for achieving the results as well as steps taken to develop and apply new skills. A leader can receive feedback from all members with whom he/she is striving daily and other persons around. The feedback raises the accountability of a leader. Periodic progress review meetings are another way to raise accountability.

PROFESSIONAL DEVELOPMENT

To facilitate managers to move on the right track, they need professional development comprising coaching, mentoring, and counselling, so we can say that managers are the vehicles moving on the track. The track needs check-up and maintenance. The periodic check-up is performance review and if any shortfall is noticed, it needs gap analysis for the purpose of bridging the gap.

Coaching

Coaching is the process of equipping people with the tools, knowledge, and opportunities they need to develop and become more successful. Coaching involves helping employees or followers in equipping organizational persons with the tools, knowledge, and opportunities that they need for development and success. Coaching demands development of a trusting relationship between the coach and the coachee. Broadly, coaching can be one-to-one or one-to-many or group coaching. In organizations, the common practice is group coaching. In today's business scenario, coaching needs are identified to fulfil specific shortcomings, which are termed as 'niche coaching'.

Coaches are trained to listen, observe, and customize their approach to individual clients, and they believe that clients are creative and resourceful (Mukherjee 2007). Coaching facilitates clients in one or more of the following ways:

- discovering the answers within
- clarifying their purpose, values, and aspirations
- challenging their existing views or perspectives
- brainstorming
- co-creating a plan for action
- expanding or challenging their vision
- identifying future directions
- using coach as a source for new ideas
- identifying resources required or obstacles to be managed
- making decisions
- getting encouragement and acknowledgement
- using role-plays

Types of coaching

The most common types of coaching practised in organizations are personal/life coaching, career coaching, mentor coaching, spiritual coaching, business coaching, and executive coaching.

Personal/life coaching   A person may suffer from a lack of self-awareness. A coach may help him/her to gain that awareness, gaining clarity of personal goals and prioritize them to better understand the thoughts. Life coaching supports clients in choosing new perspectives and establishing new beliefs. Clients, with help from the coach, can identify strengths and weaknesses. In fact, life coaching builds a bridge between where the client is and where he/she wants to be.

Career coaching   Career coaching helps employees to fulfil their career aspirations. The employees take decisions, contact the coach, receive directions, and take actions to achieve their career objectives. Career coaching is primarily meant for job or career transition. But it extends to overall career direction and helps in job search, résumé writing, interview practice, and negotiation actions.

Mentor coaching   Mentoring is meant to develop work leadership. Mentor coaching is another powerful form of guidance coaching. It is believed that behind a successful person, there must be at least one mentor. Through knowledge and experience sharing, a mentor restores confidence and develops employees. The focus of a mentoring relationship is specific to the expertise of the mentor. A mentor provides the wisdom minus the pain of acquiring it.

Spiritual coaching   This coaching is different from all other types of coaching as it taps the power centre within both the client and the coach. Giving credence to this intelligence, coaches aid clients listening to their heart, and support them to take action and effect changes from that place of 'inner strength' (Mukherjee 2007). A spiritual coach does his/her job by intuition.

Business coaching   Business needs include increase in sales, enhancing productivity, promoting teamwork, conflict resolution, quality improvement, and so forth. Aspirants come to business coaches for inspiration in desperation. They want the coach to help them. Businessmen in trouble come to a coach for solution of problems they are encountering.

Executive coaching   Executive coaching is an experiential and individualized leader development process to enhance a leader's capacity to achieve short-term and long-term business goals. Characteristics of this type of coaching includes one-to-one interaction, driven by data, facts, and figures. The coach and client must develop mutual trust. This coaching differs from other types as a partnership develops between the coach, the executive (client), and the organization. During coaching, examples are drawn from the organization itself.

Five steps of informal coaching

The term 'informal coaching' applies in a case where a leader helps the followers in behaviour modification by initially developing a partnership and gradually making it grow stronger through trust, sympathy, empathy, and other means. Hughes et al. (2008) postulate five steps of informal coaching: forge a partnership, inspire commitment, grow skills, promote persistence, and shape the environment.

Forge a partnership   A client/employee receives messages from a coach. Unless he/she accepts the messages wholeheartedly, development would be at stake. Coaching only works if there develops a trusting relationship between the coach (leader) and the client (follower). In this step, the coach determines the goals of followers and the drives needed.

Inspire commitment   A leader coach helps followers to determine the skills or behaviours that would give the biggest payoffs. The skill gap or knowledge gap may be ascertained from 360-degree review reports or conventional appraisal reports.

Grow skills   The leader and the follower develop and build up the development plans jointly to capitalize on on-the-job experiences and coaching plans to realize the follower's development.

Promote persistence   Development is a steady and continuous process. As such, a leader meets his/her coaches at intervals to keep the wheel of development moving, providing new tasks, projects, or assignments, whichever is needed to achieve the plans.

Shape the environment   The leader must keep track through reviews of how the followers are doing to foster development in the workplace. Unless this is done, there might be distraction.

The various steps of high-impact development plans are formulating career and development objectives, determining the criteria for success, detailing action steps, identifying persons to be involved, giving assignments, mobilizing resources, and reflecting with a partner to review the progresses.

Having become acquainted with various facets of coaching, we will now turn our attention to mentoring.

Mentoring

Mentoring is an old concept of developing leadership skills. Mentoring refers to developing work leadership and structured and methodical processes whereby the less experienced members of an organization develop the necessary skills and leadership abilities. Mentored employees discharge their duties and responsibilities effectively, performing better in the workplace. Leadership is different from performing managerial tasks. All organizational leaders are managers but all managers are not leaders. Managers get work done by their subordinates while most leaders work with their followers as a 'leading hand'. Leaders involve themselves with the work as they prefer to work in teams.

Leadership characteristics include insight, initiative, inspiration, involvement, improvisation, individuality, and implementation. To survive and grow in the competitive business environment, organizations are keen to develop leadership potential for which they arrange mentoring programmes. Mentoring can be both natural mentoring, and planned or structured mentoring. Mentors and mentees have different views about the quality that mentors should have. In the process of mentoring, a mentor performs a variety of roles: sponsoring, teaching, advocating, coaching, advising, counselling, negotiating, and whatever else is required to bring up the mentees and change their life. A mentoring relationship develops in four phases—initiation, cultivation, separation, and redefinition or re-translation.

The concept of 360-degree mentoring encompasses steps like defining goals and expectations, selecting the mentoring coordinator, encouraging reciprocity, evaluating mentoring progress regularly, and fostering a mentoring-friendly culture. Mentoring is about supporting, propping up, buoying up, and developing an employee through experience sharing to enhance his/her problem-solving skills. The benefits of mentoring are many. Both mentoring and coaching are professional development tools. Mentoring is a useful adjunct to coaching; yet these two tools have certain differences. Organizations must implement mentoring practices methodically complying with steps like specifying the objectives, building a mentoring support structure, training mentoring coordinators, identifying mentors and mentees, training them, matching mentors and mentees, and installing guidelines for evaluation.

Benefits of mentoring

As discussed, mentoring is about supporting, propping up, buoying up, and developing an employee through experience sharing to enhance his/her problem-solving skills. It is evidenced that mentoring works best if the mentor is someone other than a direct supervisor and is not from the department the mentee is working in. There are numerous benefits of mentoring, for example,

- Ensuring career growth through training and helping employees in a systematic way
- Developing new recruits, namely, younger generations of the workforce
- Making management trainees and junior managers rise up the organization ladder, and making them high-flyers
- Moderating entry shocks, helping newcomers cope with cultural shocks, and providing socialization
- Inculcating organization citizenship behaviour among new recruits
- Providing on-the-job-training and mentoring-coaching

A comparison of mentoring and coaching is provided in Table 7.1.

TABLE **7.1** **Mentoring and coaching—A comparison**

Mentoring	Coaching
Developing leadership among managerial personnel	Helping one to perform role better without ambiguity
Ongoing relationship that can last for a longer period of time between the mentor and the mentee	Relationship generally has a set duration. The duration varies depending on the phase
Can be informal or formal. In informal mentoring, meetings can take place as and when the mentee needs some advice, guidance, or support	Generally more structured in nature and meetings are scheduled on a regular basis as per fixed programme
More long-term and takes a broader view of the person	Short-term (sometimes time-bound) and focused on specific development areas or issues
Mentors are usually more experienced and qualified than the mentee. Often a senior person in the organization who can pass on knowledge, experience, and expertise to the mentee, which may otherwise remain as out-of-reach opportunities	Coaching helps to develop occupational roles. Thus the coach needs to have direct experience of the work area of the coachee and the role required to be performed
Focus is on career and personal development	Focus is generally on developmental issues at work
Organization benefits indirectly following the personal development of the employees	Organization benefits directly from coaching-enhanced role performance
Agenda is set by the mentee, and the mentor provides support and guidance to prepare the mentee for future roles	The agenda is focused on achieving specific, immediate organizational objectives and business goals
Mentoring revolves more around developing the mentee	Coaching revolves more around specific development areas or issues

Counselling

Counselling is essentially a discussion of a problem that usually has an emotional dimension to it and improves the well-being of the employee. It seeks to cultivate good mental health, which means that people feel comfortable about themselves and are able to face the problems at work and in personal life. Corporate employee counselling programmes began in 1936 in the Western Electric Company in Chicago. Employee counselling resulted in improvement of employee job satisfaction. Counselling is the means of assisting, developing, and helping employees/ workers, staff, and managers. It refers to professional guidance of individuals by utilizing structured methods, especially in collecting case history data, using various techniques of the personal interview, and testing interests and aptitudes. Counselling is a form of guidance in which a trained or experienced person offers advice or education about specific problems in the work area. It is the process by which a professional counsellor helps a person cope with mental or emotional distress, understand and solve personal problems, and takes him/her from distress to de-stress. The counsellor gives the individual his/her opinion, direction, advice, etc., for coping with the situation after consulting and understanding the employee.

The purpose of counselling is to provide people with a better understanding of themselves and establish links between their thoughts, feelings, and behaviour. Sometimes, people in need of counselling feel so depressed and hopeless that they cannot imagine someone or something being helpful. Some people see themselves as self-reliant and find it difficult to ask someone for assistance. To them, asking for help is a sign of weakness. However, it actually takes strength and courage to initiate counselling and focus on solving one's problems.

The central goal of counselling is to help the person to see, feel, value, and understand his/her own 'soul' in order to move forward. Rapport-building and trust are essential to this process. The counsellor must provide a passionate yet detached safe space for unfolding the psychic drama—as if he/she holds the employee's heart in his/her hand. An important issue is to maintain the necessary respect for emotional resistances, which at times need to be maintained, and at other times be removed. The counsellor must be open to rendering experience-based intuitive guidance. Counselling is also possible for a family member or friend but it requires care for emotional safety.

There may be a superficial similarity in coaching and counselling as both are one-to-one conversations and are used for professional development, but their tone and purpose are very different. The following are the differences between counselling and coaching (Table 7.2).

TABLE 7.2 **Counselling and coaching—A comparison**

Counselling	Coaching
Counselling and therapy deal with personal problems	Coaching addresses workplace performance of the counsellee
Counselling begins with a problem	Coaching generally begins with a goal or aspiration
Counselling is sought by employees facing some sort of difficulties	Coaching is used mostly by high achievers as much as by beginners or people who are stuck in some problems
Counselling, in many situations, focuses on the past and the origin of problems	Coaching focuses on the future and on developing a workable solution
Counselling has a broader focus and greater depth	Coaching has a narrower focus
Counselling is meant to help people understand the root causes of long-standing performance problems/issues at work	Coaching is extended to improve an individual's performance at work, to perform the tasks assigned better
Counselling is primarily a short-term intervention, but can last for longer time periods depending on the breadth of issues to be addressed	Coaching is goal oriented and tends to be a short-term intervention once the goal is achieved
Counselling can be used to address psycho-social as well as performance issues	Coaching assumes that a person does not require a psycho-social intervention. As such, it does not seek to resolve any underlying psychological problems
Counselling session's agenda is generally agreed to by the counsellee and the counsellor	Coaching's agenda is typically set by the coach, but in agreement or in consultation with the organization
Counselling sessions do not involve other persons	Coaching involves other personnel in the process

LEADER–MEMBER EXCHANGE THEORY

Professional development processes like coaching, mentoring, and counselling that demand close interactions of the leader with the followers have been discussed. Considering this, the leader–member exchange (LMX) theory is discussed in this section. This theory is formally known as 'vertical dyad linkage' theory and was introduced in the mid-1970s. It has been revised over time. This theory illustrates the role processes between a leader and each follower, and the exchange relationship that exists between them developed over time. LMX theory is based on the understanding that leaders establish individual relationships as well as mutually exchanged relationships with those in a follower position. All followers do not receive the same treatment from the leader though a leader typically has one major prevailing style of leadership.

According to the LMX theory, followers or subordinates fall into two different categories. The first category is composed of a group termed as the 'in-group'. Followers of this category are individuals who have a special exchange relationship with the leader. They have greater access, influence, and favour and are typically considered the trusted followers, consultants, assistants, or lieutenants of the leader.

The other category includes a group of individuals considered to be the 'out-group'. The subordinates in this group have a low level of favour or mutual influence with the leader. The 'out-group' typically complies with the formal role expectations of the leader but lacks the special built-in relationship available to the 'in-group' members. The question that comes to the mind is regarding the determining factors that make a member getting placed in the leader's 'in-group' or 'out-group'. Unfortunately, there is no answer to this question and it is usually based on bias, prejudice, or perceived similarities rather than valid information. Because of this special relationship with the leader, 'in-group' followers have certain responsibilities and obligations beyond those required of the 'out-group' members. They are expected to have a greater sense of commitment, deeper loyalty to the leader, and share difficult administrative responsibilities. Within this relationship, both the leader and subordinates mutually gain more personal power because of reciprocal trust, respect, and interdependence.

Originally, the theory proposed that these relationships were developed early in the leader–follower relationship and were due to perceived competence, dependability, and personal or astrological compatibility. Later propositions interpreted this relationship as more of a 'life cycle' model or one that has ups and downs as in most of our social relationships. Some research scholars have indicated that those subordinates who have a positive exchange relationship with the leader are more likely to have a positive exchange relationship with those who report to them.

A recent version of the LMX theory proposed by researchers George Graen and Mary Uhl-Bien (1995) has correctly added the recommendation that leaders who desire to be most effective will strive to create special exchange relationships with all their followers. It is not necessary to treat all subordinates exactly in the same manner. The leader should have a deeper exchange relationship with those who can be trusted with regard to sincerity and regularity, and have been entrusted with greater responsibility or administrative functions. Yet, it is possible and desirable that the leader cultivates a relationship of mutual supportiveness, respect, and trust with all subordinates. It is important that every follower is respected like a valued member of the team. They should be able to thrive in an environment of equal opportunity where their skills are evaluated because of their competence rather than because of favouritism. Leaders must tell performers to 'keep it up' (encourage performance). At the same time they must adequately endeavour to bring up those who are trailing behind so that they too can 'come up'.

The LMX Process

These relationships, if they are going to happen, start very soon after a person joins the group and follow three stages: role taking, role making, and routinization. Let us study these stages.

- **Role taking**: A member joins the team and the leader assesses his/her abilities and talents. Before assigning any task, the leader may offer the member opportunities to demonstrate his/her capabilities. Based on the capabilities tested, the leader proceeds.
- **Role making**: In the second phase, the leader and member take part in an unstructured and informal negotiation on role assignment. Thereafter, the leader creates a role for the member and the often-tacit promise of benefit and power in return for dedication and loyalty takes place. Trust building is of paramount importance in this stage, and any felt betrayal, especially by the leader, can result in the member being downgraded to the out-group. This negotiation includes relationship factors as well as pure work-related ones, and a member who possesses likes and dislikes similar to those of the leader is more likely to succeed. This perhaps explains why mixed-gender relationships are less successful than same-gender ones (it also affects the seeking of respect in the first stage). The same effect also applies to cultural and racial differences.
- **Routinization**: In this phase, a pattern of ongoing social exchange becomes established between the leader and the member.

Measurement of LMX

The way in which LMX has been defined varies substantially from study to study (Yukl 2007). Mutual trust, respect, love, affection, support, drive, obedience, loyalty, dedication, etc. are usually involved in determining the quality of relationship. Measurement of the LMX relation is a subjective approach. But we can reasonably establish objectivity using questionnaire and asking the respondents to express their opinions on the Likert Scale. A questionnaire is proposed (Table 7.3).

TABLE **7.3** **Measure LMX relation**

Instrument to Measure LMX Relation (Follower Perception)		
Read the statements and express your views on a 10-point Likert Scale		
S. No.	Statement	Point
a)	The leader extends full support to you in your need	
b)	At meetings and other decision-making points the leader values your opinion	
c)	The leader does not differentiate one member from another	
d)	The extent to which the leader appreciates your competency	
e)	In case you were absent for a meeting, the leader gives feedback about the matters discussed and decisions taken	
f)	In case you are entangled in some other work, the leader sends a messenger to get you to the meeting	
g)	Before assigning any task, the leader explains the importance, criticality and need of that task	
h)	While progressing in an assignment, the leader periodically seeks feedback and extends support	
i)	You have made a mistake which has resulted in financial loss; the leader will caution you but use his/her power to safeguard you	
j)	The leader is considering the weaknesses of a member and consciously trying to protect his/her image	
k)	Your extent of overall satisfaction with the leader's behaviour	
l)	The extent of trust of the leader in various spheres of work as you perceive it	
m)	The leader's likes and dislikes match with your own	
n)	The leader sometimes makes positive remarks about you to your team-mates	
o)	You identify yourself from many perspectives with the leader	

Add the scores against all the statements. Next, analyse the total score for each member. The scale is not validated. The reliability has also not been ascertained so far. But the scale can be used to measure the LMX relation.

Score below 60—Poor leader–member relationship; need for improvement. Top management immediately needs to initiate steps like organizing trust building workshops, attitudinal change or attitude building workshops, finding the root causes for poor relationship and eliminating these causes. Refresher courses must also be frequently conducted. Leader and all members need continuous monitoring.

Score between 60 and 89—Good relationship exists. Top management needs to initiate steps like organizing trust building workshops, attitudinal change or attitude building workshops, finding the root causes hindering relation building, and eliminating these factors. Refresher courses also may be conducted once a year.

Score between 90 and 119—Very good relationships exists. Management needs to initiate steps like organizing trust building workshops, attitudinal change or attitude building workshops. Refresher courses may also be conducted.

Score 120 and more—Excellent leader–member relationships, which must be maintained.

Members' average may be calculated.

Leader-member relations may be measured using multiple option scales also. Not many studies have been pursued on LMX relations from the perspective of both leader and follower.

Promoting Leader–Member Relations

No concrete methods can be prescribed to promote leader–member relationships. However, certain soft means are suggested. Organizations should organize 'social gatherings' inside the company. Sometimes organizations may also arrange gatherings outside the organization, say, in an open space or a resort. Recognition or attention, appreciation, one-on-one coaching, training, good work environment, on-the-spot praise, leadership roles, team spirit, casual dress day, time off, outside seminars, additional responsibility, theme contests, stress management, idli-dosa-pizza-popcorn days, and gags and gimmicks, etc. may help to bring the leader and the member psychologically closer. The leader must socialize to bring all the members together, should have knowledge of how to be an inspiration, and harmonize natural talents. The organization needs to motivate people by

- creating conditions where people's energies are not expended in meeting their basic needs;
- ensuring an organizational climate for interdependent work rather than dependency;
- facilitating a competitive, but healthy, climate through recognition of good work;
- providing a productive climate practising what you preach;
- generating a climate of problem-solving rather avoidance.

Organization may use instruments to measure determinants of mutual relationship.

Evaluation of LMX Theory

Yukl (2007) evaluates LMX theory from various angles considering various research outcomes. LMX theory began as a descriptive theory, but over time, it has become more prescriptive. The theory has been revised but unfortunately the revisions have still not been as precise as a theory from which benefits can be derived. LMX theory has a number of conceptual weaknesses that limit its utility. Revisions of the theory attempted to enhance its utility and remedy some deficiencies, but more improvements are needed. A continuing problem over the years has been the ambiguity about the nature of the exchange relationship. The LMX scale measures a theoretical construct (quality of relationship) that is conceptually meaningful and distinct from more traditional constructs such as satisfaction with the leader, trust of the leader, and identification with the leader. The theory needs more elaboration regarding the way exchange relationships evolve over time. The theory would be improved by a clear description of the way a leader's different dyadic relationships affect each other and overall group performance.

Yukl (2007) adds that at some point, increasing differentiation of dyadic relationships begins. This leads to the creation of feelings of resentment among the low exchange members. There is ample scope of improving the LMX theory by incorporation of processes relating to attribution that explain how leaders interpret subordinates' actions and subordinates interpret leaders' actions. Attribution theory describes the cognitive processes used by leaders to determine the reasons for effective or ineffective performance and the appropriate reaction. Successful members are thus similar in many ways to the leader (which perhaps explains why many senior teams are all-male, middle class and middle aged); the reason behind success may be homogeneity of the members. They work hard at building and sustaining trust and respect. Towards this end, they are compassionate, patient, reasonable, sensitive, and are good at seeing the viewpoint of other people (especially the leader). Aggression, disdain, and an egocentric view will mean inclusion in the out-group.

The overall quality of the LMX relationship varies with several factors. Curiously, it is better when the challenge of the job is extremely high or extremely low. The size of the group, financial resource availability, and overall workload are also important.

SUMMARY

Early studies revealed five core leader behaviours: supportive, directive, participative, reward and punishment, and charismatic. Managers change behaviours according to situations. Leaders can make or mar a business and hence assessing and measuring their potential is vital. Sometimes good managers also are derailed and adopt self-defeating behaviour, which leads to their increasing frustration. They should actually perform a realistic analysis to prevent recurrence of failure. In fact, leaders should develop plans to achieve one or two needs at a time and not multiple goals all at the same time.

Leaders should follow a development pipeline describing five components: insight, motivation, new knowledge and skills, real-world applications, and accountability. Professional development encompasses coaching, mentoring, and counselling. Leader interact and work closely with followers. As such, they must have healthy relations. According to LMX theory, formerly known as 'vertical dyad linkage', followers are categorized as 'in-group' and 'out-group'. LMX theory began as a descriptive theory, but over time it has become more prescriptive. Leader–member relations need be healthy for team effectiveness. Research on LMX can further improve this.

KEY TERMS

Managerial derailment refers to the situation when top executives on an apparently clear track fail to achieve organizational goals.

Mentor qualities signify good communication skills, empathetic listening, interpreting mentees' needs, dedication to develop people, deriving joy from the process of mentoring.

Natural mentoring or informal mentoring occurs through friendship, affection, collegiality, psychological closeness, and congruent likes and dislikes.

Niche coaching refers to coaching to eradicate identified specific shortcomings of a person enabling him/her to develop in his/her role.

Planned mentoring is organized through structured programmes in which mentors and mentees or protégés are selected and matched through a formal organizational process.

EXERCISES

Concept Review Questions

1. Discuss how the effects of leadership may be measured in organizations. Discuss the end use of measuring the effects.
2. What is managerial derailment? Discuss the characteristics of derailment.
3. What is professional development? Discuss the various tools that can be used for professional development.
4. If derailed, what action should the derailed manager take? What is self-defeating behaviour? Discuss development pipeline.
5. Discuss LMX theory and the process involved. How can we identify 'in-group' and 'out-group' members? How can the quality of relationships be measured?

Critical Thinking Questions

1. Discuss the various roles of mentors and correlate them with the activities they are actually performing in your organization or in any other organization known to you. Describe the organization in brief.
2. Suppose you are working as an engineering manager in an IT company employing 700 employees. You have been assigned the task of counselling 20 employees out of a total of 85 employees under your control with the designation of (a) software engineer, senior software engineer, and (b) technical leader. How would you do this? Discuss the various steps.

Assignments

1. Approach two or three companies that have persons responsible for organizing leadership development programmes. Contact the person responsible. Collect the names and other details of about five teams striving to achieve their team goals. Apply LMX theory, identify whether there exists any member who appears to be in the 'out-group' category and justify your findings.

2. Select three teams that were formed some two years back, working to achieve the team goals, but not very effective in the view of management. Administer a questionnaire to ascertain the leader–member relationships. Ascertain whether the relations are responsible for the team being 'not very effective'.

REFERENCES

Clark, Donald (www.skagit.com/~donclark/leader/survstyl.html, accessed on 26 December 2008).

Gary, Ukil (2007), *Leadership in Organizations*, Pearson Education, Delhi.

Ghosh, Lipi (2009), Leadership and Team Building, Unpublished dissertation, Master of Business Administration, Indian Institute of Social Welfare and Business Management for evaluation by University of Calcutta.

Haldar, U.K. (2009), *Human Resource Development*, Oxford Higher Education, Oxford University Press, New Delhi.

Howell, Jon P. and Dan L. Costley (2006), *Understanding Behaviours for Effective Leadership*, Prentice-Hall India, New Delhi.

Hughes, Richard L., Robert C. Ginnett, and Gordon J. Curphy (2007), *Leadership Enhancing the Lessons of Experience*, Tata McGraw-Hill, New Delhi.

Mukherjee, Sraban (2007), The New-age Manager's Doctor: How Coaching is Slowly Emerging and Fulfilling Felt Needs, *Indian Management* (Journal of the All India Management Association), Vol. 36, No. 9, September, p. 166.

Sen, Sureeta (2008), Leadership and Patterns of Leadership Behaviour, Unpublished dissertation, Master of Business Administration, Indian Institute of Social Welfare and Business Management for evaluation by University of Calcutta.

CLOSING CASE

Developing Leadership Qualities in Managers

A leadership awareness programme was organized in Elite Engineering. A renowned consultant, Mr M.B.S. Shastry was the faculty. He designed the programme curriculum and showed the same to the CEO of the company. The curriculum included topics such as:

- Core leader behaviours (for all managers)
- Assessing leadership potential (for senior managers)
- Why managers fail to achieve goals (for all managers)
- Making development plans (for all managers)
- Measuring leader–member relations (for senior managers)

- Tools of professional development (for senior managers)
- Identification of strengths and weaknesses (for junior managers only as senior managers attended a management development programme on a similar theme)
- Importance of documentation and record maintenance in line with ISO 9001 Quality Management System procedures
- Solving cases (the cases were written by Mr Shastry based on problems faced by the company and its sister concerns)
- Developing the leader within you (in the second phase of the programme)

The leadership programmes for all levels were conducted in seven batches. The managers received three-hour inputs in the company conference room. However, managers, by appointment, consulted Mr Shastry for clarification and to discuss work-related problems. Feedback was collected from all the participants in all the programmes.

The CEO expressed his utmost satisfaction with the programmes. In fact, he was casually interrogating participants in different ways about the programme and its utility. The CEO requested Mr Shastry to conduct refresher courses. He specifically requested Mr Shastry to design and develop formats and undertake post-training-impact measurement at a suitable periodicity.

Discussion Questions

1. Propose any topic that Mr Shastry could have included. Justify your answer.
2. Narrate the necessity of post-training-impact measurement over feedback. Clearly distinguish between impact and feedback in the context of leadership programmes.
3. Some learning points have been mentioned after the opening case. Do you feel that while designing the programme content Mr Shastry considered all of them? Critically analyse.

ANNEXURE 7.1

A Modified Scale of Howell and Costley

Sir,

I am pursuing a dissertation in partial fulfilment of the master's in Business Administration (Specialization–HR) from IISWBM, University of Calcutta, Kolkata. My dissertation includes identification of leadership pattern.

I have chosen an instrument from a textbook. The objective is to identify the leadership behaviour that may be used when leading a task group. I am reproducing the instrument to collate your valued responses against the items.

Direction (as given in the book): Circle the number on the 1 to 5 scale that best indicates how you would normally behave as a leader of a group that is responsible for completing some task.

S. No.	Statement	Almost Never		→		Almost Always
1	I assign specific tasks to others	1	2	3	4	5
2	I show consideration and acceptance to others	1	2	3	4	5
3	I get others involved in making decisions	1	2	3	4	5
4	I provide others with benefits and rewards	1	2	3	4	5
5	I display high expectation and confidence	1	2	3	4	5
6	I explain methods and set goals for the group	1	2	3	4	5
7	I show concern for the feelings of others	1	2	3	4	5
8	I consult others to get their ideas and suggestions	1	2	3	4	5
9	I punish others for undesirable behaviour	1	2	3	4	5
10	I communicate a vision for the group	1	2	3	4	5
11	I explain what each group member needs to accomplish	1	2	3	4	5
12	I help develop the abilities of others to contribute to the task	1	2	3	4	5
13	I encourage subgroups to handle certain aspects of the group	1	2	3	4	5
14	I compliment those who do a good job	1	2	3	4	5
15	I attempt to inspire others by pointing out the importance of the group's task and their part in accomplishing it	1	2	3	4	5

Source: Based on Jon. P. Howell and Dan L. Costley (2006), *Understanding Behaviours for Effective Leadership*, Prentice-Hall India, New Delhi.

Scoring and ranking behaviour patterns (for each respondent)

Leadership Behaviour	Statements	Scores			Total	Rank
Directive	1 + 6 + 11					
Supportive	2 + 7 + 12					
Participative	3 + 8 + 13					
Reward and punishment	4 + 9 + 14					
Charismatic	5 + 10 + 15					

ANNEXURE 7.2

Leadership Style Survey
(Developed by Donald Clark)

Directions

This questionnaire contains statements about leadership style beliefs. Next to each statement, circle the number that represents how strongly you feel about the statement by using the following scoring system:

5	AAT	Almost Always True
4	FT	Frequently True
3	OT	Occasionally True
2	ST	Seldom True
1	ANT	Almost Never True

Be honest about your choices as there are no right or wrong answers—it is only for self-assessment.

S. No.	Statement	AAT	FT	OT	ST	ANT
1	I always retain the final decision-making authority within my department or team.	5	4	3	2	1
2	I always try to include one or more employees in determining what to do and how to do it. However, I retain the final decision-making authority.	5	4	3	2	1

Contd

Table contd

S. No.	Statement	AAT	FT	OT	ST	ANT
3	I and my employees always vote whenever a major decision has to be made.	5	4	3	2	1
4	I do not consider suggestions made by my employees as I do not have time for them.	5	4	3	2	1
5	I ask for employee ideas and input on upcoming plans and projects.	5	4	3	2	1
6	For a major decision to pass in my department, it must have the approval of each individual or the majority.	5	4	3	2	1
7	I tell my employees what has to be done and how to do it.	5	4	3	2	1
8	When things go wrong and I need to create a strategy to keep a project or process running on schedule, I call a meeting to get my employees' advice.	5	4	3	2	1
9	To communicate any information, I send it by email, memos, or voicemail; very rarely is a meeting called. My employees are then expected to act upon the information.	5	4	3	2	1
10	When someone makes a mistake, I tell them not to ever do that again and make a note of it.	5	4	3	2	1
11	I want to create an environment where the employees take ownership of the project. I allow them to participate in the decision-making process.	5	4	3	2	1
12	I allow my employees to determine what needs to be done and how to do it.	5	4	3	2	1
13	New hires are not allowed to make any decision unless it is approved by me first.	5	4	3	2	1
14	I ask employees where they see their jobs going and then use their vision where appropriate.	5	4	3	2	1
15	My workers know more about their jobs than me, so I allow them to take their own decisions while doing their job.	5	4	3	2	1

Contd

Table contd

S. No.	Statement	AAT	FT	OT	ST	ANT
16	When something goes wrong, I tell my employees that a procedure is not working correctly and I establish a new one.	5	4	3	2	1
17	I allow my employees to set priorities with my guidance.	5	4	3	2	1
18	I delegate tasks in order to implement a new procedure or process.	5	4	3	2	1
19	I closely monitor my employees to ensure they are performing correctly.	5	4	3	2	1
20	When there are differences in role expectations, I work with them to resolve the differences.	5	4	3	2	1
21	Each individual is responsible for defining their job.	5	4	3	2	1
22	I like the power that my leadership position holds over subordinates.	5	4	3	2	1
23	I like to use my leadership power to help subordinates grow.	5	4	3	2	1
24	I like to share my leadership power with my subordinates.	5	4	3	2	1
25	Employees must be directed or threatened with punishment in order to get them to achieve organizational objectives.	5	4	3	2	1
26	Employees will exercise self-direction if they are committed to the objectives.	5	4	3	2	1
27	Employees have the right to determine their own organizational objectives.	5	4	3	2	1
28	Employees seek mainly security.	5	4	3	2	1
29	Employees know how to use creativity and ingenuity to solve organizational problems.	5	4	3	2	1
30	My employees can lead themselves just as well as I can.	5	4	3	2	1

In the cells below, mark the score of each item on the questionnaire. For example, if you scored item 1 with a 3 (Occasionally), then enter a 3 next to item 1. When you have entered all the scores for each question, calculate the total of each of the three columns.

Item	Score	Item	Score	Item	Score
1		2		3	
4		5		6	
7		8		9	
10		11		12	
13		14		15	
16		17		18	
19		20		21	
22		23		24	
25		26		27	
28		29		30	
Total		Total		Total	

Source: www.nwlink.com/~donclark/leader/survstyl.html, accessed on 26 December 2008).
Permission granted by Donald Clark vide email dated 28 December 2008.

CHAPTER **8**

Leadership Development

========= **Learning Objectives** =========

After studying this chapter you will be able to

▶ State the difference between leader and leadership
▶ Discuss the concepts and objectives of leadership development
▶ Understand leadership development techniques and mechanisms
▶ Distinguish leader profiles
▶ Develop an understanding of leadership development drives
▶ Understand the need for leadership pipeline

OPENING CASE

Need for Behavioural Modification

Mr Ganapathy was a non-resident Indian (NRI) based in New Jersey in the United States. He was an engineering graduate and had completed an M. Tech. (production engineering) from an institute of international repute. He had lucrative offers from several organizations during the campus interview but he rejected them all and decided to launch a consultancy firm so that he could be his own boss and remain independent. Within a short time, Ganapathy Technology Limited (GTL) gained reputation and had a thriving practice in New Jersey. However, Mr Ganapathy harboured thoughts of returning to India. He had married an Indian woman who was born and brought up in India and had a master's degree in economics, and doctorate in arts (economics) from an Indian university. She visited India frequently and was probably urging Mr Ganapathy to settle in India. Mr Ganapathy too had been waiting to return to India.

In 1981–2, the Government of India appealed to NRIs to invest in various businesses in India. Many NRIs responded to this request and Mr Ganapathy viewed this as his opportunity. The idea appealed to him and he too invested substantial amounts in a few businesses flourishing in India. The rate of return on investments was high. He discussed this with an Indian businessman and having decided to return to India, he conveyed his decision to some of his clients in New Jersey. The clients tried hard to persuade him to continue in New Jersey as his advice was result oriented and his practice was well established. However, Mr Ganapathy eventually returned to India after spending about fifteen years in the United States.

He built close contacts with the companies in which he had invested, and studied the profit and loss statements, income/expenditure accounts, balance sheets, and other related financial documents in depth. Mr Ganapathy gradually became inclined towards starting a business. During his stay in New Jersey, many firms had benefited from his consultancy advice. The majority of the clients were producing special purpose hydraulic and pneumatic pumps. He provided advice regarding design and manufacturing of the components, assembling and quality control parameters. The products never failed and as such, the clients never received any customer complaints. The clients only benefited from the expertise of Mr Ganapathy.

Mr Ganapathy decided to start an organization to design, manufacture, and sell hydraulic and pneumatic pumps. Accordingly, he selected land in an industrial area in the state he belonged to, applied for a trade licence, registered his firm, and appointed personnel, both technical and administrative. It took about six months to procure the machines, and another four months for erection and commissioning. He appointed an expert mechanical engineer to look after the quality control department. Meanwhile, he secured orders for the pumps. Thereafter, he gradually started production and sales, initially in the domestic market. He recruited salespersons—fresh diploma holders in sales management—from a local management institute to deliver the pumps directly to customers without the help of any distributor or dealer. Gradually, the business grew, and customers vigorously started to contact him for expediting delivery. Mr Ganapathy advised his team to take immediate actions. They put in their best efforts to cope with the demand.

In view of the urgent need for production, Mr Ganapathy appointed a production manager (Mr PM), but the pressure continued. Mr PM was a qualified person and disciplined as well. He seldom reached the factory late. At the same time, he was a task-oriented manager. At the end of the day, he would walk around the production department to collect the production figures, which his supervisors could have done. But Mr PM had little trust in juniors. He was also overstaying in office to organize data, prepare statistical graphs, and endorse decisions regarding short-term and long-term production planning. He never allocated duties to his immediate junior, Mr APM, assistant production manager. Rather, Mr APM approached Mr PM to extend a helping hand. But due to lack of confidence, Mr PM neither allocated any decision-making duty nor transferred some of his powers to Mr APM.

One day, while walking around, some operators tried to express their difficulties and grievances. But Mr PM was not very keen to hear them and rudely said, 'I don't like to hear any story.' This statement led to labour problems and the episode consumed ample time before settlement by the industrial relations officer with the intervention of Mr Ganapathy.

Once, Mr Ganapathy convened a meeting to discuss multiple organizational issues including introduction of multi-rater feedback system for managerial personnel. Mr PM objected forcefully to this proposal stating, 'I don't like to be evaluated by any junior. What do they know about evaluation?' He passed this comment in the presence of some managers.

On one occasion, Mr APM approached Mr PM with certain technical problems and requested his intervention for a solution. Mr PM told Mr APM not to approach him again. Mr APM felt insulted by this statement and started avoiding Mr PM.

Learning outcomes

1. A senior person must involve juniors and trust them.
2. Leaders should be empathetic listeners.
3. A senior manager should make comments cautiously.
4. Task orientation must be supported by willing participation of juniors.

INTRODUCTION

In Chapter 1, we studied the differences between managers and leaders from multiple angles. Managers focus on day-to-day activities, render services to survive, and strive to ensure that the business runs smoothly. Leaders on the other hand look and think ahead, go beyond the normal domain of work, extend their vision, and make certain that the business grows. An effective leader foresees the future, sets a vision, and prepares to march towards excellence. Thus, leaders require a high degree of emotional intelligence—a strong 'people sense' to understand how to motivate, stimulate, and encourage individuals and teams to drive the organization forward.

The nature of duties of administrators, managers, and leaders appear to be similar. But if observed closely, one can identify the differences. Pareek (2008) brings out very lucidly the distinct differences in tabular form (Exhibit 21.1, p. 551) in his book titled *Understanding Organizational Behaviour*. The table is reproduced below (Table 8.1).

TABLE **8.1** **Three managerial modes**

	Administration	Manager	Leadership
Main concern	Follow procedures	Get results	Excel
Emphasis on	Conformity	Interaction	Creativity
Focus on	Status quo	Stability	Trend setting
Norms	Quantity	Quality	Pushing benchmark
Assessment criteria	Efficiency	Effectiveness	Boundary management
Driven by	Past (tradition, precedence)	Present (competence)	Future (vision)
Approach	Tactics	Strategy	Vision
Structure	Hierarchy/Protocol	Matrix	Network
Response mode	Reactive	Proactive	Preactive (making others play your game)
Managing by	Developing procedures	Building systems	Building culture
HRD approach	Supervision	Coaching	Mentoring
Dominant need	Control dependency	Achievement power	Power extension
Concept of power	Limited/Unshareable	Shareable	Multiplying
Source of power	Status/Authority	Competence	Empowerment

Source: Understanding organizational behaviour, Udai Pareek, Oxford University Press, 2008.

From the above table, you can understand the important roles of leaders. In this chapter, you will study concepts, objectives, and mechanisms of leadership development, and role of crucibles, and gain an overview of leadership pipeline.

LEADER DEVELOPMENT

All people are not born with the same potential to lead well; rather some may not have the ability to lead at all. Different personal characteristics help or hinder a person's leadership successes that require formalized programmes for developing leadership competencies. Leaders have to make a difference. Leader development is a matter of great concern. A leader has to perform different roles. Leadership failure happens when one or more roles are not performed effectively. Ramnarayan (2007) underscores four challenges of leadership—leader as cognitive tuner, leader as a people catalyser, leader as systems architect, and leader as efficacy builder.

Leader as cognitive tuner   As cognitive tuner, a leader has to appreciate changes. An organization may decide to pursue the objective to strengthen interface management among the key functions for developing new products. For the success of the change effort, employees need behavioural modification; they need to behave in ways that would be qualitatively different from the manner in which they are used to. Juniors must be empowered to express difficulties, talk openly and voice opinions without fear at meetings, go beyond functional boundaries, and act assertively in multiple directions. On the other hand, seniors have to accept opinions on scrutiny, encourage juniors, and support efforts to modify dysfunctional procedures. Thus, people at all levels have to tune themselves to suit the organization's emerging needs. Obviously, then, mindset changes are the need of the day.

Leader as a people catalyser   Leaders need to mobilize support and the support should be spontaneous. They must be skilled in initiating dialogues to both understand prevailing mindsets and make the people aware of their mindsets. Top management should not confine themselves within the limited perspective of education and exhortation. It is needless to mention that change is a long and difficult journey, and during this journey, managers need to listen to diverse views, enact the changes in a variety of settings, and keep up the momentum of the change campaign. Leaders are required to build supporting coalitions, evaluate interests of people in different set-ups, alter people's incentives for change, frame and create change messages in a way that evokes support, institute a process that is open, transparent, and inclusive, consulting as widely as possible. In view of the foregoing, it is concluded that a leader must be a people catalyser.

Leader as systems architect   As a systems architect, leaders create cross-functional linkages in the organization, create new routines for improvement, and execute change (Ramnarayan 2007). A leadership challenge is to facilitate modification of mindsets by attending to four requirements—exposing people to alternative perspectives, enabling people from different functions to work together, identifying and removing roadblocks to modify existing routines, and creating new routines to focus the organization's attention on continuous improvement. Leadership is essential to establish contexts that facilitate these four requirements. This is achieved through the creation of an appropriate architecture made up of roles, responsibilities, systems, and procedures.

Leader as efficacy builder A leader has to build change capacity. Following the liberalization process, Indian organizations are also operating in a global village. In the changing business scenario, to cope with the changes, a leader has to ultimately build change capacity. Modern business history is littered with examples of changes though success stories are few. The steps taken by Tata Steel are exemplary in this regard (Box 8.1).

Box 8.1   Tata Steel—Steps taken for improvement

Tata Steel mobilized more than a hundred teams to bring about improvements in different areas. The company entrusted around 5000 people with the challenge of carrying out initiatives to 'modernize the mindsets' of 40,000 employees of the company. Improvements were sought in multiple areas—enhancing quality, bringing about radical performance improvements, augmenting total operational performance (TOP), creating a market-oriented organization, de-bottlenecking facilities, phasing out technologically obsolete plants, adding new facilities for manufacturing value-added products, capacity expansion, and so forth.

Tata Steel trained the entire workforce in certain improvement techniques and in changing the pattern of thinking. The company raised the aspiration levels of the workforce. It termed the initiative as 'ASPIRE', denoting 'Aspirational Initiatives to Retain Excellence'. Tata Steel formed teams, ignited the members, and used teams as instruments and a source of innovation in the company.

The intention of the Tata Steel management was to enhance the 'insights' of the workforce and their capabilities, make them look at the objects and operations with 'new eyes', be innovative, think and transform the thoughts into actions, dream and translate dreams into reality, finally doing work efficiently.

The result of the phenomenal drive to accomplish the above mentioned is known to all of us. Not surprisingly, Tata Steel has now been rated among the top five steel producers in the world by World Steel Dynamics. Tata Steel was ranked the best company in the world in 2005.

It is leadership shown by leaders that can make impossible things possible. An effective leader understands his/her strengths and limitations and teams up with other leaders having complementary strengths so that the leadership team can perform all the four roles. Their orchestral efforts navigate through the complex challenge of altering mindsets. The altered mindsets dare to accept any challenge and march to achieve the goal. They are not 'slow and steady'; rather they are 'fast and consistent'.

Everyone in an organization can develop their leadership skills and effectiveness. Classroom-style training, workshops, and associated reading can contribute to developing leadership skills. It can inform one about about what he/she has in possession and what else is needed, and what is involved in leading well. Leader development is person-oriented action and focuses on the development of managers as leaders, such as the personal attributes, desired ways of behaving, and approach to thinking.

Leader development focuses on three main areas: (a) providing opportunities for development, (b) stimulating the ability to develop including motivation, skills and knowledge for change, (c) and providing a supportive context for changes to occur. The leadership development process encompasses leader development and follower development. Traditionally, leadership development has focused on developing the leadership abilities and attitudes of individuals. A leader must have qualities like integrity, loyalty, commitment, energy, decisiveness, and selflessness.

Integrity Full devotion to the highest personal and professional standards.

Loyalty Faithfulness to superiors, peers, and subordinates, and, above all, to the organization.

Commitment Attachment and dedication to duty to achieve team goals, and objectives of the organization to the maximum extent.

Energy Enthusiasm, enterprise, and drive to take initiative.

Decisiveness Willingness to act and courage to decide.

Selflessness Preparedness to sacrifice personal objectives and gains in the larger interest of the organization.

Leader Profiles

A leader has to show concern for excellence, lay emphasis on creativity and innovation, set trends, push benchmarks, pursue boundary management, be a visionary, build network and culture, mentor and counsel, and multiply employee excellence through empowerment. Some organizations which excelled; have become examples. So, the question that comes to our mind is, 'what should be their profiles?' The characteristics of organizational leaders need analysis and such analysis shows that they have the distinguishing qualities of internality, creativity, humility, values, and networking (Pareek 2008).

Internality

Internality comprises a grand vision, internality, optimism, and professional will.

Grand vision   It is the vision of a leader by virtue of which he/she can devise strategies and prioritize. Moreover, the leader has to create a unified vision out of diverse visions of various groups, departments, cost centres, in the organization; articulate it, inspire people with it, and ultimately translate it into reality.

Internality   A leader makes people want to do what he wants them to do. Leaders make things happen as they want them to happen. This is so because leaders' internal locus of control is high.

Optimism   Optimism leads a person to effectiveness in any sphere of work life.

Professional will   Leaders with a strong professional will become effective in their career. I have discussed this in Chapter 5 in the section on 'Level 5 Leadership'.

Creativity

Creativity is the bringing into being of something that did not exist before, either as a product, a process, or a thought. A person needs opportunity to be creative and apply creativity. It drives the generation of ideas, and you need new ideas constantly. It is the ability to discover new relationships and ideas. It must be followed by innovation.

Innovation   Creativity is the ability to discover new relationships and ideas; innovation refers to the practical implementation of the ideas at the workplace. You have searched out the idea that a causal relationship exists between assertiveness and performance. You could search, as you are creative. An organization needs innovation to survive, grow, and thrive in today's competitive environment. You are to generate your own methods for creative thinking to vitalize your organization's quality process.

Humility

Humility means humbleness, modesty, an unassuming nature. It comprises self-restraint, empowerment, and culture building.

Self-restraint   It is a key characteristic of most successful organizational leaders. It is further a part of the ethos of most Asian cultures. This part of humility refers to the tendency to postpone gratification, satisfaction, fulfilment of one's immediate needs for the sake of achieving a long-term goal. It is of vital importance to be rewarded with success.

Empowerment   Empowerment is the process of passing authority and responsibility to individuals at lower levels in the organization hierarchy. Empowerment ensures a greater degree of involvement and a higher degree of responsibility. However, junior colleagues cannot just be empowered. Managers must be sure that employees at lower levels in the organizational hierarchy have the right mix of information, knowledge, power, and reward.

Culture building   Culture is an environment in the organization in which employees breathe without trouble, see innovative ways of doing work, freely exchange ideas, view the positive aspects but not the negative, learn from experiences, and so forth. It is the moral responsibility of leaders to develop an enabling and empowering culture.

Values

Organizations of this millennium need value-based leadership. Values incorporate four characteristics–value orientation, ethics, people first, and social concern.

Value orientation   In conformance with organizational needs, a leader will be value driven. The leader will uphold the image of the organization and ensure effectiveness. The essential components of value orientation are personal integrity, sense of equity and justice, and obviously ethics at the core. Research findings show that effective leaders lay much emphasis on values, place high value on empowerment, participation and involvement, and sharing of credits and gains. Leaders discuss 'failure stories' for learning and share success to enthuse others.

Ethics   These are moral values, codes, and principles. Great leaders rely heavily on ethics. They always establish norms and fight corruption. They preach ethics and practise what they preach. For them, preaching is not merely words. In distress or in bad times of personal life or the organization, they do not forgo ethical approaches to problem-solving. Companies like Infosys, Tata, and Wipro relentlessly pursue ethical practices. Leaders of these companies are role models not only for their employees, but also for many persons outside the firm. For example, the great living legend, N.R. Narayana Murthy of Infosys is a role model to umpteen people and even to a few competitor company executives.

People first Material resources depreciate but human resource appreciates. Narayana Murthy says: 'Our core corporate assets walk out every evening. It is our duty to make sure that these assets return the next morning, mentally and physically enthusiastic and energetic.' We need to direct a sharper focus on searching, recruiting, retaining, and developing talent. We need to constantly expend our energy to energize them and gain sharp edge, and finally execute.

Social concern An organization functions within society. It gets people from society. Achieving its goals should not be an organization's only concern. It must also consider the problems of the community, develop the community, and discharge its corporate social responsibility. If the community develops, business also develops. That is why 'social welfare' and 'business management' are intertwined. These two aspects are complementary.

Networking

Networking is building bridges of relationship. It has four characteristics—communication, networking competence, synergy building, and customer orientation.

Communication An administrator tells about the procedure to be followed, a manager tells about strategy, quality, and building systems. A leader tells about vision to share that. Leaders share visions and ideas. All the messages must reach the targets without any absorption in the communication chain.

Networking competence Networking and partnering are key success factors. Networking with companies within the industry and beyond the industry is common. Through networking, each of the networked companies enhances its strength. Networking benefits both companies. Leaders network with key individuals and strategic groups outside.

Synergy building Synergy implies that 'the total is greater than the sum of its parts'. That is why effective leaders encourage working through teams. Many organizations today are team based, conventional system of departmentalization. You will study more about teams and team building in the following chapters.

Customer orientation Quality of products or services is the main concern of businesses. Quality is not 'what excellent things the organization can give'. Quality is meeting customer demands and fulfilling them. Customer focus is the most vital quality management principle. Customer-oriented companies win by translating customer needs and expectations, called 'voices', into actions through design parameters, and delivering products and services in accordance with customer-specified needs.

NEED FOR LEADERSHIP

Pareek (2008) states that 'everybody can lead at every level; there are two excuses. It does not matter if you're on the front line or top line. If you are given an office with the powers of that office, what do you add to the office above and beyond those powers? Do you excite or motivate people? Do you bring excellence and vision to what ultimately is the objective or even the whole country? Everybody should be good at leading, whatever be their level in the company.' Survival of a business is not the only requirement for an organization. It has to grow keeping pace with the global economy. 'Survival of the fittest' is the law of jungle.

At present, the industrial scenario demands 'survival of the fastest'. The maxim 'slow and steady' has been superseded by 'fast and consistent'. Thus, leadership development is necessary for the following reasons:

- Customers today are cost sensitive and quality conscious.
- There is high attrition, careerism, and declining employee morale and loyalty.
- There are decreasing organizational citizenship behaviours.
- Rapid changes are taking place in the technological and industrial scenario. Managers are facing multifaceted problems arising out of automation, intense market competition, growth of new markets, rising customer consciousness, enhanced labour participation, and the like.
- Leaders are increasingly recognizing the company's social and public responsibility.
- The size and complexity of organizations are ever increasing.
- Labour union management relations are becoming more and more intricate.
- The socio-economic forces, effective market forces, changes in public policy and concepts of social, industrial democracy, ecological imbalances (smog or pollution), ekistics (problem of human settlements), and ergonomics (human engineering) are changing with time.

Leadership Development

In view of the need for leadership, organizations must initiate actions to develop leadership. Now, while leader development is person oriented actions focused on the development of managers as leaders, leadership development focuses on the development of leadership as a process (Pareek 2008).

Leadership development refers to the strategic investment in, and utilization of, the human capital within an organization. Henry Ford said, 'Burn my company, destroy everything I have, ruin all my assets—just give back my men. I will create another Ford.' The gamut of leadership processes will include the social influence process and the team dynamics between the leader and each team member at the dyad levels, and the contextual factors surrounding the team such as perception of the organizational climate and social network linkages between the team and other groups in the organization.

Pareek (2008) emphasizes that both leader and leadership development may mutually influence each other. The development drives are interacting, interrelated, and interdependent. Later in this chapter, you will come across highlights of organizational practices in developing leadership. To develop leadership, you must know the generic concept of leader's development. Certain perceptions, conceptions, and notions give rise to leader development. Some of the underlying concepts behind leader development are the following:

- An executive needs development throughout his/her work life and his/her professional career. Thus management development is an ongoing activity.
- There always exists a gap between 'required performance level' and the 'capacity' of an individual. Management must fill the gap to provide an opportunity for improvement.
- Some personal variables (age, habits, level of motivation, state of mind, etc.) retard the growth of an individual.
- In a work situation, growth involves stresses and strains. Development can seldom take place in a completely peaceful atmosphere.
- Involvement and participation is inescapable for growth.
- There must be defined objectives and goals required to be achieved in addition to the methodology of achievement.
- Shortcomings must be identified. Feedback and counselling to junior colleagues by apprising them of their shortcomings along with relevant HRD instruments to overcome such shortcomings are essential.

Leadership development objectives

Based on perceptions and notions, organizations arrange leadership development programmes with the aim to achieve objectives like the following:

- To provide the organization the required number of leaders having the ability to meet present and future organizational needs
- To instil leader capabilities among managers—sense of self-dependency, achievement, and affiliation to team members
- To encourage leaders to keep themselves up to date and grow to meet the challenges, cope up with the changes, handle complex situations and greater problems.
- To discharge their responsibilities with improved performance.
- To sustain good performance and gain distinctive competence.

Leadership development techniques

The techniques lay emphasis not on the skill of leaders but on their capacity to handle complex situations, deal with tough-minded and negative persons, and solve managerial problems. The techniques generally used are:

- Creation of 'Assistant to' position—The junior colleague (the follower) can perform the activities of the senior colleague (the leader). In turn, the senior colleague discharges a teacher-like role while judging the decision-making ability, and leadership skills, traits, and other potential.
- Making member of junior boards of management—The behavioural dispositions of junior managers are observed, their views/decisions are very often implemented. This is done to instil a sense of responsibility among prospective leaders.
- Coaching and counselling—Adopt to transform the new subordinate, to make him/her job-oriented in order to accomplish the goals.
- Syndicate—Team of persons of mature judgement and proven ability drawn from different functional areas exchange and share their experiences and ideas. Large numbers of new recruits are divided into small groups of 7–10 persons each. A facilitator observes and guides the group.

You have studied leadership development and its objectives, and a few techniques of development. You should now know what an organization does to develop leadership talent and global leadership talent (Box 8.2).

Process of leadership development—Role of crucibles

Bennis and Thomas (2002) use the term 'crucibles' and define it as follows: 'Crucibles refers to an experiential dimension in the lives of all the leaders— an intense, transformational experience that set them on the road to where they are now' (Pareek 2008). They identified four major types of crucibles:

Box 8.2　Develop global leadership talent

Dr Kumar Mangalam Birla answers self raised question, 'What is Aditya Birla Group doing to develop Global Leadership Talent?' He states the following:

- The hallmark of our overall development efforts has been our belief in taking 'bets on our people'. This largely stems from our innate trust in people's ability to stretch and learn.
- Our leadership development initiatives are specifically tailored to the business context. We have defined the process by identifying competencies needed to succeed in critical roles.
- The Aditya Birla Group assesses people early in their career on their potential to hold leadership roles. To the extent possible, all the key positions in our organization are staffed by talent pool members.
- Our in-house university 'Gyanodaya' is a globally benchmarked institution that leverages resources from among the world. Our e-learning network creates a seamless learning environment for our global workforce.
- We have institutionalized global career paths driven both by the individual and the organization's needs. This allows an individual to take charge of his own career.

(Dr Kumar Mangalam's speech at the AIMA, New Delhi, 21 February 2009).

mentoring relationships, enforced reflection, experiencing a new world, and disruption and loss.

Mentoring relationships　Mentors have always been found to influence and develop leadership in their protégés or mentees. Some mentors attract protégés when the process of mentoring happens automatically. This is termed as 'natural mentoring'. In many cases, organizations, in a planned way, select employees to be mentored by one senior, which is termed as 'planned mentoring'. In the knowledge industry, often a younger person mentors an elder person and this is termed as 'reverse mentoring'. Mentors offer valuable advice to protégés, develop work leadership, and help them to advance in their professional career.

Enforced reflection　This crucible refers to an opportunity for both exploration and reflection, found in such events as going away to a school or to an *ashram*. 'Through these crucibles, individuals learn preparedness— an alertness to the rich signals that surround them—and a willingness to experiment in the interest of advancing self-knowledge and, by extension, knowledge of the world around them.'

Experiencing a new world　Leaders demonstrate a remarkable capacity not only to survive in new situations, but also to derive profound insights from them. Leaders capture insights and means to advance from their own experimental tapestry, from one's own understanding, familiarity, and experience. For Mahatma Gandhi, the crucible experience was his stay in South Africa.

Disruption and loss   Remember what Gautama Buddha asked the person who approached him following the death of a near one. Personal loss of a parent, a grown child, bankruptcy, failure in an important assignment or undertaking, marriage of a girl whom one loves very much, cheating by a wife, or any similar loss or defeat can stimulate a search for greater understanding of self and relationships, a striving to explore, venturing into problem-solving and larger webs of affiliation.

A good student affected by chickenpox had to appear in a university examination from hospital. During the examination, due to mass copying, all the students were 'reported against'. One year was spoiled. This 'shocking step' of the university was the first 'crucible' for the students. But the student did not get frustrated. Instead he pursued a realistic analysis, and accepted the crucible as a simple roadblock in his career. As on date, he is an accepted academician. Again, many persons have transformed following untoward incidents, for the crucibles produced negative impacts. Thus, the effects of crucibles can be positive as well as negative. A leader should react to crucibles in a positive manner and help his/her followers likewise.

LEADERSHIP DEVELOPMENTAL MECHANISMS

Leadership development is the process adopted to supply knowledge, skills, attitudes, and insights to managerial personnel discharging roles of leaders to help them manage the work effectively and efficiently. Manager may be transformed into leaders, and leaders are further developed through certain structured mechanisms like recruitment, training, delegation, 360-degree appraisal, mentoring, and other developmental mechanisms (Pareek 2008).

Recruitment

Leadership development may start with selecting people who are interested in learning, unlearning, and relearning. They definitely need to have the capability to develop qualities of leadership very fast. Potential leaders need to be identified during the process of selection using psychometric tests, interviews, simulation exercises, assessment centres, or other suitable means.

Training

Systematic training programmes are widely used to improve leadership skills of people. Any leader needs certain traits like integrity, loyalty, commitment, energy, decisiveness, and selflessness. Leadership training can take many forms, from a short one-week workshop to induce a particular skill or to induce a trait, to a long programme of six-month duration even to induce several required skills and traits. Leadership at different levels of an organization need different focuses.

Leaders need to tackle a variety of problems in multiple situations. As such, the true sprit of leadership training is to inculcate a variety of skills and traits to enable them to innovatively deal with complex issues. Need identification is of paramount importance. After this step, relevant experts must carefully design the training curriculum. Curriculum design must specify the topics, mode of transferring the intended knowledge, faculty deployment, training infrastructure, preparation of handouts, and so forth. A matrix showing 'Time and Facilities Required' may be of great help (Haldar 2009). After the programme, you need to perform post-training work for references.

Delegation for Leadership Development

Delegation is the process of transferring powers to junior colleagues such that the senior person can utilize the time saved in performing higher-level innovative activities and productively use his/her time. Another important reason for delegation is developing juniors. This process relies heavily on the assumption that every person in the organization has some assets with him/her like physical strength, competency, persuasive skills, convincing skills, interpersonal relation building skills, etc. All these form the power base of any person. If power is delegated, the decision-making abilities of the junior can be tested. Further, getting the power, one feels empowered, decides, and applies discretion in the better interest of the organization. Furthermore, the power can be seen as expanding and multiplying. Delegation is a formal way of enhancing enabling capacities. Before delegating, a leader must assess the capacity and willingness of the junior to accept more responsibility.

Making Delegation Effective

Delegation is not simply passing on the workload; rather it is a deliberate process. In order to delegate effectively, the scope of role boundaries should be decided upon jointly. The senior must make gap analysis with regard to skill and knowledge and arrange to fill the gap. The delegate should undertake self-assessment of the skills and knowledge required and what he/she possesses. He/she may need human resource to prepare documents and records to undertake analysis. Being empowered, he/she will try to execute the task and need many resources that the senior must provide. To keep the organizational wheel moving, the senior needs to monitor. But he/she must abstain from close supervision.

Mentoring

Mentoring is to develop work leadership. Mentoring has been discussed earlier.

Experiential Learning

Experiential learning requires no teacher and relates solely to the meaning-making process of the individual's direct experience. Experiential learning enables positioning of the individual in the focus of the learning process. The process goes through four stages of experiential learning: concrete experience, observation and reflection, forming abstract concepts, and testing in new situations. Experiential learning is the process of learning from direct experience. This is highly suited to the acquisition of practical skills, where trial and error and the opportunity to practice techniques related to real tasks is essential. Experiential learning, the way of acquiring skills, is integral to vocational education in many countries. Knowledge is continuously gained through both personal and environmental experiences. The learning method is focused on the learner and his/her experience as experiential education focuses on communicative relationship and the exchange of information between teacher and learner.

In order to gain genuine knowledge from an experience, a person needs certain abilities like (a) the learner must be willing to be actively involved in the experience, (b) the learner must be able to reflect on the experience, (c) the learner must possess and use analytical skills to conceptualize the experience, and (d) and the learner must possess decision-making and problem-solving skills in order to use of the new ideas gained from the experience. On-the-job-training, equipment simulators, games and simulation, case study and analysis, role-playing, behavioural modelling, sensitivity (or t-group) training are a few examples of experiential methods of learning.

360-Degree Appraisal

This appraisal system provides adequate inputs to decide upon the shortcomings of a person and initiate steps to overcome those. TV Rao Learning System (TVRLS) is an expression with a few decades of experience, study, review, reflection, and action combined with a desire to discover more about the behaviour of people in different settings and ways of making them give their best. The advisory board of TVRLS includes eminent personalities like Udai Pareek, R.S. Ramnarayan, and other renowned professionals and academicians. TVRLS has developed a model for Indian top and senior management levels in terms of managerial and leadership competencies needed. TVRLS terms it as the RSDQ model (Roles, Styles, Delegation, and Qualities). This model of leadership and managerial effectiveness views effective management and leadership as a combination of four sets of variables: roles, style, delegation, and qualities. The 'RSDQ Model of 360 Degree Feedback' is often referred to as 'Indian Model of Leadership Development'.

Roles   Role is the extent to which the individual plays various leadership and managerial roles and activities. There are a number of roles which have to be played by every manager in order to be effective. These are both transformational roles (leadership roles) and transactional roles (managerial). Some of these are the following:

- Articulating and communicating vision and values
- Formulating long-term policies and strategies
- Introducing and managing new technology and systems
- Inspiring, developing, and motivating juniors
- Managing juniors, colleagues, and seniors
- Culture building
- Internal customer management
- External customer management
- Managing unions and associations

The standard base questionnaire generally covers nine dimensions: vision and values; policy formulation and goal-setting; technology and system management; inspiring, developing, and empowering staff; culture building; teamwork and team building; management of colleagues/internal customers; liaison with boss and top management, and external customer relations and client management (total 55 questions).

Style   Style is one element of the 'McKinsey 7S Framework'. Effective managers recognize all the leadership roles and perform them well. It is not only the roles or activities that determine the effectiveness but also the way in which they are played. The model envisages that managers may play most roles well, devote time and effort, but they could be insensitive to the style with which they carry out these activities. Rao, in his research at the Indian Institute of Management, Ahmedabad, classified the styles in three categories: benevolent or paternalistic leadership style, critical leadership style, and developmental leadership style.

Benevolent or paternalistic leadership style The strategic apex believes that all employees should be constantly guided and treated with affection like a parent treats his/her children, and it is relationship-oriented, assigns tasks on the basis of the likes and dislikes of the subordinates, constantly guides and protects them, understands their needs, salvages situations of crisis by his/her active involvement, distributes rewards to those who are loyal and obedient and produces results, shares information with those who are close to him/her, etc.

Critical leadership style This style is characterized by its closeness to 'Theory X' belief pattern where the manager believes that employees should be closely and constantly supervised, directed, and reminded of their duties and responsibilities. The practitioners of this style are short-term goal oriented and cannot tolerate mistakes or conflicts among employees. They are personal power dominated, keep all information to himself/herself, work strictly according to norms and rules and regulations, and are highly discipline oriented.

Developmental leadership style Managers possessing this style believe in empowerment and the development of their employees' competencies, treat their subordinates as mature adults, leave them on their own most of the times, are long-term goal oriented, share information with all to build their competencies, and facilitate the resolution of conflicts and mistakes by employees themselves, with minimal involvement on his/her part. It has been found that the developmental style is the most desired organization-building style. However, some individuals and some situations at times, require the benevolent and critical styles. Research shows that some managers are not aware of the predominant style that they tend to use and the effects of their style on the employees.

Delegation The RSDQ model considers level of delegation as an important part of a senior executive's effectiveness. A senior executive delegates not only for offloading his/her own work, but also for managing the time in performing creative higher order tasks. Rao included this dimension because most senior managers seem to have difficulties in delegating, especially those who get promotions fast in their career. In view of these experiences, delegation was isolated as an important variable of leadership. Those who do delegate and continue to perform lower-level tasks suppress their leadership qualities and managerial effectiveness.

Qualities The model envisages that managers should exhibit qualities of leaders and world-class managers (proaction, listening, communication, positive approach, participative nature, quality orientation, etc.). Such qualities not only affect the effectiveness with which top-level managers perform various roles but also have an impact on the leadership style and hence are very critical.

ORGANIZATIONAL DRIVES TO DEVELOP LEADERSHIP

The modern (Western) management concepts of vision, leadership, motivation, excellence in work, achieving goals, making work meaningful, decision-making, and planning are all discussed in the Bhagavad Gita. Though, there is one major difference. While Western management thought too often deals with problems at the material, external, and peripheral levels, the Bhagavad Gita tackles the issues from the grass-roots level of human thinking. Once the basic thinking of humans is improved, it will automatically enhance the quality of their actions and results. Organizations are keen to impart leadership potential to its managers for obvious reasons. Let us study the initiatives taken by some organizations.

Nowadays organizations have realized that leadership can also be developed by strengthening the connection between and alignment of the efforts of individual leaders and the systems through which they influence organizational operations. Leadership development can work on the grooming of individuals (including followers) towards becoming leaders. Accordingly, organizations are keen to impart leadership potential and develop leaders in many ways.

Lakshmi et al. (2008) are of the opinion that leaders are made, and submit that some multinationals and their Indian subsidiaries like General Electric (GE), IBM India, and Hindustan Unilever Limited (HUL) have been at the cutting edge of leadership development for many years. Lakshmi et al. further say that Indian growth companies like Infosys Technologies, Tata Consultancy Services (TCS), Bharti Airtel, and Wipro have also been pioneers in this field and have been putting more emphasis on it, particularly, in the last few years. Eureka Forbes Limited (EFL) has also established its leadership development centre. A recent global survey by consultancy firms Hewitt and RBS International, along with *Fortune* magazine, has placed two Indian companies, HUL and Infosys, in the top ten. ICICI, Wipro, and TCS are amongst the top twenty. Further, the Indian subcontinent has been classified as one of the global hotspots. Indian companies have grown in scale and global exposures requiring new mindsets. Leadership development, proactively and innovatively, has emerged as a readymade solution to address the issue of the acute talent crunch. The drives of HUL, Infosys, TCS, IBM, and EFL are briefly discussed below.

HUL is a pioneer in the field of leadership development in India and was one of the first multinationals in the country to have developed a base of homegrown talent. The company strongly believes that the genesis of its performance culture lies in its leadership behaviours defined on the Standard of Leadership (SOL) framework, that are clearly aligned to business needs and realities. As HUL's executive director opines, 'Leadership is fostered in a culture where individuals are provided a chance to grow in their own way. The foremost job of leaders is to produce more leaders.' As such, there is sharp focus on six key leadership behaviours that need to be demonstrated by HUL managers. The behaviours are assessed through the performance management process (line manager feedback) and 360-degree feedback (mandatory only for senior leadership).

Infosys has developed a leadership matrix to measure its people on nine dimensions. Infosys on its part develops leaders from an early phase by measuring them against a customized nine-part leadership trait model. In addition to these dimensions, Infosys uses nine leadership pillars and six leadership traits. These will be discussed in detail in the chapter-end closing case on 'Leadership Development at Infosys Technologies'.

TCS is organizing classroom and web-based strategic leadership development programmes for its senior leadership team with the assistance of the M Ross School of Business, University of Michigan. TCS is making sustained and incremental investments, to the tune of 2 per cent of its revenue to build infrastructure for leadership development. Ambassador Corps is a comprehensive learning and development programme that prepares TCS employees in global sales roles. An intensive residential programme helps to lay emphasis on knowledge sharing, and conceptual, practical insights gleaned from the TCS leadership.

Bharti Airtel has a succession planning exercise for managers who are identified for the next 12 months. The company looks for traits such as entrepreneurship and the ability to think big. Bharti Airtel empowers the leaders to the maximum. The company's leadership strategy is closely intertwined with its corporate mission. The company strongly focuses on building a unified culture at the workplace to enable its leaders to gain entrepreneurial zeal and stretch themselves in terms of their execution capabilities.

IBM has some basic tenets and principles around which its leadership initiatives revolve. IBM provides a ten-day training programme a year per employee (six technical and three non-technical). It focuses much more on leadership training. The top team, from India and Global Leadership Development Team and Vice President (HR), has a monthly cadence calls to track progress. The company focuses on all levels without any gender bias and is keen to promote women to diversify leadership. IBM provides rotational assignments to its identified potential leaders, which are not limited to the country, and include global exposure. For example, a fresher can be identified as high potential, just after two years in IBM, and sent on an assignment to IBM headquarters in Armonk where he/she is exposed to the top management of the corporation to gain a deeper insight into leadership skills and styles. In essence, IBM tries to inculcate local and global skills and best practices among its employees.

Wipro, formerly known as Western India Vegetable Products, started its operation 1916. Now the company is a highly people-focused information technology corporation and has been one of the early companies to have launched cutting-edge leadership development programmes for its leaders. The leaders well understand the responsibility invested in them and adequately address it with respect to clients and employees. Wipro Infotech creates an environment where individuals can work in an unstructured manner and develop the self-initiative to succeed in any situation. Strong customer orientation and strategic thinking are the key to balance short-term and long-term goals. It specifically looks for strategic thinking, self-confidence, ability to work in teams, and inculcating leadership among others, and achieving orientation. See Box 8.3.

The company spends significant time and efforts to instil this confidence among employees through extensive leadership development programmes and these initiatives have paid rich dividends. Through this, Wipro brings its leadership closer to the client and builds trust and reliability in its service offerings. Adaptability across cultures and geographies has made Wipro the ideal partner to work with. Wipro Infotech's leadership reflects the global outlook and commitment to excellence, at the same time grooming new leaders who can make the company more agile to address new challenges. Wipro, while having both individual and team development initiatives,

Box 8.3 Wipro leadership qualities

Wipro concentrates on eight pillars:

Strategic thinking: Anticipating the future through an articulated vision.

Customer orientation: Customer at the centre of the vision.

Aggressive commitments: Pursue stretched commitments with determination and focus.

Global thinking and acting: Global cultural synchronization with respect to issues and trends.

Self-confidence: Belief in the ability of self and the team.

Commitment to excellence: Commitment to surpass the best with respect to global standards.

Working in teams: Encouraging harmony and synergy for getting multiplier effect from the team.

Building future leaders: Spending time with team; coaching and pursuing developmental needs of the team.

(Based on a lecture by Ranjan Acharya, Vice President—HR, Wipro, on 25 April 2008 at the All India Management Association, New Delhi.)

also believes that leadership development is a continuous journey and not just an event.

EFL uses multi-source assessment and feedback system reports for leadership development. EFL has leadership development centres in many places in the country. The primary focus of the company is on observing the potential and ability of the employees viz-à-viz their performance. The process objectively analyses leadership competencies through multiple simulations or exercises, and trained assessors. It gives feedback on an individual's ability to display behaviours related to the competencies. EFL has leadership development centres in fourteen cities in India. The 360-degree format of EFL incorporates leadership factors—vision and strategic thinking, business acumen, influence, planning and execution, collaboration and teamwork, and people development. EFL is laying emphasis on thinking factors (analysis and judgement, and innovation and continuous improvement), relationship factors (interpersonal, communication, and customer focus), and self-management factors (initiative and drive, result orientation, resilience, integrity and ethics, and self development).

Titan (Tata group's watch manufacturing company) implemented 360-degree feedback way back in 2001 for senior management as a development-focused tool for leadership development, team building, potential development, in addition to training needs identification and internal customer relations building. The 360-degree feedback was extended to middle management in 2004. The company launched the web-based application in 2004 for senior management, and in 2005, it was introduced for the middle managers.

Titan is using the RSQ model where RSQ indicates role, style, and quality. As regard to role, Titan is trying to identify 'How well the manager is able to exhibit Tata Leadership Practices in the leadership and managerial roles that he/she plays.' The company is instrumental in locating critical managerial and leadership qualities. In order to identify style, the company is collecting information on the manner in which managers carry out their roles as supervisor/boss.

Titan has classified three styles: benevolent or paternalistic leadership (acts like a parent, relationship oriented, plays favourites, and guides and protects), critical leadership (belief in 'theory X' of Herzberg motivation theory that emphasizes the negative aspects of an individual, close and constant monitoring, short-term goal orientation, does not share information, and high discipline but low tolerance), and developmental leadership (empowering style, develops competencies, long-term orientation, open communication, and delegation). The qualities considered Titan are at organizational commitment, interpersonal relations and teamwork, leadership and employee development, values, and strengths and weaknesses.

With the growing need to develop leaders, companies can achieve this by setting up leadership or management development centres. The oldest is the Tata Management and Training Centre (TMTC) established in 1966, in Pune. TMTC has always been instrumental in developing its personnel who significantly contribute to the Tata group's operations.

Challenges Faced by an Organization

Considering the utmost need for leaders, leadership development organizations are instrumental in initiating programmes and are facing challenges in creating a global leadership pool. Kumar Mangalam Birla narrates his experience in creating global leadership pool in the Aditya Birla Group:

'I believe the more you invest in talent development, the more you run the risk of raising aspirations. This may turn into dysfunctional internal competition. The efforts required to manage expectations have to be as robust as the talent development itself. One important feature of our employer brand is that talent from anywhere in the organization is able to bubble up through the layers to the top based on merit. We will see that top management of ABG in the future being multinational as opposed to being only Indian. This would need more flexibility—culturally and in working methods.

We are acutely aware that we have a long way to cover in our quest of creating global leaders. I would like to emphasize that the brand of leadership that we seek to build combines the virtues of professionalism with the commanding powers of heart, mind and soul. Our biggest strength has been an emotional bonding that our employees have with the groups, that makes the paradigm of duty truly without boundaries.'

The salient point is that the talent development drive is likely to end in managing expectation; managers' need to adopt flexible culture and methods. A critical challenge for organizations today is the leadership bandwidth needed to access all opportunities and execute ideas for value creation. Today, most successful organizations are realizing that they have been good at management development, but have not done enough towards leadership development. Excellent managers need to be transformed to leaders. Recognizing these imperatives, the AIMA organized a workshop on 'Developing Global Leadership Skills: A Pipeline Approach'. The key takeaways from the workshop are the following:

- Achieve breakthrough profitability
- Create organization capacities to manage hypergrowth and hypertransformation
- Institutionalize leadership programmes
- Maximize stakeholder satisfaction
- Develop execution excellence
- Catalyse people engagement and development
- Use 'style flex' for diverse groups
- Calculate return on investment on leadership

The takeaways indicate the need for organizations to take leadership development initiatives. Managers move up the organizational hierarchy step by step. A movement to the next higher position is a passage. Organizational leaders should be aware of the passages.

LEADERSHIP PASSAGES: AN OVERVIEW

The six turns in the leadership pipeline are major events in the life of a leader (Ram Charan et al. 2001). Each turn represents a significant passage, which needs adequate time to understand and master. Each passage demands familiarization with the skills, time applications, and work values. On understanding the need of each passage and the challenges involved in each transition, one can facilitate self-growth as a leader and can assess the organization's leadership pipeline. When a person moves through the passages, he/she takes up tasks of increasing responsibility and complexity. While moving through the passages, leaders gain emotional strength as they take on tasks of increasing complexity and scope.

Awareness of the six passages provides one with ideas and tools to achieve optimal performance at all leadership levels in the organization. Ram Charan alerts that one may find a turn or passage in his/her organization not addressed in the leadership pipeline model. They say that the passage may not be a major one. Transition from team member to team leader is not worthy of a passage as this is usually a subset of the passage 'managing self to managing others'.

Furthermore, team leaders commonly lack the decision-making authority on selection and rewards that first-line managers receive. Also, team leaders usually focus on technical or professional matters (getting a project or programme completed) and are not tested in more general management areas.

The six passages are:

Passage One: From Managing Self to Managing Others
Passage Two: From Managing Others to Managing Managers
Passage Three: From Managing Managers to Functional Manager
Passage Four: From Functional Manager to Business Manager
Passage Five: From Business Manager to Group Manager
Passage Six: From Group Manager to Enterprise Manager

Passage One: From Managing Self to Managing Others

New recruits after joining an organization spend time in learning professional skills in their job functions such as sales, accounting, engineering, or marketing. Apart from gaining job-related skills, they learn planning, and appreciate punctuality, content, quality, and reliability. In course of time, they understand values, accept company culture, adopt professional standards, become good organizational citizens and individual contributors, and demonstrate an ability to collaborate with others and receive additional responsibilities. They further demonstrate an ability to handle responsibilities to plan work, assign work, motivate, coach, and measure the work of others adhering to the company's values. They do these when they are in passage one.

It is evidenced that high performers continue to do what made them successful; they transit from individual contributor to manager without making a behavioural or value-based transition. Skipping this turn, moving from transitory team leadership to business leader may lead to disaster at a later stage. Actually, they must shift from 'doing work' to 'getting work done through others'. Some managers at the initial stage prefer to spend time on their 'old' work even after taking charge of a group though they should spend more time in managing. At this passage, the most difficult change involves values. Managers are required to value managerial work rather than just tolerate it. They must view other-directed work as mission critical to their success. Changes in skills and time applications can be seen and measured but changes in values are more difficult to assess.

Ram Charan et al. (2001) add that, 'Value changes will only take place if upper management reinforces the need to shift beliefs and if people find they're successful at their new jobs after a value shift.'

Passage Two: From Managing Others to Managing Managers

Managers manage a group of subordinates or lead a group of followers. Managing such managers definitely needs expertise and capabilities. The biggest difference from the previous passage is that managers must be pure management persons. To manage managers, one needs to divest oneself of individual tasks. At this stage, managers need to think beyond the normal domain of function and concern themselves with strategic issues that support the overall business. A manager needs to forgo individual contributions and functional work for the greater interest of the company. He/she should not change the skills, time applications of work value, and thus avoid clogging the leadership pipeline. He/she must prefer and choose highly technical people as first-line managers. He/she cannot differentiate between those 'who can do' and 'who can lead'. If he/she continues to do so, he/she would poison managerial reserves.

A 'software designer' developing superb products, an expert technician solving many production problems, or a maintenance engineer reducing machine downtime is unlikely to move up to a leadership role. To become a leader, they need both coaching and mentoring skills. But, unfortunately coaching ability in not rewarded and not even recognized.

Passage Three: From Managing Managers to Functional Manager

Functional heads need to manage some areas outside their own domain and experience. They need to understand and learn to value the 'foreign' work. In this passage of moving from 'managing managers' to a functional manager, new communication skills are required. Functional managers report to general managers who perform multifunctional duties, or at least manage managers of many functional areas. As such, functional managers must consider other areas and gain skills in developing knowledge of other functional concerns. They are at play with other functional managers and compete for resources based on business needs. They should become proficient strategists, for their function as well as for blending their functional strategy with the overall business strategy. Obviously, functional managers cannot devote time to purely functional responsibilities. They need to delegate responsibility or overseeing of many functional tasks to those who directly report to them. They have to decide whom to delegate a task and to what extent. This leadership passage requires an increase in managerial maturity, that is, thinking and acting like a functional leader rather than a functional member. They design long-term functional strategy, such as state-of-the-art, futurity of present plans, and long-term consideration of their functions. The strategies include designing more innovative products, penetrating new customer groups, deriving sustainable competitive advantages, etc.

Passage Four: From Functional Manager to Business Manager

The sphere of duties, responsibilities, and job requirements of business managers is wider compared to that of functional managers. The passage from functional manager to business manager is most satisfying as well as the most challenging in the professional career of a manager. Business mangers usually receive significant autonomy. People with leadership intuition and instinct find this passage most liberating and can see a clear link between their efforts and marketplace results. Due to the sharp turn in this passage, people need a major shift in skills, time applications, and work values as they are going to be an in-charge of integrating functions. They must look at plans and proposals functionally and must get responses to questions like 'can we do it technically, professionally, or physically?' Thus, they have to carry out techno-economic feasibility analysis with the aim of achieving sustainable profit. Business managers perform this journey in unexplored territory, as at this position they become responsible for many unfamiliar functions and outcomes. Top management expects business managers to manage quarterly profit, market share, product and people targets, and at the same time plan for goals three to five years into the future. Ram Charan et al. (2001) alert managers to stop acting at the last moment and reserve time for reflection and analysis as incomplete tasks result in the leadership pipeline quickly becoming clogged. Business managers must learn to trust, accept advice, receive feedback from all functional managers, and analyse situations and outcomes irrespective of their background.

Passage Five: From Business Manager to Group Manager

The term group manager applies to a manager managing more than one business or different strategic business units, producing different types of products. For each unit, there may be one business manager and a group manager heads the group of units. A business manager values the success of his/her own business. A group manager will obviously value all the businesses under his/her control. Moreover, group managers have to value the success of other people's businesses. Unless they value and derive pleasure from the success of other's businesses, they would not be able to inspire and support the performance of the business managers who report to them. This spreads the essence of community leadership.

Four skill sets are essential for the critical shift in this passage.

1. Group managers must become proficient at evaluating strategy for capital allocation and deployment purposes.
2. The second skill cluster involves development of business managers. Group managers need in-depth knowledge of people down the hierarchy. A group manager needs to know who among the functional managers are ready to become business managers. Coaching is an important role for this level.
3. The third skill set has to do with portfolio strategy, which is quite different from business strategy. This skill demands a perceptual shift. This is the first time when managers have to ask questions like 'Do I have the right collection of businesses? What businesses should be added, subtracted, or changed to position us properly and assure current and future earnings?'
4. Group managers must become astute, be perceptive and perform self-assessment to evaluate whether they have the right core capabilities to win. They need to initiate a systematic approach, look objectively at their range of resources, and make judgements based on an analysis of facts and figures, and experience. It is needless to mention that leadership becomes more holistic at this level. People may master the required skills but may not be able to perform at full leadership capacity unless they begin to see themselves as broad-gauge executives. This is so because group managers are required to run multiple businesses, and

think in terms of community, industry, government, and ceremonial activities. In small companies, CEOs usually undertake the group manager's responsibilities.

Passage Six: From Group Manager to Enterprise Manager

Unlike the five previous passages, transition during the sixth passage is much more focused on values than on skills. People must reinvent their self-concepts as enterprise managers to a greater extent than at the previous level. As institution builders, they must aim at long-term objectives and be visionary thinkers. They need to develop operating mechanisms to know and drive business performance at short intervals. They can act locally but need to think globally in tune with long-term strategy. The trade-offs involved can be mind-bending, and enterprise leaders learn to value these trade-offs. Enterprise managers need to ascertain the direction and speed of changes in the global business environment. Therefore, leaders require a well-developed external sensitivity, innate or learned ability to manage external constituencies, sense significant external shifts, and act accordingly.

Enterprise leaders need to realize that their performance as a CEO will be based on three or four high-level decisions each year. They must set these three or four mission-critical priorities and focus on them. During this passage, there is a subtle but fundamental shift in responsibility from strategic to visionary thinking and from an operation to a global perspective. Enterprise leaders need to focus sharper attention on the whole to find an answer to the question 'how well do we conceive, develop, produce, and market all products to all customers?'

At the enterprise leader level, a CEO needs to assemble teams of high-achieving and ambitious direct reports. This is also the only leadership position in the organization where inspiring all the organizational citizens through a variety of communication tools is essential. Leadership pipeline problems occur at this level for two common reasons:

- CEOs are often unaware that this is a significant passage that requires changes in values that they can develop these values through a strong will and conscious efforts. A leader may fail if he/she sustains the same set of skills, time application, and values as that of a group manager.
- Preparation for the chief executive's position is the result of a series of diverse experiences over a long time. The developmental approach must be steady, providing carefully selected job assignments to stretch

the CEOs over a prolonged period of time. Otherwise, it is difficult to develop a CEO for this particular leadership transition.

If the business needs more people and offices or products, the owner must again go through a leadership passage. Because he/she cannot be everywhere at once, he/she must appoint additional managers and hold them accountable for various managerial responsibilities. The work of the entire enterprise needs integration to properly serve customers and ensure that resources are used efficiently. In this role, the leader must make sure that the total effort is profitable and sustainable.

Passages through the Pipeline

Any manager needs knowledge of all the passages to be successful at the highest level. Therefore, he must pass through each of them to understand their respective gravity and need. While functioning in a passage, he/she learns the hidden leadership problems. The manager, as well as the organization need to realize this. At one level, he/she should perform duties essential for that particular level. An organization, if it is acutely aware of these leadership passages, can quickly diagnose any problem hindering the passage and initiate actions to aid and develop the manager. A development programme could be created targeting to bridge the identified deficiencies. Managers in one level are responsible and accountable for developing managers in the immediate junior level.

The pipeline model does not allow any passage to be skipped. The unique advantage of the pipeline model is that it provides a measurement system to identify when someone is ready to move to the next leadership level. The model reduces the typical time-frame needed to prepare an individual for the top leadership position in a large corporation. The beauty of the model is that it clearly defines what is needed to move from one level to the next, and there is thus little or no wastage, of time on jobs that merely duplicate skills. From a pure talent perspective, however, the most significant benefit of the pipeline methodology is that one does not need external expertise to prime the leadership pump. An organization can create its own exports up and down the line, beginning at the first level when people make the transition from managing themselves to managing others.

FLOWCHART OF LEADERSHIP DEVELOPMENT

Leader and leadership development need systematic approaches. Organizations must determine acquaintance of the leader with the organizational leadership pillars, dimensions of leadership, generic leadership traits, position in leadership pipeline, and specific skills needed to accomplish a task.

The process of leadership development is represented through the flowchart in Figure 8.1. The process, which incorporates training curriculum design, has been explained through a separate flowchart in Figure 8.2.

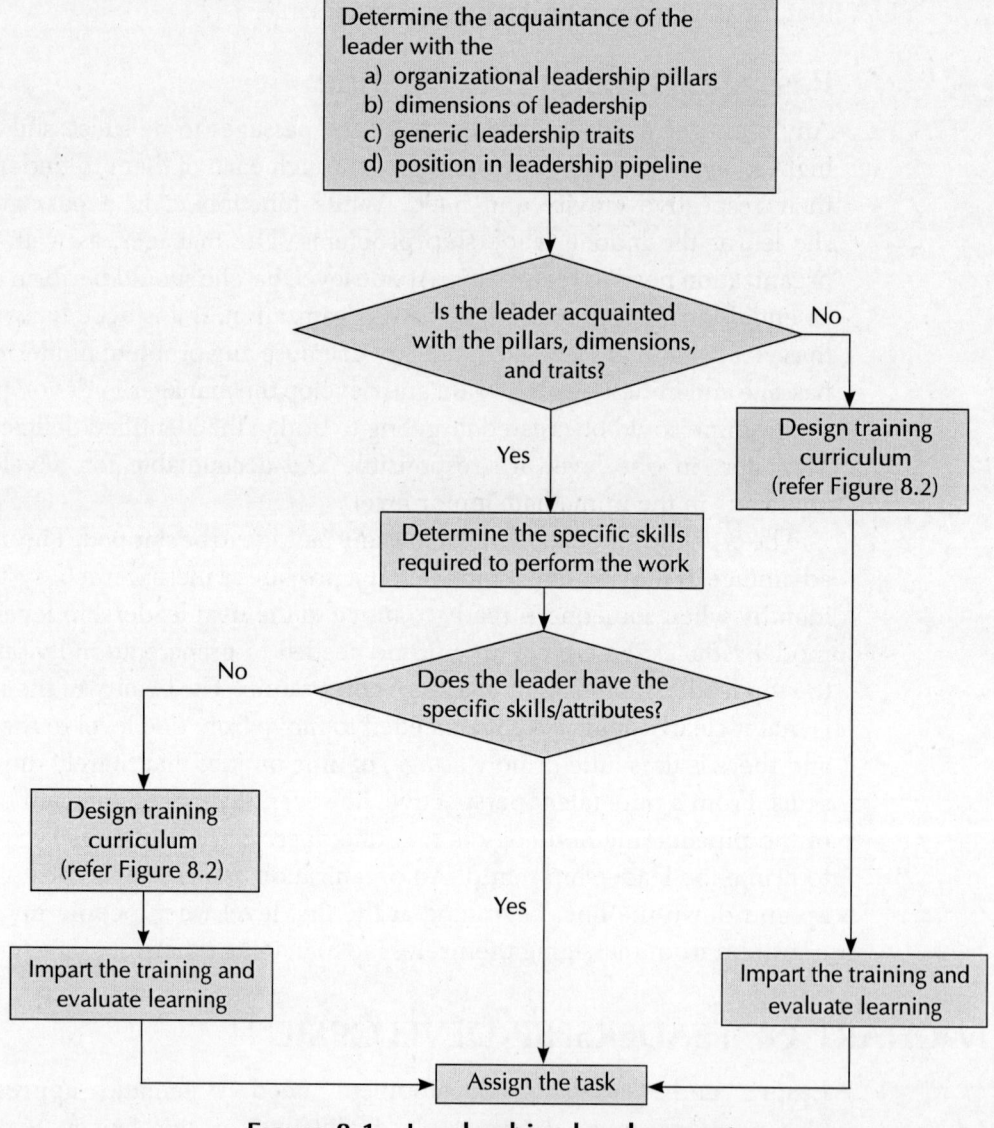

FIGURE 8.1 **Leadership development**

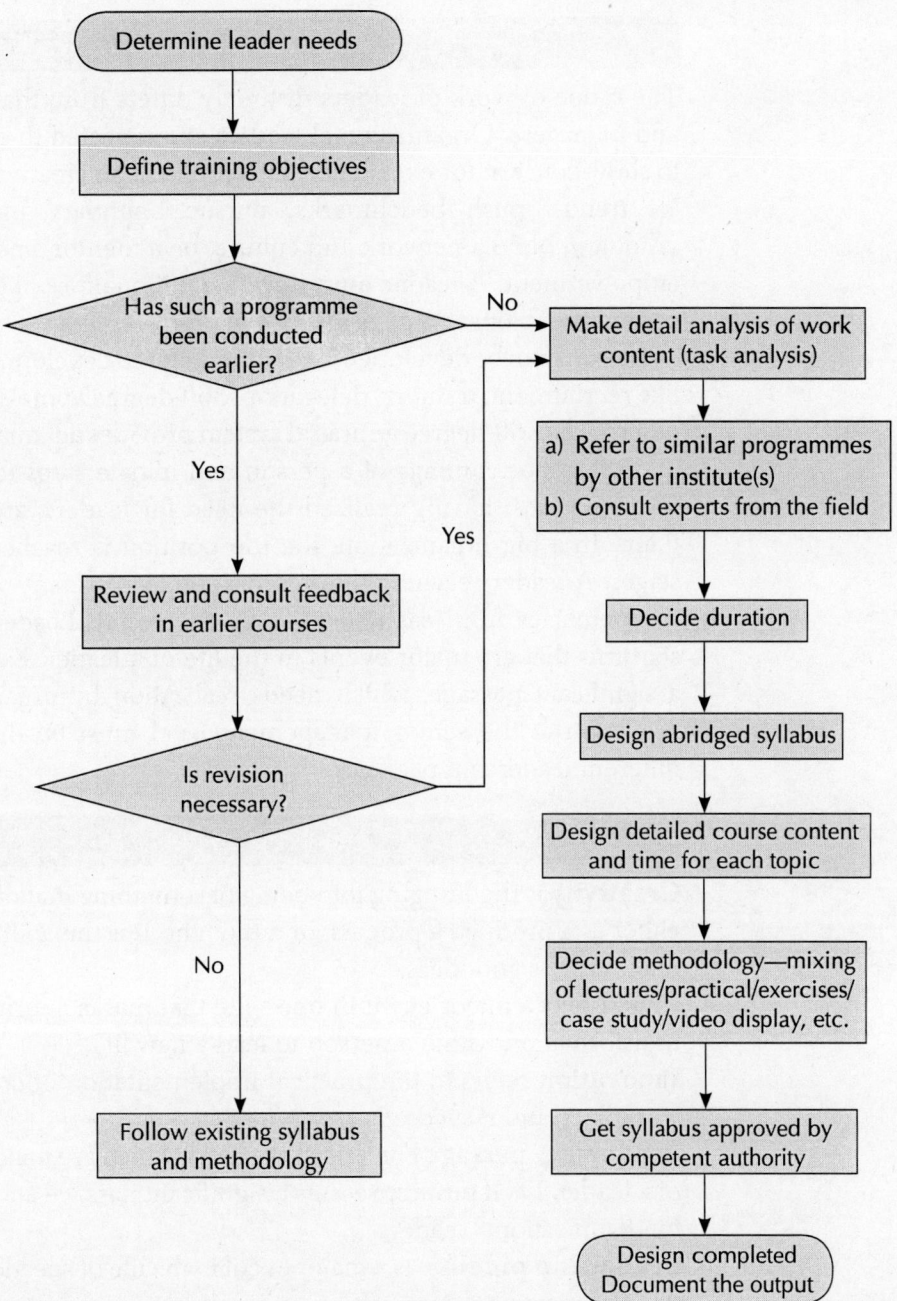

FIGURE **8.2** **Designing training curriculum**

(Based on OFILIS Model in Uday Kumar Haldar, *Human Resource Development* [2009], Oxford University Press, New Delhi.)

SUMMARY

The scope of work of leaders distinctly differs from that of administrators and managers. Organizational leaders are expected to excel. A leader has to show concern for excellence, lay emphasis on creativity and innovation, set trends, push benchmarks, pursue boundary management, be a visionary, build a network and culture, be a mentor, and multiply through empowerment. A leader must have certain qualities like integrity, loyalty, commitment, energy, decisiveness, and selflessness.

Leaders can be developed through structured developmental mechanisms like recruitment, training, delegation, 360-degree appraisal, mentoring, and others. The 360-degree appraisal system provides adequate inputs to decide upon the shortcomings of a person and initiate steps to overcome those. Organizations, having realized the need for leaders, are keen to develop them. In a big organization, the top position is reached through various stages. A leader reaching the top position learns many skills and develops competencies from each stage to be successful. Leadership pipeline has six turns that are major events in the life of a leader. Each turn represents a significant passage, which needs realization by organizational leaders. A person at the senior management level must be thorough about the different leadership passages.

KEY TERMS

Creativity is the bringing into being of something that did not exist before, either as a product, a process, or a thought. It is the ability to discover new relationships and ideas.

Crucible is a major event in one's life that marks a turning point or helps transformation within a person to lead a new life.

Innovation refers to the practical implementation of creative ideas at the workplace and it succeeds creativity.

Leadership passage consists of six turns, which are major events in the life of a leader. Each turn represents a significant passage and needs realization by organizational leaders.

Leadership pipeline is a major event in the life of a leader while ascending the organizational hierarchy that comprises six turns and the final turn is the top position.

EXERCISES

Concept Review Questions

1. Mention the qualities a leader must have. What might be the consequences in the absence of a particular quality? Consider the functions of a leader and discuss with examples.
2. Discuss the need for developing leadership and the concepts behind this drive. How does a leader distinguish himself/herself from an administrator or a manager? Narrate your answer citing five dimensions.
3. What are the techniques used by organizations to develop leadership?
4. What is meant by 'crucible'? Discuss the principal crucibles in the context of leadership development.
5. Name the various mechanisms used by organizations for leadership development. How do you conceive the mechanism 'experiential learning'?

Critical Thinking Questions

1. Discuss all the possible effects of 'crucibles' in one's organizational life. Can you remember a crucible from your past that has an effect on the present?
2. Develop a questionnaire to ascertain whether the style of working of five managers has changed after attending leadership development programmes. While designing the questionnaire, assume that he/she attended the programme about a year back.
3. Consider the leadership pipeline with six leadership passages. Comment on how an organization can derive benefits from them.

Assignments

1. Organizations are engaged in developing leaders. Visit any two organizations and prepare a list of activities they are adopting. The list must show methods of identifying the needs and mechanisms commonly used for evaluating developmental programmes. Compare the lists and draw a conclusion.
2. Visit an organization that has implemented 360-degree feedback system. How is the organization identifying the deficiencies of the leader? Prepare an exhaustive list of points that are considered as weaknesses by the organization.

REFERENCES

Bennis, Warren G. and Robert J. Thomas (2002), *Geeks and Geezers: How Ero, Values, and Defining Moments Shape Leaders*, Harvard Business Press, US.

Birla, Kumar Mangalam (2009), J.R.D. Tata Memorial Award Lecture delivered at the All India Management Association on 21 February, *AIMA News* (Newsletter of All India Management Association, New Delhi).

Charan, Ram, Steve Drodder, and Jim L. Noel (2001), *The Leadership Pipeline: How to Build the Leadership Powered Company*, Wiley (Jossy-Bass: A Wiley Reprint), New Delhi.

Haldar, Uday Kumar (2009), *Human Resource Development*, Oxford Higher Education, Oxford University Press, New Delhi.

Lakshmi, S., Shyamal Mazumdar, and George Skaria (2008), Building Future Leaders, *Indian Management* (Journal of the All India Management Association), January, Vol. 47, No. 1.

Maxwell, John C. (2001), *Developing the Leader Within You*, Magna Publishing Co. Ltd, Mumbai.

Pareek, Udai (2008), *Understanding Organizational Behaviour*, Oxford Higher Education, Oxford University Press, New Delhi.

Ramnarayan, S. (2007), The Four Challenges of Leadership, *Indian Management* (Journal of All India Management Association), Vol. 46, No. 3, pp. 62–64.

Rao, T.V., Raju Rao, and Soumya Dixit (2002), 'A Study of Leadership Roles, Styles, Delegation, and Qualities of Indian CEOs', in Ashad M. Osmani, S. Ramnarayan, and T.V. Rao (eds), *Human Resource Development in Asia: Trends and Challenge*, Oxford and IBH, New Delhi.

Tharappan, Shushant (2008), Record of Discussion, dated 13 October 2009 (Infosys Technologies, Bangalore).

Leadership Development at Infosys Technologies: The Infosys Model

About the Company

Infosys Technologies does not need any introduction. However, a point needs to be mentioned. Infosys believes that 'aspiration is the main fuel for progress. Aspirations transform a set of ordinary people into extraordinary achievers.' The company has become a role model for its value-based leadership, exemplary corporate governance, best-in-class processes, caring and development of people, commendable wealth creation, and delivery of world-class products and services. Infosys believes in the power of talent.

Vision behind Infosys Leadership Programme

The vision of Infosys is to create an organization that is 'built to last', and has the agility and liveliness to manage ambiguity and uncertainty under all circumstances. The vision is in continuance with the ideal set by N.R. Narayana Murthy, the founder and former CEO of the company and currently chairman and chief mentor. He carefully put together at the Management Council, an advisory body that took strategic decisions about the company. The company observed the people of the younger generation hesitated to come forth with their suggestions. On encouraging them to speak, Murthy found their suggestions and thoughts had a lot of substance and could help the company significantly. These people had not contributed to the discussions not because they had nothing of value to add, but because they were afraid of transgressing hierarchy.

The hesitations bothered Murthy significantly and from this concern was born his grand plan to build a leadership institute that would groom and develop leaders from among promising employees of Infosys (Infoscions), irrespective of hierarchy, and give them the opportunity to shape the future of the company they were helping to build. Infosys went through an assessment to look at all the aspects of its business, as well as how it was doing. It discovered one of the areas for improvement, which was the need to have a structured way of developing leaders.

As a result, the company established its leadership institute in 2001 at Mysore and named it Infosys Leadership Institute (ILI). The fundamental goal of the ILI is to fulfil this stated need: to enhance the enabling capacities in responding to specific challenges of the present and future. The vision behind setting up the leadership institute was to create leaders of tomorrow. The various programmes focus on nurturing leaders with a global perspective. ILI grooms leaders and provides them the opportunity to shape the future of Infosys. Infosys believes in empowering its employees.

Infosys was the first Indian company to set up a formalized leadership institute. The company has developed a three-tier leadership model, based on the belief that 'the company is the campus, the business is the curriculum, and leaders shall teach'. Senior members of the Infosys management conduct courses on leadership at the institute, drawing from their experiences. This drive helps the company to attract, retain, and motivate the best and the brightest talent from India and abroad. Each year, it grooms about 700 to 800 employees.

Leadership Development in Infosys

The company does not have any specific mechanism to identify leaders though it has a structured system. It invites applications from employees at the middle- and senior-level management to undergo the leadership programmes. The leadership competency department evaluates these applications on the basis of nine leadership competencies formulated by the company and selects employees for different sets of programmes. So, the entire initiative starts from identifying what are the competencies that the organizational leaders need.

The ILI ensures that talent is optimally harnessed to stay ahead of the innovation curve. Its dedicated campus in Mysore, India, offers courses on leadership and management. ILI grooms high-potential candidates under a three-tier mentoring process. Tier 1 includes business leaders and leaders of business enabler functions, Tier 2 has people who can take on Tier 1 responsibility in three to five years, and Tier 3 consists of Infoscions expected to reach Tier 1 category in six to ten years. Every Infoscion in the leadership programme has a mentor. A member of the board of directors mentors a Tier 1 leader, whereas Tier 1 and Tier 2 leaders mentor Tier 2 and Tier 3 leaders, respectively. As on July 2009, 45 executives are a part of Tier 1 council. Each of the leader undergoes exhaustive and sustained trans/development through the company's personal development programmes. Other ILI initiatives are 'Pravesh', a programme for first-time project managers, and the 'Global Business Finishing School'.

Nine Leadership Pillars

Infosys uses nine pillars for leadership development: (1) 360-degree feedback, (2) development assignments, (3) Infosys culture workshops, (4) development relationships, (5) leadership skills training, (6) feedback-intensive programmes, (7) systemic process learning, (8) action learning, and (9) community empathy.

1. 360-degree feedback—The multi-source assessment and feedback system, a long-felt organizational need, emphasizes the softer dimensions of performance like leadership, creativity, originality, innovation, teamwork, initiative, emotional intelligence, entrepreneurship, etc. This is the mechanism through which the company gathers data about an individual's performance and abilities. This information is collected from co-workers, including peers, subordinates, managers, and customers. Personal development plans are prepared on the basis of this feedback. Then, each of these individuals is assigned an ILI faculty member to help prepare the personal development plan and to follow it.
2. Development assignments—Infosys identifies high-potential employees (Infoscions) at various functions of the company and trains them through job rotation and cross-functional assignments. This helps employees to acquire new leadership skills outside their own areas of expertise and experience.

3. Infosys culture workshops—These tailor-made workshops help to fortify and strengthen the Infosys culture among the participants, help instil better communication skills through sustained interaction among participants, and identify with the values and processes involved in leadership development.
4. Development relationships—The company believes in healthy relationships among various levels of personnel. This includes one-on-one interaction in actual on-the-job work climate and leads to better sharing of knowledge and camaraderie/companionship among individuals. Mentoring forms an integral part of this exercise that strengthens camaraderie or friendship.
5. Leadership skills training—The 'Leaders Teach Series' are workshops that the company's Tier 1 members, including Narayana Murthy (Chairman and Chief Mentor) and Kris Gopalakrishan (CEO and MD), hold to acclimatize the next rung with leadership roles and to groom them through their own rich experience.
6. Feedback-intensive programmes—These are similar to 360-degree feedback, but based on formal and informal feedback from employees that an individual interacts with.
7. Systemic process learning—Infoscions gain an overall view of the company and its diverse and complex systems, businesses, operations, and processes. It is a continuous process and helps improve the individual and also the systems.
8. Action learning—Infosys believes and encourages working in teams. Action learning is an exercise constituting solving real problems in real-time conditions, but as a team.
9. Community empathy—A company functions in society. Infosys stresses the need to give back to society through involvement in various developmental, educational, and social causes. This programme helps nurture a social conscience among its leaders.

Leadership Traits

The company looks for six leadership traits in its employees.

1. High penetration for self and organization—An employee, as a leader, can penetrate deeper through self-assessment, which is a process to assess what one is doing, why he/she is doing it, and what he/she must do to improve the organization's performance. There are five essential questions in the process: What is our mission? Who is our customer? What does the customer value? What are our results? What is our plan?
2. Passion for excellence—Without enthusiasm and excitement of its people, an organization cannot gain excellence, become a role model, display

value-based leadership, exhibit exemplary corporate governance, and so forth.

3. Team player—Each team player must have role clarity, should know his/her role, and how his/her job fits in with the others. No matter what the office politics is, each team member must do the assigned work. If each person on the team makes it a point to treat each member of the team with respect no matter what personal matters or matters of office politics are between them, they can still operate as team players working to get the job done.

4. Desire in learnability—Infosys, believing in continuous learning, inculcates the spirit of learnability among Infoscions and fulfils its organizational commitment to continuous personal and professional development. This keeps Infosys at the forefront in a fast-changing industry.

5. Courage to take risk—One cannot avoid taking risks in the workplace. A person with high risk-taking propensity ultimately wins the game even if the playing field is the work area. But one should take calculated risks. A good leader has the courage to take risks. Of course, organizational environment matters.

6. Focus on results and attention to detail—The result or outcome and the process are important. Process approach to an activity helps to complete it with perfection.

Nine Dimensions of Leadership

Infosys believes that the leadership must drive the creation of a leadership funnel at different levels of the organization, must be cantered on the Infoscions, and must be rooted in the organizational context. There cannot be any single mantra to develop leadership: it needs multiple methods and multiple directions. Strategic leadership, change leadership, operational leadership, talent leadership, relationship/networking leadership, content leadership, entrepreneurial leadership, transactional leadership, and adversity leadership are the nine dimensions Infosys is looking for. These nine dimensions are explained for an in-depth understanding, whatever the nature of business maybe.

1. Strategic leadership—It is about unique positioning: how one can create a unique position for the company. Strategic leadership is about creating an agile and flexible organization which can cope with changes in the business environment and suitably respond to them.

2. Change leadership—It is about changing the context and making change effective. A leader, particularly a top-level leader, must have the vision to anticipate the direction and speed of changes in the business environment. Accordingly, he/she has to finalize steps to bring changes in the organization, and communicate the reasons behind the internal

changes to various levels of personnel. While incorporating the changes, many issues would emerge, which he/she must handle with a combination of firmness and flexibility.

3. Operational leadership—It is about achieving a high degree of effectiveness and productivity. This leadership refers to defining operational excellence in the organizational context, considering the framework used to achieve operational excellence and judging the used parameters for rightness.

4. Talent leadership—It is about creating a top-quality leadership team, globally best in class in the relevant area. A top-level manager must understand the need for nurturing talent and develop a system to identify talent of middle- and junior-level managers and provide them with the required inputs so that their potentials are realized. A top-level organizational leader has to see himself as a teacher or coach and devote time to developing the next level of leaders.

5. Relationship/networking leadership—It is about building bridges of relationship, and developing, maintaining, and leveraging long-term internal and external relationship networks. In fact, relationships operate at different levels in an organization and with various influential agencies that can impact the business. A leader must understand the difference between the breadth and depth of a relationship grid. A suitable communication strategy needs to go hand in hand, with the relation-building strategy.

6. Content leadership—It is about thought leadership, which can be applied for intellectual property rights. Content leadership needs assessing the level of domain expertise of the business. The domain can be banking, insurance, advertising, software development, etc. If the domain is banking technology, the content includes core banking, internet banking, and customer relations management.

7. Entrepreneurial leadership—It is about having entrepreneurial zeal and showing ownership for business outcomes. The entrepreneurial zeal of a manager takes him/her from a humdrum and monotonous state to a state in which he/she can contribute effectively to the organization. This skill encompasses power of imagination and commitment in the face of challenges.

8. Transactional leadership—It is about acquiring and integrating new lines of business. Transactional leaders create clear structures whereby it is clear what is required of their subordinates, and the rewards that they would get for following orders. They do not always propose the type of punishment for non-conformance or when things go wrong. The transactional leader often uses management decisions by exception, working on the principle that if something is operating to an expected and defined performance level, then it does not need attention. Beyond expectation performances

require praise and reward for exceeding expectations, while some kind of corrective action is applied for performance below expectation.

9. Adversity leadership—Adversity may arise from differences in region, religion, language spoken, gender, belief system, cultural and social backgrounds, etc. Adversity is a part and parcel of any business organization. It can be small or big, and is likely to impede the functioning of business. As a leader, you have to handle adversity, whatever be its intensity. A leader learns from his/her experiences and initiates steps to prevent recurrence of such situations. However, Infosys has an adversity centre to manage problems arising out of diversity.

Leadership Journey

Infosys selects high-potential personnel through structured systems. The leadership journey starts from this point as the company keeps track of their performance. It identifies a pool of employees (Infoscions) on the basis of past performance and leadership potential. The duration of leadership is long enough. The company classifies a segment of Infoscions as 'high potentials'. One ILI faculty member is attached with each high-potential employee. The former guides the latter through the leadership journey and helps to develop the employee. The faculty member provides all-round support in implementing the individual change objectives. All high-potential employees are trained at ILI. The faculty member acts as coach, mentor, counsellor, and internal consultant to enhance enabling capacities, which helps the employee become capable of undertaking complex assignments and resolving real business issues efficiently and effectively.

(Case written by the author based on a discussion with Dr Shushant Tharappan, Associate Vice President and member of the senior leadership of Infosys Leadership Institute, on 13 October 2008.)

Discussion Questions

1. How does Infosys involve people, particularly new recruits, and get their opinions in formal meetings? Comment on the action plans of the company to develop them.
2. Consider the nine pillars of leadership and discuss the role of developmental assignments in the context of 360-degree feedback.
3. Community empathy is one of the nine pillars of leadership. Does this pillar contribute to leadership development? Discuss critically.
4. 'Relationship/networking leadership' and 'operational leadership' are two dimensions of leadership. Do you feel that these dimensions are complementary?

Part 2

TEAMBUILDING

CHAPTER 9

Essentials of Building and Managing Teams

Learning Objectives

After studying this chapter you will be able to

▶ Understand the need for working in teams

▶ Define the strength of mutual support among team members

▶ State the various roles of leaders

▶ Have a knowledge of the types of teams and their contribution

▶ Understand the importance of delegation

▶ State the role of collective wisdom in teamwork

▶ Discuss the concept of virtual teams and associated aspects

▶ Develop an understanding of the skills required for team progress

Organizing Work Teams
Apollo Engineering Works

Albert Engineering Works (AEW) was formed in mid-1994 by a non-resident Indian, Mr K.P. Basu, who is still in the US. He appointed a general manager, A.C. Mazumdar, and delegated the sole responsibility of managing the company to him. Mr Basu decided the location, planned the factory, invested capital for developing infrastructure, purchased capital items, etc. He obtained the trade licence and completed all required formalities, and was present during the start of the company. He invited all his contacts from India and abroad on the day of the inauguration.

Mr Basu never believed in departmentalization; rather he preferred to work in teams. He conveyed the same thing to Mr Mazumdar also. Mr Basu left for the US, and after some time came to know about a management development programme on leadership and team building that was organized by a very reputed business school in US in early 1995. Accordingly, he sponsored and requested Mr Mazumdar to attend the four-week programme. Mr Mazumdar understood the underlying concepts and was truly convinced. Till that time only a few machines had been erected and commissioned. Most of the machines were under procurement and orders were placed with various manufacturers. Recruitment of managers, engineers, and machinists was in progress. Some offices including the IT cell were functioning. The IT cell was instrumental in populating the employee database immediately after joining of an employee at any level. On his return from the US, Mr Mazumdar referred to the employee database and started planning for forming work teams. He desired to form teams to undertake processes forgoing departmental affiliation.

Mr Mazumdar formed teams considering the academic background and experience and the planned processes of the company. In the process of team member selection, he was very much involved with the production, maintenance, quality, and purchase managers. He named the teams Einstein, Newton, Galileo, Jagadish Bose, Nagarjuna, and after other scientists. In the course of two years, he formed nearly forty process teams and the team size varied from minimum five to maximum twenty, depending on the tasks assigned to them. All the team members and team leaders were trained by Indian experts. All the teams started functioning to achieve the team goals. While some of them were functioning smoothly without any problem and achieving the team targets, some were facing problems. Some of the problems encountered were the following:

· Conflict among members
· Dominating attitudes of some members
· Jealousy of an expert team member
· Gross mutual mistrust
· Blaming the team leader
· Concealing of information by one member from others
· Lack of dedication to achieve the team goals
· Passing the buck to others
· Fault finding rather than fact finding

The leaders of the teams were at a loss about what to do. Mr Mazumdar took the matter up and paid undivided attention to the composition of the teams. He brought this to the notice of an expert (Mr Vikram) with adequate experience in team forming and analysing team performance.

Mr Vikram noted that out of the total of forty teams, seventeen were unable to achieve their targets. His first observation was that in most of the unsuccessful teams the number of members was ten or more. Then he concentrated on the leaders' ability but could not find anything significant and attributable to them. Mr Vikram consulted the leaders individually and also in groups. They unanimously opined about the strengths of the teams. When the expert pointed out the problems encountered, the leaders opined in consensus that it was due to the size of the teams. They further confirmed that if the teams were split, these problems might disappear. However, Mr Vikram expressed the desire to explore other issues including team effectiveness.

Learning outcomes

1. Team size should be small.
2. Mutual mistrust disrupts team functioning.
3. Leader must ensure that members are concentrating only on fact finding.
4. Concealing information makes a team dysfunctional.

INTRODUCTION

Interdependence is a common feature of large and complex organizations. Team interdependence is applicable for functions, departments, and organizations too. But interdependence of individuals is by far the most important practice in today's competitive business environment. The globalization of the Indian economy has led to the environment of Indian organizations becoming much more complex and turbulent. World-class organizations rely heavily on team building. When we heat a solid, the intermolecular binding force decreases, resulting in its conversion into liquid, which is an example of change of state. On the contrary, when a group is formed, the interpersonal binding force increases and the members start functioning.

Effectiveness of organizations, therefore, depends on teamwork at different levels. This chapter explores the various facets of teamwork and helps the reader acquire an understanding of the skills needed for development of effective teams in organizations. This chapter will explore factors that determine effectiveness of teams, the concepts of team leadership, skills needed for team effectiveness (problem-solving, decision-making, communication, conflict resolution, etc.), the role of empowerment, and culture for team building. It will also discuss interdepartmental coordination with a focus on employee orientation, and working and finding strategies for improving team effectiveness.

When a group or team is formed, there is a lot of enthusiasm. But most often, it does not continue. The main reason is that a sincere member finds that another member is not contributing to the extent required. He/she is unable to work keeping pace with the former, being engaged in extra-curricular activities such as participating in social functions or organizing cultural events and similar other non-academic activities. He/she might be interested in writing a book, to be exposed and known in the academic arena, and for getting intellectual happiness. He/she might have enormous ability to do this, but cannot withdraw him/her from other activities and as such his/her desire remains unfulfilled. Of late, he/she joins a group for obvious reasons.

INDIVIDUAL VS GROUP VS TEAM

Individuals are important entities or units of any organization. By understanding the behaviour of individuals, we can predict their outcomes, and it becomes easy to manage their behaviours in desirable directions to achieve organizational objectives and goals. In order to get the best from individuals, we have to look at three individual variables—biographical characteristics, ability, and learning. Training keeps the abilities of incumbents up to date or provides new skills as times and conditions change. Any observable change in behaviour is prima facie evidence that learning has taken place.

Learning, further, suggests that reinforcement is a more effective tool than punishment. Tasks are assigned to individuals to achieve the goals of the business, small or medium or large. If individuals work in a group, the output increases. A group is defined as two or more interacting and interdependent individuals who come together to achieve particular objectives. The group helps an individual to feel stronger, have fewer self-doubts, and be more resistant to threats. An individual gains personal fulfilment from the feeling of accomplishment, recognition, authority and, purpose (Williams 1997).

A group develops in various stages. A team is a mature group with highly independent members who are totally committed to a common goal. Though they are independent members, they believe in interdependence for the effectiveness of their combination. Organizations today are facing cut-throat competition. As such, organizations encourage forming work teams and investing efforts as a member of team rather than working as an individual. The aim and purpose of a team is to perform, get results, and achieve business goals in the workplace and marketplace. The purpose of forming a team is to accomplish bigger goals that would not have been possible for the individuals working alone.

THE NATURE OF GROUPS

The nature of a group encompasses the group size and the roles played by members, group norms, group cohesion, group dynamics, group processes, and group performance in relation to an individual's performance.

Group Size and Role

The size of a group plays an important role. A group takes more time to take a decision if the size is large. Moreover, consensus can seldom be achieved with more members. Since it is easier for fewer people to agree on goals and to coordinate their work, smaller groups are more cohesive than larger groups. Task cohesiveness may suffer, though, if the group lacks enough members to perform its tasks well enough. Some managers are of the opinion that a difficult set of criteria for becoming a member of a group tends to present the group in a more exclusive light. The more elite the group is perceived to be, the more prestigious it is. A person strives to get entry to that group. The members continue in these groups. Incidentally, it is also known that alumni of prestigious universities tend to keep in touch for many years after they graduate. They also contribute substantially to the respective universities/institutes for obvious reasons.

However, elite groups develop difficult criteria to ensure exclusive entry. This type of group increases the value of group membership to its members and influences members to identify more strongly with the team and to want to be actively associated with it. Individuals, as members of groups, perform a variety of group roles. Some of the group roles are task-oriented roles, relationship-oriented roles, and individual roles. Task-oriented roles demand an individual, as a member of a group, to initiate and contribute, and seek and give information to other members. In order to discharge relationship-oriented roles, a member must encourage and harmonize others. Individual roles are roles performed for self while accomplishing group tasks. Further discussion on roles is presented later in the chapter.

Group Norm

Norm refers to standard, custom, or model. At the developmental stage, the members of a group prefer to settle the rules to coordinate and govern their behaviour. The most fascinating aspect of people is that they do this only after a few minutes of interaction. The group norm is the shared and agreed upon rules of behaviour established by group members after discussion among themselves.

When members cannot reach consensus, they accept and adopt the decisions of the majority of members. The norms comprise the kind of behaviour that is expected from a member, what a member should not do, the kinds of situations when a member should be expelled, willingness to listen to each others' problems, prohibiting excessive demands from a particular member, and similar other issues that are likely to make the group function smoothly. Obviously, then, norms not only prescribe, they proscribe also.

Group Cohesion

Group cohesion is the most fundamental of all the aspects that arise out of the process of communication and interactions among members in a group. Group cohesion is the force that brings group members closer together. The basic dimension, which defines the degree of 'groupness' or unity, is the solidarity or strength with which a group is bound together.

At the extreme low end of the cohesiveness scale is 'a collection of people tenaciously linked together by organizational superiors' where the members are loosely bound and cannot be considered as a group. On the other end of the same scale are closely knit members, a unified set of people who seem to embody what we call a 'group'. With the passing of time, the members gradually become psychologically closer and become a 'team'.

Broadly, cohesiveness has two dimensions—emotional (or personal) and task-related. The emotional aspect of cohesiveness, which has been studied more often by researchers, is derived from the connection that members have with other group members and with their group as a whole. That is, how much do members like to spend time with other group members? Do they look forward to the next group meeting? Task cohesiveness refers to the degree to which group members share group goals and work together to meet these goals. That is, is there a feeling that the group works smoothly as one unit or do different people pull or move in different directions?

Group Dynamics

Group dynamics refers to the study of the nature of groups. The dynamics develop from the quality and extent of interactive behaviour, style of communication, and the nature of the individuals forming the group. Interactions between individuals within the group are distinctly different from one-to-one interactions. Group dynamics are formed by the level of satisfaction and fulfilment of the people involved. The dynamics is positive when the group enjoys the work that they do and the members get the recognition they aspire for. Positive group dynamics, in turn, mostly influence the behaviour of individuals depending on their position within the group, their task within the group, and their behavioural patterns in the group. The personalities of each of the group members influence the dynamics of any group. The influence of the group on the individual can be strong or weak, influential or ineffective, and overwhelming or insignificant depending on the nature of the group and the participation level of the individual.

Human beings exhibit some characteristic behavioural patterns in groups. People involved in managing groups and group members themselves can benefit from studying theories and doing practical exercises. It would help them to better understand people's behaviour in groups and group dynamics.

Ginnett et al. define group dynamics as the interactions among team members, including such aspects as how they communicate with each other, how they respond to others' needs, how they accept challenges, etc.

Group Process

A group is a dynamic entity and therefore it must have a process, that is, a chain of events with a beginning, a middle, and an end linked sequentially. Some understanding of group processes is essential to analyse what happens in group situations. The analysis helps identify the reasons behinds things that happen and to gain assurance that some measure of control is possible in future. The control may be in terms of understanding and the response to the happenings. Thus, the analysis leads to the development of an increased understanding of group functioning and the development of techniques for modifying the functioning deliberately and purposefully.

In fact, group process is described as the study of groups remembering that a group is not just a collection of some people; rather it is a different system level and a function of member interactions. Williams (1998) defines group process as the understanding of the processes that determine group behaviour and effectiveness, and actively facilitate these processes to ensure that groups work well together. Group process is a key aspect in managing groups and teams.

Group Performance

Individual and group performances differ significantly. The performance of a group is not merely the sum of the performances of its members; it is much more. This is so due to the concerted and orchestral efforts of the members and their synergy. Job performance or work performance is a special case of psychological measurement that provides a quantitative description of the extent to which individuals demonstrate or exhibit certain characteristics, properties, or traits (Ghiselli 1964).

Work performance measurement involves the methods or procedures that provide quantitatively the extent to which employees demonstrate certain work behaviours and the result of those behaviours (Landy and Farr 1983). Performance is a measurement for effective and efficient work, which also considers personal data such as measures of accidents, turnover, absence, and tardiness. The work performance of a group of individuals employed in common jobs reveals considerable individual variation.

In a group, the members are united around a common goal. They are structured to work together, share responsibilities for their task, work interdependently, and be empowered to implement consensus decisions (Pokras 2004). In group working, the leader leads the group as a developmental supervisor to accomplish the task and for effective boundary management. And a developmental supervisor delegates, empowers, and transfers the planning process to the team; he/she works as a member of the team keeping aside status symbols and gets involved in task accomplishment. He never says 'go and work' and rather says 'let us work'. Because of his/her involvement, he/she can read the pulse and never allows the work to slow down. Thus, a developmental supervisor views his/her task as boundary management, that is, facilitates the work of his/her junior colleagues and procures the resources needed to complete the task in compliance with the plan (Haldar 2009).

The performance of individual members affects in a positive way the team's performance goals if he/she completes his/her fair share of the work; members assist other team members in completing tasks as necessary and/or as requested; learn and share new skills and knowledge; and contribute ideas for improving the team's performance.

Having studied the nature of groups and the aspects that reflect such nature, one should be aware of the reasons behind forming a group, and the urge of an individual to join a group.

GROUP FORMING

Groups are collections of human beings working together, investing efforts to accomplish tasks. Influence is a very common phenomenon when there are more than two people interacting with one another.

Reason behind Group Forming

People form and come together in groups primarily to deal with shared problems to make best use of collective wisdom and to benefit from one another's expertise. A positive reinforcement comes from group membership, such as friendly interaction and the ability to achieve something that cannot be achieved otherwise. Working in a group leads to goal accomplishment, affiliation, emotional support, social validation, and physical factors.

Goal accomplishment

Individuals feel a lack of knowledge, skills, and technical know-how in the workplace. When they form a group, members contribute to group success by suggesting new thoughts, ideas, proposals, and process outline and similar other intangibles. Collectives achieve the goal much faster and more easily. A group on accomplishing goals celebrates the success during which all the members are enthused. The success itself is a reward, of course non-financial, for the members. It is needless to mention that a winning team can co-opt new members who derive a sense of pride in being a part of it.

Affiliation

Attachments and relations with other group members give joy to a member particularly, when their likes and dislikes match. The most common derivables are friendship, association, social stimulation, and most importantly personal acceptance. A person starts his/her journey beyond his/her physical self and achieves a sense of belongingness, and exerts beyond individual limits. One success generates the will to achieve the next one, gives encouragement to undertake another challenging task in conformance with the maxim 'success breeds success'.

Emotional support

Support from peers cannot be compared with anything else and when the support is spontaneous, one can probably attain the hitherto impossible. Threatening situations are common in organizational life, but emotional supports help to convert threats into opportunities, translating the uncertainty into certainty, and anything into its antonym. One member becomes the coach, mentor, and counsellor of another, giving knowledge, leadership, and mental and emotional support. Thus a member helps another one to come out of stressful situations, puts him/her in a comfortable position for individual gain and for organizational gains too.

Social validation

People want to enhance self-esteem through self-identity. We want to rediscover ourselves getting feedback from others because we believe 'how others see me' is more important than 'how I judge myself'. The feedback comes as a pointer from the people whom we love and respect. Their comments give us the unique opportunity to introspect and thus pave the way to self-improvement. Furthermore, a person is identified by the company he/she keeps. Membership of a group augments social respect and social validation in the organizational context.

Physical factors

We are acquainted with the proverb 'out of sight, out of mind'. Proximity of some people influences formation of a group. They sometimes meet after working hours, interact on many issues related or unrelated to their work, and become psychologically closer. Exchange of facial expressions also brings people closer. They feel a mutual attraction for each other. As time passes, they unknowingly form a group. Anything that blocks face-to-face interaction, such as separate cubicles, file cabinets, etc. disrupts group formation. A group functioning well and on a spree of achieving can think of increasing the size of the group to enhance the scope of activities, getting an additional expert, or just to increase the group strength. People may like to join an existing group for various reasons.

Reasons of Joining Groups

Individuals join groups for multiple reasons. Particularly if the group is a highly valued one, membership raises feelings of self-esteem after being accepted in the group. Security reflects strength in numbers. Self-esteem conveys people's feelings of self-worth. Association and attachment with groups can fulfil one's social and affiliation needs; work groups significantly contribute to fulfilment of the need for friendship and social relations. The following are some reasons for joining or forming groups:

- One of the appealing aspects of groups is that they represent power.
- What often cannot be achieved individually becomes possible through group action.

- People might want power to protect themselves from unreasonable demands of competent authority.
- Informal groups additionally provide opportunities for individuals to exercise power through collectivity.
- Finally, people may join a group for goal achievement.
- There is a need to pool talent, knowledge, or power and influence in order to get a job completed.

Joining a group needs some adjustments such as surrendering some amount of personal freedom. This is so because members are spontaneously willing to accept the standards of the group and conform to group norms. History is littered with examples where group members sacrificed and surrendered individual interests. While writing a book under joint authorship, one author must endeavour to keep pace with the other while framing the contents, to develop the chapters, collecting organized and relevant case studies, interviewing organizational leaders, and various such activities.

Formal and Informal Groups

Groups are categorized as formal and informal. Formal groups are those established, at a broader level, by the organization or the society to achieve some specified business goals. The behaviours in which one should engage are stipulated by and directed towards achieving organizational goals. For example, task forces, command groups, project groups, standing committees are the most common formal groups in organizations.

Whereas, informal groups emerge naturally, without management intervention, in response to something similar like common interest, likes and dislikes, identical social nature, shared values of individuals, fondness of same personalities, and so forth. Examples include interest group, friendship groups, reference groups, fan clubs, etc.

ROLES

The concept of roles applies to all employees in organizations, irrespective of whether they are working individually or as members of a group, and to their life outside the organization as well. A role refers to a set of behaviour patterns expected from someone who occupies a given position in a social unit. One should remember that

- Employees as individuals play multiple roles.
- Employees attempt to determine the behaviours expected of them.

- An individual who is confronted by divergent role expectations experiences role conflict, which is a common organizational phenomenon.
- Employees in organizations often face such role conflicts.

A manager generally performs three broad types of roles, namely, interpersonal roles, informational roles, and decision-making roles. These roles have been discussed in Chapter 1. The roles that leaders are required to perform are discussed under group roles.

Group Roles

Group members perform a variety of group roles like task roles, personal and/or social roles, and dysfunctional and/or individualistic roles (Benne and Sheats; www.mindtools.com) are discussed in Table 9.1.

Task roles

These are roles that relate to getting the work done by the group members. They represent the different roles needed to take a project step by step from initial conception through action. Task roles include initiator/contributor, information seeker, information giver, opinion seeker and giver, elaborator, coordinator, orienter, evaluator/critic, energizer, procedural technician, and recorder.

- *Initiator/Contributor*—Gets the group moving; offers new ideas; suggests ways to approach a task or problem; reminds others that there is a task to perform. Members who are creative propose original ideas, different ways, or alternatives to approaching group problems or goals. They initiate discussions and move groups into new areas of exploration.
- *Information seeker*—Encourages others to raise issues; asks them to justify their argument; asks for further information from them. He identifies data deficiency and requests clarification or comments regarding terms of factual adequacy; seeks expert information or facts relevant to the problem. Information seekers scrutinize data and establish what information is missing and needs to be collected before moving forward.
- *Information giver*—Clarifies important facts; brings in knowledge from personal experiences; raises issues; supports opinion with fact; provides factual information to the group. Information giver is seen as an authority on the subject and relates own experience when relevant.

- *Opinion seeker*—Seeks clarification of the values, attitudes, and opinions of group members. Checks to make sure that different perspectives are considered.
- *Opinion giver*—Expresses his/her own opinions and beliefs about the subject being discussed. Often states opinions in terms of what the group should do. He/she does so assertively to maintain group cohesion.
- *Elaborator*—Takes and interprets other people's initial ideas and builds on them with examples, and relevant facts and data. Further, he/she looks at the consequences of proposed ideas and actions. Thus, elaborators explore the consequences.
- *Coordinator*—Brings together the activities of others; schedules activities; analyses and combines activities. Identifies and explains the relationships between ideas. Pulls together different ideas, establishes their relationships, and makes them cohesive.
- *Orienter*—Reviews and clarifies the group's position and provides a summary of what has been accomplished; notes where the group has deviated, and finally suggests how to get back on track to achieve the target.
- *Evaluator/Critic*—Helps the group assess the quality of its suggestions or solutions; tests to see whether the ideas will work in reality; points out consequences of implementation; guesses how parties external to the group will view the solution. Evaluates the proposals against a predetermined objective standard as the yardstick; assesses to justify the reasonableness of a proposal and looks at whether it is fact-based and manageable as a solution. He/she evaluates to validate the proposal.
- *Energizer*—Concentrates on the group's energy on forward movement; challenges and stimulates the group for further action.
- *Procedural technician*—Contemplates the infrastructure to facilitate group discussion by taking care of logistics like where meetings are to take place and what supplies are needed for each meeting.
- *Recorder*—Acts as the member secretary and prepares the record of discussion. Specifically lays emphasis on recording ideas and keeping track of what goes on at each meeting. He monitors and critiques the group process as an outsider who is not responsible for task accomplishment.

Personal and/or social roles

These roles contribute to the positive functioning of the group and comprise the roles of encourager, harmonizer, compromiser, gatekeeper or expediter, observer or commentator, and follower.

- *Encourager*—Affirms and encourages support, praises the efforts of fellow group members, endeavours to boost their morale. Demonstrates warmth and provides a positive attitude at meetings. Approaches assertively to take care of any lapses.
- *Harmonizer*—Helps members see past their differences; reduces tension with humour and friendliness; helps members work together and appreciate divergent viewpoints. Appeases as a conciliator to eliminate or reduce problems that arise out of individual differences. Seeks ways to reduce tension and diffuse a situation by providing further explanations or using humour.
- *Compromiser*—Offers to change his/her position for the good of the group, and manages situations.
- *Gatekeeper or expediter*—Asks for opinions from everyone; maintains 'open gate' to others' participation; ensures that all members have opportunities to share their ideas and feelings; uses statements such as 'Let's hear him out'. Regulates flow of communication. Makes sure all members get a chance to express their viewpoints by encouraging shy and quiet members to contribute their ideas. Also exercises control and limits on those who tend to dominate the conversation, and may suggest group rules or standards that ensure everyone gets a chance to speak up. Obviously prefers to adopt structured brainstorming at idea collection stage.
- *Observer or commentator*—Provides feedback to the group about the functioning of the group. Is instrumental when a group wants to set, evaluate, or change its standards and processes.
- *Follower*—Accepts what others say and decide even though he/she has not contributed to the decision or expressed his/her own thoughts. He/she is mostly a good listener, though not a contributor.

Dysfunctional and/or individualistic roles

Certain roles disrupt group progress and adversely affect group cohesion. Some disrupting roles are aggressor, blocker, recognition seeker, self-confessor, disrupter or playboy/playgirl, dominator, help seeker, and special interest pleader.

- *Aggressor*—Does not hesitate to make personal attacks, or use offensive and insulting comments, for example, 'You are always talking like an engineer though you are merely an…', 'You are always giving ridiculous and ambiguous ideas; truly disgusting'. His actions are usually an attempt to decrease another member's status.
- *Blocker*—Appears as a roadblock and opposes every idea or opinion that is put forward and yet refuses to make his/her own suggestions, for example, 'That idea is not at all acceptable'. The statements stall the group from proceeding in a healthy manner.
- *Recognition seeker*—Person with high recognition motive tries to draw others' attention to him/her at meetings. He/she always highlights and discusses his/her past accomplishments or relates irrelevant stories that paint him/her in a positive light. Sometimes he/she pulls off crazy stunts to attract attention like acting silly, making excess noise, or otherwise directing members away from the task at hand.
- *Self-confessor*—Frequently uses group meetings as an avenue to disclose personal feelings and issues. He/she tries to slip in these comments under the guise of relevance, such as 'that reminds me of a time when I succeeded in accomplishing…' He/she often tries to relate group actions to his/her personal life.
- *Disrupter or playboy/playgirl*—Treats the group meeting as a country club and uses the forum as fun time, to relax, and a way to get out of real work. Distracts other people by telling jokes, playing pranks, or even reading or talking about unrelated issues.
- *Dominator*—Places in high position, gives direction, tries to control the conversation, and dictate what people should be doing. Often exaggerates his/her knowledge and strives to monopolize any conversation claiming to know more about the situation and having better solutions than anybody else. He/she generally speaks in a high voice.
- *Help seeker*—Actively looks for sympathy by expressing feelings of inadequacy and inability projecting weaknesses. Acts helpless, self-deprecating, and unable to contribute, saying 'I cannot undertake this assignment as I have never done this type work before'. Persons with high dependency motive are generally help seekers.
- *Special interest pleader*—Makes suggestions based on what others would think or feel. Avoids revealing own biases or opinions by using a stereotypical position instead, offers complimentary comments in support of others or otherwise. For example, 'I am sure that this idea will not be accepted by the production department', 'Our registered suppliers will definitely disagree with this proposal'.

TABLE **9.1** **Managerial roles**

Task Roles	Personal and/or Social Roles	Dysfunctional and/or Individualistic Roles
· Initiator or contributor · Information seeker · Information giver · Opinion seekers · Opinion givers · Elaborator · Coordinator · Orienter · Evaluator/Critic · Energizer · Procedural technician · Recorder	· Encourager · Harmonizer · Compromiser · Gatekeeper or expediter · Observer or commentator · Follower	· Aggressor · Blocker · Recognition seeker · Self-confessor · Disrupter or playboy/playgirl · Dominator · Help seeker · Special interest pleader

When managers form a group or a group like a task force, decision-making body, fact-finding board, etc. is formed with managers, they bear in mind the group roles for effective outcomes. However, to get a better insight, one should know the theoretical approaches to groups.

THEORETICAL APPROACHES TO GROUPS

Social scientists use the term theory to indicate a set of logically related concepts or propositions describing the relationship among phenomena under study. There are theories with regard to groups which attempt to provide the basis of group forming.

- Field theory
- Exchange theory
- Social system theory

Field Theory

Kurt Lewin (1890–1947), a German psychologist by birth who emigrated to the US before the Second World War, observed that a person's psychological state influences the social field or milieu. He viewed the social environment as a dynamic field, that impacted human consciousness in an interactive way. He emphasized the discovery of the laws through the knowledge of the field of psychological and sociological process serving at any moment a cause of action. He is the proponent of the field theory and believed that human behaviour, no matter how idiosyncratic, was lawful.

In the field theory, a 'field' is 'the totality of coexisting facts which are conceived of as mutually interdependent'. Lewin not only described group dynamics, but also investigated the conditions and forces that bring about change or resist change in groups.

Lewin and his associates created different groups with known characteristics. They put them under different styles of leaders and then observed sequentially the actions of the leaders, responses of the members, and finally compared the results and drew empirical conclusions about the dynamic effects of leadership. The steps were simple, yet followed scientifically sound procedures. The researchers demonstrated that theoretically relevant hypothesis could be tested in an experimental set-up.

The study by Lewin had tremendous impact on the study of groups and group dynamics mainly for three reasons:

(a) He took a phenomenological position towards behaviour.
(b) He showed great ingenuity in research design.
(c) He was influential because of his theoretical system.

Due to the phenomenological position towards behaviour, Lewin felt that to understand a person's behaviour, it must be analysed in terms of what that person subjectively perceives, rather than in terms of what an outside observer thinks. Lewin pioneered the use of laboratory settings and relied on experimental design to study group phenomena. He meticulously blended experimental control with the creation of a realistic, meaningful context in which to study important group processes such as leadership climate and decision-making. The theoretical system adopted by Lewin had its roots in the school of psychology.

Contextually, it needs to be mentioned that Lewin also looked at the power of underlying forces (needs) to determine behaviour and, hence, expressed 'a preference for psychological as opposed to physical or physiological descriptions of the field'.

The salient features of the field theory as observed by Hall and Lindzey (1978) are as follows:

• Behaviour is a function of the field that exists at the time the behaviour occurs.
• Analysis begins with the situation as a whole from which the component parts are differentiated.
• The concrete person in a concrete situation can be represented mathematically.

Lewin states, 'A successful individual typically sets his next goal somewhat but not too much above his last achievement. In this way he steadily raises his level of aspiration.' Lewin further stated: (a) 'Learning is more effective when it is an active rather than a passive process,' and (b) 'If you want to truly understand something, try to change it.'

Exchange Theory

Influencing is a common organizational phenomenon in a group. The exchange theory is one of the most influential approaches to interpersonal relations. In a group, members control one another's behaviour by exchanging rewards and costs. The exchange theory assumes from the start that people in relationships as well as in the economic market try to maximize the rewards they receive and minimize the costs they incur, by seeking rewarding experiences and avoiding painful ones. The theory emphasizes that rewarding others requires that one should be ready to give up time, effort or something else.

Social System Theory

This theory emphasizes that the key to understanding groups is to focus and consider them as a network of people functioning together as a holistic entity. From the standpoint of system theory, a system comprises five characteristics:

First, a group is composed of members who are independent of one another.

Second, the theory specifies that to form a system, the collection of people must have interaction among themselves, as interaction clarifies issues and interaction that can have its effect.

Third, through interaction what develops is interdependence which in turn creates characteristic of systems, an emergent property. This property exemplifies the group as 'whole' rather than the members as individuals, leading to the creation of a distinctive group identity.

The fourth characteristic of social system theory is an offshoot of the first three. The group members forge themselves through adequate interaction into a unified entity, a district developing a boundary between themselves and the 'outside world'. The boundary makes the distinction between 'we' comprising the group members and 'they' comprising outsiders.

The fifth characteristic refers to the dynamism of the system evidenced from the constant changing and evolving. The group attains a relatively stable pattern of behaviours along with a leadership pattern. The members maintain a continued balancing and rebalancing of restraining forces in the group. From the standpoint of social system theory, groups are like waves of the ocean wherein the patterns only appear through continual motion of the components.

GROUP DEVELOPMENT STAGES

Tuckman (1965) propounded his 'Forming-Storming-Norming-Performing' model to explain team development and behaviour. He elucidated that as the team develops, its maturity, ability, and interpersonal relationships also develop. Consequently, the team leader changes his/her leadership style. The leader begins with a directing style, moves through coaching, then participates, finishes delegating, and slowly detaches himself/herself to take over and develop a new team. At this point, the team may produce a successor leader and the previous leader can move on to develop a new team.

Forming   At this stage, members meet and form a team. They learn what the team opportunities and challenge will be. Individual members may be confused about their role or not understand the need for the team. Members will agree on goals and assign actions for work, often working independently. Slowly, ground rules or team guidelines are established. At the start, the team leader may be a member of the group, a supervisor, a manager, or a consultant who will facilitate the team-building process. Leadership will help the team to define their processes. At this stage, the leader needs to be directive and understand the requirements for team training to move through each stage.

Storming   During this stage, the members express ideas. Individual expression of ideas occurs and there is open conflict between members. Members tend to focus on details rather than the issues and start competing for influence. Furthermore, conflict arises due to non-homogeneous contribution towards the group. One member notices that another one is giving lowest priority to the group. The second member might be passionate about responding to activities of his/her liking. Individual differences of this type 'storm' the group when the episode of conflict starts. These feelings lead to low trust among team members, which is an obvious indicator at this stage. The team needs to select their desired leadership style and decision methodology. The team leader can help through fostering endurance and tolerance between members. The leader further should guide the team process towards clearly stated goals, defined individual roles, acceptable team behaviour, and a mutual feedback process for team communication.

Norming Some time after team formation, this is the stage when the team develops certain work habits that support group rules and values. They use established tools and methods and exhibit good behaviours. Mutual trust and motivation develop. Open communication among members increases followed by positive teamwork and group focus. The team relationships grow and individual characteristics are understood and appropriately utilized. The team leader continues to encourage participation, involvement, and professionalism among the team members.

Performing The fourth stage is characterized by high levels of loyalty, participation, motivation, concerted efforts, and group decision-making. Knowledge sharing, mutual trust, and interdependence increase. The team is self-directing in developing plans and strategies to achieve its goals and carry out work. Personal growth and sharing is encouraged through membership. The leader becomes a facilitator, aiding the team in communication processes and helping if they revert to a prior stage.

Adjourning Later, Tuckman added the fifth stage implying break up of the group on completion of the task. Everyone can move on to new things, feeling good about what has been achieved. However, the adjourning step also applies in the case of temporary groups like a task force. At the adjourning stage, the members wrap up activities. With disbandment in mind, the group's focus shifts from high task performance to closure. The attitude of members varies from excitement to depression. Tuckman's theory is an elegant and helpful explanation of team development and behaviour.

There exist other way of explaining group and team formation and development. A group is initially formed. After it is formed, it does not immediately function effectively until it has gone through various stages of development. At this point of time, you must note that there are no prescriptive guidelines for the stages of group development. However, development generally follows a basic model for most of the groups. The model specifies four stages—orientation, confrontation, differentiation, and collaboration (Figure 9.1). Some groups never advance to the later stages, and due to internal problems and interpersonal conflicts, cease to work.

- *Orientation*—This is the stage when the members of the group learn about the purpose of the group and the roles of each member to achieve the team objective. Individual members want to achieve consensus, decide how the group will be structured, and how much they are willing to commit themselves to the group. The leader plays a vital role to structure the group, and shape and mould member expectations.

Subsequently, members need to be acquainted with one another and shape their expectations about the goals and objectives of the group. This stage predominantly demands openness, collaboration, empathy, trust, authenticity, etc.

- *Confrontation*—Altercation, conflict, disagreement are part and parcel of organizational life. Team members are struggling to gain control over the group, extending influence over other group members arising out of the power motive are common. Challenging the group's objective and goals can very often lead to a healthy process, but conflict on this ground is likely to affect group cohesiveness and acceptance. In most cases. confrontation is an undesired stage of group development as it might turn into intense conflict. The leader must take care of this aspect.
- *Differentiation*—The modality of distribution of tasks and responsibilities among members is a major issue of this stage. Another concern is the evaluation of each other's performance. The task accomplishments of group members may differ widely as they depend on individual skills, expertise, and experience. Individual differences are recognized at this stage. Group cohesiveness can be achieved if the group members can resolve conflicts arising out of individual differences and create shared expectations regarding the goals. Otherwise, the group may dissolve at this stage even. If, however, the group can resolve the conflicts, members start functioning for long-term effectiveness when it requires re-establishing shared expectations.
- *Collaboration*—After crossing the barrier of confrontation and then differentiation, the group gains maturity and at this stage, collaboration

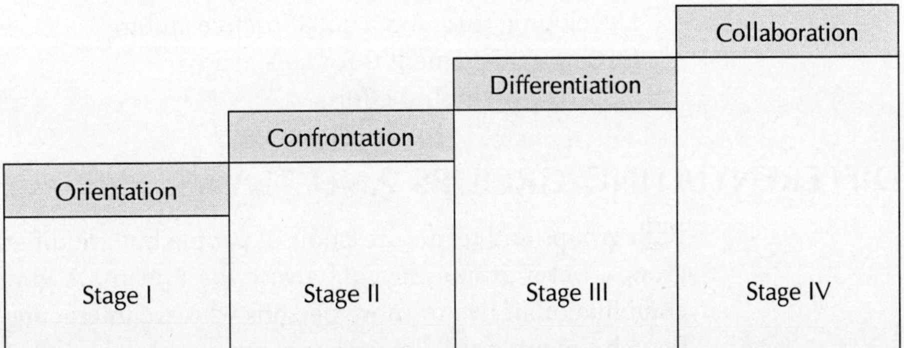

FIGURE **9.1** **Stages of group development**

starts. This stage is characterized by a feeling of cohesiveness and commitment to the group. One must note that interpersonal conflicts due to individual differences can never be eliminated but they can be resolved through group discussion. Sometimes conflicts, keeping emotional issues aside, act as a catharsis that helps the group to function effectively. The members take decisions through rational and balanced group discussions.

UNDERSTANDING TEAMS

A group of people do not make a team. A team is a group of people with a high degree of interdependence focused on the achievement of some goal or task. All the members in a team agree on the goal and the process of achieving it. Thus, a team is a mature group with highly independent members in terms of capability but works interdependently and is completely committed to achieve a common goal.

All teams start out as groups, but not all groups become teams. Teams are groups of people who co-operate to carry out a joint task. They may be assigned different work roles, or be allowed to sort them out between themselves and change jobs when they feel like, for example, crews of ships and aircraft, research teams, maintenance gangs, and groups of miners.

The elements that distinguish teams from groups are the following:

- Exhibiting full commitment to achieve a common goal and mission
- Feeling that they are interdependent
- Believing that they have mutual accountability
- Accepting shared leadership
- Developing trust and a collaborative culture
- Getting achievement through synergy
- Applying orchestral efforts

DIFFERENTIATING GROUPS AND TEAMS

Both groups and teams are pools of people but are different. All teams are groups, but a group may not always be a team. A group is formed by a combination of two or more persons who are interacting with one another in such a manner that each person influences and is influenced by the other. A team is always distinguished by the fact that its members are committed to a common purpose, a set of performance goals, and an approach for which they hold themselves mutually accountable.

Group vs Team

A team differentiates itself from a group on various dimensions. The website www.1000ventures.com identifies ten dimensions: understanding, ownership, creativity and contribution, trust, common understanding, personal development, conflict resolution, participative decision-making, clear leadership, and commitment.

The understanding between team members is the unique feature, and members possess a sense of ownership. Each member acknowledges the creativity and contribution of another member. Mutual trust and understanding help accomplish team goals. Members receive knowledge inputs and utilize that in the workplace. They view conflict as part and parcel of organizational life, look at the positive aspects of the conflict, and resolve it quickly in a constructive manner. They believe in participative decision-making and strive for a win–win result. The leader sets mutually agreed high standards of performance for the team. Turnover of members is seldom experienced in a team. A band of committed members create the team identity. The differences between a group and a team are summarized in Table 9.2.

TABLE **9.2 Differences between group and team**

Dimension	Group	Team
1. Understanding	· Members think they are grouped for administrative purposes	· Members recognize their interdependence and understand both personal and team goals
2. Ownership	· Members focus on themselves · They are less involved	· Members feel a sense of ownership · They are committed to value-based common goals · They derive pride from the job
3. Creativity and contribution	· Members need instructions about what to do · What would be the best approach	· Members apply talents and creativity and decide on/identify tasks
4. Trust	· Members cannot understand the motives of colleagues · They generally cannot trust others	· Members work in a climate of trust · Express ideas, opinions, disagreements, and feelings

Contd

Table 9.2 contd

Dimension	Group	Team
5. Common understanding	· Members speak cautiously · They do not try to understand others' viewpoint	· Members practice open and honest communication
6. Personal development	· Members receive good training · They can apply only limited knowledge in the work area	· Members continually develop skills · They perceive they have the support of the team
7. Conflict resolution	· Members do not know how to resolve conflict · Supervisors/Leaders intervene	· Members realize conflict is a normal aspect of human interaction · They view conflicts as an opportunity for new ideas and creativity
8. Participative decision-making	· Member's participation in decision-making is unlikely · Win–Lose situations are common	· Members participate in decisions affecting the team performance · Positive win–win results are the goal at all times
9. Clear leadership	· Members tend to work in an unstructured environment · Leaders cannot exercise proper control	· Members work in a structured environment · Leader sets agreed high standards of performance
10. Commitment	· Members are not so committed towards excellence · Member turnover is high	· Members are committed to and strive for excellence · They work in a harmonious environment

Source: www.1000ventures.com

Dimensions of Teams

A basic work team comprises a manager and those who directly report to him. Teams can also be ad hoc groups such as task forces or committees, which come together for a specific purpose and a limited time. A recent phenomenon is the cross-cultural team, which brings together experts from a variety of disciplines and departments to develop new products, systems, or other results.

We may also distinguish teams by three dimensions:

- Purpose—product development, quality, marketing, systems, etc.
- Duration—permanent or ad hoc.
- Membership—functional or cross-functional.

The most challenging teams are cross-functional and ad hoc teams. The challenges are intensified when the purpose is unclear. Although the payoff is potentially great, the difficulty of forging an effective team is complicated by the different styles that the people from the various disciplines bring to the table. And the temporary nature of the relationship often decreases the motivation to work hard on building an effective team (Parker and Richard 1999).

A team is a distinguishable set of two or more individuals who interact dynamically, interdependently, and adaptively to achieve specified, shared, and valued objectives (Bowers et al., www.team-wise.co.uk). This is a fairly general term that is used in a number of different ways. It can cover either what you are trying to achieve or how you are trying to achieve it—or both. The following cover most of the options:

- Team building is meant to develop working relationships.
- Team building is for promoting team performance.
- Team building is a fresco effort that confronts the individuals within the team.
- Team building is meant to increase motivation, communication, support, and interpersonal trust, and reduce individual differences within a team.

Types of Teams

Organizations generally use four types of teams, which differ according to the complexity of their task and the fluidity of their membership:

- Process teams
- Self-managed teams
- Cross-departmental or cross-functional teams
- Quality improvement teams or quality circles
- Virtual teams

Process teams

Many organizations today are team based and rely heavily on process teams. These organizations do not have departmental affiliation but function independently to undertake broad organizational-level process improvements. In many cases, organizations that implement process teams later partially or totally disband or disperse their traditional departments.

Self-directed or self-managed work teams

A self-managed work team is a formal mature group of employees who work without a supervisory personnel and are responsible for a complete work package that delivers good product or service to an external or internal customer. Self-managed teams are process teams of employees. This kind of team has control over its work pace, determines work assignments, and is capable of producing results, etc. Fully self-managed work teams even select their own members and evaluate team performance. As a result, supervisory positions decrease in importance and may even be eliminated.

However, a team leader provides internal facilitation to remove any hurdle and obtain the needed resources. The leader considers himself/herself as a team member, and coordinates and cooperates with other teams and individuals who are affected by their decisions and activities. Self-managed work teams require a total change in organizational structure; not surprisingly, lack of commitment is the common reason for failure.

Cross-departmental or functional teams

You have evidenced that in a declining market, salespersons blame marketing personnel and marketing personnel in turn blame salespersons. Also, you have definitely experienced that production blame the maintenance department and the maintenance people hold production responsible for machine breakdowns. Organizations prefer to form cross-functional teams to study, analyse, and offer solutions that they are required to implement. The team members cannot divert the responsibility on to others. Cross-functional teams are regarded as the means to manage social collaboration and concept creation.

A cross-functional team is a small group of interdependent employees from various functional areas of the organization—research, planning, production, maintenance, marketing, sales, finance, human resources, and operations—depending on the organizational need. Cross-functional teams work, operate, or communicate across different functions within an organization.

A team is formed to handle a specific problem. Such teams work on simpler tasks and their membership fluidity is high, which means that members come and go over time. Process teams, which address complex tasks, have highly fluid membership. Cross-functional teams must be given freedom to work and be empowered. Such teams become essential when the organization:

- struggles with a problem that impacts many sections of the organization,
- needs to improve the operation or system or process, demanding close coordination from more that one section or department,
- reveals that multi-skilled persons cannot take up the work, and
- requires simultaneous application of multifarious skills, expertise, and judgement of persons from different sections (crossing the boundaries) to accomplish the goal.

Problem-solving team

A problem-solving team is also known as a 'quality improvement team' or 'quality circle', or simply 'work team'. Whatever be the name, the team generally consists of eight to ten members from a common work area who meet at fixed intervals, say once a week, to find solutions to specific problems about the work processes, products, or services. A problem-solving team has a clear and specific focus on process improvement within a single work unit. Such teams have limited power to implement their ideas. Organizations can establish such teams without making major organizational changes, because they operate in parallel with the rest of the structure.

Virtual teams

In an era of information technology, we are aware of teleconferencing—two members located in the US, three members in Pakistan, two in Canada, and four in India participating in a meeting. Instead of being geographically dispersed, they work in the same company and take part in decision-making. A virtual team allows the members to meet without concern for space or time and enables organizations to link the workforce together, which could not have been done in the past. Team members rely heavily on the use of technology advances to receive tasks, achieve business goals, solve day-to-day problems, provide feedback, keep all members aware, share success, encourage achievements, and so forth. Geographic dispersion never appears as a roadblock. More about virtual teams will be discussed later in this chapter.

CHARACTERISTICS OF A TEAM

The characteristics of a well-functioning and effective group are manifold. The team members share openly and authentically their feelings, opinions, thoughts, and perceptions about problems and conditions, and work for consensus on decisions. Trust, support, and involvement are genuine concerns of each team member. Each member encourages the development of other team members. Every member focuses on the ultimate goal of the project and gathers underlying details. Members give realistic time-frames for team goals. They do not hesitate to take calculated risks. All members communicate assertively. Some other characteristics are as follows:

- Members are relaxed, comfortable, and maintain an informal atmosphere.
- Members accept the work willingly and understand their roles and responsibilities.
- Members exhibit patience, listen well, and participate in the given assignments.
- Members perform assigned tasks considering their background, strengths and weakness, what they accept willingly and enthusiastically.
- The team is aware of its operation and function.
- People do not hesitate to express feelings and ideas.
- The team mostly achieves consensus in decision-making.
- Conflict and disagreement centre on ideas or method, and never impair personal relationships.

ROLES OF TEAM MEMBERS

Astrological compatibility between team members is an essential prerequisite of high-performing work teams. Mature groups are teams. Organizations properly match people to various roles. There are nine potential roles that work team members often 'play' (www.vulms.vu.edu.pk). The website has mentioned roles like creator-innovators, explorer-promoters, assessor-developers, thruster-organizers, concluder-producers, controller-inspectors, upholder-maintainers, reporter-advisers, and linkers.

(a) Creator-innovators are imaginative and initiate ideas or concepts. They are typically very independent and prefer to work at their own pace in their own way and very often in their own time.

(b) Explorer-promoters take ideas from the creator-innovator, find resources to implement the ideas, and thus they promote the ideas gathered. However, they often lack the patience and control skills to ensure that the ideas are implemented.

(c) Assessor-developers are persons with strong analytical skills. When they gather several brainstormed options or alternatives, they evaluate and analyse them before taking a decision. They significantly contribute to the decision-making process.

(d) Thruster-organizers like to set up operating procedures to get things done. They obviously rely on system theory. They set goals, establish plans, organize resources including people, and establish systems to ensure that deadlines are met. They are obviously target oriented. Their role focuses on insisting that deadlines are kept and commitments fulfilled.

(e) Concluder-producers take pride in producing a regular output to a standard. They strive to produce the planned results. Like thruster-organizers, concluder-producers are also concerned with results. They also insist that deadlines are kept and commitments fulfilled.

(f) Controller-inspectors have a high concern for establishing and enforcing rules and policies. They possess the expertise to examine details and make sure that inaccuracies are avoided. They want to check all the facts and figures to make sure these are complete. They are obviously good problem solvers.

(g) Upholder-maintainers are process oriented and hold strong convictions about the way things should be done. They defend their teams, remain ready to face all consequences, and strongly support fellow team members. They provide stability to the respective teams.

(h) Reporter-advisers are good listeners and they never try to press their viewpoints on others. They try to gather more information before taking decisions. They perform an important role in encouraging the team to seek additional information and discouraging the team from taking hasty decisions.

(i) The linkers overlap the others. Anyone can play the role of a linker provided he/she understands others' views. Linkers possess the unique capacity of creating psychologically bonded people. They believe in mutual cooperation, can inculcate mutual trust, take care of individual differences, resolve interpersonal conflicts, and manage diversity. They are excellent coordinators and integrators.

MAKING TEAMS EFFECTIVE

In team building, organizations apply the principle of group dynamics to select complementary members, support more cohesion, manage stages of group development, and establish constructive norms that foster high performance. While paying attention to task accomplishment, organizations also strive to improve the internal work, create cohesion, promote interpersonal relationships, maintain harmony, build mutual trust, and so forth.

Turning Individuals into Team Players

A team has it own dynamics. The characteristics of a team are that it operates with clearly defined goals and expectations, gives a great deal of personal freedom to members, makes decisions, shares information among team members, and sets high standards; its members are disciplined, possess a sense of commitment, and share successes. A system of developmental supervision encourages working in a team to derive benefits from the synergistic effect of inputs. Members mostly solve the problems on their own (Haldar 2008). An individual can be converted into a team player on careful considerations of certain points.

In order to perform well as team members, individuals must be able to communicate openly and honestly with one another, to confront differences and resolve conflicts, and to place lower priority on personal goals for the good of the team. The challenge of creating team players and making a team function effectively will be greatest if

- the national culture is highly individualistic,
- the system of recognizing individuals is encouraging and strong enough, and
- the teams are being introduced into an established organization that has historically valued individual achievement.

On the contrary, the challenge for management is less when teams are introduced where employees have strong collective values. Collectivism in organizations in Japan or Mexico is worth mentioning. In new organizations, the challenge of forming teams will be less as they start the journey using the concept of working in teams as their initial form. These organizations structure the work system and form departments accordingly.

Shaping Team Behaviour

Productive teams require careful selection of personnel, and their training, development, and management. Guidelines for building effective teams include seeking employee input, establishing rules and norms, and enhancing their skills to act in a team. The behaviours of team members can be shaped in three popular ways including proper selection of personnel, employee training, and rewarding appropriate team behaviours.

Role of selection—When selecting team members, the organization should ensure that applicants can fulfil their team roles. Some personnel may lack team skills. A person should not be selected as a team player if he/she lacks team skills. Otherwise the effort may go astray.

Role of training—A candidate who has some basic team skills may be selected on a temporary basis and developed through training. Performing well in a team involves a set of behaviours, which can be induced by an experienced trainer or coach. The people who were raised or promoted based on and considering individual accomplishment can be trained to become team players. A feeling can be inculcated among them, highlighting the essence and importance of working in a team.

Experienced trainers can administer exercises to let employees know and experience the satisfaction that teamwork can provide. Some organizations conduct workshops to elucidate such topics as problem-solving, communication, negotiations, conflict resolution, and coaching skills. In case of non-availability of internal experts, engaging external consultants is in practice. He/She can provide a learning environment in which workers can gain practical skills for working in teams.

Role of rewards—Organizations should preferably design the reward system with the ultimate aim to encourage cooperative efforts rather than competitive ones. Rewards must be structured to return a percentage increase in the bottom line to team members on the basis of achievement of the team's performance goals. Organizations must set performance goals and then link promotions, pay hike, and other forms of recognition with the performance. It is needless to mention that rewards are extrinsic motivation. Employees, at the transition stage, must be developed to appreciate the utmost need of working as collaborative team members. Individual contribution needs to be balanced with selfless contribution to the team. Managers cannot forget the inherent rewards that employees can receive from teamwork. Work teams provide camaraderie or championship. There are inherent rewards from being on a team; it is exciting and satisfying to lead a pleasant work life.

Maintaining a Mature Team

With the passing of time, the team undertakes more complex problems and begins to tackle the more difficult issues. Teams do not automatically continue to perform at their peak. Mature and effective teams also sometimes become dysfunctional and stagnant on various grounds. Initial enthusiasm can give way to apathy. Time can diminish the positive value from diverse perspectives as cohesiveness slowly increases. Recurring successes of a team can lead to contentment and complacency. Mature teams also often suffer from smugness. A team's early successes are often due to having taken on easy tasks. Teams need refreshing and bolstering periodically and to do that, a manager can use the following tools.

- Prepare team members to deal with the more and more complex problems with the enhancement of team maturity.
- Remind the team members occasionally that they are not unique; they have much more to contribute to the organization.
- Provide them with training and retraining in communication, conflict resolution, team processes, recent developments, technological advancements, and so forth. The scope of training should also include the area of their expertise.
- Experienced team members interact with the trainer actively. Mature teams must benefit from training or workshops to develop stronger problem-solving, interpersonal, and technical skills.
- Encourage teams to treat their development as a constant learning experience and as stepping stones to further successes.
- Just as organizations are adopting organizational development (OD) initiatives and using continuous improvement programmes, teams should approach their own development as part of a search for continuous improvement.
- Teams must be encouraged to gain distinctive competence and differentiable identity.

Managing Dysfunctional Teams

Some teams function well and achieve team and organizational goals, whereas some cannot and ultimately become dysfunctional. These teams take a long time to complete their projects or their projects are of poor quality; members complain to the leader of the team, the leader complains to the team facilitator. The team members feel that they do not get the opportunities that they deserve. As such, a team gradually becomes dysfunctional.

The various reasons behind a team becoming dysfunctional are weak or autocratic leadership, culture of blame, indistinct roles, lack of transfer of skills; experts jealously guard their positions; and the size of the team (Tina Erwee, www.dotnet.org.za/tina).

Weak or autocratic leadership—A leader with little or no leadership skills cannot motivate members and inculcate the spirit of working in teams. A manager has to have strong leadership skills to inspire a team to greater heights.

Culture of blame—If something goes wrong, and the first question is 'who did this work?' and not 'how can we fix it?' it would be extremely difficult for the team to be successful. In fact, one should lay emphasis on the task rather than the doer.

Indistinct roles—Role clarity, role expertise, multi-tasking and multiple skills are all equally vital for effective team functioning. If the planner does only planning, the designer only designing, and the analyst only analysing, then they will not understand the importance of each other's role and the associated complications. This causes stagnation in a team and it also makes it easier to pass the blame on to someone else, and the effect is that all the blame falls on the person at the bottom of the pyramid since he/she cannot pass on the blame any further.

Lack of transfer of skills—People always hunt for learning something new. If skills are not transferred, people get frustrated because they are not learning. This can lead to a high turnover of key personnel or to a despondent work atmosphere.

Experts jealously guard their positions—When an expert in a team conceals his/her knowledge due to jealousy, the interdependency of members is disturbed and the whole team suffers. The success of a project can also become too dependent on one person who is highly capable, which poses a high-risk scenario.

Size of the team—The bigger the team size, the more is the chance of it being dysfunctional. People come from various cultures with variety of backgrounds. The members will compete against each other instead of cooperating with each other. The optimum size is six to eight members.

A team may become dysfunctional for various other reasons like inadequate education and training, lack of top management commitment, shortage of time, and inadequate budget. Literature review confirms that due to poor communication and undefined purpose, many teams became dysfunctional. It is truly a hard task for a team to function without having authority and empowerment. An organization needs restructuring during a change process. Lack of an implementation or organizational restructuring plan often makes the teams dysfunctional.

A team gains maturity through various stages. If some members have the tendency of passing the buck to the leader or other team members, then also the team will not achieve the target it is meant to. So, handling dysfunctional teams need careful attention of the top management. Eric Berkman (2004) suggests six ways to handle dysfunctional teams: (1) understand team members' motives and motivations, (2) define roles and responsibilities, (3) set measurable team goals, (4) provide a forum for regular feedback, (5) set and enforce consequences, and (6) practise random acts of kindness.

A person needs a driving force to execute a task. In a team-based organization, understanding the motives and motivations of team members is as essential as anything else. Psychometric tools can be used to analyse the motives. But equally important is having one-on-one meetings to get a better feel of team members' motivation.

The manager or team leader must define the roles and responsibilities of each member. Role overlaps and confusion over responsibilities can lead to ugly turf wars. It can even leave critical tasks unfinished, with everyone pointing the finger at someone else. The expectations, in terms of actual deliverables, must be made clear while defining the roles. Team goals must be set unambiguously. Individual goals and the team goal must be congruent and understood by all the members. If the goals are set in measurable terms, then it would be easier to carry out the performance audit and initiate remedial measures. A forum for regular feedback is inescapable to keep track of the team environment. One cannot ward off internal fighting without detecting emerging conflicts. There must be a level of trust that would take care of interpersonal differences. A team member by virtue of his/her relationship with one significant personality in the organization may not contribute to the team's progress. Such a team may become extinct through resentment.

The team leader has to foresee the consequences and discuss these with the team. The leader will have to handle the issue tactfully. Token gestures can go a long way in preventing the worst kind of dysfunction: group animosity or hostility towards the manager. Honest team management, fair evaluation, and open communication help to a great extent in such a situation. In the interest of the team and organization, the leader should practise random acts of kindness to eliminate or reduce psychological distance.

MANAGING VIRTUAL TEAMS

You have read about virtual teams, which are a group of people within the same organization or from different organizations who work together for a common goal. Like any other team, a virtual team comprises a small number of people with complementary skills who are committed to a common purpose, performance goals, and approach for which they hold themselves mutually accountable, although they are geographically separated. As such, being at different work sites, they travel frequently and rely upon communication technologies (such as telephone, fax, teleconferencing, computer, groupware, Internet, etc.) to share information, collaborate, and coordinate their work efforts. Virtual teams are driven by an urgent need to work together, share accountability, commitment to teamwork, and active communication instead of being dormant (Jude-York et al. 2004) and respond to new realities that organizations face. The main objective of forming virtual teams is breaking the barriers of time and place. In fact, the needs behind virtual teams are manifold, some of which are as follows:

- Gaining global competence
- Fast pace of work
- Strategic alliance and partnering
- Cross-organizational teamwork
- Decentralized decision-making
- Traffic and commute challenge
- Work–home balance
- Cost saving to the organization (less office space)
- Accelerated learning and knowledge sharing
- Cultural diversity
- Customer focus
- Flatter organizational structure
- The 'team' as the unit of performance
- Merger and/or acquisition

Barriers to Functioning

Jude-York et al. (2004) remind that nothing is perfect and that the success of virtual teams depends on the individuals forming the team. They further point out the barriers in the functioning of virtual teams, some of which are as follows:

- Limited opportunity of daily interaction
- Less focus and more distraction
- Increased difficulty for leaders/coordinators/managers to motivate members
- More difficulty in establishing team spirit
- Technological challenges and associated learnings
- Social isolation

- Some non-verbal cues could result in miscommunication and misinterpretation

Potential Communication Challenges for Virtual Teams

Special communication challenges any virtual team face very often revolve around technology. The potential challenges include:

- Technophobia (fear of working with technology)
- Lack of technical skills
- Incompatibility of software or hardware or both and team members
- Lack of technical support (from other teams or the organization)
- Uncertainty among team players about when to use the various communication channels
- Information overload
- Natural disasters on account of inability to access technology due to multiple reasons

Strategies for Virtual Teams

Some researchers have recommended certain strategic guidelines to make virtual teamwork effective

- Holding an initial face-to-face introductory meeting
- Arranging periodic face-to-face meetings, especially to resolve conflict, and maintain and enhance team cohesiveness
- Establishing a transparent 'code of conduct' or set of norms and protocols for behaviour of members within the group and with others
- Recognizing and rewarding performance
- Using audio-visual presentation, to the extent possible, to avoid communication distortion
- Recognizing that most communications will be non-verbal—use caution in tone, intonation, and language
- Seeking confirmation, in case of verbal communication, through paraphrasing

Leading Virtual Teams: Ten Principles

The needs of virtual teams, the barriers to their functioning, potential communication challenges, and strategies for such teams have been discussed. To lead these teams effectively, one should follow certain principles. Hughes et al. (2007) provide ten principles:

1.   Be proactive—A virtual team may face challenges due to diversity, variation in time zones, psychological distractions, and so forth. Identify and welcome the challenge, but initiate remedial measures, for example, be diversity conscious to manage diversity, provide the option of working from home, organize occasional meetings, etc.

2.   Focus on relationship before tasks—Interpersonal relationship development and maintenance is a task to which the leader must pay prime importance.

3.   Seek clarity and focus early on—Clarify team purpose; clarity of purpose and accountability supports group cohesion.

4.   Create a sense of order and predictability—Uncertainty creates anxiety, phobias, and demotivation, which may even cause withdrawal. Communicate suitably to handle such situations. Use psychological threads to connect separate minds.

5.   Be a cool-headed, objective problem-solver—Isolation of a member from others may lead to distorted perception, and ultimately a problem may develop. Your fairness, impartiality, pragmatism, and maturity will help to solve the problem using problem-solving tools. Remember that panic is a virus and it breeds exceptionally well in silent and isolated places.

6.   Develop shared operating agreements—Involve your members in process selection, finalizing operating agreements, and other issues, and try to reach consensus. Make them want to do what you want them to do.

7.   Give team members personal attention—Understand your people, recognize their problems and shortcomings, endeavour to develop them, and, most importantly, share success to enthuse others.

8.   Respect the challenges of the virtual environment—Members are always tempted to carry over habits from one environment to another. Recognize individual differences and adapt to them. You have to enhance listening, empathizing, communicating, coordinating, engaging, energizing, involving, and enabling.

9.   Recognize the limits of available technologies—Virtual teams depend heavily on technology. You may aspire for a tailor-made facility and that particular technology may not be available. Technologies have limitations, and you must recognize that. Even if available, the cost may be prohibitive on budget considerations. Technology is a tool, excellent for some and not so much for others.

10. Stay people focused—People are the most vital entities of any team. They need belonging, accomplishment, and recognition. They also

suffer from frustration, anxiety, anger, excitement, and boredom. You have to humanize the virtual workplace, though it is dispersed.

FOSTERING TEAM CREATIVITY—COLLECTIVE WISDOM

A leader has to make efforts to turn individuals into team players, make teams effective, shape team behaviour, maintain a mature team, manage dysfunctional teams, and undertake many such tasks. Therefore, leaders need to foster team creativity, gaining and utilizing collective wisdom.

Creativity

People are imaginative, inventive risk-takers and challengers. But such attributes differ in magnitude from one person to another. The value of what people produce depends on their originality and creativity. You may recall that 'winners do not do different things, but they do things differently'.

Creativity is the ability to solve problems that are worth solving. It is the ability to create knowledge and use that to solve a specific problem. Creativity is the bringing into being of something that did not exist before, either as a product, a process, or a thought. A person needs opportunity to be creative and apply creativity. Creativity drives the generation of ideas, and you need new ideas constantly. Everyone is creative to a lesser or greater extent. You must have the urge, drive, or motivation to create something new, and you need to have the talent to carry out and materialize this urge and drive. These two factors, your drive and talent, although seem complementary to each other, are in fact independent.

Many individuals may be endowed with only one of the factors, and therefore never succeed in being really creative. You will notice that many talented persons due to a lack of motivation cease to create something new and original. They rather devote themselves only to performing, teaching, studying, reviewing, or criticizing creations by others. A review of the literature establishes that imagination, purposefulness, originality, and value are the four distinct characteristics of creativity.

Imagination, the output of a widespread thought process, is definitely a key part of creativity. But all imaginative ideas may not be creative. In an organizational context, a creative idea must lead to the achievement of a certain objective. The characteristics of creativity always involve thinking or behaving. Thus creativity calls for imaginative activities that are directed to achieving an objective. It is a process that must generate something original and the outcome must be of value in relation to the objective.

'Creativity is the connecting and rearranging of knowledge in the minds of the people who will allow themselves to think flexibly to generate often new and surprising ideas that others judge to be useful' (Joseph McPherson 1964). Creativity depends on a number of abilities: originality, fluency, variety, sensing, and analysing the phenomenon. Creative abilities include the ability to elaborate a theme, ability to go behind the surface features of the problem to investigate the real problem (Telsang 2002). The following are three examples of creativity.

Examples of creativity

Example 1 Kingdom Fine Metal Ltd (KFML)—KFML is one of the first companies in its industry to obtain ISO 9002 and ISO 14001 certification in 1995 and 1998, respectively. To continuously improve its products and services, the company has implemented a tailor-made management system that integrates total quality management; Ricoh's source assurance programme, 10-ppm quality improvement programme, statistical process control, and 5S practice.

KFML maintains a close partnership with its international customers that play another key role in organization improvement. Effective application of benchmarking has enabled the company to keep abreast of information regarding best practices in production processes, administration, innovation management, information technology, etc. KFML is enthusiastic about environmental protection. Besides using recycled materials, exhausted air and wastewater treatment facilities are well established. Implementing its recycling and management strategy, KFML strives to keep its promise to environmental protection. KFML received the Hong Kong Award for Industry: Quality in 1995, (www.tid.gov.hk).

Example 2 Swire Technologies Ltd—The company provides semi-conductor assembly and testing services to the electronics industry. To achieve continuous improvement, its cross-functional Quality Improvement Program (QIP), adopted since 1989, has actively combined total quality management applications, quality systems, training, teamwork, statistical process control, and benchmarking. The company received the Hong Kong Award for Industry: Quality in 1995 (www.tid.gov.hk).

Example 3 Motorola Semiconductors Hong Kong Ltd—The company is a wholly owned subsidiary of Motorola, Inc., US, which is the third largest semiconductor company in the world as well as a leading provider of electronic equipment systems, components, and services. Every step of operations was precisely engineered and managed to the ISO 9002 quality management system, with a distinctive road map for continuous improvement. Motorola bagged the Governor's Award for Industry: Quality in 1994 (www.tid.gov.hk).

Fostering team creativity

Large organizations today encourage people to work in teams and strive to foster creativity in the teams. They take up an already existing team and try to make the team more creative than it would otherwise tend to be. Brainstorming is the tool that is mostly used to foster creativity leading to problem-solving. However, 'synectics' or 'lateral thinking' is encouraged to add to the gamut of means to support the accelerated flow of ideas.

Synectics is an approach to creative thinking that depends on understanding that is apparently different and its main tool is analogy, equivalence, or similarity. Workgroups use synectics to help develop creative ideas that lead to problem-solving. Synectics helps its users break existing mindsets and think in a different way. It combines a structured approach to creativity with the freewheeling problem-solving approach used in techniques like brainstorming.

Lateral thinking is a heuristic for solving problems. It looks at the problem from many angles instead of remaining stuck with one only. It means a set of systematic techniques used for changing concepts and perceptions, exploring multiple possibilities and approaches and generating new technique for solving a problems. Not all people are creative. Creative thinking, an instinctive talent a person possesses, can be learned, developed, and utilized in the work area.

Phases of creativity

Creativity, the instinctive talent of a person, develops in phases like preparation, immersion, incubation, illumination, evaluation, and application (Goman 2004).

- Preparation—First of all, one has to do the groundwork like information gathering, data collection, opinion survey, etc., whichever one feels is relevant to the project or assignment undertaken.
- Immersion—This is the stage when one should be totally absorbed in the situation or problem. Concentration on all the appropriate and significant facts, figures, concerns, angles, and opinions is the elements of the immersion stage. While your imagination will be free and open, your thinking process may be juxtaposed by many unusual and unlikely elements. But that will not cause any hindrance.
- Incubation—When a person takes rest, his/her subconscious, which is a

far more fertile ground for creativity, becomes active. The subconscious mind has no judgemental or censoring elements in which ideas are free to recombine in unique ways, emerge in noble ways. You turn off the process and do not think about the solution of a problem.

- Illumination—In the subconscious mind, you may suddenly get the solution. The sudden appearance of the answer to your problem in the form of an image, an insight, a thought breaks through your conscious awareness and comes to you.
- Evaluation—At this stage, one has to test the practicability of the idea in reality considering all possible consequences.
- Application—This is the final phase when creativity is translated into an innovative reality, tangibility, value, usefulness, and meaningfulness. A creative workgroup or team differentiates itself from others based on its achievements.

Collective Intelligence, Wisdom, and Consciousness

The hallmark of a creative group is the extent to which a prolific flow of ideas can take place in it (Belbin 1981). Collective intelligence, collective wisdom, and collective consciousness are all different (Macdonald 2008).

Collective intelligence refers to the external, methodological, and operational aspects of social organizations to raise their intelligence as a whole. The astounding and surprising effects of collective intelligence are appearing as a topic of interest worldwide, in the natural sciences as well as the social sciences, under such names as group wisdom, co-intelligence, transpersonal-creative knowledge, or the zero point fields. In various areas of enquiry, information from a shared field offers solutions that extend far beyond the best efforts of an individual and, at the same time, exercise a strong developmental influence on the individual.

Collective wisdom is the access to and the manifestation and demonstration of wisdom at a collective level. A group of wise individuals do not necessarily know how to work and behave wisely together, because of a lack of collective intelligence. Therefore, collective intelligence is a necessary (but not exclusive) condition for collective wisdom to emerge. The meaning of collective wisdom, a collaborative knowledge and acumen of a group, is simple but it is difficult to put into practice. You have your own firmly established beliefs about individual, social and political developments, and their effects on organizations. You also believe in working in teams as synergy plays its role.

The wisdom of shared fields contributes to the understanding of organizational phenomena, accelerating the transformation process and advancing the organization towards improvement. This shared wisdom has immediate, practical importance. The shared field phenomena are being researched and utilized to create solutions based on a more complete and more human one foundation in many areas—in new approaches to therapy such as in the new, expanded development of family constellations as well as other transpersonal methods, in peace and reconciliation work, in communal initiatives for the improvement of local politics, in business, political advisement, and in art, music, and theatre as well.

Hewlett-Packard is bringing together a wide range of members from different divisions and customers of multiple products to create new strategic planning and innovative products. Similarly, Ford is putting designers, engineers, lawyers, finance people, suppliers, dealers, distributors, market researchers all together under one roof. Companies all over the world are learning the creative power of well-run teams. Successful and excellent companies are enjoying the benefits of collective wisdom.

Collective consciousness is the sense that each member of a team, each participant of a brainstorming session has about the consciousness of the group. It is a space one can access at any time to sense what the context is and what is likely to emerge. Three key conditions necessary for the manifestation of collective consciousness are a shared wealth (the perception of qualities and contributions of each one), a shared vulnerability (the humanness in the other), and a shared language (for understanding each other). Something new has recently begun to emerge—the wisdom of our shared fields, in which we all participate and which bind us more intimately than we ever might have imagined.

A few examples on collective wisdom are appended to elucidate collective wisdom.

Example 1: Locating the missing submarine

The former president of India, Dr A.P.J. Abdul Kalam, in his convocation address on 6 December 2006 at the Indian Institute of Social Welfare and Business Management, emphasized the need for 'collective wisdom' and cited an example from his Defence Research and Development Organisation (DRDO) experience. In his language, 'I read a book in which a methodology is described for solving a complex problem pertaining to a lost submarine. This book describes how the management held meetings with four experts who made suggestions. When the search was made using these suggestions, no positive result was found. Then the top management decided to call a meeting of all the 40 people from multiple disciplines for working out a comprehensive search process. All the 40 members were asked to give a mutually exclusive suggestion for progressing towards the search. The resultant 40 suggestions gave five alternatives. Based on these five alternatives, parallel teams were developed to carry out the search process. This finally led to the detection of the missing submarine. This type of problem-solving technique is followed in our Indian institutions like the Indian Space Research Organisation and the DRDO, where the programme review meetings are attended by specialists in multi-discipline, leading to precise determination of the problem area and finding satisfactory solutions. The message for graduating students from this institution is that they have to keep their eyes and ears open and try to seek guidance from all possible avenues for solving organizational problems.' Thus, collective wisdom gives result.

Example 2: Breaking of a 40 kg weight

You have been told that a 40 kg weight has broken into four pieces. Using the four pieces, it is possible to measure any weight ranging from unity to 40 kg. You are to tell the individual weights. You are not able to answer immediately. After some time, you get a clue from your friend. The clue specifies that the individual weights be in geometric progression. On getting the clue, you could answer that the weights would be 1, 3, 9, and 27.

Example 3: Golomb rulers

Imagine a six-inch ruler with marks inscribed not at the usual equal intervals but at 0, 1, 4, and 6 inches. Taking all possible pairs of marks, you can measure six distinct distances: 1, 2, 3, 4, 5, and 6 inches. A ruler on which no two pairs of marks measure the same distance is called a Golomb ruler, after Solomon W. Golomb of the University of Southern California. He described the concept more than 25 years ago. The '0-1-4-6' example is a perfect Golomb ruler, in that all integer intervals from 1 to the length of the ruler are represented. On rulers with more than four marks, perfection is not possible; the best you can do is an optimal Golomb ruler, which for a given number of marks is the shortest ruler on which no intervals are duplicated.

Example 4: Supercomputer

The most powerful computer in the world, according to a recent ranking, is a machine called 'Janus', which has 9216 Pentium Pro processors. That is a lot of Pentia, but it is a pretty puny number in comparison with the 20 million or more processors attached to the global Internet. The 9216 Pentiums are all conveniently housed in a single room at the Sandia National Laboratory in Albuquerque. Setting them to work on the task of your choice is a simple matter; all you need is an account on the machine, a password, an allocation of CPU time, possibly a security clearance, and a little knowledge of programming in a specialized dialect of FORTRAN or C (www.americanscientist.org, Brian Hayes 1998).

After creativity, the need of fostering team creativity, and collective intelligence, wisdom, and consciousness, you should now study the basic skills of team leaders.

BASIC SKILLS OF TEAM LEADERS

In order to drive the team and accomplish the targets, a leader must have certain basic leadership skills, some of which are communication, listening, assertiveness, technical competency, setting goals, reprimanding for behavioural modification, etc.

Communication

A leader has to communicate to exchange ideas, concepts, opinions, thoughts, plans, and judgement to one person, a group, or a mass of people. The process of transfer of information as discussed above is communication. Communication skills are essentially required to address, arbitrate, arrange, brief, collaborate, consult, contact, convince, correspond, demonstrate, develop, direct, draft, edit, enlist, explain, familiarize, formulate, influence, inform, interpret, listen, market, mediate, moderate, motivate, negotiate, persuade, present, publicize, reconcile, recruit, report, respond, secure, sell, solicit, summarize, translate, etc. The communicator must know the purpose of communication, choose the appropriate context and medium, transmit clear signals and ensure that the receiver understands them. Any distortion in the communication is likely to pose a threat to organizational decision-making.

Hughes et al. (2008) mention knowledge, behaviours, and criteria to evaluate communication skills. The knowledge component 'communication skills' concerns the intention of the leader, knowing what medium is most effective, and knowing where the message was heard and understood. The quality of communication can progress or retreat, make or mar a team's advancement. Some people have a high level of awareness of how they are behaving when they are interacting with others.

Communication effectiveness

Technology has made a great impact on communication. Estimates show that 50 per cent of interpersonal messages in any organization are communicated through telephone (Pareek 2008). With the advent of mobile phones, this has become a frequent mode of communication.

Another mode of communication is e-mail; in contrast to 'snail mail', e-mail accounts for 40 per cent of all acts of communication and the advantages of using e-mail for attaching files of different types and formats, as a means of communication are known to all of us. Teleconferencing is now a common means of meeting with members from cross-functional teams. Browsing to search for information and download files has become an easy task. Internet technology has brought a revolution in the communication system. In conventional face-to-face communication, on studying the non-verbal signals or body language of the other person or members, one can interpret the thinking process of others.

Apart from what a person says, how he/she delivers a message (its non-verbal aspects) and receives a message (non-verbal responses during exchange of communication) influence the quality and effect of communication (Pareek 2008).

Promoting effective communication

We spend most of our communication energy on telling others what we need them to hear and when we need them to hear it. Effective communication requires us to balance this with what they need to hear from us and when they need to hear it. As a team leader, consider the following strategies or approaches:

- Formulate and organize a survey of satisfaction ratings on different forms and directions of communication within your team. Use the data to target aspects of communication that have the greatest potential for improvement. Avoid embarrassment by telling people why you are doing it. Do not criticize any person, only discuss the process.
- Encourage rephrasing as an approach or a strategy to enhance active listening. Empathetic listening is vital.
- Try to finish conversations with the question 'Is there anything else you want to talk about?' or 'Am I clear to you?' These questions will provide opportunities for others to ask about what they need to hear. Look into their eyes constantly.
- Management means communication. Though many factors may hinder team performance, communication is the most crucial of these. To make a team better, and achieving common goals and vision, the ability to harness diversity and gaining mastery over communication are the key differences between a group and a team.

Listening

Listening is a vital component of communication. While performing the role of coach, mentor, counsellor, or a family member, one has to be an active listener. Active listening (crs.uvm.edu/gopher/nerl/personal/comm/) makes communication helpful, meaningful, telepathic, motivational, inspirational. In our daily work life we spend most of the time listening, but we seldom endeavour to enhance our listening skills which is most important in teamworking.

Ten discrete skills for listening

Listening empathetically needs certain skills. The listener has to attend to or acknowledge what the other person is saying by nodding the head or other non-verbal messages in addition to verbal messages. He has to respond to the person's basic verbal messages. Marisue (1986) identifies ten discrete skills for empathetic listening.

(a) Attending—Acknowledging what the other person is saying through verbal and non-verbal messages and setting eye contact.

(b) Reiterating—Paraphrasing what the person is briefing, responding to his/her verbal messages.

(c) Reflecting—Replicating your own experience, feelings, and content perceived through cues and signals corresponding to what you have heard.

(d) Interpreting—You must offer tentative inference about the other person's feelings, desires, and meanings.

(e) Synthesizing—In order to express your seriousness about his/her briefings, you should summarize and provide a focus.

(f) Probing—You must frame messages in a supporting way and ask questions requesting further clarifications or getting your doubts clarified; when he/she is likely to vent out more for your benefit.

(g) Providing feedback—To get you have to give; share perceptions of the other person's ideas and disclose relevant personal information.

(h) Supporting—To make the process of communication more effective, create an environment of warmth, friendship, and caring in your own way.

(i) Verifying perception—In verbal communication, there can always be a certain gap or distortion; therefore, get your interpretations and perceptions verified for accuracy and validity.

(j) Being quiet—Give the other person time to think and talk; interruption will lead to disruption of his/her thoughts.

In order to develop listening skills one has to be careful about the following:

- Developing the desire to be directed by others, the team members, rather than to project one's own feelings, thoughts, and ideas on to others.
- Sacrificing behaviour to protect self—unless this is done it would be difficult to focus and honour other persons' views.
- Respecting others' experience, credentials, thoughts, viewpoints, etc.
- Interpreting the importance of the roles, perspectives, or responsibilities of others rather than assuming they are the same as one's own.
- Cultivating the habit of listening as a receiver, and not as a critic, and the desire to understand other persons and their strengths and weaknesses for their constructive uses.

Anyone can learn, practice, and master these skills. One advice that I offer is that if you find someone is influencing you and others in a discussion, do not be demoralized. Pay more attention on the spoken side of the communication equation of the person; notice with care how he/she listens to others and react accordingly. A communicator needs to affirm that the person in front him/her is listening to what he/she is saying.

In the communication equation, one is the spoken side and the other is the listener side. We all will agree that we lay emphasis on the spoken side and mostly ignore the other one. Communication is conveying true messages, and in this active listening plays a dominant role. You need to communicate that you are listening. You can do that through eye contact (non-verbal method). You can encourage by asking questions—both open (how? what? when? would you clarify?) and closed (is it so? are you?). The questions must be relevant, focusing on the speaker, topic, listener, or anything else. In a coaching session conducted by a quality manager, the answer to an open-ended question like 'how to handle the situation if the components are beyond the control limits?' must be listened to carefully. Another open-ended question maybe, when should we feel that the machine operator needs training or would you clarify how exactly to carry out the force field analysis?

Assertiveness

Assertiveness is social 'boldness' and is a dominant determinant of performance in any work sphere—manufacturing or service. Assertiveness is essential for human beings who desire to achieve success, irrespective of the nature of engagement, as an assertive person can execute his/her duties efficiently and effectively. The level of assertiveness greatly affects the performance of an individual and is a dominant factor responsible for the successful accomplishment of a job.

Assertive employees participate more broadly, take on greater responsibilities, express their ideas and interact with greater varieties of people, solve problems objectively, find solutions and implement them with little or no resistance. Assertive persons get the willing support of their team-mates and colleagues. They can manage conflict effectively. They do not avoid but accommodate, do not compromise but collaborate with others. Assertiveness is a quality required in the area of quality management in teamwork.

Assertiveness is a positive and constructive way of relating to other people, respecting their needs, wants, and rights, as well as one's own needs, wants, and rights. Thus, teamwork needs assertive people. Assertive behaviour enables people to act in their own best interests, to stand up for themselves without undue anxiety, to express honest feelings comfortably, or to exercise personal rights without denying the rights of others. Assertiveness directly helps an individual to get what he/she wants, thus making himself/herself heard and known without trampling on the rights of others.

Gillen (1995) states that assertive interaction is the beginning of a rational, non-accusatory conversation, and assertiveness helps achieve results, respect people, build confidence and self-esteem, reduce stress, and gain people's liking. Assertiveness emphasizes expressing one's needs, opinions, and feelings with the confidence that he/she will not be dominated, exploited, or coerced. Tone of voice, intonation, volume, facial expression, gesture, and body language, all play a part in assertive communication (Bishop 2000).

Assertiveness is an antidote for fear, shyness, passivity, and even anger, and so there is an astonishingly wide range of situations in which assertiveness is appropriate (Schimmel 1976). He suggests several kinds of assertive behaviours:

- To speak up, make requests, ask for favours, and generally insist that one's rights are respected as a significant, equal human being to overcome the fears and self-deprecation that keeps one from doing these things.
- To express negative emotions (complaints, resentment, criticism, disagreement, intimidation, the desire to be left alone) and to refuse requests.

- To show positive emotions (joy, pride, liking someone, attraction) and to give compliments, and accept compliments with a smile and a 'thank you'.
- To ask 'why' and question authority or tradition, not in order to rebel but to assume responsibility for asserting one's share of control of the situation, and to make things better.
- To initiate, carry on, change, and terminate conversations comfortably, and share one's feelings, opinions, and experiences with others.
- To deal with minor irritations before one's anger builds into intense resentment and explosive aggression.

Assertive communication

You must have been convinced that you and your team mates should be more assertive. Do you think you will gain from being more assertive? And where will you start? Think of the areas or actual situations where you want to apply your assertiveness skill. Assertiveness hierarchy (or assertiveness ladder) implies starting with the least difficult and working upwards to the most difficult change that you would like to bring about in yourself. As usual, you should start at the bottom and progress up through the list.

In the workplace or elsewhere, you will come across many awkward situations. You should not worry. If you remain passive, you will burn internally. On the other hand, do not be aggressive and quit. Be assertive. Remember that there are 201 ways to say 'No' effectively and gracefully. Learn assertiveness and apply it right from today. Your assertive behaviour will enable you to reach a 'win-win' situation (Haldar 2008) (Figure 9.2).

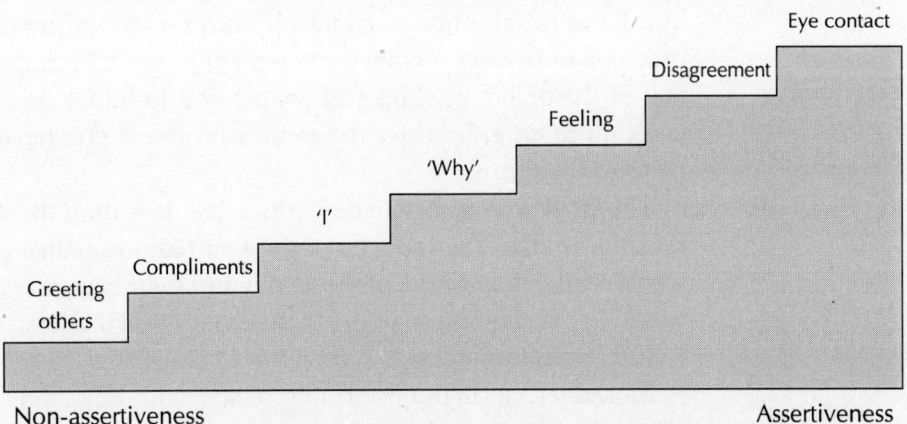

FIGURE **9.2   The steps to be assertive**

Technical Competency

Leaders need a variety of competencies to achieve team goals, of which technical competency is one. This competency helps them in direct interaction while communicating and building personal networks and relationships with others. In fact, leadership competency comprises skills and behaviours concerned with building teams and getting results through team members. The competencies that relate to analysing issues, generating alternatives, selecting the best, considering financial positions, thinking strategically, and making decisions fall in the category of business skills.

Technical competencies refer to knowledge about systems, processes, procedures or methods, and techniques for conducting a specialized activity as in the case of engineers, doctors, musicians, players, accounts, and other professionals. This competency is also the ability to select and use equipment, a procedure, standing instructions, technique, and knowledge.

Setting Goals

Setting goals for self, a team member, or the team as a whole needs experience, maturity, and pragmatism. If the goals are specific and the roles are clear and unambiguous, members can perform better. Specific goals lead to higher performance. Each goal must be split into its elements and time allotted for its achievement. Completion of each element must be closely monitored.

Consider the objective of productivity enhancement. To achieve this objective, you are first required to consider the product range and logically segregate that. Consider a particular group of products, estimate the level to which you can enhance the output or reduce the resources required. You have to take into account all constraints you might encounter. The time you estimate to achieve an element or work package must be less than that of the objective. This will enable you to initiate action if any element takes more time. In order to monitor progress, you have to set the goal in measurable terms.

The goal should be neither more nor less than attainable. If the goal set is more than the capacity of the team and remains unachieved, then it would lead to frustration of the leader and members, and team performance would become questionable. On the contrary, if it is less, members' capacity would remain unutilized.

Moreover, a high-performing team with talented members prefers challenging tasks and innovative activities to derive intellectual joy. Such a team cannot prove itself if a routine task is assigned. Targets must aim to produce superior performance, for which a considerable degree of stretch is required. But they must also be realistic to motivate the manager. Unrealistic targets tend to demotivate and also create a climate of 'fear of failure'.

Goals (Tables 9.3, 9.4, and 9.5) must be relevant to specific business objectives, and be accomplished within the time stipulated for them. Otherwise, even if a goal is achieved within time, it will not lead to achieving a business objective. Targets must be 'measurable' even if not necessarily 'quantitative'. Some examples of quantitative targets are as follows:

- Improve sales by 8 per cent in one year
- Achieve profit to the extent of Rs 20 million in the coming financial year
- Improve yield to 5 per cent in one quarter
- Reduce costs by 2 per cent in six months
- Recruit 50 management trainees within four months
- Cut overtime to zero in two years

TABLE **9.3** **Guidelines to setting specific targets**

How NOT to set targets	How to set targets
Initiate cost saving programmes	Reduce transport rates by 5 per cent in the coming annual estimates
Achieve 40 per cent market share for product 'roller bearing'	Achieve average 'roller bearing' market share of 40 per cent
Liaise with information technology department to automate payroll	Install the software on 'Production Planning and Control' in second quarter, train people, and use in third quarter
Conduct many staff training workshops	Conduct quarterly staff workshops focusing on…

TABLE **9.4** **Guidelines to setting measurable targets**

How NOT to set targets	How to set targets
Successfully launch the product 'Front Axle' in second quarters	Launch 'Front Axle' in second quarter and achieve exit value market share of 5 per cent
Provide commercial support to business head	Submit Monthly Commercial Review docket
Launch product 'Dove' if import rules are relaxed	Launch product 'Dove' in second quarter since imports are now allowed
Sign a good welfare system with workers	Sign four-year welfare system before third quarter with 20 per cent productivity improvement

TABLE **9.5** **Guidelines to setting time-bound targets**

How NOT to set targets	How to set targets
Increase market share to 40 per cent in product 'Flange Coupling'	Increase exit market in product 'Flange Coupling' to 40 per cent by third quarter
Advance target dates for accounts closing	Complete accounts closing and audit by 30 June
Reduce absenteeism in the factory	Reduce absenteeism in the maintenance department from 12 per cent to minimum 8 per cent by October

(Tables 9.3, 9.4, and 9.5 designed based on a lecture on 'Target Setting for Superior Performance' delivered by P.K. Chatterjee, Senior Vice President [HR], Duncans Group, on 4 December 2008 at Indian Society for Training and Development (ISTD), Kolkata Chapter.)

Chatterjee (2008) also spoke on the acid test of target setting, review of targets, agreeing on review mechanism at the beginning, and encouraging self-review and continuous review.

Acid test of target setting

Will the deliverable and the level of target achievement be crystal clear at the end of the year to the manager to whom you report, the HR department and to you?

Review of targets

- Often, the most contentious and problematic aspect is review of performance.
- Consideration of some of the common objections and pitfalls will help prepare the ground for success
- Advice: Start long before the review itself.

Agree on review mechanism at the beginning

- Clarify success criteria unambiguously
- Description of outcomes
- Tendency to show leniency at the evaluation stage; this can be minimized if targets and success criteria are specific
- Extra preparation needed especially when the target involves qualitative measures

Encourage self-review and continuous review

- As in target setting, the employee has a key role in own review
- Several advantages of self-review
- Tone will be more participative and employees are likely to be more committed

- Easy to discuss shortfalls
- Continuous review should be encouraged, with emphasis of final review on summarizing issues already discussed

A team cannot use any 'magic bullet' to accomplish tasks. Goals require commitment of each member and the leader. Organizational commitment is a state in which an employee identifies with a particular organization, its mission, policies, objectives, and goals, and wishes to maintain membership of the organization.

Commitments are emotional reactions of employees towards an organization and its policies. Feelings of alienation and helplessness influence the commitment of team members. Organizational goals or team goals are most likely to be achieved if there is commitment towards them at the level of the workforce concerned. Persons higher in the hierarchy must be committed to extend leadership, provide resources, continue support, identify member weaknesses and help eliminate them, encourage through rewards and compensation, etc. In turn, the working members must spontaneously extend support to achieve team goals. To build subordinate acceptance and commitment to goals is to have subordinates participate in setting the goals.

Gathering feedback is essential to assess, in the true sense, the extent of achieving feedback. If the goals are precisely measurable, then it is an easy task to decide about completion of the goals. But goals cannot always be set in precisely measurable terms. In such cases, gathering feedback helps decide about completion of the goal. Hughes et al. (2008) highlight that one of the most effective ways to improve performance is to assess how closely a person's behaviour matches some criterion, and research shows that performance was much higher when goals were accompanied by feedback than when either goal or feedback were used alone.

Thus the primers of goal setting are as follows:

- Goals should be specific and measurable.
- Goals should be attainable but challenging.
- Goals should be relevant, realistic, and time bound.
- Goals require commitment of all levels of workers.
- Goals require feedback.

ADVANCED SKILLS OF TEAM LEADERS

Apart from the basic skills just discussed, leaders must also have certain other skills generally called advanced skills. Time management, delegation, managing conflict, persuasiveness, negotiation, problem-solving, team building for work teams, building high performance teams, development planning, and developing commitment are some advanced skills a leader must have.

Time Management

Leaders very often suffer from stress due to work pressure. Gradually, the pressure leads to burn-out stress syndrome and then to health problems. Thus, managing time is an essential need of a leader. A leader performs urgent as well as important activities in addition to many normal activities. He/she should entrust most of the activities to junior colleagues. He/she should not be afraid thinking that the junior may keep aside some important work and delay execution of something urgent. Team leaders must assess and consider the strengths and weaknesses, and regularity and sincerity of team members. They should monitor but desist from close supervision. Leaders should prepare an exhaustive list of activities they are performing and classify them based on urgency (urgent and very urgent) and importance (important and very important). Leaders can do the very urgent work themselves and assign important tasks to a sincere junior. The rest of the activities can be allocated to other juniors.

Certain steps are suggested that may enable leaders to manage time (Haldar 2009).

Step 1 Classify the activities based on urgency (urgent and very urgent) and importance (important and very important).

Step 2 Prepare a matrix and place the activities in the respective cells (Figure 9.3).

Step 3 Concentrate only on activities in the category VI-VU, that is, very important and very urgent.

Step 4 Assign the VI-U tasks to a junior who is regular in his/her work.

Step 5 Delegate the I-VU tasks to a sincere junior.

Step 6 Detail staff members to carry out the I-U tasks. Develop a system and procedure, and issue work instructions for these tasks. Assign the task of monitoring to the junior managers.

Step 7 Oversee the system occasionally.

Figure 9.3 elucidates categorization of activities based on two parameters: degree of urgency and degree of importance.

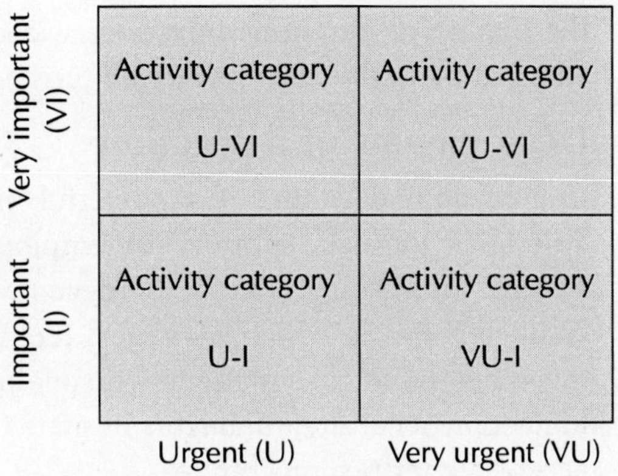

FIGURE **9.3** **Time management matrix**

Delegation

Delegation is transferring authority from one organizational level to another lower level, assigning authority for work to junior colleagues, allowing them to make decisions that enable the senior person to manage time more effectively. Delegation is basically a four-step process: allocation of duties to subordinates, delegation of authority, assignment of responsibility, and creation of accountability. In fact, on receiving authority, responsibility develops from within.

Allocation of duties means set of activities and tasks that one desires to get done by junior colleagues. Allocation of tasks precedes delegation of authority. Delegation of authority refers to passing on tasks, and empowering another to carry out tasks acting on behalf of his/her senior. Delegation is a formal step that helps develop juniors. Assigning the person a corresponding obligation to perform follows the delegation of authority. From this obligation, what develops is responsibility. The delegation process is complete on the creation of accountability of the person delegated.

On receiving authority, a junior feels responsible and boldly accepts accountability. Furthermore, the relationship between the dyads, the senior who has delegated and the junior who has received the authority, is enhanced.

Purpose of delegation

Delegation helps develop juniors and enables them to make decisions. In addition, delegation frees up the senior's time which he/she can utilize in doing creative activities. Juniors can consider all inputs meticulously and the quality of decisions improves. Needless to mention, subordinates get stimulation and energy, which in turn enhances their commitment.

Determinants of delegation

Organizational culture is a powerful influencer of managers' delegation. Tolerance for risk, support for employees, a high degree of autonomy, system of working, extent of decentralization are some organizational characteristics in which managers feel more comfortable to delegate. On the other hand, in risk-aversive situations, and in a non-supportive and high control culture, managers hesitate to delegate. Also, juniors hesitate to accept higher responsibilities.

Principles of effective delegation

A leader, in order to manage his/her team and produce results, has to follow certain principles like deciding what to delegate and to whom to delegate, making the assignment clear, specific, and measurable, assigning an objective, giving credit but sharing the blame, allowing autonomy but monitoring performance (Hughes et al. 2008). However, sharing success to enthuse others is another principle a leader must observe after delegation. The leader need not necessarily communicate the procedure as he/she must have taken into account the ability in this regard. But he/she must be vigilant about how things are moving without interfering too much as that retards the velocity of work.

Deciding what to delegate—You can make this decision fairly easily just by maintaining a record of the activities and the time required to complete them. As a leader, you must consider each activity one by one and justify the time spent to complete that. You must further judge critically. This will enable you to decide what to delegate and to whom. Refer to the time management skills of leaders discussed earlier in this chapter.

Who to be delegated—Any team comprises excellent, good, and fair performers. Delegating only to excellent performers will overburden them. As a leader, you have to balance the developmental opportunities among all the followers. Followers of all levels must be assigned series of assignments commensurate with their capabilities. Otherwise, they will ultimately become parasitic on the team and the organization. A good leader delegates to all team members based on individual capabilities.

Making the assignment clear, specific, and measurable—Having decided what you will delegate and to whom, your next duty should be to ensure that the assignments are clear to the delegate. You have to clarify, preferably in writing, what is expected of them, both the quantitative target and the qualitative requirements. Verbal communication, though it cannot always be avoided, can often lead to disaster. A good leader invites and welcomes questions to ensure whether the communication interpreted by the team members conforms to what actually has been communicated.

Assigning an objective—Assign the tasks to be performed; do not tell the procedure they are to follow. This will give them a chance to brainstorm and help them grow. Otherwise, their growth vector will cease.

Give credit but share blame—Recall the old proverb, 'to err is human'. A sincere and dedicated member of your team can also a commit mistake. If juniors do something commendable, praise them to motivate them. However, if anyone makes a mistake, criticize the work but not the person; rather share the blame so that the junior feels your greatness as a leader. This will definitely yield positive results. Follow the practice, 'praise in public; criticize privately'.

Allow autonomy, but monitor performance—Empowering juniors and giving them a degree of autonomy, as well as authority, in carrying out their new responsibilities must also include the freedom to make certain kinds of mistakes. Hughes et al. (2008) emphasize that punishment for mistakes suppresses initiative and innovation. As a leader-manager, remember that mistakes are important sources of development. Create an organizational environment conducive to learning from mistakes.

Share success to enthuse others—You might be the main architect behind an achievement. But if you share the success with your team members, you will ultimately win, be able to transmit a silent message to them and uphold your image among them. Remember that image building is an essential prerequisite for successful accomplishment. The sharing will not only motivate them, but will also enhance your charisma.

Leader delegation skills

A team leader delegates authority for multiple reasons. Delegation needs certain skills for its effectiveness—clarifying the assignment, specifying the range discretion, allowing subordinates to participate and develop, informing that delegation has occurred, establishing feedback controls, and insisting on recommendations from subordinates when problems occur (Robbins 2008).

Clarify the assignment—This has been discussed earlier in a different way. The process of delegation starts with what is to be delegated and to whom.

Identifying the right person is a critical task for the leader. The person must be capable of performing the delegated task. He/she has to be trustworthy and motivated to willingly accept challenging and higher-order tasks. However, he/she needs clarity about the assignment.

Specify the range discretion—All organizational phenomena cannot be brought under the umbrella of system, rules, and procedures. As such, subordinates need empowerment to apply discretion, which obviously must have a certain boundary. The leader must specify the range. Preferably all the parameters should be categorized and then a category-wise range specified.

Allow the subordinate to participate and develop—It may not be possible to assess at the start how much authority will be necessary for task accomplishment. But the person who will be held accountable must have authority. Therefore the subordinate may be cautiously allowed to participate while taking decisions on how much authority will be required.

Inform that delegation has occurred—All members of the group, and other relevant persons of the organization who are likely to be affected should know about the delegation. Preferably a circular mentioning who has been delegated and the extent of authority given may be issued under the signature of the competent authority. Delegation cannot take place in secrecy. Failure to inform others often generates conflict.

Establish feedback control—Having received the authority, one inadvertently makes a mistake, not to speak of misusing authority. This demands feedback control. The control may be exercised by instituting a system of feedback on work progress. Ideally, the control system should be planned and designed at the time of initial design.

When a problem occurs, insist on recommendations from the subordinate. Once delegated and authorized, the member should share the total responsibility. He/she should not run to the team leader for solution to the problem. The leader should not encourage this either, otherwise the member will continue to be dependent and never develop.

Managing Conflict

Conflict is part and parcel of organizational life. It can be intra-personal or interpersonal. Conflict does not develop all of a sudden. When one individual perceives that another individual is dynamic and making some conscious effort to frustrate him, then the conflict episode begins. The second stage begins when the individual experiences feelings of threat, hostility, mistrust, or fear of loss and so on. In the third stage, a conscious attempt is made by one to block the goal or achievement of another. The endeavours for conflict resolution may start from this stage. The fourth or last stage refers to the consequences that different conflict-handling strategies may have on the antecedent (ground) conditions. The attempt may either resolve the conflict or reduce it.

To manage conflict, the leader may impose a solution, choose diffusion strategy, smooth out the same, or appeal to the team goal.

Imposing a solution—The team leader should study the antecedent conditions, finalize a solution, and impose the solution on the conflicting members.

Conflict diffusion strategy—This strategy attempts to keep the conflict in abeyance. The emotions of both the parties are allowed to precipitate down.

Smoothing—This strategy has been found to be successful where the conflicting members have some similarities. In this technique, the leader may highlight the similarities between the members. This enables both the parties to realize that they are not basically much apart from each other with regard to their viewpoints, perception and psychological bases.

Appealing to team goal—In order to appeal, the leader may uphold the status of the team, its achievements in the recent past, and other positive aspects.

Conflict resolution principles

Different authors have given different taxonomies like conflict avoidance strategy, conflict diffusion strategy, conflict containment strategy, and conflict confrontation strategy.

Conflict avoidance strategy encompasses either ignoring the conflict or imposing a solution. Considering the gravity of the conflict and parties involved it can be reduced by ignoring it altogether. Again, considering the antecedent conditions, a solution can be finalized and imposed by a higher-level manager. However, in either case, the conflict will disappear for some time but can reappear in some other form or guise or in another situation.

Conflict diffusion strategy attempts to keep the conflict in abeyance. The emotions of both parties are allowed to precipitate down. Conflict smoothing, appealing to team goal, and conflict containment strategy are adopted. The smoothing strategy has been found to be successful. The superordinate goal of any organization is basically its survival and then its growth. If the superordinate goal is highlighted and discussed to the conflicting parties, then the current problem appears insignificant. This sometimes helps the leader to tackle the situation.

In the conflict containment strategy, the issues are selectively discussed through mediators or through bargaining or by restructuring the interaction patterns. Conflict may stem between two parties or groups on various issues. They may be asked to depute their chosen representatives issue-wise. While explaining the case to the representative, the party or group may discover lapses. The representative may also react with and influence the party or group whereby the intensity of conflict will get diluted. The rationale is that only when the representative will be fully convinced, will he/she argue the party's point forcefully and accurately.

Conflict is very often managed by structuring the interaction or restructuring the system. This may be effected by (a) decreasing the amount of direct interaction between the groups (in the early stage of the conflict), (b) decreasing the time for problem-solving meeting or by organizing it very quickly, (c) decreasing the formality of the presentation of the issue, (d) limiting submission of historic events and precedence, (e) using a third party mediator, and (f) and forcing the group to focus on current issues and goals.

Conflict confrontation strategy is designed in such a way that all the issues are first 'uncovered' and then a mutually acceptable solution found. This strategy deals with the conflict more openly and thoroughly. The two techniques incorporated are 'problem-solving' and 'comprehensive organizational redesign'.

Problem-solving emphasizes finding a mutually satisfactory solution that will reconcile and integrate the needs of both parties who work together. If lack of coordination of work is the source of conflict, then organizational redesign helps conflict resolution. While redesigning the task, interdependence may be eliminated or reduced, and clear work responsibilities may be assigned. This is restructuring of the organization that leads to an effective inter-group conflict resolution.

While handling conflicts, certain points must be kept in mind. Differences and divergent views of members can always be there. Find something positive in the every divergent view and bring it to the limelight. React assertively and positively, use empathy and positive feedback, confront problems, and negotiate solutions together.

Persuasiveness

Persuasiveness refers to conscious manipulation mainly through face-to-face communication to induce and stimulate others to take action that helps achieve a goal. Persuasion means influencing but it differs from authority and power. It does not encroach in others area of interest as it preserves his/her freedom. When authority does not work, persuasion often can.

Credibility: In order to be successful in persuasion, you must establish your credibility, use logical reasoning, and appeal emotionally. The leader can establish credibility by demonstrating competence, knowledge, and ability. Credibility cannot be earned immediately. It takes time to develop a reputation for competence. Credibility can also be established by having trustworthy intentions. An ethical, industrious, and dependable person can earn credibility among his/her colleagues. If a team leader strikes others as friendly, positive, enthusiastic, and caring, his/her credibility starts growing. Credibility is enhanced personal charisma.

Logical reasoning: Persuasion demands others to behave and act as one wishes. A team wants to achieve its goal for which it needs the efforts of its members. A team needs helps from other functional areas. Logical reasoning makes the persuasion process easy. For this, you have to gather data, facts and figures, and submit them sequentially during discussions.

Emotional support: This approach, in addition to credibility and logical reasoning, helps a lot in persuasion. You need to be psychologically closer and use a language that touches their emotions. Appealing language penetrates deeper, supplements credibility and logic, when they extend their helping hands to help you to achieve the team's goal. From the standpoint of transactional analysis, you may start discussions from the adult ego state. At the end you may apply your transaction from the child ego state to get what you want. I have found the sandwich technique to be successful in many instances.

You must remember that whatever you are doing is for the sake of the team and ultimately for the organization. Thus, you should not hesitate to adopt many means or any combination. Learn and practice assertive communication throughout to achieve a win-win situation. Develop your style.

Negotiation

Negotiation implies compromise or conciliation, but for team functioning, it mainly means cooperation. It is the process by which two parties exchange goods or services or ideas leading to a contractual agreement. Negotiation occurs when someone else has what you want and you are prepared to bargain for it and vice versa (Hindle 2000). Hindle emphasizes the utmost need of creating the right atmosphere to make a negotiation effective. The duration should not exceed two hours without a break. If the negotiation encompasses several agendas and more time is essential to discuss all the points in detail, then a break must be organized. The location must be mutually decided, which can be the office of either party. The organizing party must arrange facilities like overhead projector, LCD projector, flip-charts, voice recorders, etc.

Negotiation is an attempt by the parties to achieve a mutually acceptable solution and should lead to a win-win situation. It should not result in a winner and a loser; if that happens, then the negotiated agreement will not work. While negotiating, both parties should understand the principles of negotiation. You should prepare well before going for a negotiation, gather all the relevant documents and records that might be needed, collect information about the other party, assess the other party, anticipate the possible direction of the process, choose your own strategy, proceed as per the agenda, maintain an environment conducive to effective discussion, consider and honour the other party's interest, understand body language, try to understand the tone and judge the mood, and strengthen your position. Try to identify the weaknesses of the other party to gain leverage.

Hindle (2000) identifies many facets of successful negotiation. Preparing for negotiation and the location and corresponding factors to be considered are discussed.

Preparation for negotiation

At the negotiation table, you must remember certain points (a) incorrect information is worse than no information at all as this will lead to wrong decision, (b) annual reports or accounts are a mine of valuable information, for example Infosys, (c) estimate the information available to the other party, (d) too many statistics may only lead to confusion, and (e) it is worth developing sources of information and lines of access to information. Keeping these points in mind, assemble the data and prepare an index to help you to retrieve the information you want to refer to as the negotiation proceeds. Preferably, one should store the data in relational database management system (RDBMS) environment so that you can use structured query language (SQL) scripts to get the information you want.

Possible direction of a negotiation

A negotiation process might have three possible outcomes: sudden death due to breakdown, an acceptable compromise, or an ideal outcome for which the negotiation had been organized. Hindle (2000) elucidates the various steps of the above outcomes. Even if the opening position is carefully planned, a negotiation can follow the planned as well as an unplanned route. If the negotiation follows the planned route, an ideal outcome is achieved. If the negotiation follows an unplanned route, then it may lead to a wasting of time. It can even move through a dangerous route with a lot of arguments ending in a breakdown of the negotiation. On the other hand, in the case of an unplanned long-winded route, more time may be spent but it may lead to finding an acceptable compromise and achieving an ideal outcome (Figure 9.4).

It is essential for an executive to anticipate the possible direction of a negotiation.

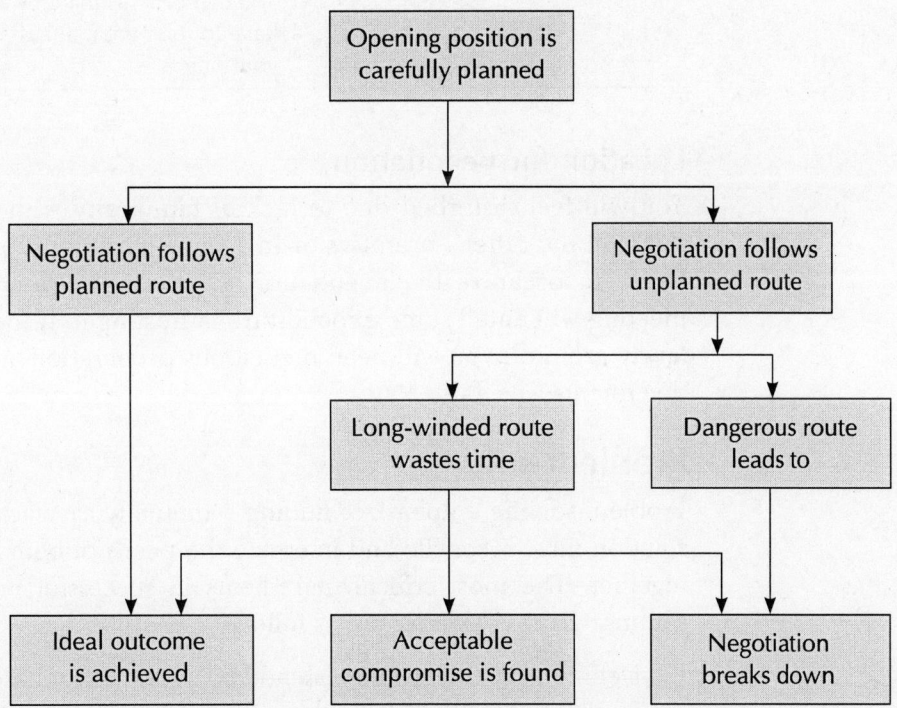

FIGURE **9.4 Direction of a negotiation**

TABLE **9.6** Types of location for negotiation

Location	Factors to consider
Home ground—An office or room in your company building.	· It is easy for you to organize strategic interruptions. · It is difficult to avoid unplanned interruptions. · It is easy for your in-house experts to collect information needed for contributions to the negotiation.
Neutral ground—The office of a third party or a hired public space is considered neutral ground.	· Neither party gains the upper hand because of their unfamiliarity with the location. · Both sides have to 'ship in' their experts and any background material they might need.
Away ground—an office or room belonging to the other negotiating party.	· Lack of familiarity with the surroundings may be disturbing. · You have no control of the logistics. · You can procrastinate by saying that you have to refer the matter back to someone in your office.

Location for negotiation

You will feel disturbed due to lack of familiarity with the surroundings if it is in the other's premises or in a third-party location. It is invariably better to organize the negotiation at your own premises. But such a meeting will entail some expenditure in hosting it. If the negotiation is in 'away ground', you will need meticulous preparation and compilation of documents (see Table 9.6).

Problem-solving

Problem-solving emphasizes finding a mutually satisfactory solution. The solution must reconcile and integrate the needs of both parties who work together. The most critical ingredients in successful problem-solving as summarized by Alderfer are as follows:

* Definition of the problem should be a joint effort based on shared fact-finding rather than on the biased perceptions of the individual groups.
* Problems should be specific and not abstract.
* Points of initial agreement and also the differences in the goals and benefits of both the parties should be identified.

- Discussion between the groups should consist of specific but non-evaluative comments. Any question may be asked for clarification of information but not to humiliate the opponent.
- Groups should work together in developing alternative solutions. Each group may present a range of solutions.
- Solutions should be evaluated objectively in terms of quality and acceptability. In some cases, the solution may maximize joint benefits but favour one party. To make the solution equitable, someone should oversee that neither party gets any special benefits over the other party.

All agreements on separate issues should be considered tentatively until all the issues are dealt with. The issues may be interrelated.

TEAM BUILDING FOR WORK TEAMS

You have so far studied various aspects of teams, different types of teams, fostering team creativity and collective wisdom, and basic and advanced skills required in the context of a team approach. However, it may be repeated here that a team is a collection of people who agree on the goal and the process of achievement, and feel a high degree of interdependence. A team is a mature group in terms of capability and entirely committed to achieving a common goal. A paradigm shift is visible in the workplace. The focus primarily on individual work has changed to team-centred work. A team should not be blamed and held responsible for non-performance if the organizational environment is not conducive to teamwork. Further, team building needs certain considerations. Hughes et al. (2008) propose three aspects—team building interventions, what a team building workshop involves, and examples of interventions.

Team building interventions Team building ideally creates a harmonious, efficient, and productive work group, study its own process of working together and act to create a climate that encourages and values the contributions of team members. Their energies must be directed towards problem-solving, task effectiveness, and maximizing the use of all members' resources to achieve the team's purpose. Sound team building recognizes that it is not possible to fully separate one's performance from that of others. Obviously, there exists the utmost need for training members individually and the team as a whole, on interpersonal relations. Organizational training also required to build, promote, and maintain organizational culture.

What a team building workshop involves   Teamwork is the heart and soul of an organization. Team comprises individuals; and individual drive, skills, and motivation are essential to the success of the group. A key role of every leader is to continually build teamwork within her/his organization. Unfortunately, most managers and supervisors unwittingly sabotage their own team building efforts on a daily basis through a lack of awareness. Team building workshops involve team building activities, interactive training and exercises, assessments, role play, and facilitated group discussions.

Examples of interventions   Ginnett conducted an intervention with three interdependent teams from a state youth psychiatric hospital. (Ginnett is a partner with Impact [a leadership consulting organization] who earlier worked with Centre for Creative Leadership.) The teams comprised members of the administrative services, professional staff, and direct care providers. The members of each team were dedicated to their roles in providing high-quality services to the youth under their care, but the three groups experienced great difficulty in working with each other. On extensive diagnosis of the groups, Ginnett observed two underlying problems. First, each group had a very different vision of what the hospital was or should be. Second, each of the groups defined themselves as 'care givers', thus making it difficult for them to ask others for help since, in their minds, asking for help tended to put them in the role of their patients.

Ginnett and others conducted a series of workshops to arrive at a common vision for the hospital, but the second problem required considerably more work. Since the staff members needed to experimentally understand that asking for help did not place them in an inherently inferior position, a 'Wilderness Experience' was designed where the entire staff was asked to spend four days together in a primitive wilderness environment with difficult tasks such as hiking, climbing, and mountaineering. At the end of the experience, everyone had found an occasion to ask someone else for help. Even more important, everyone found that actually asking for help—something they had previously resisted—enhanced the team's ability to perform. Considerable time was spent each evening linking the lessons of the day with the work in the hospital. (The example is from Hughes et al. 2008.)

The main learning point from this example is that staying for four days in a primitive wilderness environment developed a deep 'sense of togetherness', which is by far the most essential ingredient while working in a team. It reduces individualism, attitude towards others, and treating team members as members of a family with whom close relations exist and private information is shared.

To give another example of the 'feeling of togetherness': the West Bengal Tourism Development Corporation (WBTDC) organized a six-day tour to places of historical, cultural, and religious interest. The luxury tourist coach started from the WBTDC office at Kolkata. WBTDC invariably allots seat numbers, but for some reason it did not do so this time. Tourists occupied seats wherever available. They visited the first spot in the afternoon after which there was quite a scramble among them for seats of their choice. They reached the hotel at about 7 p.m. Dinner was scheduled at 9.15 p.m. The tour officer organized a cultural function asking the tourists to volunteer to perform something. On request, one tourist volunteered to conduct the function and announce the events. Most of the tourists participated and displayed some events of their choice. All the tourists liked the performances of the amateur artists from among them.

While the function was in progress the tour officer twice announced that dinner was ready to be served. But the tourists did not bother to go to the dining hall as they were all enjoying the function. The tour officer could take them to the dining hall only at 10.45 p.m. He reminded them of the next day's schedule.

On the second day the tour officer was present to manage occupying seats to the tourists on rotational basis. To his utter astonishment he did not notice any competition among the tourists and thus did not need to intervene.

He noticed that some tourists who had been aggressive and argumentative on the first day were sacrificing convenient front seats to elder persons, ladies were sitting together without their husbands; men were engaged in gossiping, and so on. He realized that the fellow feeling must have arisen from the participation at the cultural function. In fact, what evolved was a 'feeling of togetherness', an essential ingredient of a team.

BUILDING HIGH-PERFORMANCE TEAMS

Teams drive organizational progress. Building and leading high-performance teams is one of the most complex challenges that a leader comes across. The processes need best insights from research and case studies, tested in the context of hands-on sessions and experiential learning. Commitment, mutual trust, purpose, effective communication, involvement and participation, process orientation, and continuous improvement are the key requirements for building and leading a high-performance team. The requirements extend to team belongingness; commitment enables each member to perform his/her role in the team. The leader has to take initiative to eradicate individual differences.

Not all teams can perform at their peak. A business manager needs to achieve a coherent and congruent management approach to build and deliver high performance and achieve outstanding results. The achievements must be visible and accountable. McLean (2008) proposes four principles to be adopted and practised consistently to be successful for high-performing teams:

- Possess a personal sense of mission, vision, and values
- Develop a personal sense of responsibility and accountability
- Sharpen personal skills in sharing information and communicating effectively
- Learn to identify gaps and manage them

The mission statement of an organization gives the basic purpose of the organization. The vision describes where a company wants to be in the future. The vision guides, controls, and encourages the organization as a whole to reach the desirable state of the organization. In other words, vision helps to cross the 'delta state', a state that indicates the gap between the current state (where we are today) and the desired state (where we want to be tomorrow). In a changing business scenario, teams and the whole organization must respond to changes. A team in order to perform at its peak has to accommodate necessary changes. Members call for preparedness accordingly and need exposure to:

- building capacity to accept changes,
- forming and sustaining successful teams,
- aligning individuals around team goals,
- realizing team dynamics,
- leading from the front, middle, and behind, and
- encouraging experiential learning.

Leader of a High-performing Team—A Model

There cannot be a prescription on how to build and lead a high-performing team. However, the following are the attributes leaders should have.

Assertiveness   Assertiveness is social boldness that enables a person to express his/her viewpoint without fear. An employee participates more broadly, takes on greater responsibilities, expresses his/her ideas, and interacts with greater varieties of people, solves problems objectively, finds solutions and implements them with minimum or no resistance.

Assertiveness can be measured using a psychometric scale. The level of assertiveness should be high.

Job satisfaction   You have read in Chapter 6 that satisfaction is just a constellation of attitudes about the job, that is, the extent to which people like versus dislike the various aspects of the work (Spector 1994). Pay, promotion, supervision, fringe benefits, contingent rewards, operating procedure, co-workers, nature of work, and communication are the nine facets that determine the total job satisfaction of a person. For leaders, a high score in the facet 'colleague' indicates improved relations. For members, a high score in the facet 'supervision' is an indication of a healthy team (the ability of the leader).

Motive   The dominant motives should be achievement, affiliation, independence, and activity. If these motives are high, leaders are likely to be successful. Very high affiliation motive of a leader helps him/her to transform subordinates into followers and then to improve relations with followers in line with the leader–member exchange theory. The motives can be conveniently measured through a questionnaire and then the motive system can be structured (Haldar 2009).

Johari window   A leader has to gather information and disseminate it to the team members. Moreover, he/she has to gather information about self. That is why a leader's 'arena' should be high. Four cells of a person can be measured (Haldar 2009). The 'blind area' and 'private area' should be smaller. The 'dark area' must be minimal. The area of each cell helps to identify training need.

Personality trait   The personality traits of an ideal team leader should be teacher, thought leader, tolerant, unbiased, risk-taker, persuasive, rational, negotiator, open, inquisitive, initiator, adaptable, energetic, and enterprising. The leader will further excel and reach the peak if he/she is a visionary, wise, innovative, and spiritual.

The leader must clearly state his/her expectations from each member, establish channels of communication, resolve conflict, anticipate consequences, and celebrate achievements as a team. The purpose of assembling a team is to accomplish bigger goals. The best managers are those who can assemble a group of individuals and mould them into a team. To keep the wheel of excellence moving at a fast speed, a leader must develop a sense of commitment among members. In a team, only those committed to excellence should be hired. Prospective team members approaching the organization for employment should be recruited on the basis of their high levels of hard and soft skill sets. Everyone working together in a harmonious environment contributes his/her best. The leader has to establish his/her credibility.

Emotional Intelligence for High-performance Teams

To build and manage a high-performing team, leaders need a high level of emotional intelligence. Singh (2000) mentions the emotional intelligence base of leadership styles (Table 9.7).

TABLE **9.7** **Emotional intelligence base of leadership styles**

Leadership Styles	Emotional Intelligence Base
Coercive	Desire to achieve, initiative, self-control
Authoritative	Self-confidence, empathy, change catalyst
Affiliative	Empathy, building relations, communication
Democratic	Collaboration, team leadership, communication
Pace setting	Conscientiousness, drive to achieve, initiative
Coaching	Developing others, empathy, self-awareness

MANAGING GROUPS AND TEAMS

Managing groups and teams needs concentrating on identity, processes, and skills (Williams 1997).

Identity—Identity helps one to reflect on his/her role and contribution as a team leader. You have to consider three perspectives: requirements of the team, your strategic choices, and the aspects of your personality that influence these choices. You have to know the influencing members of the team and whether your expertise matches the influence. Next, you must define the responsibilities of each member, and select your strategies and the requisite leadership style. You have studied leadership styles earlier. Adopting a style that takes into account the internal work environment, nature of members, and extraneous forces is of paramount importance.

Process—This includes product and process, managing process, and work process and the individual (Williams 1997). The product is the ultimate outcome of the concerted efforts put in by the team leader and members. The product must be commensurate with the objectives and activities. On the other hand, the process is the ways and means through which people work to get the planned output. While designing the process, the team has to make conscious choices considering all the issues—existing ones as well as those that may emerge as the work progresses. The process must be finalized, duly taking into account the knowledge foundation, skill bases, and other human attributes of individual members. Otherwise, the initiative may turn out to be futile.

Skills—The skills essential to managing teams are facilitation skills, achieving consensus, interactive skills, group working skills, process management skills, influencing skills, and influence tactics.

(a) **Facilitation skills**: Facilitation simply means smoothing the progress of teamwork. Facilitators are mainly organizers and communicators. This skill involves planning team meeting and equipment required, interrogating, being a good and empathetic listener, encouraging member involvement and decision-making, sharing information, developing team culture, tolerating and diffusing conflicts, linking team to management, etc.

(b) **Achieving consensus**: Achieving consensus is a journey that begins with multiple points of views and ends with mutual agreements (Scott and Flanigan 2004). A team leader needs to understand members, leave behind ego and position in organizational hierarchy, accept member opinions, and throughout keep in mind the objective. He/She must plan a checklist to control the proceeding of the meeting comprising destination and the route.

(c) **Interactive skills**: In a team, many people work to achieve a common goal. The leader has to consider the astrological compatibility of the members. He/She has to understand individual and group behaviours, be alert about his/her own behaviour (a leader is not what he/she thinks about self but he/she is how the follower members think about the leader and view his/her various behavioural dispositions). You need to identify the root cause of a problem (using a cause–effect diagram for your own convenience) at the behavioural level of process, and manage key interactions. You would be able to manage effectively with the help of the cause–effect diagram.

(d) **Group working skills**: Airtime, information, ideas, reaction, and clarity are the five aspects of group working skills (Williams 1997). Of these, airtime refers to the opportunity members have to express their opinion and speak during the meeting. Other skill components include the way in which information is exchanged, means of generating ideas, members' manner of expressing reactions, the way members ensure that they understand the discussion proceedings. Telling and asking are the two blocks of behaviour during information exchange. As a leader, you must be aware of the amount of telling in the first phase. More telling at a stretch leads to ineffective communication. Communication skills includes listening also. Asking is a very good way to get clarification. In fact, you have to strike a balance between telling and asking.

(e) **Process management skills**: A process is a set of interrelated activities. In any organization, there will be many systems like planning, material management, production, quality control, maintenance, storage, etc. A system is a set of interrelated processes. In the context of managing groups and teams, process management skills are applicable at: (a) the procedural level and the management of meetings and group discussions and (b) the social level and management of group dynamics. A team leader needs to manage the direction and structure of the meeting, levels of participation and involvement, and most importantly, clarity about the content of the meeting.

(f) **Influencing skills**: These are interactive skills involved in persuading people to make them want to do what the leader wants them to do, overcoming their psychological barriers, and developing an openness to accept changes. Persuading people needs both push style and pull style. Identifying outcomes, persuasion scenarios, and some persuasive questions comprise the elements of persuasion skills. Influencing people needs tactics. Use of power base to influence is no longer valid in today's work environment. What is prevalent is the use of situation-specific behaviours to influence. It is further evidenced that this sort of influencing is long-lasting. Impression management tactics, political tactics, and proactive influence tactics are extensively used currently for team success.

SUMMARY

Many organizations today are switching over to working in teams giving up departmental affiliations. This trend is growing in view of benefits like cooperative behaviour and synergy, ease in goal accomplishment, affiliation, emotional support, social validation, and physical factors. Individuals prefer to join groups for multiple reasons. Groups develop in distinct stages like orientation, confrontation, differentiation, and collaboration.

A team is a group of people with a high degree of interdependence focused on the achievement of some goal or task. Ownership, creativity and contribution, trust, common understanding, personal development, conflict resolution, participative decision-making, clear leadership, and commitment are various dimensions in which teams differ from groups. There can be various types of teams including virtual teams. Individuals turn into team players when a team becomes effective.

Dysfunctional teams can also be managed. Virtual teams face certain obvious problems. They can be led following ten principles. Fostering team creativity is essential to derive the best from the team. Team leaders need certain skills like communication, listening, assertiveness, technical competency, setting goals, time management, delegation, managing conflict, persuasiveness, negotiation, problem-solving, team building for work teams, building high-performance teams, development planning, and developing commitment. Some teams are differentiated as high-performing teams. Leaders need competence and emotional intelligence.

KEY TERMS

Collective wisdom is a demonstration of wisdom collectively, applying orchestral thoughts to find a solution to a critical problem.

Cross-functional team comprises members from different departments to solve a specific problem. The members are drawn considering the expertise required.

Delta state indicates the gap between the current state (where we are today) and the desired state (where we want to be tomorrow) in the context of changes in an organization.

Team is a group of people with a high degree of interdependence focused on the achievement of some goal or task.

Virtual team is a collection of members located in geographically dispersed areas. Such teams enable organizations to link workforce together. Members of virtual teams rely heavily on the use of technology.

EXERCISES

Concept Review Questions

1. What are the stages of group development? Elaborate the 'collaboration' stage, citing examples from the company you are working for.
2. Discuss the various roles of team members to make a team effective. Also discuss how the behaviour of team members can be shaped.

3. What is creativity? Discuss the stages of creativity.
4. What should be the attributes of a leader of a high-performing team? How can these attributes be imparted to a team leader? Discuss critically.
5. Discuss the managerial roles in teamwork. Distinguish between social roles and individualistic roles. State the effects of these roles from the standpoint of effectiveness of a team's progress.

Critical Thinking Questions

1. In the context of teamwork, to what extent do you believe knowledge and human power to be the same? Justify your answer.
2. What are the circumstances under which a team is formed, stormed, and directly reaches the adjourning stage? Bring out the reasons. How can this be eliminated?
3. What should be the profile of the leader of a high-performing team? When can a team be termed high performing? Bring out the criteria pointwise.

Assignments

1. Visit five information technology or BPO organizations in your city. Ask them whether they have virtual teams. Record the problems they are facing in leading and managing such teams. Find out the steps they are taking to tackle the problems. Prepare consolidated lists of the problems and the actions to solve the problems. Share your findings with your teacher of leadership.
2. Select five senior managers who are heads of production, maintenance, or other functional areas. Discuss with them and attempt to identify the 'crucible' that has led them to encourage teamwork. Next, observe how they are facilitating the teams to progress. What are they doing to enhance the skills of the team leaders and team members? Compare your findings referring to any book on leadership and team building.
3. Contact an organization and ask for permission to be present as an observer at a team meeting. Get introduced to the leader prior to the meeting and express your academic interest to observe and record interactions (behaviours of the leader and members). Prepare a format as given to record the interactions. Use a scale of 1 to 5, where 5 indicates an area of strength and 1 indicates an area in which the leader lacks strength.

	Leader interaction	1	2	3	4	5
1	Active listener					
2	Briefs from previous record of discussion					
3	Empathetic					
4	Controls anger					
5	Resolves hot discussions					
6	Wise					
7	Remains calm throughout					
8	Involves members					
9	Allows members to express					
10	Follows the agenda					
11	Summarizes at the end					
12	Can influence with logic					
13	Seeks suggestions					
14	Gives information					
15	???					
16	???					
17	???					
18	???					
19	???					
20	???					

Note: Add any number of aspects of interaction you feel necessary. Find the total score. You can extend your survey to four or five more leaders of the same organization or different organizations. Compare the results and draw your conclusion. Share your findings with your teacher.

REFERENCES

Belbin, R. Meridith (1981), *Management Team: Why They Succeed or Fail*, Heineman, London.

Bishop, Sue (2000), *Develop Your Assertiveness*, Kogan Page India Private Limited, New Delhi.

Haldar, Uday Kumar (2003), 'Job Performance of the Operational Agents of L.I.C.I—A Study in 24 Parganas (North), West Bengal'. Unpublished doctoral thesis, University of Burdwan, Burdwan, West Bengal.

Haldar, Uday Kumar (2008), *Understanding Assertive Communication*, *MANAV*

(Journal published by Department of Human Resource Management during 'Genesis 2008'), Indian Institute of Social Welfare and Business Management, Kolkata.

Haldar, Uday Kumar (2009), *Human Resource Development*, Oxford University Press, New Delhi.

Hindle, Tim (2000), *Negotiating Skills*, DK Publishing (Dorling Kindersley Limited, New York).

Human Technology, Inc. (2004), *Building a Team Based Organisation*, Jayco Publishing House, Mumbai.

Katzenbach, J.R. and D.K. Smith (1993), *The Wisdom of Teams: Creating the High-Performance Organization*, Harvard Business School, Boston, MA.

Leigh, Andrew and Michael Maynard (1995), *Leading Your Team—How to Inspire Teams*, Nicholas Brealey Publishing, London.

Macdonald, Copthorne (2008), *A Brief Introduction to Collective Wisdom* (www.wisdompage.com; accessed on 16 November 2008).

McLean, Peter (ezinearticles.com/?Leadership-Skill-Development-Four-Principles-of-a-High-Performance-Business-Person&id=441663; accessed on 23 September 2008).

McManus, John (2007), *Leadership Project and Human Capital Management*, Butterworth-Heinemann, Oxford.

Osborn, Alex F. (1953), *Applied Imagination*, Charles Scribner, New York.

Pareek, Udai (2008). *Understanding Organizational Behaviour*, Second Edition, Fourth Impression, Oxford University Press, New Delhi.

Pickering, Marisue (1986), *Communication in Exploration* (A Journal of Research of the University of Maine), Vol. 3, No. 1, Fall 1986, pp. 16–19 (www.sustainability networker.org).

Robbins, Stephen P. and Phillip L. Hunseker (2008), *Training in Interpersonal Skills*, Fourth Edition, Prentice-Hall India, New Delhi.

Scott, Jon and Eileen Flanigan (2004), *Achieving Consensus Tools and Techniques*, Viva Books Private Limited, New Delhi.

Singh, Shailendra (2000), Leadership in High Performing Organizations. In *Transformational Leadership—Value Based Management for Indian Organizations* (2002), Bhargava, Shivnagesh (ed). Response Books (a division of Sage Publications), New Delhi.

Spector, P.E. (1997), *Job Satisfaction: Application, Assessment, Causes, and Consequences*, Sage, Thousand Oaks.

Telsang, Martand (2002), *Human Dimension of Total Quality Management*, Indian Society for Training and Development, New Delhi.

Williams, Hank (1997), *The Essence of Managing Groups and Teams* (Ed. Adrian Buckley), Prentice Hall India, New Delhi.

Web Resources

Centre for Rural Studies (crs.uvm.edu/gopher/nerl/personal/comm/e.html; accessed on October 7, 2008). (Active listening)

www.americanscientist.org, Brian Hayes, 1998. (*Supercomputer)*

www.wisdompage.com/GroupWisdom.html (accessed on 16 November 2008)

www.tid.gov.hk (accessed on 16 November 2008).

CLOSING CASE

Turning Individuals into Team Players
Apollo Engineering Works

Mr Vikram is a person who does not leave any work halfway. In this regard, he is very stubborn. He contacted an Indian university that conducts a certificate programme on 'Team Building and Leadership'. The programme comprises five units and each unit has eight sessions. The five units are as detailed below.

- Overview of groups—Formation of group; group dynamics; group structure and group cohesiveness; managing group and inter-group dynamics in organization
- Team building process—Overview of teams: definition, types, stages of team development: storming, norming, forming and performing; quality circles and self-managed teams; evaluating team's performance; teams and high-performing organizations
- Goal setting for team—Defining roles and responsibilities of team members; developing interpersonal skills; interpersonal communication barriers and gateways to communication
- Leadership and management of team—Sources of powers and influence; leadership models and styles
- Leadership styles—Contingency approach to effective leadership; situational leadership; transformational leadership; leadership in decision-making process; leadership in times of change

Mr Vikram discussed at length with the departmental head of the university and drafted a tentative syllabus for 30-hour knowledge inputs. On the second day, Mr Mazumdar accompanied Mr Vikram, studied the draft syllabus, and finalized it. Mr Mazumdar said that some employees had already attended a few in-house programmes on leadership, group dynamics, team building, etc. Mr Mazumdar requested some changes and stated the modality of conducting the training session:

- Enhancing the duration
- Daily 3-hour input in the post-lunch session (from 2.30 p.m. to 5.30 p.m.)
- Class days—From Monday to Friday
- Duration—3 weeks
- Cases studies on Apollo Engineering Works without using the company name.

In course of discussion, the departmental head spoke about the effects of individual differences in teamwork, aggression of members, and further used a proverb—'Too many cooks spoil the broth'. Mr Mazumdar and Mr Vikram finalized the honorarium for each batch of the programme that the university agreed to. They left the university department happy.

Discussion Questions

1. The opening case discusses some problems encountered by the company. Consider each problem and match the topic that might solve through the knowledge inputs.
2. The head said something casually during the concluding discussion. Does his statement address any 'learning points' mentioned in the opening case. Discuss critically referring to the text.
3. Why did Mr Mazumdar request to give cases anonymously for analysis? Discuss the possible reasons.

CHAPTER 10

Team Effectiveness

Learning Objectives

After studying this chapter you will be able to

▶ Define group processes
▶ Develop a knowledge of shared objectives, coordination, and support
▶ Discuss the role of facilitation in teamworking
▶ Understand the role of interpersonal competence
▶ State the need for measuring team effectiveness
▶ Define the measurement of team effectiveness

OPENING CASE

Organizing Work Teams

The company Elite Hydraulic Works (EHE) was formed in mid-1997. Mr Bhaskar was the general manager since the company was started. He is a mechanical engineering graduate and a postgraduate in hydraulics. He was involved with the company from the site selection stage. Mr Bhaskar closely monitored the erection and commissioning of the machines in the departments during the initial project stage. Gradually, production started and products went for sales as planned. Managers, engineers, supervisors, machinists were recruited in phases. Some offices including the IT cell were functioning. The IT cell was instrumental in updating the employee database immediately after joining of an employee at any level.

Mr Bhaskar, in a production meeting, expressed his desire to encourage teamwork, forgo departmental affiliation, and form teams for certain critical jobs. He delegated the task to four deputy managers. Mr Bhaskar directed them to form teams considering the academic background of the employees and area of experience. In the process of team member selection, the deputy managers involved the production, maintenance, quality, and purchase managers. Mr Bhaskar laid emphasis on cross-functional teams; accordingly, he requested the deputy managers to select certain critical jobs requiring involvement of people from multiple disciplines. They undertook job evaluation and selected members based on their skills and knowledge. They identified twelve jobs and for accomplishing them, they formed one team for each job. The team size varied from a minimum of eight members to a maximum of fifteen depending on the tasks for which the team was formed. All the team members and team leaders were trained in-house, but the faculty for training was invited from outside. All the teams started functioning to achieve the team goals. While some teams were functioning smoothly without any problem and achieving the team targets, some teams were facing problems. One team completed a task and started the next one. While the second job was in progress, the team needed to refer to a process they followed in the first task. But, it could not find any record relating to the process they improved in the first task for use as guideline. Mr Bhaskar nominated one facilitator to identify the problems and suggest remedial actions. The coordinator listed the problems. Some of the problems were:

· Low performance of many teams
· High sentiments of certain members
· Inability to accept opinions of fellow members
· Dominating attitudes of members at higher positions
· Different opinions to achieve the goal
· Lack of clarity in work roles and overlapping of roles
· Difficulties in resource mobilization
· Lack of commitment and dedication to achieve team goals
· Achievers not getting due recognition
· Unavailability of documentation system and records

The facilitator, who was dynamic person, decided to take the help of an expert, Mr Pratap, to formulate a course of action.

Learning points

1. Relationships between members should be healthy.
2. Members must develop a network to get resources and political support.
3. A leader must review the reasons for failure.
4. Teams should not lack in external coordination.
5. Concealing information from team members should be avoided.

INTRODUCTION

In the previous chapter (Chapter 9), we discussed some aspects of building and managing teams; how a team becomes dysfunctional; and the skills and other human attributes needed by leaders. Several characteristics of a team influence the group process. When a team performs methodically, exerts team efforts in a concerted way, and members have knowledge and skills, it is likely to be successful. But it may not always be so. It may fail to achieve the goal. The leader conducts a review meeting to analyse the possible reasons behind failure, which is a post-mortem activity. But the leader should conduct review meetings even if the team succeeds. Different types of teams need different leader skills and behaviours. You need to know the determinants of team performance and role of facilitators in a team.

DETERMINANTS OF GROUP PROCESSES

The success of a team depends on the group process. Group size, status differentials, cohesiveness, individual differences, emotional maturity, physical environment, and communication technology are the determinants of group processes.

It is an established finding that as the team size increases, more time is taken to reach a decision. In fact, the time required is proportional to the square of the number of members. As such, group size should be minimal though the members should be included for various types of expertise.

In a team meeting juniors hesitate to express their views when a member, senior in position in the organizational hierarchy, states something irrelevant or wrong. Thus, status differentials or differences in positions create problems to juniors in being expressive. Junior employees seldom criticize seniors. This is so because people higher in the hierarchy often dominate juniors' opinions.

Team members with similar likes and dislikes, and similar backgrounds, values, and attitudes tend to be cohesive. A cohesive group of people generally reach consensus faster. They do not prefer objective evaluation of alternatives for arriving at decisions. This determinant has both good and bad sides.

Individual differences generate diverse opinions. On the positive side, members do not easily accept the judgment of others that leads to perfection in the decision. On the negative side, diversity leads to variety of opinions with regard to language used, perspectives, experiences, jargon, etc., sorting of which consume time.

People with low emotional maturity exhibit disruptive self-oriented behaviours, thereby reducing team cohesiveness. Unsuitable physical environment impedes decision-making. Work environment should be ergonomically acceptable. Other aspects include shape and size of infrastructure. A round table is excellent for exchanging ideas and conducive to team meetings. But a long rectangular table induces formality, hinders communication, and emphasizes status differential.

Communication technology plays a vital role in today's business. In the case of teleconferencing, some groupware allows members to suggest, criticize, evaluate ideas, without revealing their identity. Thus, irrespective of their status, members enjoy the freedom of expression.

In view of the above, it is obvious that the determinants of the group processes must be considered while selecting the team members. The team has to produce results. That is why you need to know the determinants of team performance.

DETERMINANTS OF TEAM PERFORMANCE

Some determinants of team performance are as follows: commitment in shared objectives, member skills and role clarity, internal organization and coordination, external coordination, resource and political support, mutual trust and cooperation, and collective efficacy and potency (Yukl 2007).

Commitment in Shared Objectives

Commitment is a state in which an employee identifies himself/herself with a particular organization, its mission, policies, objectives, goals, and wishes to remain employed in the organization. Recent workforce trends, such as downsizing and re-engineering, have jeopardized employee commitment and morale in organizations.

Commitment depends on the loyalty of members, and trust in the leader and team management. Feelings of alienation, helplessness, and isolation influence the commitment of a member. Team performance will be higher when the members are involved and motivated to attain the shared team objectives. The objectives must be clear to the members for them to make high task commitments. On clarifying the team objectives, targets must be split into its elements, corresponding strategies must be finalized, and then tasks should be assigned. A shared understanding about what is to be done and how, and the importance of doing that work increases member commitment. This, in turn, promotes interdependence among the team members.

Member Skills and Role Clarity

The ability of a person is a function of his/her knowledge and skills. He/she must have knowledge of what is expected of him/her, the importance of the task assigned to him/her, the consequence of poor quality of performance and inability to complete the task in time, and how he/she should perform the task. He/she will able to perform the job if it is simple. But if the task is new and challenging in nature, he/she may need additional learning to enhance his/her level of competency. The leader bears the responsibility of identifying skill requirements, verifying whether members have the requisite skills, and impart or arrange to impart the knowledge and skills. Leaders have to do this while forming the team, when inducting new members, and when replacements are needed.

Internal Organization and Coordination

Careful selection and organizing of members considering their 'astrological compatibility' apart from their skills, enthusiasm, and motivation determine team performance. Members will be able to accomplish the tasks assigned to them efficiently and effectively if the work roles are designed suitably. Thus, organizing members is a vital performance strategy. The relevant leader behaviours encompass planning how to make efficient use of personnel and resources, planning effective performance strategies, involving members with relevant expertise in planning operations for the team, and, most importantly, team learning practices.

Furthermore, the leader must gather and analyse information about effective performance strategies. If you assign a task to a talented and innovative person where the skill possessed by the person is not relevant to the job, then there will be a setback in the performance. Synchronous execution of work of interdependent members determines team performance. For effective team performance, the coordination effort of the leader is an important criterion. Coordination is determined by decisions taken during the planning phase before undertaking any new task and adjustments made during the execution of the task.

A good leader anticipates bottlenecks and hurdles that might hinder the progress of the work and strategizes before beginning the work. Motivation and skills of team members definitely enhance team performance; but these must be backed by organization and coordination of the members. The leader's activities include selection of members, making efficient utilization of them, foreseeing hurdles and emergencies, involving members and formulating strategies to gain their willing participation, and leading to solve problems using their collective wisdom. Improved coordination prevents unnecessary delays. In case of any complex task in the changing business scenario, the leader should select an able team member as coordinator to share his/her duties. The added advantage is that as coordinator the member will also get a unique opportunity for development.

External Coordination

The success of a department in an organization depends upon adjusting its activities consistently with the activities of interdependent departments. Likewise, the performance of a team also depends upon adjusting its activities with other interdependent teams. A team leader needs to identify strategies to deal with the environment comprising teams, sections, or departments. The leader decides on the strategies in team meetings, taking all the members into confidence. Methodically finalized and tactfully applied strategies smooth out the path to achieve team goals. More external coordination is needed when a group has high lateral interdependence with other parts of the organization or it is highly dependent on powerful outside clients whose viewpoints must be considered, accommodated if applicable, and rejected tactfully. The leader must meet and consult clients and users about plans and decisions that affect them, gather feedback from clients for customer service improvements, promote a favourable image of the team members and performance among outsiders, and play the role of mediator or conciliator to resolve conflicts between team members and outsiders.

Resources and Political Support

In a manufacturing organization, any department depends on many other departments. For example, the material management section depends on the design section and material planning for initiating procurement actions; the production section depends on material management for right quantity and right quality materials at the right time; the design office for quality plan; tool planning for tool schedule; the industrial engineering section for flow charts; the store for drawing of materials; etc. Most interestingly, the assembly section depends on all production units for manufactured components and also the material management section for procured items. The planning section depends on external sources for information on requirements, on the market survey section for customer feedback. Thus, it is obvious that all the sections are interdependent. The efforts at producing outputs must be synchronous. In the production section, there will be many production teams.

The success of team performance depends on gathering information, resources, and support from other relevant sections. The support are inescapable for task accomplishment. Resources include budgetary funds, tools/equipment, supplies/materials, utilities and facilities, and the like. All the resources needed for a special project need meticulous planning, lobbying with superiors to provide additional materials and other resources, preparation of budget, providing justification, and obtaining approval. Furthermore, to gain political support, establishing, maintaining, and promoting relationships with relevant outsiders are essential. The team leaders have to sustain cooperative relationships with the personnel who are a potential source of necessary resources and assistance. Further, leaders have to negotiate favourable agreements with resource providers.

Mutual Trust and Cooperation

Mutual trust is a shared belief that one can depend on another to achieve a common purpose. More inclusively and comprehensively stated, trust is 'the willingness of a party (the trustor) to be vulnerable and exposed to the actions of another party (the trustee) based on the expectation that the trustee will perform an action important to the trustor, regardless of the ability of the trustor to monitor or control the trustee'. In a trusting relationship, people sense how you feel about them. If you want to change their attitudes towards you, first change the negative attitudes you have towards them. Remember that trust begets trust.

Team performance obviously depends on the factors discussed above. But mutual trust among team members and cooperation play a dominant role in achieving team goals. Whatever be the talent, qualification, skill bases of the members, unless they are psychologically bonded, the team cannot achieve its mission. Apart from the involvement and task commitment of your team, member skills and role clarity, and performance strategies, you should especially pay attention to mutual trust and cooperation and resources. If the team is constrained by friction or lack of trust among members, a sequence of trust-building exercises needs to be implemented. You must be instrumental in clearing bad feelings by discussing negative aspects in a constructive manner before starting a project in a team. Otherwise, the team will not be able to work under stressful condition for a long period effectively.

In the previous chapter, you have read that a team develops in stages. At the forming stage, members try to get to know one another; lack of trust and group cohesiveness emerge at this stage. Furthermore, frequent changes in membership, members of diverse cultures as in the case of virtual teams, and members with less emotional stability and maturity create mistrust, leading to non-cooperation. Members will be cohesive and cooperative only when they identify with the team, feel a sense of togetherness, feel pride at being members of the team, and are intrinsically motivated.

Collective Efficacy and Potency

Members of a team endeavour to carry out the team mission and achieve specific task objectives. Member commitment depends in part on the shared belief of members that the team is capable of successfully carrying out its mission and achieving specific task objectives (Yukl 2007). This shared belief is the collective efficacy or potency. Team performance will be higher when its members are highly motivated to attain shared objectives, have adequate skills, possess trusting relationship, cooperate with one another, and follow a well-designed performance strategy. The team will perform even better if it gets the needed resources.

The task commitment of members plays a predominant role in team performance, which will be higher when the team considers the objectives as very important and members have confidence in their ability to achieve them. Leader behaviour helps enhance commitment by articulation of an appealing vision of what can be accomplished by the team, relating the task objectives to member values and ideas, building member confidence in the ability of the team to accomplish the objectives, and celebrating progress made in attaining those objectives.

You have learned many aspects of leadership including skills of leaders and leader behaviours in the previous chapters. Now we wil discuss the skills and behaviour for driving particular types of teams.

TYPES OF TEAM VIS-À-VIS LEADERS' SKILLS AND BEHAVIOURS

In Chapter 9, we discussed various aspects of a team, and that collective processes determine the performance of a team. We had further studied different types of teams: cross-departmental or cross-functional team, self-managed teams, virtual teams, and quality improvement teams or quality circles.

The role of leaders will be different for different types of teams although some leadership roles are similar irrespective of the type of team. For the convenience of readers, each type of team is discussed briefly. Some organizations do not have departmental affiliation but prefer to function independently to undertake broad organizational-level process improvements through process teams. A self-managed or self-directed work team is a formal mature group of employees capable of achieving team objectives and results without supervisory personnel.

A cross-departmental or cross-functional team is a combination of people with varying expertise from different functional areas who manage social collaboration and concept creation, and who operate or communicate across different functions within an organization to handle a specific problem. A problem-solving team (or quality improvement team or quality circle or simply work team) consists of a few members, generally eight to ten, from a common work area who meet at fixed intervals, say once a week, to find solutions to specific problems about work processes, products, or services. Virtual teams comprise a group of people with complementary skills from geographically dispersed units of the same organization or countries, who work together to achieve common goals, but hold themselves mutually accountable. Now we will look at the skills required and leadership styles that might be effective for each of the teams.

Cross-departmental or Cross-functional Team

In these types of teams, members having the requisite knowledge and skill are drawn from different areas to accomplish a specific task. But it is the leader's duty to communicate the task requirements and related technical details to the members. He/she must possess 'technical expertise'.

To lead a cross-functional team, a leader needs both intelligence and emotional intelligence, creativity, and knowledge about systems (set of interrelated processes) to resolve complex problems, which needs 'cognitive skill'. To pursue a project, he/she needs to plan and execute the plan, mobilize resources, and arrange budgets, and must therefore have 'project management skills'. The leader has to develop networks and collaborate to get support for which he/she must have 'political skills'. Lastly, to deal with people, the leader should bond with them, eliminate individual differences, and create harmony—in other words, he/she must have 'interpersonal skills'. Thus, his/her skill set must comprise technical expertise, cognitive skills, project management skills, political skills, and interpersonal skills.

Cross-functional teams face multiple hurdles, which may not be possible for a formal leader to tackle. He/she has to communicate tactical objectives, develop mental models, and suggest creative and imaginative thoughts to his/her people. These are of course required in all types of teams and need much attention to be applied in cross-functional teams. This calls for exhibiting envisioning behaviour. As usual, the leader has to organize planning and scheduling activities, help the members to develop standards of output, and conduct problem-solving meetings.

The most challenging task for a leader is developing trust, cooperation, collaboration, and mutual acceptance among the members drawn from different functional areas. He/she has to facilitate open communication and arbitrate conflicts. Obviously, he/she has to display a socially integrating behaviour. He/she has to discharge the role of a spokesperson to promote the image of the team, and interact with clients or recipients of products and services, influence outsiders for multiple reasons, which constitute his/her external spanning behaviour. Envisioning, organizing, socially integrating, and external spanning are the behaviours essential for the leader of a cross-functional team. In these tasks, getting commitments of diverse members is difficult as they are engaged in performing many other activities apart from the activities of the cross-functional team.

Self-managed Teams

In a self-managed team, the members select a leader from among themselves. All members share leadership on a rotational basis. Shared leadership is a unique feature of self-managed teams. All quality circle teams formed voluntarily in the early 1980s are examples of self-managed teams. The member-leaders of such teams are 'internal leaders'. The members perform routine technical and administrative works. For such a team, an external leader is attached to oversee, execute managerial responsibilities that are not delegated to the team members, and extend administrative support. The external leader serves as a coach, mentor, counsellor, facilitator, and consultant to the team. He/she further helps members acquire interpersonal skills, build self-confidence, and get the necessary information, resources, and support from the organization. Obviously, he/she happens to be the link pin to self-managed teams.

Virtual Teams

Members of virtual teams cannot have face-to-face interactions and remain psychologically detached from one another. As the members are dispersed, it becomes difficult to monitor their performance. Members may have different objectives and aims or priorities. Moreover, they work from different places located in different time zones and cultures. Leadership becomes a challenge for virtual teams. Virtual team members and leaders depend heavily on information technology; teleconferencing facility makes the tasks somewhat easier. If a leader can visit the locations frequently, leading a virtual team becomes easier to some extent. But travel expenditure prohibits frequent movements.

Quality Improvement Teams or Quality Circles

In these teams, members select the leader on a rotational basis. Like the external leader, a facilitator extends all support to the members.

FACILITATING TEAM BUILDING

Learning is a continuous process. A team needs to learn both from failures and successes. The process needs facilitation. Team learning originates from team review meetings, which is a type of experiential learning. Experiential learning is the process of making meaning from direct experiences. It focuses on the learning for an individual and a group of individuals working in a team. Experiential learning occurs through observation, simulation, and/or participation. It provides depth and meaning to learning when the mind or body or both are used. Experiential learning can take place in many different settings and have many objectives. A team performs a variety of activities. The leader with his/her members must review the activity or set of activities performed to assess, evaluate, and analyse and to find related facts. A review of failure brings out the reasons behind failure so that its recurrence can be prevented. It is not true that only failures need reviews. Successes also need review to understand how success was achieved, what processes were followed, which obstacles were encountered and how they were overcome, the skills and knowledge required to achieve success, etc. Finally, everything must be documented for reference in the future. The leader or an internal or external facilitator may conduct the review meeting. They have to guide the review process.

Leader behaviour should be supportive and democratic. He/she must seek free and frank opinions of his/her followers. It is evidenced that followers seldom like to point out a mistake committed by the leader, particularly if the leader's position is high in the organizational hierarchy. Moreover, followers seldom suggest improvement measures in a meeting though some of them are capable of doing so. Good interpersonal relations of the leader reduce this tendency of followers remaining passive in coming out with their suggestions. Improved leader–member exchange accelerates involvement and participation, and obviously idea generation.

Understanding between members is an important prerequisite for team learning. Yukl (2007) quotes that members who understand each other's perceptions and role expectations are able to coordinate their actions more easily. Mutual understanding is another vital aspect. Improved understanding makes their assumptions collinear, which is helpful during problem-solving. Yukl (2007) outlines the guidelines for conducting an after-activity review, which is given below:

1. A leader should make a self-critique that acknowledges shortcomings.
2. Encourage feedback from followers and accept the feedback in a non-defensive manner.
3. Ask members to identify both the effective and ineffective aspects of team performance.
4. Encourage members to examine the flaws that impact team performance.
5. Focus only on results and lapses and not on members.
6. Provide own assessment of team performance.
7. Recognize and appreciate improvements in team performance.
8. Seek suggestions on improving team performance.
9. Propose improvements not already included in the team's suggestions.

A leader has to constantly motivate members and convert subordinates into followers. A major part of a leader's facilitating role extends over building interpersonal competence.

INTERPERSONAL COMPETENCE

Interpersonal competence relates to self-awareness, empathetic listening, communication skills, and leads to organizational success. Transformational leaders recognize the need for interpersonal competence and endeavour to build this competence. Regardless of the industry, everything that is achieved, to some extent, depends on people. It is therefore the quality of the relationships within an organization that ultimately impacts the quality of the output.

Increasing interpersonal competence in an organization enhances the outcome in certain situations including:

- getting the work done right the first time,
- disciplinary issues,
- resolution of interpersonal conflict,
- staff and workgroup development, and
- coaching/mentoring/counselling

Interpersonal competence is the foundation for success and its components are the following:

- Self-awareness—How well do you know yourself?
- Listening—How effective are you as a listener?
- Empathy and understanding—How effective are you at reading beyond the words?
- Communication skills—Do you have and use the skills of paraphrasing, perception checking, describing feelings, and describing behaviour?

Interpersonal competence will make the people in an organization more effective at:

- setting goals and objectives and holding individuals accountable for the results,
- encouraging exploration of options and giving people free choice in deciding whether or not to change,
- providing appropriate information and instructions and meaningful feedback when needed,
- listening to problems, identifying feelings, and legitimizing them,
- confronting problems, and
- teaching new skills and capabilities.

If anyone wants to become interpersonally competent, he/she needs to do three things—(a) get to know himself/herself: his/her likes and dislikes, strengths and weaknesses; (b) build strong relationships with the people he/she meets; and (c) resolve conflict positively.

The model of Bud Bilanich (2008) on interpersonal competence has three factors:

(a) Interpersonally competent people are self-aware. They use this awareness to better understand others and to adapt their behaviour accordingly.
(b) Interpersonally competent people build and nurture strong, lasting, mutually beneficial relationships.
(c) Interpersonally competent people resolve conflicts in a positive manner.

Bilanich (2008) mentions that in 1988, researchers at the Department of Psychology at University of California, Los Angeles (UCLA), suggested five dimensions of interpersonal competence:

- Initiating relationships
- Self-disclosure
- Providing emotional support
- Asserting displeasure with others' actions
- Managing interpersonal conflicts

Out of the five dimensions initiating relationships, self-disclosure and providing emotional support create avenues to build, nurture, and maintain a relationship. On the other hand, asserting displeasure and managing conflict promote a healthy work environment in a positive manner.

Bilanich believes and argues that self-awareness is the foundation of interpersonal competence and the first step in building positive relationships and resolving conflicts in a positive manner. Self-aware people understand how they are similar to and different from other people. Their insights help them to build relationship with a variety of people; determine how much they should disclose about themselves at various points in a relationship; and determine the appropriate amount of emotional support they should offer others. This proactive approach makes them effective and successful.

Interpersonally competent people develop collaborative capacity that cannot be transmitted in a 'single loop' learning process. It needs several journeys and explorations. It develops through experience and reflection, new knowledge and insight, conscious practice, and credible feedback.

Role of Interpersonal Competence in Team Building

Interpersonal competence and interpersonal relationships are interwoven. Promoting interpersonal relationships and the capacity of working as a team member is of paramount importance. Measuring interpersonal relationships using a psychometric scale is essential. Measuring the interpersonal competence for effective functioning of the team is an essential organizational task.

Measuring Interpersonal Competence: FIRO-B

Fundamental Interpersonal Relations Orientation-Behaviour (FIRO-B) assessment helps people unlock the mysteries of human interaction at work and in their personal life. Schutz (1958) propounded this theory and questionnaire (FIRO-B) to quickly gather critical insights into how an individual's needs for inclusion, control, and affection to shape his/her interactions with others. This psychological instrument manifests its use in many areas including one-on-one coaching, small groups, or teams.

The FIRO-B tool kit includes a number of narrative and graphic reports, a technical guide, booklets, and other resources that highlight ways to use the assessment as an integral part of team-building initiatives, management training programmes, and communication workshops.

FIRO-B is a highly valid and reliable tool that assesses how an individual's personal needs affect that person's behaviour towards other individuals. This highly valid and reliable self-report instrument offers an insight both into an individual's compatibility with other people as well as into that his/her own individual characteristics.

FIRO-B measures a person's need for expressed behaviour and wanted behaviour.

- Expressed Behaviour (E)—What a person prefers to do, and how much that person wants to initiate action
- Wanted Behaviour (W)—How much a person wants others to initiate action and how much that person wants to be the recipient

The instrument also measures a person's need for inclusion, control, and affection.

- Inclusion (I)—recognition, belonging, and participation
- Control (C)—influence, leading, and responsibility
- Affection (A)—closeness, warmth, and sensitivity

Benefits of FIRO-B

FIRO-B is an ideal tool to use for interpersonal behaviour measurement and assessment, including

- Management and supervisor development
- Leadership development
- Identifying leadership preferred operating styles
- Employee development
- Team building and explaining team roles
- Improving team effectiveness
- Advancing career development

TEAM EFFECTIVENESS

Effectiveness is the extent to which the planned activities are realized and planned results are achieved. The literature review confirms that defining team effectiveness is a difficult task and also shows disagreements in the definition. However, a definition by Hackman (1990) is that team effectiveness is not a function only of the team's ability to work together interdependently and effectively, but also of the personal well-being or satisfaction of the team members; the team's output must also meet the standards of quality of the people who receive or review that output.

Dimensions of Effectiveness

Effectiveness has several dimensions. Some of these are:

- Loyalty to other members and the leader
- Confidence of leader and members
- Members communicate with openness
- Members do not hesitate to take decision; they feel secure
- Activities of the group occur in a supportive and encouraging manner
- Group goals and individual goals are more or less congruent
- Satisfaction of team members

Influencers of Team Effectiveness

Effectiveness of a team depends on many factors like loyalty of members to the leader, quality of mutual interaction, level of confidence, challenging attitude, organizational climate, OCTAPACE (openness, collaboration, trust, authenticity, proactivity, autonomy, confrontation, and experimentation/experiencing), skills to perform interpersonal roles, informational roles and decision-making roles of the leaders, and similar other factors.

Measuring Team Effectiveness

Measuring effectiveness of team is as essential and as encouraging as working in teams. Unless it is measured, how can it be monitored? Organizations must develop means to measure team effectiveness and continuously evaluate it. The importance of teams for the ultimate success of organizations is unquestioned today. Organizations should develop guidelines and implement systems of team assessment.

Two specific reasons that justify the utmost need for measuring team effectiveness are:

(a) Identifying quickly where things are going wrong, in order to put them on the right track
(b) Knowing when they are in the right so they can get on with their work confidently

Therefore, it is a prime obligation of an organization to have a simple framework to guide the teams to self-assess their effectiveness in the way they need to be assessed. The website workplaceculture.suite101.com has developed a simple framework called PERFORM—an acronym for seven dimensions of effectiveness: productivity, empathy, roles and goals, flexibility, openness, recognition, and morale.

Productivity (or Outcomes)

Productivity is obviously the most important of all the dimensions because it is about whether the team is producing the desired result to get response to questions like (a) is it achieving its goals? (b) is the team able to satisfy both internal and external customers? For an accurate assessment, the website suggests collecting data through surveys, analysing complaints, etc.

Empathy

The most vital need while working in teams is mutual trust and as such this dimension considers whether team members feel comfortable with each other. It is important because if they do not, it can drain energy and creativity, which adversely affects performance. Empathy is strongly related to the ability of the team to communicate effectively regarding difficult issues without affecting the dignity of others.

Roles and Goals

Role clarity is an essential requirement for the leader as well as team members. This dimension emphasizes that individuals must know their roles in the team and how these fit in with others' roles. Team tasks can fall through the cracks if people are not clear about who should be taking responsibility for the tasks, or if they do not know where their responsibility begins and ends.

Flexibility

This dimension considers responsiveness of the team and whether the team is sensitive to outside influence and contribution. Some teams develop a rigid way of operating, which can limit team functioning. Team members should ask themselves questions to verify (a) whether they respond to the changes, (b) does the extent of communication with the teams around them fulfil team needs, and (c) whether they listen, respond as well as tell, to clarify various issues.

Openness

This dimension refers to transparency and to free and ready communication between team members by way of information giving and opinion sharing. The team must find answers to key questions like (a) do we tell other team members everything they need to know, including information about difficulties, mistakes, risks, and problems? (b) Do we share what we are thinking and planning?

Recognition

A person whose recognition motive is dominant aspires to get something, tangible or intangible, when he/she does some good or innovative work. This dimension is important for the long-term health of the team and takes into account whether the team members celebrate successes and praise one another. Members must remember that 'success breeds success', which may happen more frequently if team members enthuse each other. The important inference is team members 'feel good' when their work is recognized.

Morale

Morale or self-esteem helps team members to derive pride from the output of the team and more so from their being members of the team. Members with high morale utilize their abilities to the maximum possible extent, achieve recurring successes, and contribute positively to the organization.

As the foregoing discussions make clear, periodically measuring effectiveness helps to bring out the weaknesses of a team, any deviation in its functioning, deficiency in problem-solving skills, inability to communicate, behaving in a way leading to misperception, etc. Thus, it enables initiation of remedial measures that ultimately pave the way to organizational success.

Team Effectiveness Scale

Pareek (2002) designed a scale to assess thirty aspects of team effectiveness. Some of the aspects are mutual trust, mutual support, communication, handling conflicts, decision process, external linkages, team member satisfaction, attitude of members, collaboration, team cohesion, and creativity. The scale contains thirty bipolar items, and each item has answer choices on a five-point scale; there are positive and negative items. To make all items unidirectional, Pareek suggests reversing the scores of negative items.

Pareek's Team Effectiveness Scale (Table 10.1) takes into account various team requirements and characteristics. For example, mutual trust may vary from high suspicion to high trust, communication can be open or cautious, members may take responsibility always or rarely, leadership can be shared or centralized, external linkages can be low or high, and so forth.

A few items from the thirty item scale and corresponding answer choices are reproduced for clarity.

TABLE **10.1 Team effectiveness scale**

Goal of the team	Very vague	1	2	3	4	5	Very clear
Decision process	Arbitration	1	2	3	4	5	Consensus
Team assessment	Seldom	1	2	3	4	5	Periodical
Team climate	Relaxed	1	2	3	4	5	Tense
Work assignment	Clear	1	2	3	4	5	Ambiguous

Team Effectiveness Assessment Measure (TEAM)

Pareek (2002) designed a 28-item scale titled Team Effectiveness Assessment Measure (TEAM) to assess seven components of a team. These components are:

- Task clarity
- Cohesion
- Autonomy
- Confrontation
- Support
- Collaboration
- Accountability

The instrument has four items to assess each component. Pareek (2002) suggests that the team/group be rated on the following options:

- Write 4 if this is highly characteristic of the group, and/or this always happens.
- Write 3 if this is fairly characteristic of the group, and/or this frequently happens.
- Write 2 if this is slightly characteristic of the group, and/or this sometimes happens.
- Write 1 if this is very little true about the group, and/or this occasionally happens.
- Write 0 if this is not at all true about the group, and/or this never happens.

Some of the items/statements are as follows:

- The goals of this team are well defined.
- The team has enough freedom to decide its ways of working.
- The team is given adequate resources to carry out its functions.
- The sense of responsibility and accountability is pretty high amongst the team members.

- The team generates alternative solutions for a problem.
- The members of the team have enough freedom in their areas.
- The team has enough competent persons needed for its work.
- The team does not have autonomy in vital aspects of its working.

The responses allow calculating 'team functioning' and 'team empowerment' objectively.

Ginnett's Team Effectiveness Leadership Model
About the model

Leadership is a group or team function aimed at achieving team objectives. Obviously, then, it is essential to assess whether the team is achieving that what it should. Robert Ginnett, a Senior Fellow at the Center for Creative Leadership, developed the TELM in 1993. The model provides a mechanism to first identify what a team needs to be effective, and then to point the leader either towards the roadblocks that are hindering the team or towards ways to make the team more effective than it is now. The unique features are that the model

(a) identifies leverage points for change and then points the way to pragmatic solutions,
(b) resembles system theory approach with
- inputs on the left (that is, individual, team, and organizational factors),
- processes or throughputs in the centre (that is, what one can tell about the team by actually observing team members at work), and
- outputs on the right (that is, how well the team did in accomplishing its objectives).

TELM thus follows the process approach to management (Figures 10.1 and 10.2).

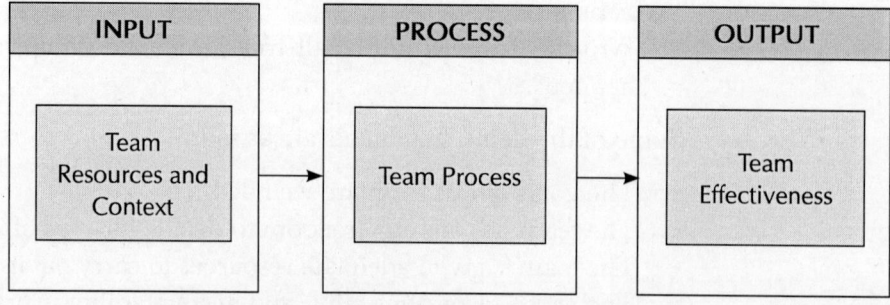

FIGURE **10.1** **Systems theory for teams**

Output—Team members put in concerted efforts for success. Outputs are the results of their efforts. The accomplishments differ widely based on the objectives of the teams. A work team strives to accomplish business goals, leading to the achievement of organizational objectives. A team of social workers might be trying to save people in an area hit by an epidemic or a natural disaster. The Indian cricket team tries to win match. All the examples cited are raw data and insufficient for assessing team effectiveness and will not help measure effectiveness, neither in an absolute sense nor in a relative sense.

Hackman (1990) emphasizes that a group is effective if (a) the team's productive output (goods, services, decisions) meets the quantitative requirements and also the qualitative standards, and the schedule for the delivery of the output to the people who use it; (b) the group process that takes place while the group is performing its tasks that enhances the ability of the people to work as a team (either in the team where the person is a member or some other team that he/she is assigned to); and (c) the group experience enhances the growth and personal well-being of the individuals who compose the team.

Process—A process is defined as a set of interrelated activities. A team leader must have process orientation. It is the process that is greatly responsible for the output. The leader has to pay adequate attention to the team's process—how the team goes about the work. Selecting the process is the most important task a leader performs. Hughes et al. (2007) mention four 'process measures' of effectiveness by which one can examine the way the teams work. To perform effectively a team must

(a) work hard enough,
(b) have sufficient knowledge and skills within the team to perform the task,
(c) have an appropriate strategy to accomplish its work (or ways to approach the task at hand), and
(d) have positive group dynamics among its members.

The four process measures are fairly good diagnostic measures of a team's ultimate effectiveness. If a leader discovers deviation or a problem with any of the process measure, he/she will focus sharper attention on that process. The leader may adopt many means to tackle the problem, a unique example being a motivational speech to the members.

Input—Raw materials are inputs in a manufacturing organization; ideas, information, and some other intellectual properties are inputs in service organizations. Strategies are inputs in both types of organizations. While designing a team, we often consider the personal attributes—the psychological factors—of the members. There exists a variety of inputs, ranging from the individual to the environmental level (Hughes et al. 2007). It is ultimately the responsibility of the leader to harmonize and create the conditions for effective teamwork.

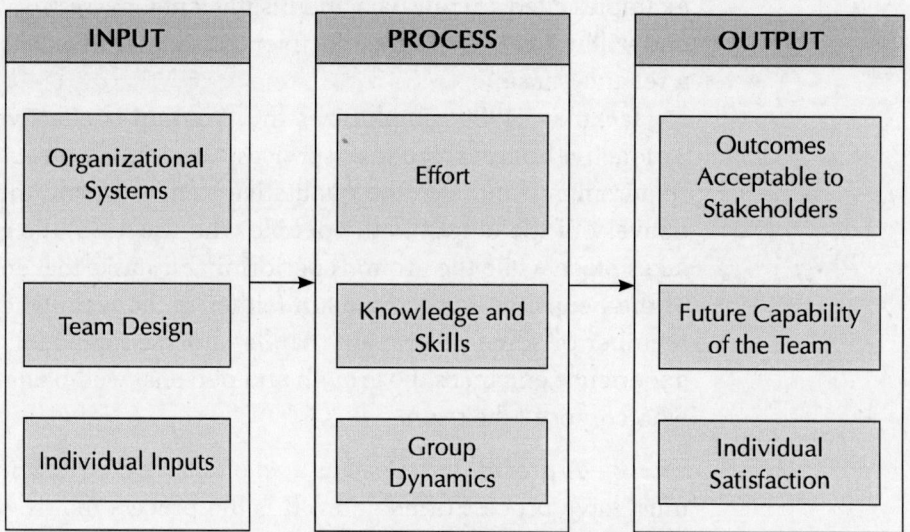

FIGURE 10.2 Basic TELM components

Leadership prescriptions of the model

Leadership prescriptions of the team effectiveness leadership model lay emphasis on building of team, and then on three functions—creation, dream, and design.

Creation Hughes et al. (2007) elucidate the leadership prescriptions of the (TELM) team effectiveness leadership model. One should start building a team with a concept, create a design, make the members want to do what the leader wants them to do, and then float a design of the team. A somewhat more complex version of the TELM leadership functions (Figure 10.3) emphasizes that a leader should begin with the 'dream', proceed with all the 'design' variables, and then pay attention to the 'development' needs of the team. As such, a leader can implement the three critical functions for team leadership, namely, dream (planning and deciding direction), design (inputs), and development (the process).

Dream In order to establish a new team, the leader has to 'dream' to set a clear and unambiguous direction. This is the most important phase in the team-building process and backed by wild thoughts and deep conceptualization. A vision statement clarifies where a team intends to reach, and what should be the path. Hughes et al. (2007) state that the communication of vision frequently involves metaphorical/symbolic language so that members actually 'paint their own picture' of where the team is headed.

Design This phase is the activity-packed phase and needs the most attention of the leader and others to ensure no component is left out, and that all tangible and intangible inputs are taken into account. In case any component is omitted, the consequence may be enhanced development cost. With adequate care and undivided attention to this phase, teams can achieve excellence and gain the benefits of being a high-performing team. It may not be possible for a team leader to exercise control on the

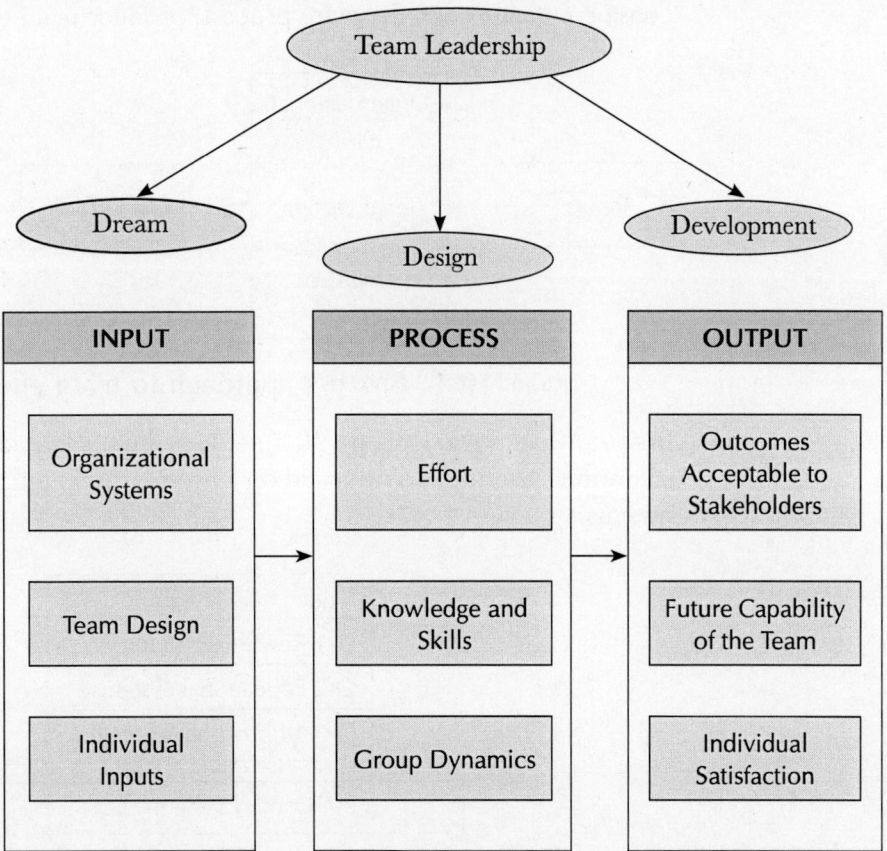

FIGURE **10.3** **Three TELM leadership functions**

organizational context and system, but he/she can do so in the team he/she is leading.

Development This is actually the process phase. While the team is functioning, the leader will have to observe whether the team has a clear sense of direction and vision. He/she has also to oversee that the input variables are contributing to team effectiveness. The inputs obviously comprise variables at the organizational as well as individual levels. Organizational inputs include reward, education, and information systems. Interests/motivation, skills/abilities, and values/attitudes are the individual inputs.

Diagnosis and Leverage Points

From Figure 10.4, it is clear that the design function incorporates three inputs: (a) organizational inputs, (b) team design, and (c) individual inputs. These inputs, through the team process, produce team effectiveness.

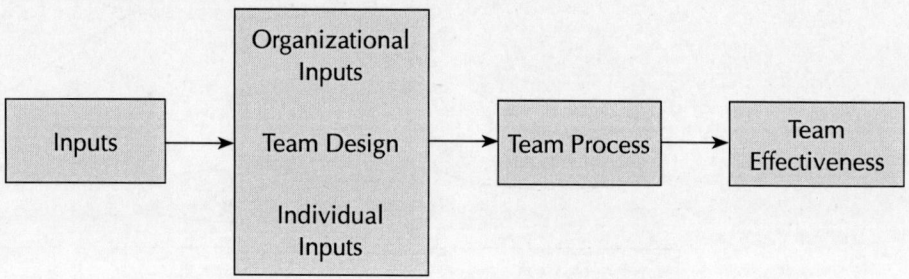

FIGURE 10.4 Process approach to team effectiveness

Organizational inputs (Figure 10.5)—These inputs include reward systems, education systems, and information systems, the foundation being control systems.

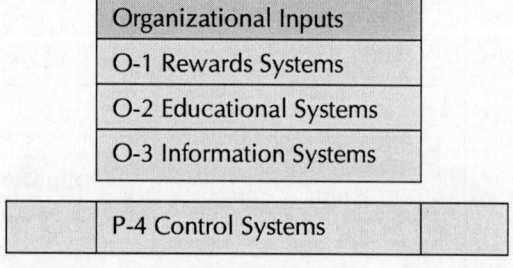

FIGURE 10.5 Components of a control system

Team design—These inputs include task, composition, and norms, the foundation being authority (Figure 10.6).

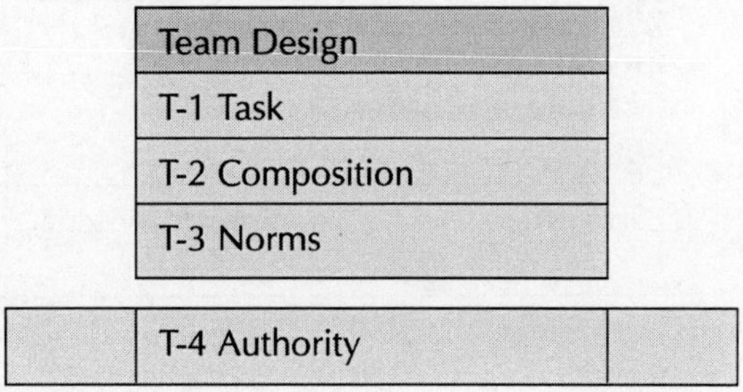

Team Design
T-1 Task
T-2 Composition
T-3 Norms

| | T-4 Authority | |

FIGURE 10.6 Component: Authority

Individual inputs: These inputs include interests/motivation, skills/abilities, values/attitudes, the foundation being interpersonal behaviour (Figure 10.7).

Individual Inputs
I-1 Interests/Motivation
I-2 Skills/Abilities
I-3 Values/Attitudes

| | I-4 Interpersonal Behaviour | |

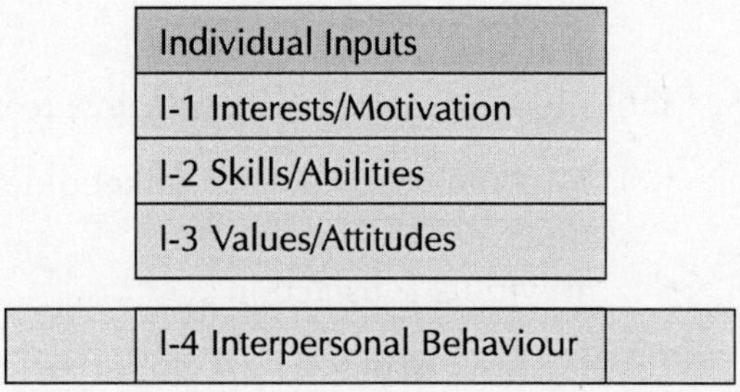

FIGURE 10.7 Component: Interpersonal behaviour

The process criteria of TELM comprises effort, knowledge and skills, and strategy, the foundation being group dynamics (Figure 10.8).

Process Criteria
P-1 Effort
P-2 Knowledge and Skills
P-3 Strategy

| | P-4 Group Dynamics | |

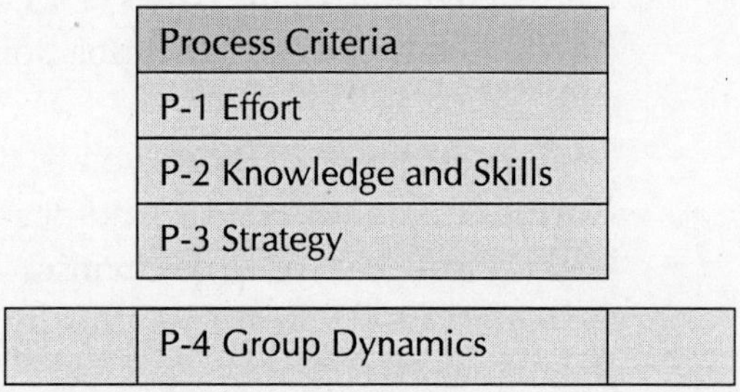

FIGURE 10.8 Component: Group dynamics

TABLE **10.2**   **Identifying the root cause of team effectiveness**

When the effectiveness measurements indicate a problem with	Look at these inputs		
	Organizational Inputs (O)	Team Design (T)	Individual Inputs (I)
Effort (P-1)	Reward Systems (O-1)	Tasks (T-1)	Interests/ Motivation (I-1)
Knowledge and Skills (P-2)	Education Systems (O-2)	Design Composition (T-2)	Skills/Abilities (I-2)
Strategy (P-3)	Information Systems (O-3)	Norms (T-3)	Values/Attitudes (I-3)
All the above are built on foundations of group dynamics			
Group Dynamics (P-4)	Control Systems (O-4)	Authority (T-4)	Interpersonal Behaviours (I-4)

Table 10.2 explains how to achieve team effectiveness.

• Outcome acceptable to stakeholders
• Future capability of team
• Individual satisfaction

To diagnose issues in an underperforming team and find the process criteria leverage points, the model is to be followed backward, starting with processes and moving back to inputs to find appropriate solutions.

• If a team is having problems with Effort (P-1), then examine Reward Systems (O-1), Tasks (T-1), and Interests/Motivation (I-1).
• Knowledge and Skills issues (P-2) require a look at Education Systems (O-2), Team Design Composition (T-2), and Team Skills/Abilities (I-2).
• Strategy issues (P-3) direct you to consider Information Systems (O-3), Norms (T-3), and Values/Attitudes (I-3).
• If the issue is Group Dynamics (P-4), then look at Team Control Systems (O-4), Team Authority (T-4), and Team Interpersonal Behaviour (I-4).

The TELM helps to identify the root cause for any observation while measuring team effectiveness. We are to move from the symptom to the root cause. The observed symptom may be an inability to achieve the target

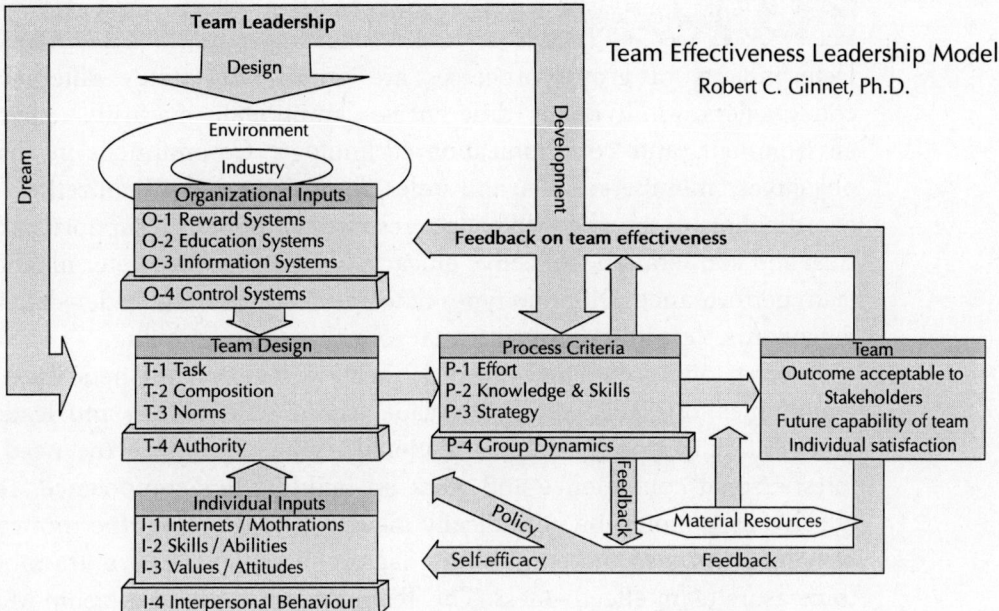

Source: Hughes, Ginnett, and Curphy (2007), *Leadership—Enhancing the Lessons of Experience*, 5th edn, Tata McGraw-Hill, New Delhi, p. 315.

FIGURE **10.9** **Ginnett's Team Effectiveness Leadership Model**

though the members are sincere and put in their best efforts. They do not gossip or loiter about. Initiating disciplinary action is not recommended as a solution. Such action will simply further lower their motivation levels. On careful investigation, it may be revealed that the reason for non-performance or underperformance is lack of knowledge and inadequate skills. From the process criteria, we get that knowledge and skills is the level (P-2). No amount of encouragement will help them to achieve the target. We should consider the corresponding level in the 'Individual Factors', which is 'Skills/Abilities' (I-2). Then we are required to move to the corresponding level in 'Organizational Factors' or control system, which is 'Education systems' (O-2). This approach clearly prompts us to examine the education system. However, team design receives inputs from the organization and the individual. Using this model, we find key leverage points at various levels of the input stage that impacted the functioning of the team (Figure 10.9).

SUMMARY

Determinants of group processes are group size, status differentials, cohesiveness, individual differences, emotional maturity, physical environment, and communication technology. Commitment in shared objectives, members skills and role clarity, internal organization and coordination, external coordination, resource and political support, mutual trust and cooperation, collective efficacy, and potency are determinants of team performance. Different types of teams need different leader skills and behaviours. A facilitator plays a vital role in team functioning.

Interpersonal competence relates to self-awareness, empathetic listening, communication skills, promotes leader–member relations, and leads to organizational success. Transformational leaders recognize the need for interpersonal competence and work on building this competence. Team effectiveness should be periodically measured to bring out the root cause of failure and also the contributing factors to success. There are models to measure team effectiveness. The Team Effectiveness Leadership Model developed by Robert Ginnett is an extremely valuable model and considers system theory and process approach to management.

KEY TERMS

External spanning behaviour incorporates the role of a spokesperson in promoting the image of the team, interacting with clients, and influencing outsiders.

Emotional support refers to morale boosting by peers and others and with this support, a member can probably attain something hitherto impossible.

Group process is the process that determines group behaviour and effectiveness and is a key aspect of managing groups and teams.

Interpersonal competence promotes interpersonal relationships, relates to self-awareness, empathetic listening, communication skills, and leads to organizational success.

Process teams are preferred by many organizations that do not have affiliation to departmental form or structure to undertake broad organizational-level process improvements.

Task cohesiveness refers to the degree to which group members share group goals, work together to meet these goals, and work smoothly together.

Team effectiveness is a complex function of the team's ability to work together interdependently and effectively, and considers satisfaction and well-being of team members, future capability of the team, and also whether the team's output meets the standards of quality for the people who receive or review that output (Hackman 1990).

EXERCISES

Concept Review Questions

1. State your understanding about group process. How does it relate to the outcomes of a group?
2. Discuss the determinants of team performance. Do you feel that these are interdependent?
3. 'Depending on the type of team, a leader has to modulate his/her role.' Do you agree with this statement? Justify your viewpoint.
4. 'A leader's facilitating role is of paramount importance for the success of his/her team.' Critically discuss this statement.
5. Discuss the role of interpersonal competence in team building. Correlate interpersonal competence and team effectiveness.

Critical Thinking Questions

1. What do you understand by interpersonal competence? Explain the components of interpersonal competence. Cite examples.
2. Discuss the components of the Team Effectiveness Leadership Model. Consider that the members of a team are seen to frequently loiter, gossip, waste time, and ultimately cannot achieve their goals. How does the model help to analyse the situation?

Assignments

1. Consider a team functioning for a long time, say five years. Observe and discuss the leader's role, especially on what basis he/she has distributed the tasks to the members. Also record the various roles played by each member to achieve the team objectives. Present your findings, preferably in a tabular form.
2. Contact the leader of the team and interview to record how he/she identifies the strengths and weaknesses of the team members. Discuss at length how he/she shapes the behaviour of a new member. If you notice any flaw in his/her approach, provide suitable advice. (Take the help of your teacher.)

REFERENCES

Bowers, Clint A., Eduardo Salas, Weaver, and Jeanne L. *Coordination & Virtual Environment* (www.team-wise.co.uk).

Berkman, Eric (2004), *Six Ways to Handle a Dysfunctional Team* (www.searchsecurity. techtarget.com/tip/ 0,289483,sid14_gci960850,00.html; accessed on 29 September 2007).

Bud, Bilanich. *Self-Awareness and Interpersonal Competence* (ezinearticles.com/? Self-Awareness- and-Interpersonal-Competence&id=1017877; accessed on 3 August 2008).

Deborah Jude-York, Lauren D. Davis, and Susan L. Wise (2004), *Virtual Teaming, Breaking the Boundaries of Time and Place*, Viva Books, New Delhi.

Ghiselli, E.E. (1956), Differentiation of Individuals in Terms of Their Predictability, *Journal of Applied Psychology*, Vol. 40, pp. 374–7.

Hackman, J.R. (1990), *Groups That Work (and Those That Don't)*, Jossey-Bass, San Francisco, CA.

Haldar, U.K. (2009), *Human Resource Development*, Oxford University Press, New Delhi.

Hughes, Richard L., Robert C. Ginnett and Gordon J. Curphy (2007), *Leadership Enhancing the Lessons of Experience*, Tata McGraw-Hill, New Delhi.

Landy, F.J. and J.L. Farr (1983), *The Measurement of Work Performance: Methods, Theory and Application*, Academic Press, New York.

Pareek, Udai (2002), *Training Instruments in HRD and OD*, Second Edition, Tata McGraw-Hill, New Delhi.

Parker, Glenn M. and Richard P. Kropp (1999), *Training Activities, Team Building—A Sourcebook of Activities*, Viva Books, New Delhi.

Pokras, Sandy (2004), *Working in Teams—A Viva Crisp Fifty-Minute Book*, Viva Books, New Delhi.

Schutz, William C. (1958), *A Three Dimensional Theory of Interpersonal Behavior*, Renehart, New York.

Stoner, J.A.F., A.E. Freeman, and D.A. Gilbert, Jr. (2006), *Management*, Prentice-Hall India, New Delhi.

Williams, Hank (1997), *The Essence of Managing Groups and Teams*, Prentice-Hall India, New Delhi.

Web Resources

www.1000ventures.com/business_guide/crosscuttings/team_vs_group.html (accessed on 5 August 2008).

wilderdom.com/theory/FieldTheory.html#Smith2001 (accessed on 3 August 2008).

www.team-wise.co.uk/benefits_of_team_building.htm (accessed on 23 May 2008).

vulms.vu.edu.pk/Courses/MGT501/HandOuts/Lecture%2005.pdf (accessed on 21 August 2008).

www.mindtools.com/pages/article/newTMM_85.htm (accessed on 23 August 2008).

www.faculty.ed.umuc.edu/~prichard/crs_guid_gen/smlgrp_process.html (accessed on 24 August 2008).

workplaceculture.suite101.com/article.cfm/measures_of_team_effectiveness (accessed on 28 August 2008).

dotnet.org.za/tina/pages/4563.aspx (accessed on 29 September 2008).

searchsecurity.techtarget.com/tip/0,289483,sid14_gci960850,00.html (accessed on 29 September 2007).

Facilitating a Dysfunctional Team

(*Note: This case is in continuation of the opening case, wherein it has been decided to take the help of Mr Pratap for settling on a future course of action.*)

The expert, Mr Pratap, carried out further analysis to diagnose issues in the teams. He concentrated on the process criteria leverage points to find appropriate solutions. He tried to identify the possible reasons hindering the functioning and progress of the teams. He observed that members had requisite knowledge and skills. As such, he ignored education systems, team design composition, and skills/abilities. The tasks assigned were not strategic in nature. Therefore, he did not consider information systems, norms, and values/attitudes.

His observations included that the teams had problems with effort. As a result, he examined the reward systems, compensation packages, tasks, interests and motivation. It revealed that the motives and motivations of the members were not identified. It came to his notice that members did not trust each other; they were passing the buck and were finding faults and not relying on facts. He therefore looked at team control systems, team authority, and team interpersonal behaviour.

There was lack of role clarity and responsibilities of members were not defined. The goals were set in non-measurable terms and hence they could not be quantified. The system of obtaining feedback periodically was not installed.

Mr Pratap came up with some suggestions:

(a) Empowering the leader
(b) Understanding the motivation of team members
(c) Assigning tasks to each member
(d) Defining roles and responsibilities of all
(e) Setting team goals in measurable terms
(f) Developing system of gathering feedback on regular basis

The expert further advised that the manager or the leader must take care of the above aspects. However, Mr Pratap proposed the need for training on interpersonal competency and team effectiveness dimensions.

Discussion Questions

1. When it was revealed that the teams had problems with making effort, the expert examined certain aspects. What might be the reason behind these considerations?
2. Had you been in Mr Pratap's position, what would you have done?
3. As an expert, what advice would you have given to Elite Hydraulic Works to revitalize the teams?

CHAPTER 11

Research Findings and Training

Learning Objectives

After studying the chapter you will be able to

▶ Understand the importance of research in team building

▶ State the need for research in the study of leader behaviours

▶ Define the structured training process

▶ Appreciate the importance of documentation

▶ Describe the use of procedures

INTRODUCTION

We had discussed in earlier chapters various aspects and components of leadership and team building. Researchers are keen to identify the contributing factors to team effectiveness, organizational outcomes, interpersonal relations, and so forth. This chapter discusses two research studies in detail showing the background, hypotheses, and discussions and conclusions. Thereafter, few research findings are discussed, which lay emphasis on some independent variables and indirectly point towards training needs. The second part of this chapter is on a range of training aspects.

RESEARCH 1: LEADERSHIP STYLES ON FOLLOWERS' SATISFACTION

(*Source: South Asian Journal of Management*, Vol. 11, No. 1, January–March 2004. Editor: Mathew Manimala

Title: Effect of Leadership Styles on Followers' Satisfaction and Perceived Effectiveness (Summary of a research)

Researcher and Author: Kum Kum Mukherjee)

Background of the GLOBE Study

The Global Leadership and Organizational Behaviour Effectiveness (GLOBE) research programme aims to examine the impact of national culture on leadership effectiveness in the organizational context. The research project was initiated by Robert House in 1993 and a score of eminent researchers from all over the world joined the project. It is essentially a multi-phase and ongoing research effort, collecting and using data from 62 countries across the world.

Mukherjee (2004) from India was the state co-investigator for the state of West Bengal. The present study is based on the data collected for the GLOBE project where an attempt was made to determine the effect of various leadership styles on overall organizational effectiveness and followers' level of satisfaction.

Aim of the Study

The study attempted to critically examine the effects of leadership styles on overall organizational effectiveness. The specific objectives of the study were the following:

- To identify the business styles of business leaders in the state of West Bengal, India.
- To measure and quantify followers' level of satisfaction and perceived effectiveness.
- To examine whether these two are linked in some way or the other.

General Hypothesis

Leadership styles have a significant level of influence over followers' level of satisfaction, perceived feelings of effectiveness, and willingness to contribute towards the achievement of organizational goals.

Specific Hypotheses

In order to test the general hypotheses, the researcher framed nineteen specific hypotheses. The leaders listed below increase followers' level of satisfaction, perceived feeling of effectiveness, and willingness to contribute towards the achievement of organizational goals:

1. Visionary leaders
2. Leaders with a high level of integrity
3. Leaders who try not to embarrass their followers

4. Leaders who are able to retain their calm even when facing difficult situations
5. Leaders who take pain in clearly identifying subordinates' job responsibilities
6. Intellectually stimulating leaders who can encourage subordinates to think and challenge basic assumptions
7. Leaders who are team-oriented and integrate subordinates into cohesive groups
8. Decisive leaders
9. Leaders who act as the information source for followers, are knowledgeable, and understand easily
10. Leaders who are open, share critical information, and communicate freely
11. Leaders who show a great deal of confidence in followers and allow them to use a considerable amount of discretion in their work
12. Leaders who are humane, kind, and compassionate towards subordinates and are always supportive
13. Leaders who are administratively effective
14. Leaders who are performance oriented and always strive for excellence

However, the following leaders will decrease the followers' level of satisfaction, perceived feeling of effectiveness, and willingness to contribute towards the achievement of organizational goals:

15. Leaders who are status conscious
16. Autocratic leaders
17. Self-protecting leaders who pursue their own interests
18. Leaders who do not reward their subordinates on the basis of their performances
19. Leaders who are not explicit and are indirect in their dealings

It is evident from the above hypotheses that the researcher analysed various facets of leaders to bring out and test followers' level of satisfaction, perceived feeling of effectiveness, and willingness to contribute towards the achievement of organizational goals.

Operational Definitions

The operational definition of any term helps an evaluator to understand the exact meaning of a term in the context of a specific research. Mukherjee (2004) defines leadership style and entrepreneurship as follows:

- Leadership style—An individual's propensity to behave in a particular way, which can be assessed through the response of his/her followers to a specifically designed questionnaire. The researcher used the Leader Behaviour Description Questionnaire (LBDQ).
- Entrepreneurship—The processes leading to new venture creation, without regard to the type or potential of the organization created.
- Followers' satisfaction, perceived feeling of effectiveness, and willingness to contribute towards the achievement of organizational goals defined by GLOBE. Parameters assessed through specific items of the LBDQ.

Method

The researcher administered two parallel sets of a 130-item questionnaire (LBDQ) to the leaders and their respective followers.

Tool

Pearson Correlation coefficient

Method of Data Collection

The unique aspects of the study are the following:

- Leader's idea about his/her own style of leading
- Leadership style as perceived by the followers in managerial position

The researcher interviewed each sample leader based on structured guidelines. The direct interview sessions were recorded for post-interview analysis. Thereafter, the researcher collected a list of subordinates at the managerial level who directly reported to or interacted with the leader interviewees. From the list, the researcher selected nine followers for each of the leaders.

Senior managers were given version E whereas junior- and middle-level managers were given versions C and D of the LBDQ.

Data Analysis

Some interesting points in the analysis are given below:

- Considerable degree of discrepancy was observed between the CEO's style of leadership as perceived by himself/herself and the followers.
- As an example, a CEO claimed to be a team-oriented person though followers actually perceived him as an autonomous leader, a loner who liked to remain aloof.

- Significant difference was found between entrepreneur and non-entrepreneur leaders in their beliefs, attitudes, and behavioural patterns.
- Entrepreneur-CEOs are risk takers, creative, and innovative. But, non-entrepreneur-CEOs are traditional and more rule-bound.

Discussion and Conclusion

The leadership style that provides the maximum satisfaction to followers and generates a feeling of worthiness, in terms of being able to contribute effectively to the attainment of organizational goals and objectives, appears to be the 'intellectually stimulating' style and the next effective style is showing 'integrity'.

The values of correlation coefficient (r) of various leadership styles and followers' satisfaction, perceived effectiveness, and willingness to contribute are presented in Table 11.1 in descending order.

TABLE 11.1   Leadership style vs correlation coefficient

S. No.	Leadership Style	r	S. No.	Leadership Style	r
1	Intellectually stimulating	0.94	11	Autocratic	0.70
2	Integrity	0.92	12	Self-protecting	0.70
3	Performance oriented	0.91	13	Decisive	0.49
4	Role clarity	0.91	14	Information source	0.46
5	Visionary	0.89	15	Follower confidence	0.46
6	Charismatic	0.88	16	Communication	0.36
7	Administrative effectiveness	0.88	17	Face-saver	0.28
8	Calmness	0.81	18	Non-contingent reward	0.16
9	Team oriented	0.81	19	Indirect	0.14
10	Status conscious	0.79			

More specifically, these types of leaders encourage followers to take up new challenges and search for newer and better ways of doing things, instead of demanding unquestionable obedience from them.

RESEARCH 2: DETERMINANTS OF TEAM EFFECTIVENESS

(*Source: Indian Journal for Training and Development* (*Journal of Indian Society for Training and Development*), Vol. XXXVIII, No. 3, July–September 2008.

Title: A Comparative Study of Team Leaders and Team Members on the Factors Affecting Team Effectiveness (Summary of a research study)

Researchers and Authors: Saurabhi Chaturvedi, Pallavi Bhatnagar, and Dr Rishu Roy

Background of the Study

The researchers exhaustively reviewed the extant literature. They perceived a causal relationship between the status of an individual in a team and team effectiveness.

Objectives of the Study

- To identify the factors that affect team effectiveness
- To identify the perceptual gaps between the team leader and team members on the factors of team effectiveness

Methodology

The researchers pursued an exploratory investigation to examine factors affecting team effectiveness. The researchers treat the status of an individual in a team as an independent variable and team effectiveness as a dependent variable.

For the study, they randomly selected an initial sample of 80 executives. They controlled extraneous variables of age, gender, functional area, and other such variables by randomization and elimination. They utilized a scale with five options per statement: strongly agree (=5), agree (=4), neither agree nor disagree (=3), disagree (=2), and strongly disagree (=1).

They classified, tabulated, and analysed the data using statistical techniques like factor analysis and two sample Z-tests to study the variables. Nine factors emerged relevant to the study. The factors are (1) Leadership, (2) Encouraging structure, (3) Team constituent, (4) Reward system, (5) Group framework, (6) Universal goal, (7) Group dynamics, (8) Performance consistency, and (9) Conflict management. The questionnaire the researchers used is given in Annexure 11.1.

Hypotheses and Findings

Hypothesis 1   Leadership—There is no significant difference between the perception of team leaders and team members.
Finding   The null hypothesis rejected. Team leaders and team members differ significantly. Team leaders perceive leadership as an important factor for team effectiveness.

Hypothesis 2 Encouraging structure—There is no significant difference between the perception of team leaders and team members.
Finding The null hypothesis cannot be rejected. Team leaders and team members do not differ significantly.

Hypothesis 3 Team constituent—There is no significant difference between the perception of team leaders and team members.
Finding The null hypothesis rejected. Team leaders and team members differ significantly.

Hypothesis 4 Reward system—There is no significant difference between the perception of team leaders and team members.
Finding The null hypothesis is rejected. Team leaders and team members differ significantly.

Hypothesis 5 Group framework—There is no significant difference between the perception of team leaders and team members.
Finding The null hypothesis cannot be rejected. Team leaders and team members do not differ significantly.

Hypothesis 6 Universal goal—There is no significant difference between the perception of team leaders and team members.
Finding The null hypothesis is rejected. Team leaders and team members differ significantly.

Hypothesis 7 Group dynamics—There is no significant difference between the perception of team leaders and team members.
Finding The null hypothesis is rejected. Team leaders and team members differ significantly.

Hypothesis 8 Performance consistency—There is no significant difference between the perception of team leaders and team members.
Finding The null hypothesis cannot be rejected. Team leaders and team members do not differ significantly.

Hypothesis 9 Conflict management—There is no significant difference between the perception of team leaders and team members.
Finding The null hypothesis is rejected. Team leaders and team members differ significantly.

Conclusion

The researchers concluded that the factors (a) leadership, (b) encouraging structure, (c) team constituent, (d) reward system, (e) group framework,

(f) universal goal, (g) group dynamics, (h) performance consistency, and (i) conflict management affect team effectiveness. They further concluded that the perceptions of team leaders and team members about the impact of each of the factors are not the same.

SOME RESEARCH FINDINGS

Some interesting research findings are discussed to indicate the diverse types of aims and objectives.

Leader Behaviour—Small Business Houses

On extensive review of the literature on leadership and team building, Ghosh (2009) undertook a research on small business houses to identify the most popular and widely used behaviour out of the five core leadership behaviours, namely directive, supportive, participative, reward and punishment, and charismatic.

Ghosh developed a questionnaire based on Howell and Costley (2008) for this investigative study. The observation is that leaders exhibiting supportive, participative, and reward and punishment behaviours are very common. Leaders displaying directive styles are not uncommon. But, followers or subordinates do not identify any leader as charismatic in small business houses. In the study extended on followers' satisfaction, Ghosh (2009) observes that subordinates or followers prefer to work under supportive leaders; do not hesitate to work under leaders exhibiting the participative style of behaviour; do not have an aversion to working with leaders with the reward and punishment style. But, they are not inclined, rather dislike, to work under leaders who exhibit the directive behaviour style. Most interestingly, the researcher did not find any leader with charismatic style in small business houses.

Reward and Punishment—Inclination of Male and Female Leaders

Transactional leadership begins with negotiating the contract whereby the subordinate is given a salary and other service-related benefits, and the company and the subordinate's manager get authority over the subordinate. This style assumes that (a) people are motivated by reward and punishment, (b) social systems work best with a clear chain of command, and (c) when people have agreed to do a job, a part of the deal is that they give up all authority to their manager.

Transactional leadership is based on contingency that reward or punishment is conditional upon performance. Northwestern University conducted a study with respect to transactional, transformational, and laissez-faire leadership styles. The study revealed that female leaders used the transactional leadership style and were more likely to focus on the rewards component of that style. On the other hand, when men utilized the transactional style, they were more likely to focus on the punishment aspects of that style (money-zone).

Transformational Leadership and *Gunas*

Indian philosophy provides a composite framework to aid the understanding of the mental make-up of a person (Agrawal 2008). It offers the *guna* theory, alternatively termed as tri-dimensional personality theory. The three *gunas* are *sattva* (awareness), *rajas* (dynamism), and *tamas* (inertness or passivity). These are the fundamental constituents of every being. The transformational leader's effectiveness is based on the leader's ability to inspire and raise the consciousness of followers by appealing to their higher needs utilizing the *rajas guna.*

In a study, Agrawal (2008) collected information from secondary sources and considered inspirational motivation, intellectual stimulation, idealized influence, and individualized consideration as factors of transformational leadership. The findings show that *sattva* and *sattva-rajas* enhance transformational leadership whereas *tamas* reduces transformational leadership. The study, however, did not reveal any support for the claim that *rajas* when combined with *sattva* would enhance transformational leadership more than *sattva* alone would do. Agrawal suggests that companies organize training programmes around the *guna* framework to develop *sattva* and reduce *tamas* and suggests encouraging sattvic food like fruits and fresh juices considering the subtle implications diet has on a person. Suggestion also includes building corporate culture recognizing knowledge as the status mechanism and not power and wealth. The benefits of *sattva guna* will grow in leaps and bounds and will not only be helpful for organizations but for the entire society (Agrawal 2008).

Leadership Behaviour and Psychological Empowerment

A group of researchers attempted to find out the association between participative leadership behaviour and psychological empowerment. They collected data from 173 employees of two Chinese state-owned enterprises.

They found a strong association between participative leadership behaviour and psychological empowerment. The four dimensions of psychological empowerment they considered were meaning, competence, self-determination, and impact. The researchers did not find a strong association with any of the four dimensions individually. They further found that participative leadership behaviour tended to make short-tenure employees feel competent and thus more committed to an organization. They further commented that this behaviour did not have a significant impact on competence or organizational commitment for long-tenure employees (*Asia Pacific Journal of Management*).

Leadership Styles—Measured vs Perceived

Sen (2008) formulated hypotheses to identify whether leader behaviours vary by (a) organizational hierarchy and (b) functional area, and concludes that the styles are dependent neither on organizational hierarchy nor necessarily on the functional area. Sen (2008) further attempts to investigate whether the styles identified through the questionnaire match the behaviours actually exhibited by managers and observe that the objectively identified style does not match with the exhibited behaviours based on observational analysis.

RESEARCH QUESTIONS

Many developments take place in organizations; many managers see these developments. They ask some questions: Why did it happen this way? What might be the reasons behind this? What else could have happened? Why did the people become violent? Why did the leader fail to control? Why could the team not achieve its targets? What do the members lack? How can the members be developed? What type of power should the leader have been used? After generation of research question a person may ignore or forget. The journey of a dynamic researcher starts from this point. He/She takes up these questions as 'research questions'.

Kalpa (2007) in his paper titled 'Creating Value out of Values' discusses some such questions from the viewpoint of 'impact of value on values' and 'development of values'.

Impact of Value on Values

Some questions from this viewpoint are the following:

- What are tangible linkages between value and creation? How do we measure value and creation?

- Are there particular values that are more important than others? Why?
- How can we make ethics, honesty, and integrity an integral part of leaders and organizations at large?
- How do we ignite inner and outer energy and passion and thereby commitment and innovation in people?

Development of Values

Some questions from this viewpoint are the following:

- How do we develop values in leaders? What sustains and strengthens the values? When and why are they ignored?
- Do we know what conditions allow people to opt for the creation of values out of values?
- Do most values emanate from leaders who operate with the heart and spirit? What is the role of the head?
- Is there a role of silence and self-reflection in developing values? What is the role of having a calm, focused mind? What other tools/techniques exist?

You can also search several such questions from many areas and then select a few clustered questions to pursue your research. Research is a fairly long journey during which researchers face hurdles. They can overcome all the hurdles with ingenuity. At the end of the journey, they derive intellectual joy on getting answers to the research questions.

TRAINING

Academicians, industrial leaders, B-school students doing internships and needing to write dissertations opt for topics on leader development, leadership development, leadership styles, impact of style on followers' satisfaction, causal relationship between leadership style and organizational effectiveness, team building, team effectiveness, leading virtual teams, and many such topics of this nature. While undertaking research, researchers interview people in organizations, hunt for data, bewilder how to proceed, and often see that data have either not been preserved or are not in order. But organizations need research results. At this point, the training for generation and preservation of documents for reference and analysis emerges as indispensable. This validates the utmost importance of training and documentation. If you take a look at the opening and closing cases in the respective chapters, you will be convinced about the need for training. You have observed that the opening case studies underline certain shortcomings in different situations. You have also seen in the closing cases that experts invited in a variety of situations suggested training as a remedial measure. You might be interested in relearning the meaning and essence of training now.

Training enhances employee retention. Recall that 'training is costly; non-training is costlier'. As training is inevitable for the survival and growth of an organization, training evaluation is essential. Training is the procedure or HRD intervention that an organization adopts by which people acquire knowledge and/or skills aimed at achieving definite purposes. Training is 'the systematic development of the knowledge, skills, and attitudes required by an individual to perform adequately a given task or job' (Armstrong 2001). It is 'the act of increasing knowledge and skills of an employee for doing a particular job' (Flippo 1984). Training is a tool to revitalize the trainee imparting knowledge and skills, to motivate him/her to promote all-round organizational growth, sustain competitive advantage, gain distinctive competence, help an organization survive and grow amidst cut-throat competition in today's business environment (Haldar 2009).

Primarily, the training manager must be aware of the principles of learning and training, the components of training, and treat training as a system. The system approach to training makes training effective. In any training system, there must five distinct phases:

20. Pre-training work
21. Designing curriculum
22. Appropriate pedagogy
23. Evaluating training
24. Post-training work for making training effective (Haldar 2009).

The effectiveness of a formal training system depends on the extent of care with which a training programme has been designed.

Pre-training Work

The need for training comes to the surface if you develop and study the training need identification checklist. You have to focus sharper attention on the identified needs as opposed to the desires of employees or their supervisor. To identify the training needs for all personnel of your organization, you should first stratify them as the mode of training differs for different levels of the workforce: the top management, middle management, junior management, and the staff members and the operating core.

In the pre-training work, the training manager must consider the organization's training policy and objectives and treat training as a tool for developing work culture. He must develop, document, and use the procedure of identifying training needs. (Two procedures on 'Training Need Identification' for two levels of employees followed by Ordnance Factories Institute of Learning (OFILIS) Ishapore, are given in Annexures 11.2 and 11.3, respectively). He/she has to formulate the phases of training, develop the training curriculum, and design appropriate pedagogy. He/she has to decide upon whether a training programme should be modular or single phase. Training on leadership and team building is not an exception. These trainings can also be other modular or single phase.

The most important aspect of training is that it must be linked to organizational needs and business goals. For training need identification, you have to consider aspects like whether training will make a difference in the bottom line, develop the ability of marketing and sales people, promote human relations skills, build up leadership skills, what specific training the employees need and what (the parameters) will improve his/her job performance, differentiating between the need for training and organizational issues and bringing about a match between individual aspirations and organizational goals—the goal congruency.

To support the achievement of business objectives and develop the people, planning for education and training, you should consider the experience of people, tacit and explicit knowledge, leadership and management skills, planning and improvement tools, problem-solving skills, team-building capacity, attitude to work as a member of team, communication skills, creativity and innovation, culture, and social behaviour. You have to make it a practice. Sometimes the number of persons in a particular training module may be too prohibitive on cost consideration and economy of scale. In such a case, you can take a 'make or buy' decision—whether to conduct the training programme in-house or to depute it to an external institute. Suppose you need to develop the leadership potential of your people at all levels. For example, the Ordnance Factory Board was keen to develop the leaders and leadership potential. Based on organizational needs, the board directed OFILIS, Ishapore, to develop a syllabus in 2001. OFILIS finalized the objectives and the syllabus as follows.

Objectives of the course

After attending the full course, the participants should be able to

- Appreciate the importance of leadership in the workplace
- Learn and attempt to apply leader skills
- Recognize the significance of working in teams and forming a team

Syllabus on leadership and team building

OFILIS conducts many training courses and management development programmes, one of which is 'Leadership and Team Building', to develop leadership potential of ordnance factories personnel and encourage working in teams. OFILIS conducts two or three courses every year since 2001. The institute has reviewed and revised the course considering the changing needs. The syllabus and the duration for each topic are appended in Tables 11.2 and 11.3.

TABLE **11.2 Syllabus of the course on leadership and team building**

Topic	Time (hours)
Leader—Definition, types, how leadership influences behaviours, leadership process, brief introduction to scientific management, human relations movement (Exercise and quiz)	3.0
Leadership—A situational approach, flexibility, diagnosis and contracting, followers' development level, appropriate leadership style (Exercise and quiz)	3.0
Continuum of leader behaviour, Blake and Mouton managerial grid and five leadership styles, effectiveness dimensions (Exercise and quiz)	3.0
Leader—Personal expressiveness, leader as good communicator to influence behaviour, overcoming the barriers of communication, superior–subordinate communication (Exercise and quiz)	3.0
Work ethics and work culture—Leader behaviour in improving work, ethics, and work culture of followers, role model or image building, self-development (Exercise and quiz)	3.0
Team building—Organizational environment, team building, team development process, leadership qualities vis-à-vis team building (Games, exercise and quiz)	3.0
Leadership games and emotional intelligence	3.0
Video show on leaders, leadership, and team building	3.0
Leadership—A situational approach, leadership skills (Exercise and quiz)	1.5
Managing change for success (with examples)	3.0
Motivation—Abraham Maslow theory	1.5
Total course duration	30.0

TABLE **11.3** **Syllabus on communication in leadership**

Topic	Deliverable	Methodology	Time (hours)
Ice breaker	Setting environment	Exercise	1.0
Concepts of Communication	· What is it? · Channels of communication	Interactive session	2.0
The Communication Process	· What is the process? · How do we do it the best? · The right processes	Interactive session	2.0
· Concepts on Barriers · Art of Listening	· Understanding barriers of communication · Impact of a good listener	· Interactive session · Exercise	3.0
Interpersonal Effectiveness	· Creating interpersonal skills · Building interpersonal skills	Interactive session	3.0
Communicating with the Customer	· Effective communicating with the customer · Need of aggressive communication	Interactive session	3.0
Inspiring Communication	· How and what of it · Inspiring communication in action	· Interactive session · Video	2.0
	Total MDP duration (hours)		16.0

Designing Curriculum

Training curriculum is an action plan for a particular area of study; its design encompasses developing the prospectus, syllabus (for new courses), and programme to meet business goals. While designing the curriculum you must prepare the training specification, consider the participant profile, finalize the training methods to produce the desired result, take decisions regarding the steps in the designing training programme and competencies of trainers, develop the training routine, settle on the venue and the pedagogical aids, anticipate impediments to effective training, meticulously prepare time and facilities required, etc. The design of the curriculum needs focused attention of the training personnel laying emphasis on the training specification (an example is exhibited). You must follow the steps while designing any training programme. Competencies of the trainers, means of validating and evaluating the training, and venue and pedagogical aids also need consideration.

The role of the training designer is of paramount importance. The designer has to involve line managers and, preferably, a few trainees who have attended the course to make the course effective. Line managers are the ones who implement the learning in the workplace, whereas, the trained persons can identify the flaws in the transfer of learning. The line manager may be a sales manager, a marketing manager, a maintenance manager, or a manager from any other functional area.

In order to make the design of the training curriculum foolproof and ensure achievement of the training objectives, you should design a table showing the objectives, training method, time (for participants, preparatory, and training time for trainers), and facilities required for each objective. One such table for a course on 'Leadership and Team Building' is presented in Exhibit 11.1.

EXHIBIT 11.1   Example of training specification

Company history: Universal Hydraulic Pumps (UHP) is engaged in the design, production, and marketing of pumps since 1983. It has increased its product range, number of customers, and its markets. It has improved the quality of its products through the application of 'quality improvement programmes'. UHP believes in the power of people, 'getting more from people' than 'getting more people'.

Problem: Increasing trend of rejection in Hydraulic Pump, Model 17.

Business goal: Reducing rejection

Target population: Persons from material purchase, production, quality control, assembly, packing, and dispatch associated with the parts of the hydraulic pump and assembly of the pump

Aim of the training: To provide knowledge and skills to the selected trainees to enhance their quality consciousness and undertake quality improvement programmes

Training objectives: After attending all the sessions, the trainees will be able to

· Participate in brainstorming sessions conforming the norms
· Generate fundamental ideas
· Evaluate and sort ideas
· Construct cause–effect diagram
· Prioritize the ideas

Contd

Exhibit 11.1 contd

· Carry out techno-economic feasibility analysis (with the guidance of the supervisor)
· Implement the ideas

Training method: Lecture programmes, shop visit, interactive workshop, individual exercises, group discussion, problem-solving techniques.

Trainer skills: Must have knowledge on quality basics, running brainstorming sessions, background of handling quality improvement programmes, analytical thinking, group dynamics, encouraging and involving people in problem-solving.

Evaluation: Use 'reaction level evaluation'; measure rejection before training and after attending the training.

Time scale: The training can be conducted immediately using the expertise of internal faculty.

Method and venue: Lecture programmes, interactive workshop, individual exercises, group discussion, problem-solving techniques will be undertaken in the lecture hall.

Schedule: Eight half-days, in the afternoon starting from ....

Time and facilities required

Designing of training programme needs intensive attention of the course director and coordinator. A training plan developed meticulously makes conducting the course easier (Table 11.4).

TABLE **11.4** **Time and facilities required**

Programme—Leadership and Team Building					
		Time (hours)			
Objectives	**Training Method**	**Participants**	**Trainers**		**Facilities**
		Training	**Prep.**	**Training**	
Objective (a) Appreciate importance of leadership in the workplace	Lecture Quiz Interaction Projection Video clippings	12.00	13.00	12.00	Classroom, 2 cases PowerPoint slides LCD projector TV and CD

Contd

Table 11.4 contd

Programme—Leadership and Team Building					
		Time (hours)			
Objectives	**Training Method**	**Participants**	**Trainers**		**Facilities**
		Training	Prep.	Training	
Objective (b) Learn and attempt to apply leader skills	Case lecture Exercise Projection Video clippings	6.00	7.00	6.00	Classroom 2 cases PowerPoint slides TV and CD LCD projector
Objective (c) Recognize significance of working in teams and forming teams	Case lecture Exercise Projection Video clippings	12.00	15.00	12.00	Classroom 4 cases PowerPoint slides TV and CD LCD projector
Total	As above	30.00	35.00	30.00	8 cases Classroom for 30 hours LCD projector fixed TV and CD

Faculty members need	· 50 hours for preparing reading material, lesson plan, exercises, quizzes, power point slides, etc. · 30 hours for lectures sessions
Programme director and coordinator	· 35 hours for all arrangements

Pedagogy and Andragogy

Pedagogy is the theory and practice of helping participants achieve a critical consciousness about the subject matter to be transferred. Critical pedagogy refers to generating interest in learning and an inclination towards reading, thinking, conceptualizing, writing, and speaking. Productive pedagogy alerts knowledge disseminators to concentrate on the intellectual quality of trainees, establishing the relevance or connectedness of the topic to the work situation, creating a socially supportive classroom environment, and recognizing individual differences. Generally, adult employees from organizations attend management development and leadership development programmes. As such, faculty members must have adequate knowledge of andragogy.

Andragogy focuses on adult learners, who are self-directed, come to attend a management development programme with a richer foundation of experience, have fixed habits and patterns of thoughts and are generally less open-minded. Leadership training is about discussing specific skills or knowledge, off-site or in-house, usually with dedicated faculty members of a leadership institute or external consultants. Training elderly persons rests on certain beliefs: adults can develop and do so, adults do not generally possess unwarranted negative attitudes, and training organizers and trainers must pay attention to motivation and intimacy. The organizational climate should be conducive to training and development, and integrated with career perspectives.

Contingency approach to adult learning assesses trainees on certain dimensions: instrumentality, scepticism, resistance to change, attention span, expectation level, dominance level, absorption level, topical interest, self-confidence, and locus of control. Learning is one kind of action and it is not true that training and learning bear a causal relationship. The trainer must be conversant with the training pedagogy and discharge his/her training role, research role, consulting role, and change management role. All these roles of trainers help participants to learn effectively. Trainers need to have certain characteristics and qualities like empathy, honesty, patience, optimum pace suitable to the group, democracy, purpose, listening ability, respect for experience, and prestige.

The training designer has to identify and adopt the suitable training methodology. A trainer should introduce the course content at the beginning, define the key terms, use examples, ensure retention through short queries, administer exercises, perform evaluation, and give feedback, share real-life experiences, use facts and figures, and finally provide the participants guidelines such they can act in their respective workplaces. To make the process of learning effective, suitable pedagogical aids should be selected. Pedagogical aids are facilities essential to improving transfer of knowledge and training effectiveness and include OHP, LCD projector, slide projector, flipchart, board and erasable marker pens, video recording, poster and wall charts, models, exhibits, motion pictures, slides, educational toys, etc.

An ideal faculty member endeavours to generate interest in the programme. You may like to draw the attention of participants and find out their expectations from the course at the beginning of the course. At the end of the course, you may have a discussion, formal or informal, to establish whether the expectations have been met. It is difficult to define what makes a good trainer. However, a trainer should be aware of his/her personal qualities, know the expectations of participants, have authoritative knowledge of the subject, have good communication skills, prepare and use lesson plans, ask thought-provoking questions, and involve the students or participants in the training session. A good trainer must know his personal strengths and weaknesses, have a thirst for knowledge, and develop himself/herself continuously.

Training Evaluation and Validation

The training cycle comprises business needs, training need identification, specifying training needs, translating the needs into actions, planning the training, and finally, evaluating it. Leaders and leadership are business needs today. Obviously, the training cycle remains incomplete unless a training programme is evaluated.

Evaluation is the process of establishing the worth of the training efforts. Training validation means corroborating or justifying the rationality of conducting the training, and directly refers to and applies to the programme and its immediate results. One must plan evaluation at the training design stage. Participants, training institute, programme designers and managers, faculty or trainers, and the organizational customer are the clients in the evaluation process. The five evaluation objectives are (i) evaluating the training programme (to improve the programme as whole or the major components of the training programme, and to increase the effectiveness of specific modules or sessions), (ii) evaluating the training process (to improve the training climate, training methodologies, and team of trainers), (iii) evaluating the training programme (to improve training facilities), (iv) evaluating training outcomes/impact (to increase learning by individuals participants, to increase use of learning in work performance, to contribute data to organizational effectiveness, and to help organizational change), and (v) evaluating programme factors (to maximize effectiveness, to ensure post-training support, and to identify helping and hindering factors). Training evaluation is not merely a state of mind, nor an end product; rather, it is a set of techniques and a process. Principally evaluation should have clarity, objectivity, reliability, structured design and methodology, ensuring that the evaluation design is tailor-made.

Validation is categorized as internal validation and external validation. Validation of either type deals with a series of tests and assessments designed to ascertain both categories of validation. In internal validation, the focus is on the relatedness of the training and learning, resulting in the knowledge of skill enhancement of the trainee, which in turn, contribute to the enhancement of organizational performance.

External validation refers to the process of objectively identifying training needs and providing training to achieve business goals. External validation involves a series of analysis designed to ascertain whether the objectives of an internally valid programme are based on accurate information in relation to training needs. This is to ensure that training is carried out in the most efficient and effective manner; at the lowest or reasonable cost without compromising on the quality of training; and with high implementation value.

Post-training Works to Make Training Effective

Training, as a strategic trigger tool, helps managers to evaluate the workforce and enhance their knowledge and skills. At the same time, training and management development programmes help managers to acquire visionary skills, understand the direction and speed of changes, interpret the business scenario, sharpen the inner potential of employees at all levels, and improve business performance. Thus, training is an organization's strategic need. In order to meet this strategic need even after the conduction of the training, many activities need to be performed. Post-training work involves generation and reviewing of the documentation and records of all the activities performed at all stages of the training. Unless this is done carefully, training efforts would go waste, business goals would remain unachieved, and training would not produce the desired result.

Training records and their classification

Training records may be classified based on their usage in the various phases of training (Table 11.5). Training records are obviously organization specific. You must generate training records for analysis, decision-making, and improving training efforts and results. You can stratify the documents and records into two broad categories: course specific and independent of the course, that is, similar for all the courses. You can further classify the course-specific documents and records into three classes: (i) required in the course planning phase, (ii) required during the course, and (iii) required after the course. You are required to generate the documents and records in specific formats designed for the purpose. You may revise the formats according to the changing needs of the institute.

TABLE **11.5** **Classification of training records**

Training Records	Course-specific	· Course planning phase · While conducting the courses · After conducting the courses
	Independent of the courses	—

Documents and record at planning phase

It is necessary to refer to or generate some documents and records while planning a course. The syllabus for a course, programme, registration sheet, etc. are examples of documents and records required to be developed before the start of the course. Although these are planning-phase documents, they need review after the conducting of the course as post-training work. The review and identified lapses help to make the training system more effective and ensure continual improvement.

- Syllabus of course or MDP
- Training specification
- Time and facilities required
- Programme
- Nomination of faculty
- Reading material
- Exercises
- Books in library (course-wise)
- Journals in the library (course-wise)

Documents and record during the course

While conducting the course, you must concentrate on generating the following documents:

- Registration sheet
- Record of attendance
- Biodata of participants
- Continuous evaluation of participants
- Feedback format

Documents and record after the course

After conducting the course, you should perform certain post-training work to make the training system effective. As such, you need to concentrate on the following documents:

- Continuous evaluation summary
- Assessment test result

- Result sheet
- Average course grading and yearly course grading
- Post-training impact measurement (from trained personnel)
- Post-training impact measurement (from immediate supervisor)
- Summary of participation
- Certificate number

Documents and records—not course specific

You have seen that the documents and records are grouped in three classes. You are required to develop and use some documents and records that are not specifically required for a particular course, and which you need for all the courses you conduct in your institute.

- Faculty database
- Topic-wise faculty
- Faculty-wise topics
- Records of qualification and experience
- Training courses attended by internal faculty members
- Annual calendar of training and MDPs
- Corrective action sheet
- Preventive action sheet
- Distribution of list of documents
- Document amendment form
- Faculty hours assessment (internal and external)
- Minutes of training review meeting
- Training audit plan
- Training audit schedule
- Training audit report

Note: You are required to design the formats for all the documents and records you require in different phases of the training. All the formats must bear 'format numbers'. Formats filled in with data must be under document control through a structured procedure, say, the procedure for design and development of courses. You need to design the formats for the documents and records at each stage of the training and post-training phase to make the training system effective. Haldar (2009) in his book titled *Human Resource Development* has exhaustively discussed and provided training formats.

Documentation

All training programmes are important. But a programme on development of leader or leadership is of vital importance because the implied objective is to enhance the enabling capacities of the 'enablers'. Leaders are enablers in any organization producing goods or services. A training department receives some documents from an external origin and develops many documents internally. Documents are information and its supporting medium. Documents may be a set of activities required to be sequentially performed for a task, a set of instructions required to achieve a goal, or some information that must be preserved. Documentation is the system of analysing organizational requirements, generating, scrutinizing, approving, issuing documents, and maintaining records of issue.

Documentation further includes periodically updating documents, issuing wherever required, and withdrawing obsolete ones from the point of use. You can classify documents broadly in two categories: documents received from external origins and documents generated internally. You may receive a request to design a training programme to meet certain specific objectives, to achieve specific business goals, or to bring about a behavioural modification, to diagnose organizational culture, or improve it. The requests or needs projected by your clients are documents received from an external origin.

To fulfil the clients' needs, you may have interacted with, developed the course curriculum, designed the syllabus, decided upon the training methodology, conducted the programme, collected feedback from trainees, etc. These documents are internally generated. Irrespective of whether the documents are received from an external origin or generated internally, they need some control measures.

A training document must be controlled. The training department should preferably develop a system of documentation. ISO 9001: 2000 (clause 4.2.3) on control of documents specifies that a documented procedure shall be established to define the controls needed

(a) to approve documents for adequacy prior to issue,

(b) to review and update as necessary and re-approve documents,

(c) to ensure that changes are incorporated and the current revision status of documents are identified,

(d) to ensure that relevant versions of applicable documents are available at points of use,

(e) to ensure that documents remain legible and readily identifiable,

(f) to ensure that documents of external origin are identified and distribution controlled, and

(g) to prevent the unintended use of obsolete documents and to ascribe suitable identification to them if they are retained for any purpose.

The training organization should define the documentation including relevant records needed to establish, implement, and maintain the training system, and to support an effective and efficient training methodology. Participants attend training courses either in an individual capacity or are sponsored by an organization. Training organizations develop customized course programmes for their clients to fulfil specific training needs. The nature and extent of documentation should satisfy the contractual requirements in addition to statutory and regulatory requirements. A training organization should establish, implement, and maintain a procedure on 'Control of Documents'. A procedure followed by OFILIS, Ishapore, is given in Annexure 11.4.

Records management

Records management is the practice of identifying, classifying, archiving, preserving, and destroying records. Records management is the field of management responsible for the efficient and systematic control of the creation, receipt, maintenance, use, and disposal of records, including the processes for capturing and maintaining evidence of and information about business activities and transactions in the form of records (ISO 15489: 2001).

Records are special types of documents. As stated before, documents are information and its supporting medium. Training documents include specification (document stating requirements), training manual (document specifying the training management system), training plan (document specifying the relevant procedures and associated resources for a particular training course), and records (document stating results achieved or providing evidence of activities performed). Records are special types of documents. Documents must be under revision control. For records, revision control is not applicable. 'A record shall be established and maintained to provide evidence of conformity to requirements and of the effective operations of the quality management system. Records shall remain legible, readily identifiable, and retrievable. A documented procedure shall be established to define the controls needed for the identification, storage, protection, retrieval, retention time, and disposition of records' (ISO 9001: 2000, Clause 4.2.4, Control of Records). ISO 9001: 2000, Clause 6.2.2 (Competency, Awareness, and Training) specifies that organizations shall maintain appropriate records of education, training, skills, and experience. A training organization should establish, implement, and maintain a procedure on control of records. A procedure followed by OFILIS, Ishapore, is given in Annexure 11.5.

In many organizations, including public sector organizations, the record management system is dismal. In fact, most organizations are losing more than what they gain from the records they maintain. Some of the items of the present system of records management are:

- inordinate delay in retrieval
- records are not readily identifiable
- records are not legible
- unspecified retention schedule
- weeding out of old records is not practised
- absence of any system of record maintenance
- improper storage space
- preservation of records improperly, etc.

Record management vis-à-vis 5S

The concept of 5S embraces (1) sorting or organizing in order, (2) systematic arrangement and neatness, (3) spic and span, cleaning, or inspection, (4) a serene atmosphere, and (5) self-discipline. Each 'S' has its own importance in the workplace; the fifth 'S' has some uniqueness compared to the previous four. This step emphasizes the need for training, sincerity, and constancy of purpose in following the rules and standards developed in the earlier four Ss. The application of 5S will enable you to pick up any record, subject to analysis, make decisions for improving the training system, and proceed towards institutional excellence.

Characteristics of record management

Review of usage ratio, accessibility, speedy retrieval, and retention schedule are important characteristics of an efficient record management system.

Review of usage ratio   As manager of learning, you may classify records into three distinct categories, namely, A—frequently used, B—sometimes used, and C—rarely used. Quite possibly in terms of volume, records of the third category may be three quarters of total records in an organization. You may install a system to periodically review the frequency of usage of training records just to classify them in the categories mentioned. The holding of rarely used records simply occupies storage space, and the storage becomes inefficient. This category needs further investigation to subclassify C1—records that might be required later and C2—records that would never be required. As such, records belonging to the second category may be destroyed that would contribute to space management. But before doing this, you must prepare a list of the records and circulate it to the relevant personnel in your organization for information and comments on retention, if any. You may empower your junior colleagues to carry out the task of scrutinizing, categorizing, and preparing the list of records in each of the three main categories and further classifying the third category. Removal of unnecessary records will make the record management system, including preservation of records, efficient.

Accessibility All records, particularly category A records, should be easily accessible and within easy reach. Records of category C1 can be preserved at up to ceiling heights.

Speedy retrieval Each record must be classified, indexed, labelled, and numbered. This will ensure identification of the records. Then the records must be stored in separate spaces according to their classification. Within each class of records, they must be arranged according to the index.

Retention schedule Each record has its life cycle. You have to decide the retention period considering the usage and nature of the record. The life of records may vary widely. For example, a record of attendance is useful during the period of training. However, for analysis purposes and to prepare a database of participants trained in an academic year, you may consider retaining the record for a year or a maximum of two years. You have to decide the retention schedule for each record and review the schedule after three to five years for effective record management.

A training institute receives many documents and records from many clients. These are obviously documents received from external origin. A training institute, in turn, generates a large number of records for the purpose of administration. All the documents and records should be controlled by record management.

In regard to record management, it is said thus: 'no record without analysis; no analysis without feedback; no feedback without corrective action; no corrective action without recording'.

Record retention time

Syllabus, programme, list of faculty members, participants' feedback, need of inclusion of topics desired by participants, etc. are some of the training records. Records should not be destroyed immediately after conducting the course. They must be retained for reference and their retention time must be defined. You have to decide the retention period for each document and record based on the nature of the document and contents of the records. You may finalize this once and revise it thereafter based on actual need and experience. The retention period of some commonly used training documents and records is provided in Table 11.6.

TABLE **11.6   Record retention time**

Document or Record	Format No.	Custodian	Retention Period
Assessment test result			Forever
Attendance sheet			One year
Audit plan			Two years
Audit report			Two years
Audit schedule			Two years
Biodata of participants			One year
Continuous evaluation			One year
Continuous evaluation summary			One year
Corrective action sheet			Two years
Document distribution list			Five years
Document amendment form			Five years
Faculty assistance from external source			One year
Faculty hours assessment— External			One year
Faculty hours assessment— Internal			One year
Feedback report			Two years
Master list of formats			Forever
Master list of training records			Forever
Minutes of training review meeting			Three years
Nomination of internal faculty			One year
Participant registration sheet			One year
Post-training impact measurement (from participants)			Continuous process
Post-training impact measurement (from supervisor)			Continuous process
Preventive action sheet			Two years
Programme			One year

Contd

Table 11.6 contd

Document or Record	Format No.	Custodian	Retention Period
Record of attendance			Three years
Record of education, training, and experience			Forever (three years after retirement)
Record of lecture			One year
Summary of feedback report			Two years
Summary of participation			Two years
Syllabus			Till updating

EFFECTIVE TRAINING ON LEADERSHIP

In order to make a leadership programme successful and effective, an institute has to consider certain factors: pointed learning objectives, content, curriculum, training methods, pedagogical aids, time and facility planning, opportunity to practice, feedback and impact, raising self-confidence of participants, involving them in discussion, providing information they need, etc. Generation and revision of documents and preserving documents and records till retention time are essential. Appropriate follow-up activities are required to assess the usefulness of the course to the participants, extent of applicability in the work area, and benefits to the sponsoring organization. The leadership course content must include individual exercises, quizzes, workshops, syndicate exercises, and modelling.

Programmes on team building must be supplemented by activities. Examples on activities performed to achieve desired results clarify the methods and approaches of the topics being discussed. Activities on team building will be discussed in the next chapter (Chapter 12).

DRIVES BY ACADEMIC INSTITUTES

Academic institutes have taken and are taking initiatives to educate organizational personnel and academicians by way of conducting management development programmes. The programme coverage of two reputed houses is furnished below.

UP Technical University

Team Building and Leadership (MBA-HR 3) comprises five units, and each unit has eight sessions. The syllabus of each unit is as follows:

Unit I (8 sessions)—Overview of groups: Formation of group; Group dynamics; Group structure and Group cohesiveness; Managing group and inter-group dynamics in organizations

Unit II (8 sessions)—Team building process: Overview of teams: definition, types, stages of team development: storming, norming, forming and performing; Quality circles and self-managed teams; Evaluating team performance; Teams and high-performing organizations

Unit III (8 sessions)—Goal setting for teams: Defining roles; Responsibilities of team members, developing interpersonal skills; Interpersonal communication barriers and gateways to communication

Unit IV (8 sessions)—Leadership and management of team: Sources of powers and influence; Leadership models and styles

Unit V (8 sessions)—Leadership styles: Contingency approach to effective leadership; Situational leadership; Transformational leadership; Leadership in decision-making process; Leadership in times of change.

IIM Lucknow

The prologue and course coverage of team building and leadership development is given below.

Team Building Interdependence is a common feature of large and complex organizations. Effectiveness of organizations, therefore, depends on teamwork at different levels. This course is designed to explore the various facets of teamwork and to acquire understanding and skills for development of effective teams in organizations. This course will explore factors which determine effectiveness of teams; understand the concept of team leadership, skills needed for team effectiveness, for example, problem-solving, decision-making, communication and conflict resolution, the role of empowerment; culture for team building interdepartmental coordination with a focus on internal customer orientation and diagnosing team effectiveness and the strategies for improving team effectiveness.

Leadership Development The course is designed to explore what leaders really do to meet adaptive challenges in their environment. It looks at leadership as a process of self-transformation and organizational renewal. Taking a descriptive as well as prescriptive approach, the course distinguishes between leadership and management. Building on shared leadership experiences of students, this course will create a model of leadership that addresses the key competencies required to succeed in a complex, knowledge-driven environment. At the end of the course, students are expected to have an insight into the foundational values that determine leader behaviour; action choices for leaders who have to engage in adaptive work in organizations; and development and dispersal of leadership within the organization and community.

The course would have inputs on themes such as leadership versus management; technical versus adaptive challenges of leadership; value-based leadership model; leadership evolution; converting knowledge into action; creating synergy; transformational leadership; development and dispersal of leadership; and Indian leadership experiences.

SUMMARY

Research on leader behaviours that generate followers' satisfaction is essential to get the best from the workforce. Research on teams, team building, team effectiveness dimensions, and other related aspects is indispensable in organizations for optimal utilization of the most crucial resource—the human resource. Fundamental research initiatives should not be limited to big organizations. Research must be extended to small business houses as well. Research scope should be broad enough to incorporate all possible independent variables like gender, business nature, product and service sectors, regions, size of organization, and so on.

Training on leadership is essential to upgrade human capital to enhance enabling capacities of the 'enablers' and 'performers'. The procedure of training need identification helps an organization to initiate a systematic approach to deploying people for training and ensures proper utilization of the training budget. Procedures on control of documents and records help any institute to strengthen documentation system.

KEY TERMS

Andragogy refers to the art and science of training adults, focuses on creation of an independent, adaptable, and socially acceptable individual because the training of adults differs substantially from that of training children, given that adults bring considerably more experience to the learning arena than children.

Control of documents underscores that documents are approved for adequacy, reviewed and updated as necessary, changes and current revision status are identified, relevant versions are available at the point of use, remain legible and readily identifiable, and obsolete documents are promptly removed.

Control of records means that an organization shall maintain records to provide evidence of conformity that shall be legible, readily identifiable, and retrievable and that each record shall have a specified retention schedule.

Critical pedagogy is a teaching approach which attempts to help trainees seeking clarifications through questions to enhance their inclination to read, think, conceptualize, write, and speak.

Document is information and its supporting medium (that can be paper, magnetic, electronic or optical computer disc, photograph or master samples, or a combination thereof). Examples of training documents include training calendar, brochure, schedule of an MDP, faculty grading, etc.

Pedagogical aids are facilities essential to improve transfer of knowledge and training effectiveness and include OHP, LCD projector, slide projector, flipchart, board and erasable marker pens, video recording, poster and wall charts, models, exhibits, motion pictures, slides, educational toys, etc.

Pedagogy is the science of disseminating knowledge; it refers to the strategies or style of instruction an educator is required to follow and it deals with forming first impressions.

Training validation is the attempt to determine whether trainees have benefited from the training programme and have learned what they needed to.

REFERENCES

Agrawal, Kalpana (2008), Effect of Gunas on Transformational Leadership, *Indian Journal of Training and Development, Journal of Indian Society for Training and Development*, Vol. XXXVIII, No. 4, October–December 2008.

Armstrong, Michael (2001), *A Handbook of Human Resource (Personnel) Management*, 8th edition, Kogan Page, UK.

Flippo, Edwin B. (1984), *Personnel Management* (Special Indian edition), 6th edition, McGraw-Hill, New Delhi.

Ghosh, Lipi (2009), Leadership and Team Building, Dissertation Report, Indian Institute of Social Welfare and Business Management, University of Calcutta, Kolkata.

Kalpa, Dr Prasad (2007), Creating Value out of VALUES, *Indian Management* (Journal of the All India Management Association), Vol. 46, No. 3, pp. 62–64 (All India Management Association, New Delhi).

Mukherjee, Kum Kum (2004), Effect of Leadership Styles on Followers' Satisfaction and Perceived Effectiveness, *South Asian Journal of Management* (ISSN 0971 5428), Vol. 11, No. 1, January–March, pp. 7–19.

Saurabhi Chaturvedi, Pallavi Bhatnagar, and Dr Rishu Roy (2008), A Comparative Study of Team Leaders and Team Members on the Factors Affecting Team Effectiveness, *Indian Journal for Training and Development* (Journal of the Indian Society for Training and Development), Vol. XXXVIII, No. 3, July–September, pp. 13–19.

Sen, Sureeta (2009), Leadership and Patterns of Leadership Behaviour, Dissertation Report, Indian Institute of Social Welfare and Business Management, University of Calcutta, Kolkata.

Web Resources

www.sopringerlink.com/content/4601020u 65614w54/ (*APJM—Asia Pacific Journal of Management*) (accessed on 24 January 2009).

Annexure 11.1

Identifying Factors Affecting Team Effectiveness

Questionnaire

Qualification:	Professional [ ]	Technical [ ]	Generalized [ ]

Experience:	< 3 yrs [ ]	4–6 yrs [ ]	More than 7 yrs [ ]

Gender:	Male [ ]	Female [ ]	Team Leader [ ]	Team Member [ ]

Industry:	Service Industry [ ]	Manufacturing [ ]

Tick the most appropriate choice for the questions provided.

Q 1	You have more than three years of experience in handling the team.				
	Strongly agree [ ]	Agree [ ]	Neutral [ ]	Disagree [ ]	Strongly disagree [ ]
Q 2	Experience is the most valued criterion to be a team leader.				
	Strongly agree [ ]	Agree [ ]	Neutral [ ]	Disagree [ ]	Strongly disagree [ ]
Q 3	Meritocracy is the most valued criterion to be a team leader.				
	Strongly agree [ ]	Agree [ ]	Neutral [ ]	Disagree [ ]	Strongly disagree [ ]
Q 4	Our team has a coherent plan for achieving our vision.				
	Strongly agree [ ]	Agree [ ]	Neutral [ ]	Disagree [ ]	Strongly disagree [ ]
Q 5	The strategies we have in place will ensure we achieve our vision.				
	Strongly agree [ ]	Agree [ ]	Neutral [ ]	Disagree [ ]	Strongly disagree [ ]
Q 6	If everybody does his or her job, the team can achieve its goals quite consistently.				
	Strongly agree [ ]	Agree [ ]	Neutral [ ]	Disagree [ ]	Strongly disagree [ ]

Q 7	I believe our team and individual goals are realistic.				
	Strongly agree [ ]	Agree [ ]	Neutral [ ]	Disagree [ ]	Strongly disagree [ ]
Q 8	The success-to-failure ratio is less than one.				
	Strongly agree [ ]	Agree [ ]	Neutral [ ]	Disagree [ ]	Strongly disagree [ ]
Q 9	A good team needs a good leader, but a successful team needs a very good leader.				
	Strongly agree [ ]	Agree [ ]	Neutral [ ]	Disagree [ ]	Strongly disagree [ ]
Q 10	Team failure is an outcome of lack of proper leadership				
	Strongly agree [ ]	Agree [ ]	Neutral [ ]	Disagree [ ]	Strongly disagree [ ]
Q 11	Leadership is the only quality required to keep a good team.				
	Strongly agree [ ]	Agree [ ]	Neutral [ ]	Disagree [ ]	Strongly disagree [ ]
Q 12	Equal contribution of all team members is very necessary to make the team effective.				
	Strongly agree [ ]	Agree [ ]	Neutral [ ]	Disagree [ ]	Strongly disagree [ ]
Q 13	An effective team normally completes its work within the time limit.				
	Strongly agree [ ]	Agree [ ]	Neutral [ ]	Disagree [ ]	Strongly disagree [ ]
Q 14	An effective team normally completes its work within the budget.				
	Strongly agree [ ]	Agree [ ]	Neutral [ ]	Disagree [ ]	Strongly disagree [ ]
Q 15	A team can be successful even if 50 per cent of its members are productive.				
	Strongly agree [ ]	Agree [ ]	Neutral [ ]	Disagree [ ]	Strongly disagree [ ]
Q 16	A good team always works in synergy.				
	Strongly agree [ ]	Agree [ ]	Neutral [ ]	Disagree [ ]	Strongly disagree [ ]
Q 17	A small team is more successful than a large one.				
	Strongly agree [ ]	Agree [ ]	Neutral [ ]	Disagree [ ]	Strongly disagree [ ]
Q 18	Our team is working towards the fulfilment of business objectives.				
	Strongly agree [ ]	Agree [ ]	Neutral [ ]	Disagree [ ]	Strongly disagree [ ]
Q 19	Our team is providing a vital service to the organization.				
	Strongly agree [ ]	Agree [ ]	Neutral [ ]	Disagree [ ]	Strongly disagree [ ]
Q 20	I personally agree with the basic principles our team operates by.				
	Strongly agree [ ]	Agree [ ]	Neutral [ ]	Disagree [ ]	Strongly disagree [ ]
Q 21	I believe we have the right people in the right roles.				
	Strongly agree [ ]	Agree [ ]	Neutral [ ]	Disagree [ ]	Strongly disagree [ ]
Q 22	Team members have the information they need to set priorities.				
	Strongly agree [ ]	Agree [ ]	Neutral [ ]	Disagree [ ]	Strongly disagree [ ]

Q 23	There is respect for individuals in the team.				
	Strongly agree [ ]	Agree [ ]	Neutral [ ]	Disagree [ ]	Strongly disagree [ ]
Q 24	In our team we can rely on each other to get the job done.				
	Strongly agree [ ]	Agree [ ]	Neutral [ ]	Disagree [ ]	Strongly disagree [ ]
Q 25	I feel the members of the team value my inputs.				
	Strongly agree [ ]	Agree [ ]	Neutral [ ]	Disagree [ ]	Strongly disagree [ ]
Q 26	Team members' morale is high in the team.				
	Strongly agree [ ]	Agree [ ]	Neutral [ ]	Disagree [ ]	Strongly disagree [ ]
Q 27	I enjoy being a member of this team.				
	Strongly agree [ ]	Agree [ ]	Neutral [ ]	Disagree [ ]	Strongly disagree [ ]
Q 28	Team members have the information they need to get the job done.				
	Strongly agree [ ]	Agree [ ]	Neutral [ ]	Disagree [ ]	Strongly disagree [ ]
Q 29	Team members have difficulty in clarifying expectations with each other.				
	Strongly agree [ ]	Agree [ ]	Neutral [ ]	Disagree [ ]	Strongly disagree [ ]
Q 30	In our team when people express their point of view, they feel they have been truly heard.				
	Strongly agree [ ]	Agree [ ]	Neutral [ ]	Disagree [ ]	Strongly disagree [ ]
Q 31	Team members are encouraged to share there feelings regardless of whether they are positive or negative.				
	Strongly agree [ ]	Agree [ ]	Neutral [ ]	Disagree [ ]	Strongly disagree [ ]
Q 32	Team members are accepted for who they are.				
	Strongly agree [ ]	Agree [ ]	Neutral [ ]	Disagree [ ]	Strongly disagree [ ]
Q 33	In our team, we have clearly defined the standards of behaviour we must operate by.				
	Strongly agree [ ]	Agree [ ]	Neutral [ ]	Disagree [ ]	Strongly disagree [ ]
Q 34	Team members take ownership of their areas of responsibility.				
	Strongly agree [ ]	Agree [ ]	Neutral [ ]	Disagree [ ]	Strongly disagree [ ]
Q 35	Team members keep information to themselves that should be shared with others.				
	Strongly agree [ ]	Agree [ ]	Neutral [ ]	Disagree [ ]	Strongly disagree [ ]
Q 36	When it comes to operating by our values, our team practises what we preach.				
	Strongly agree [ ]	Agree [ ]	Neutral [ ]	Disagree [ ]	Strongly disagree [ ]
Q 37	Our team has high standard of qualities in everything that we do.				
	Strongly agree [ ]	Agree [ ]	Neutral [ ]	Disagree [ ]	Strongly disagree [ ]

Q 38	Our team finds it difficult to encourage and support each other in our efforts to get the job done.				
	Strongly agree [ ]	Agree [ ]	Neutral [ ]	Disagree [ ]	Strongly disagree [ ]
Q 39	A creative team member contributes more towards team effectiveness.				
	Strongly agree [ ]	Agree [ ]	Neutral [ ]	Disagree [ ]	Strongly disagree [ ]
Q 40	Once a successful team is always a successful team.				
	Strongly agree [ ]	Agree [ ]	Neutral [ ]	Disagree [ ]	Strongly disagree [ ]
Q 41	When team members say they will do something it gets done.				
	Strongly agree [ ]	Agree [ ]	Neutral [ ]	Disagree [ ]	Strongly disagree [ ]
Q 42	In our team it is safe to express conflicting points of view.				
	Strongly agree [ ]	Agree [ ]	Neutral [ ]	Disagree [ ]	Strongly disagree [ ]
Q 43	If there is a conflict in our team it is handled in a straightforward and constructive manner.				
	Strongly agree [ ]	Agree [ ]	Neutral [ ]	Disagree [ ]	Strongly disagree [ ]
Q 44	Virtual teams are less successful.				
	Strongly agree [ ]	Agree [ ]	Neutral [ ]	Disagree [ ]	Strongly disagree [ ]
Q 45	Similar projects are likely to be more successful.				
	Strongly agree [ ]	Agree [ ]	Neutral [ ]	Disagree [ ]	Strongly disagree [ ]
Q 46	A successful team is one which knows how to manage disruptive people effectively.				
	Strongly agree [ ]	Agree [ ]	Neutral [ ]	Disagree [ ]	Strongly disagree [ ]
Q 47	Team members accept change readily.				
	Strongly agree [ ]	Agree [ ]	Neutral [ ]	Disagree [ ]	Strongly disagree [ ]
Q 48	The variations in workload often affect the morale of team members				
	Strongly agree [ ]	Agree [ ]	Neutral [ ]	Disagree [ ]	Strongly disagree [ ]
Q 49	Our team has a clear idea of why we exist.				
	Strongly agree [ ]	Agree [ ]	Neutral [ ]	Disagree [ ]	Strongly disagree [ ]
Q 50	Our team is moving together in the same direction.				
	Strongly agree [ ]	Agree [ ]	Neutral [ ]	Disagree [ ]	Strongly disagree [ ]
Q 51	We operate by a clearly defined set of values.				
	Strongly agree [ ]	Agree [ ]	Neutral [ ]	Disagree [ ]	Strongly disagree [ ]
Q 52	Forms, reports and procurement methods are familiar to team members.				
	Strongly agree [ ]	Agree [ ]	Neutral [ ]	Disagree [ ]	Strongly disagree [ ]

Q 53	For the most part, our team has its priorities in order.				
	Strongly agree [ ]	Agree [ ]	Neutral [ ]	Disagree [ ]	Strongly disagree [ ]
Q 54	I like the direction this team is going in.				
	Strongly agree [ ]	Agree [ ]	Neutral [ ]	Disagree [ ]	Strongly disagree [ ]
Q 55	The written and verbal methods we use to move ahead on tasks are fairly simple and efficient.				
	Strongly agree [ ]	Agree [ ]	Neutral [ ]	Disagree [ ]	Strongly disagree [ ]
Q 56	Our team knows what is expected of us.				
	Strongly agree [ ]	Agree [ ]	Neutral [ ]	Disagree [ ]	Strongly disagree [ ]
Q 57	Our team clearly understands what we need to achieve.				
	Strongly agree [ ]	Agree [ ]	Neutral [ ]	Disagree [ ]	Strongly disagree [ ]
Q 58	People in our team demonstrate a clear understanding of our values through their behaviour.				
	Strongly agree [ ]	Agree [ ]	Neutral [ ]	Disagree [ ]	Strongly disagree [ ]
Q 59	Team members know who to go to to get something done.				
	Strongly agree [ ]	Agree [ ]	Neutral [ ]	Disagree [ ]	Strongly disagree [ ]
Q 60	Team members are generally aware of the way work flow proceeds around here.				
	Strongly agree [ ]	Agree [ ]	Neutral [ ]	Disagree [ ]	Strongly disagree [ ]
Q 61	Team members understand what is expected of them in their respective roles.				
	Strongly agree [ ]	Agree [ ]	Neutral [ ]	Disagree [ ]	Strongly disagree [ ]
Q 62	The systems for getting things done around here work quite well.				
	Strongly agree [ ]	Agree [ ]	Neutral [ ]	Disagree [ ]	Strongly disagree [ ]
Q 63	Team members' areas of responsibility are big enough, yet not too big.				
	Strongly agree [ ]	Agree [ ]	Neutral [ ]	Disagree [ ]	Strongly disagree [ ]

THANK YOU FOR YOUR PARTICIPATION IN THE STUDY!

ANNEXURE 11.2

Identifying Training Needs
(For all levels except managerial personnel)

Format No. TF/OFILIS/TRG/01

1. Reference: QP/OFDC/TNI/01		2. No.:		3. Date:	
4. Name:		5. Personnel No.:		6. Department:	
7. Date of birth:		8. Age:		9. Joined on:	
10. Total length of service: .... years					
10.1 Organization		10.2 Duties performed (Code)		10.3 Length	
(a)					
(b)					
(c)					

Write the code for the nature of duties performed and the functional areas.

11. Training undergone	12. Duration	13. Relevance
(a)		
(b)		
(c)		

14. Present assignment:

    ....
    ....
    ....

15. Organizational needs:

    ....
    ....
    ....

16. Training need identified:
    16.1 The person needs training on:
          ....

16.2 Approximate duration:

....

16.3 Name of the institute(s):

....

17. Proposed by:	18. Recommended by:	19. Approved by:

Date:

20. Included in HRIS database:

(*Note:* The company retrieves data on training needs from the human resource information system and arranges the training programme.)

ANNEXURE 11.3

Identifying Training and Development Needs
(For managerial personnel)

Format No. TF/OFILIS/TRG/02

1. Reference: QP/ OFDC/TNI/01		2. No.:	3. Date:	
4. Name:		5. Personnel No.:	6. Department:	
7. Date of birth:	8. Age:		9. Joined:	
10. Total length of service: .... years				
10.1 Organization	10.2 Duties performed (Code)			10.3 Length
(a)				
(b)				
(c)				

Write the code for the nature of duties performed and the functional areas.

11. Training undergone	12. Duration	13. Relevance
(a)		
(b)		
(c)		

14. Responsibility assigned:

   ....
   ....
   ....
   ....
   ....
   ....

15. Authority delegated:

   ....
   ....
   ....

	1	2	3	4	5	6	7
16. Covert and overt knowledge required	1	2	3	4	5	6	7
17. Team-building and problem-solving skills	1	2	3	4	5	6	7
18. Managerial and leadership skills							
18.1 Conceptual	1	2	3	4	5	6	7
18.2 Human relations	1	2	3	4	5	6	7
18.3 Technical	1	2	3	4	5	6	7
19. Capacity of understanding customers	1	2	3	4	5	6	7
20. Communication skills	1	2	3	4	5	6	7
21. Negotiating skills	1	2	3	4	5	6	7

22. Organizational needs:

   ....
   ....
   ....

23. Developmental need identified:

   23.1 The person needs development on:

   ....
   ....
   ....

   Approximate duration:

   ....

Name of the institute(s): ....
....

24. Proposed by:	25. Recommended by:	26. Approved by:

Date:

27. Remarks (if any): ....
....
....
....

28. Included in HRIS database:

(*Note:* The company retrieves data on training and development needs from the human resource information system and arranges the required programme.)

ANNEXURE 11.4

Procedure for Control of Documents

Format No. TP/OFILIS/COD/01

1. Purpose—To define, establish, implement, and maintain a comprehensive system for control of training documents to achieve effectiveness of the training system and improve continually.
2. Scope—The scope of this procedure covers system-related documents, for example (1) training manual, (2) training procedure, (3) training instructions, and (4) related forms/formats referred to in the various documents mentioned.
3. Responsibility and authority—The preparing, approving, and issuing authority of the quality system-related documents are defined in the 'authority matrix'. In the absence of a designated authority the same exercises are to be carried out by a higher authority. The authority matrix is shown below:

Authority	Training Manual	Training Procedure	Training Instruction	Training Formats
Preparing authority				
Approving authority				
Issuing authority				

4. Definitions of Terms—The abbreviations used are:

TM: Training manager

PD: Programme director

PC: Programme coordinator

CC: Controlled copies (The recipients of CC get amendments done on any documents)

5.   References

1.	Training manual	Doc. No. ....
2.	Training instructions	Doc. No. ....
3.	Master list of training documents	Format No. ....
4.	Document amendment form	Format No. ....
5.	Distribution list	Format No. ....

6.   Procedure

6.1   The institute maintains a master list of all training-related documents in format no. ....

6.2   The training manager maintains a master copy of the training manual and training procedures duly authenticated by the reviewing and approving authority with their signatures.

6.3   The training manager controls the training manual and records amendments through the amendment record sheet.

6.4   After revision the obsolete page is withdrawn and the revised page is issued to the recipients of controlled copies.

- The revision numbers are changed and dated.
- No amendment is implemented without its formal issue.
- If the complete quality manual undergoes change, a new issue is released.

6.5   The institute amends the training system-related documents as per format no. ...., which are maintained by the training manager. Copies of formats are maintained along with procedures, if these are referred to.

6.6   Any user can propose a change in a document and submit the request through a change request form to the training manager. The training manager includes it in the agenda of training review meeting (refer to the authority matrix). On acceptance of the change it is incorporated in the document, the revision number is advanced, superseded documents are withdrawn, and current versions are issued to the controlled copy holders.

The term 'issue number' is applicable for the procedures and formats (for all the pages).

- When a sufficient number of pages of the procedures or formats are revised, the issue number is increased by one and the revision number will be 00.
- The amendments come into force provided (a) the amendment is appropriately approved, (b) the amendment is recorded, and (c) the issue is registered by the training manager (the competent authority).
- Whenever an issue/revision is made, the obsolete documents are withdrawn.

Issue no. ...	Issue date ...	Revision no. ...	Revision date ...	Training manager

ANNEXURE 11.5

Procedure for Control of Records

Format No. TF/OFILIS/COR/01

1. Purpose—To establish and maintain a procedure for effective operation of the training management system, which provides evidence of conformity to requirements like identification, storage, protection, retrieval, retention period, and disposition of records.
2. Scope—All records referred to in the training manual, training procedure, and training instructions of the documented quality management system.
3. Responsibility and authority
   - Overall responsibility of maintaining and monitoring the procedure lies with the training manager.
   - Responsibility of maintaining each record lies with the person(s) responsible to generate the record(s) unless otherwise mentioned in the master list of training records.

4. Definition of Terms

PD: Programme director

PC: Programme coordinator

5. References

A   Training manual

B   Master list of formats   TF. ....

C   Master list of training records   TF. ....

6. Procedure

- The institute identifies each and every training record through a unique number and name.
- The institute generates legible records and maintains them at the appropriate functional area (refer to master list of training records).
- The institute identifies the records with the unique name and keeps them in an indexed manner to ensure easy retrieval.
- The institute mentions the retention period of any training record in the master list of training records.
- The institute stores and maintains the training records in order to prevent loss, damage, or deterioration (till the expiry of the retention period). After the expiry of the retention period it destroys the records.
- The institute makes the training records available to the customer and/or to his representative, if specified in the contract.
- The institute evaluates the answer scripts or assessment test papers. The respective PD or PC of the programme preserves these till disposal.

The disposing authority initiates the disposal action of any training record on expiry of the retention period. The disposing authority is mentioned in the master list of records. If felt necessary, the record(s) are retained even after the expiry period in a separate place marking/mentioning boldly the reason, until finally disposed of. The custodian of the record is responsible for disposing of the records. He may, however, retain them beyond expiry period after obtaining approval, mentioning the reason for this, from the head

| Issue no. ... | Issue date ... | Revision no. ... | Revision date ... | Training manager |

CHAPTER 12

Team Building—Activities and Outcomes

═══════ **Learning Objectives** ═══════

After studying this chapter you will be able to

▶ Explain the importance of working in teams
▶ Describe the selection of team members to meet specific organizational needs
▶ Understand the process of team proceedings
▶ Develop knowledge about after-activity reviews
▶ Define the importance of documentation

INTRODUCTION

In the workplace, we come across situations in which a task appears to be unaccomplishable for an individual though that can be successfully accomplished by a team of members. When people apply their individual thoughts, filtered through the knowledge, skill, and maturity of other team members, then the task can be completed with perfection. Thus, collective wisdom manifests its importance in the meaning and significance of team work. Working in teams produces results and team-building activities are essential along with theories, research, and training for team building. Participants attending courses on team building are engaged in activities that stimulate problem-solving skills. They are divided into small groups and each group is assigned series of tasks one after the other.

The tasks are designed to help group members develop their capacity to work effectively together. While performing the tasks, they become psychologically close. The activities generate togetherness. Team-building tasks include complex tasks designed for specific needs. More elaborate tasks can involve rope courses, night-time activities, and the exercises may last for several days even.

Team-building activities are often used in meetings, presentations, workshops, training seminars, educational programmes, and corporate training. Team-building activities are also performed at the college, high, middle, elementary and pre-school levels, in sport teams, youth work, and in therapeutic and correctional settings. The activities can be adapted for virtually any setting irrespective of age, gender, group size, culture, religion, etc.

A facilitator or an instructor plays a vital role in team-building activities. Different team-building activities facilitated in different ways with different groups lead to a wide variety of experiences and different outcomes. Under an excellent facilitator, even a simple game can prove to be a significant experience for participants.

On the other hand, with a poor instructor, even a well-designed activity can go awry. Participants may not get interested at all or not follow the purpose. The facilitator must give an opportunity to participants to discuss the learning points. The most important part of the game is participants' reflection and discussion about the activity, how they must approach the situation, and possible points of learning. Later, the facilitator should take over. The activity should be video-recorded. By playing and replaying, the facilitator has to analyse and discuss the learning points.

PURPOSE OF TEAM BUILDING

In this chapter, I have chosen a few selected team activities where each team was formed to solve or meet a specific organizational need. Members were carefully selected considering their backgrounds. The equipment used and procedure followed are mentioned. The essential after-activity review is discussed for each activity followed by approval from a competent authority and associated documentation. Readers will get to learn how to select team members in ad-hoc teams and proceed with each activity. The activities discussed are the following:

1. Formulating Quality Policy of OFDC
2. Formulating 5S Policy and Objectives of OFILIS
3. Evaluating a Course at OFILIS
4. Reducing machine breakdown time in Elite Press Works Limited
5. Formulating HRD Policy of OFILIS
6. Rejection analysis of a vital component (Block)
7. Environment Policy of Belur Chemicals Limited
8. Developing Process Analysis Document for Training Programmes by OFILIS
9. Quality Objective Documents of OFILIS
10. Improving Quality Culture in Eureka Hospital

TEN TEAM ACTIVITIES

Activity 1: Formulating Quality Policy of OFDC

1.1 *Organizational need*—Formulating the quality policy of OFDC, a public sector departmental enterprise. While preparing the quality manual and procedure manual, the quality policy had to be defined for documentation and communicating to employees at all levels.

1.2 *Purpose*—The purpose of the activity was to evaluate product range, services rendered, as well as its employees, customers, suppliers. The management representative (MR-ISO 9001 quality management system) was assigned the responsibility by the general manager.

1.3 *Materials*—The following materials were used:

- Flip charts, marker pens, adhesive tape or board pins, paper, pen, pencil, and eraser.
- Electronic gadgets—Voice recorder and/or video recorder.

1.4 *Team composition*—Senior managers and core committee members who had (a) attended quality management awareness programme (at least 5-hour duration), (b) attended quality system audit (ISO 9001) programme and qualified in the assessment test, and (c) had been associated with preparation of documentation for at least one year in his/her own department. Members could be from production, maintenance, quality control, store, or any other department.

1.5 *Phase*—Three-phase meetings.

1.5.1 *Duration of each session*—1 to 1.5 hours.

1.5.2 *Group size*—Phase 1: 30 to 40, Phase 2: 20–25, Phase 3: 7–10.

1.5.3 *Tools*
- Phase 1: Opinion seeking, Recording.
- Phase 2: Opinion seeking, Recording, Review of outcomes of phase 1.
- Phase 3: Group discussion—Review of outcomes of phase 2.

1.5.4 *Inputs*
- Phase 1: Brief by the chairperson.
- Phase 2: Record of discussion of phase 1.
- Phase 3: Record of discussion of phase 2.

1.6 *Physical setting*
- Phase 1: Conference-room-style sitting arrangement.

- Phase 2: Chairs and tables arranged in a circle.
- Phase 3: Chairs and tables arranged in a circle.

1.7 *Process*

In all the phases, the chairperson outlined the purpose of the discussion (though it had been circulated and the agenda made known to all invited members). The member secretary noted the salient points of the discussion. A stenographer also noted the details. Moreover, the entire proceedings were video-recorded. Members of phase 3 considered all the pros and cons, product and service range, strategy plan of the company, principal and other customers, suppliers, and finalized the quality policy.

1.8 *Outcome*—Quality Policy statement

We commit to supply products and services to the customers as per their qualitative, quantitative and timely requirements at a reasonable price meeting applicable statutory requirements. We commit to enhance customers' satisfaction through continual improvements.

1.9 *After-activity reviews*—After about a fortnight, a review meeting was convened that was attended by invited experts (all external). Only the chairperson of phase 3 was present as the member secretary.

1.10 *Approval seeking*—The policy was submitted through the recommending authority to the approving authority as per the company's authority matrix. The issuing authority marked the approved copy as 'Master Copy' and retained it.

1.11 *Documentation*—The issuing authority allotted document number, issue number and date, revision number and date, reproduced the document, and circulated copies (controlled copy) to all recipients.

Activity 2: Formulating 5S Policy of Ordnance Factories Institute of Learning, Ishapore (OFILIS)

2.1 *Organizational need*—The company decided to enhance service efficiencies, ensure workplace safety, utilize vertical space, reduce searching time, boost employee morale, etc.

2.2 *Purpose*—The purpose of the activity was to identify a tool and use it to meet the organizational need.

2.3 *Materials*—Flip charts, marker pens, adhesive tape or board pins, paper, pen, pencil, eraser for each participating member.

2.4 *Team composition*—Employees who had attended the 5S awareness programme and had been engaged for at least one year in implementing 5S in his/her own workplace. Members could be drawn from production, maintenance, quality control, store, or any other department.

2.5 *Duration of each session*—1 to 1.5 hours.

2.6 *Tools*—Brainstorming (initial three sessions, unstructured; last two sessions, structured).

2.7 *Physical settings*—Chairs and tables arranged in a circle.

2.8 *Group size*—6 to 8 members.

2.9 *Procedure*—The leader of the team outlined the need for developing the 5S policy and the corresponding objectives of the company. He further declared that the 5S manual would also be prepared. Though all the members had exposure to 5S, they could not readily reach a consensus. Other than the inaugural session, five more sessions were required.

2.10 *Outcome*—(a) 5S policy and (b) 5S objectives exhibited in two separate tables (Boxes 12.1 and 12.2).

Box 12.1   5S Policy

OFILIS is committed to improve continually the quality of the workplace making it serene, which, in turn, will enhance productivity through the practice of 5S.

Date: dd.mm.yyyy.

Signature
Chief Executive Officer

Box 12.2   5S Objectives

All the employees of OFILIS
- Shall maintain standard of record keeping including weeding out unwanted and obsolete documents and records
- Shall maintain a clean and hygienic work environment
- Shall ensure enforcement of self-discipline to provide better customer service

Date: dd.mm.yyyy.

Signature
Chief Executive Officer

2.11 *After-activity reviews*—The policy and objectives were reviewed by internal specialists in the presence of the team leader.

2.12 *Approval seeking*—The documents were submitted to the chief executive officer for authentication.

2.13 *Documentation*—The document was reproduced and circulated to all departments of the organization.

Activity 3: Evaluating a Course at OFILIS

3.1 *Organizational need*—OFILIS felt the utmost need for developing a single parameter to represent the quality of a training programme. OFILIS conducts about 80 programmes every year apart from direct recruit chargeman.

3.2 *Purpose*—The institute realized the need to objectively analyse the quality of courses and to ascertain its continual improvement by comparing with the previous course. The second purpose was to undertake reviews to initiate corrective action in case of degradation in quality.

3.3 *Materials*—The following materials were used:
Flip charts, marker pens, adhesive tape or board pins, paper, pen, pencil, and eraser.

3.3.1 *Inputs*—Participant feedback records.

3.4 *Team composition*—The team comprised the training manager, management representative (MR-ISO system), two co-opted regular faculty members, two course directors, and two course coordinators (on rotational basis).

3.5 *Tools*
- Brainstorming (structured)
- Nominal Group Technique

3.6 *Physical setting*—Chairs and tables arranged in a circle.

3.7 *Procedure*—In the structured idea-generation stage of the brainstorming sessions, the members contributed many ideas. While evaluating the ideas, not a single idea emerged as acceptable for implementation. The members unanimously decided to refer to the feedback form in which participants expressed their views. Accordingly, this document was included as the input to members participating in brainstorming.

3.7.1 *Extract from feedback*—In the feedback form, participants allotted point grade (PG) for each of the six parameters of the course on the 5-point Likert scale. The parameters were:

- Achievement of course objective(s)
- Following instructions
- Exercise/Practical training facilities (where applicable)

- Applicability of knowledge/skills
- Topic and presentation grading

3.7.2 *From feedback to weightage*—The team members decided to find a single parameter representing all the parameters of the feedback format. The team arrived at a representative parameter and termed it Annual Course Grading (ACG). Thereafter, they decided to allot weightage to each of the parameters. Again, they could reach a consensus and the leader proposed use of the 'Nominal Group Technique'. Members considered the pros and cons of each parameter and expressed their individual opinions and dropped the chit in the 'opinion box'. When all the parameters had been discussed and chits dropped in the box, all the chits were taken out. The leader prepared the tabulation sheet in the presence of all the members. The average weightages are presented in Table 12.1.

TABLE **12.1** **Weightage**

Feedback from the participant	W
Achievement of course objective(s)	35
Following instructions	10
Exercise/Practical training facilities (where applicable)	10
Applicability of knowledge/skills	30
Topic and presentation grading	15

3.7.2 *From weightage to annual course grading*—The team unanimously decided to compute the average of a parameter from the feedback of all the participants and indicated it as X_i and developed the simple formula for ACG (Table 12.w).

TABLE **12.2** **Annual course grading**

Feedback from the Participant	PG	W
Achievement of course objective(s)	X_1	35
Following instructions	X_2	10
Exercise/Practical training facilities (where applicable)	X_3	10
Applicability of knowledge/skills	X_4	30
Topic and presentation grading	X_5	15

$$ACG = \frac{\Sigma(PG \times W)}{\Sigma(W)}$$

3.8 *Outcome*—A measurement yardstick of the quality of a course.

3.9 *After-activity reviews*—The method was tested for 20 courses including repeat courses on (a) internal quality audit and (b) computer. Thus the method was validated for inclusion as a system.

3.10 *Approval seeking*—All records of discussions were submitted to the principal director who further discussed with his peers and the HRD division of corporate headquarters.

3.11 *Documentation*—This was documented in the 'Procedure on Evaluation of Training' of the institute.

Activity 4: Reducing Machine Breakdown in Elite Press Works Limited

4.1 *Organizational need*—Elite Press Works Limited has many sophisticated press machines: hydraulic and pneumatic presses of a vast range of capacities. In fact, the press-worked products have exemplary qualities. But in a few cases the company could not deliver products to its customers due to machine breakdowns. Machine breakdown posed a serious threat to the company. It decided to initiate a systematic approach to solve this problem.

4.2 *Purpose*—The primary purpose is to reduce breakdown time and the secondary purpose is to formulate machine maintenance policy.

4.3 *Materials*—Flip charts, marker pens, adhesive tape or board pins, paper, pen, pencil, and eraser.

4.3.1 *Inputs*—The following documents were used:
- List of press machines
- List of critical presses
- Operation manuals of critical presses
- Guidelines on troubleshooting
- Breakdown history of critical machines

4.4 *Team composition*—Maintenance manager, maintenance engineer (one each from hydraulic and pneumatic division), one experienced mechanic who worked in both the divisions and had knowledge and skills about all ranges of presses, one production engineer from each of the four production departments.

4.5 *Tools*
- Brainstorming session (Structured)
- Cause–effect diagram (See Key Terms)

4.6 *Physical setting*—Chairs and tables arranged in a circle.

4.7 *Procedure*—The first phase of the brainstorming session was dedicated to identifying the reasons behind breakdowns, classifying the reasons (based on man, method, condition, etc.) and then preparing a cause–effect diagram. This diagram showed effect (in this case breakdown) and the reasons against each classification. Then some vital decisions could be taken.

4.7.1 *Finding*—The diagram revealed that in most cases the breakdowns were due to human error (improper handling of the machine). Statistics showed that in 90 per cent or more cases the maintenance task was of a minor nature that needed minimal maintenance knowledge.

4.8 *Outcome*

4.8.1 *Decision*—The team decided in the interest of the organization that the operators would undertake repairing of their respective machines. The machine operators would be trained to enable them to undertake the repairing.

4.8.2 *Maintenance policy*—To reduce the mean time between failures (MTBFs) the practice of intensive preventive maintenance and periodical follow-up on holidays and weekends was introduced.

4.9 *After-activity reviews*—The operators of critical machines were trained in the first phase. Training of other machine operators continued in batches. A review was done after three months for critical machines. This practice initially reduced the breakdown time to about 15 per cent.

Approval seeking—No formal approval was taken.

Documentation—The decision was circulated to all production departments. Documentation was done by and preserved at the maintenance department. Responsibility to follow-up was assigned to the maintenance department.

Activity 5: HRD Policy and Objectives of OFILIS

5.1 *Organizational need*—OFILIS is an institute responsible for imparting training to its customers who are employees of factories under the corporate headquarters of OFILIS. Formulating the HRD policy was a need for quality system certification.

5.2 *Purpose*—Displaying the HRD policy and objectives in the institute's quality manual, which is an auditable document by the certification agency. To communicate the HRD policy to employees at all levels, translating it into the languages known to employees. (OFILIS translated the policy and objectives in Bengali and Hindi.)

5.3 *Materials*—Flip charts, marker pens, adhesive tape or board pins, paper, pen, pencil, and eraser.

5.3.1 *Inputs*—ISO standard on quality manual, ISO 9004 standard on guidelines on performance improvements, administrative manual of corporate headquarters, training needs of regular clients, standing instruction on training, etc.

5.4 *Team composition*—Management Representative (MR-ISO 9001), head of training coordination cell, six course directors who regularly organize training programmes.

5.5 *Tools*—Brainstorming sessions (Structured)

5.6 *Physical setting*—Conference-room-style sitting arrangement

5.7 *Procedure*—The team leader (management representative) explained the purpose of the meeting, discussed the salient points from the input documents, and started the brainstorming session to formulate the HRD policy first. In two team meetings, the team formulated the HRD policy. The sessions continued and from the third session the team focused on HRD objectives. Multiple copies of the documents were available in the mini conference room. In the middle of the fourth session, a member reiterated that the objectives must be measurable. Other members and the leader had also missed this vital aspect though the leader had said this at the beginning of the third session. Naturally, the members immediately accepted the point, applied their wisdom collectively, and could achieve the purpose of the meeting. The team could avoid wastage of further time and energy.

5.8 *Outcomes*—HRD Policy and HRD Objectives

5.8.1 *HRD Policy*
- We commit to fulfil the training needs of ordnance factories and other customers by providing effective training services.
- We also commit to enhance customer satisfaction and continually improve the standard of training.

5.8.2 *HRD Objectives*
- 100 per cent adherence to course calendar (PLAN)
- To sustain the ACG and to further improve the quality of the courses by enhancing the ACG

- Enhancing customer satisfaction by post-training impact measurement (PTIM) for core competence (metallurgy) by 5 per cent
- 100 per cent adherence to programme for all courses
- 100 per cent adherence to monthly report schedule

5.9 *After-activity reviews*—The regional director (chief executive officer) discussed the suitability of the HRD policy and objectives with the HRD division of corporate headquarters. Concurrently, senior managers (course directors) of OFILIS also reviewed the power and objectives.

5.10 *Approval seeking*—The policy and objectives were approved.

5.11 *Documentation*—The management representative allotted the document number, issue number and date, revision number, and date. The ink-signed copies were filed in the master copies of documents. He made copies and circulated them to all managers and departments.

Activity 6: Rejection Analysis of Block

6.1 *Organizational need*—The company felt the need for undertaking analysis of a component which was performing a crucial function in the assembly. The rejection of the component was always much higher than the permissible limit allowed by the industrial engineering department. Moreover, it showed an increasing trend of rejection though experienced operators were deployed.

6.2 *Purpose*—To identify the root causes of rejection and initiate remedial measures.

6.3 *Materials*—Flip charts, marker pens, adhesive tape or board pins, paper, pen, pencil, and eraser.

6.3.1 *Inputs*—Operation layout, gauge schedules, process capability, machine details, material inspection notes, etc.

6.4 *Team composition*—Four operators and their supervisor, quality control representative, and production shop in-charge. The quality control manager and production manager were the facilitators.

6.5 *Tools*—Brainstorming session (Structured)

6.6 *Physical setting*—Chairs and tables arranged in a circle.

6.7 *Procedure*—During brainstorming, several points emerged that may have been affecting the accuracy of the component: jobs not held properly, skill of the operator, holding device not accurate, improper process, chuck not aligned, vibration in the machine, mistake in drawing, job not done in one setting, etc. The team decided to collect data for all the points. The team classified the points in categories: operator, method, machine, engineering, and planning. After classifying the points, the team discussed about the mode of presentation—graph, table, or diagram—to make the presentation lucid, logical, and convincing. As such, the team represented their findings using a cause–effect diagram (see Key Terms).

6.8 *Outcome*—The cause–effect diagram (Figure 12.1) depicted the classified groups and brainstorming points in the group.

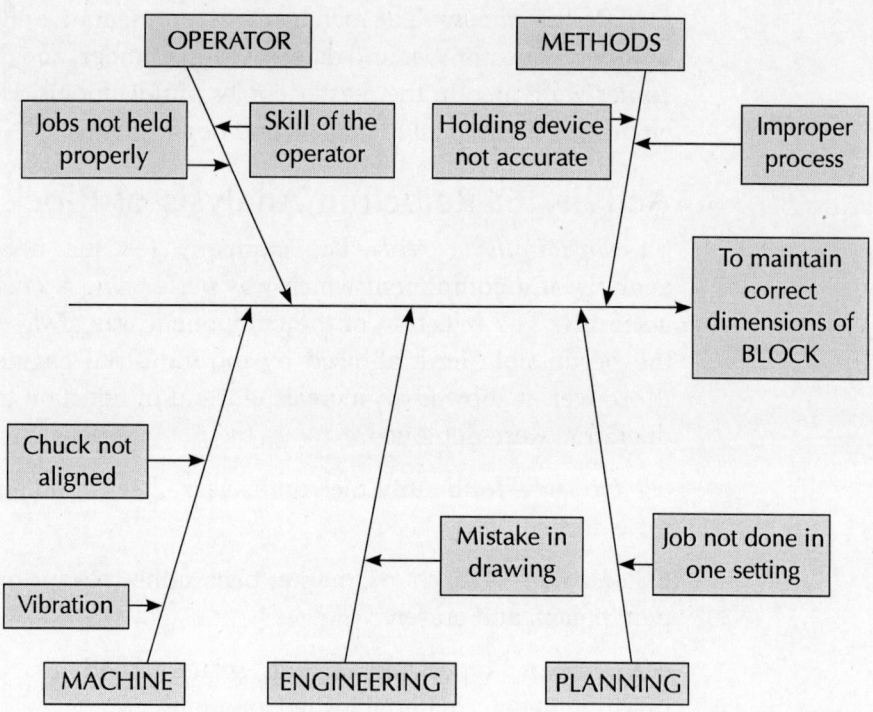

FIGURE **12.1   Rejection analysis for block—Cause–effect diagram**

6.9 *After-activity reviews*—The findings presented were not reviewed as the quality control manager and production manager were monitoring the sessions. They assigned the task of data collection to two persons.

6.10 *Approval seeking*—The method was approved and points (findings) accepted.

6.11 *Documentation*—The proceedings were documented in the quality control department.

Activity 7: Environment Policy of Belur Chemicals limited

7.1 *Organizational need*—Analysing effects of wastes in any form during the processes and activities, and adopting technological measures to eliminate or reduce their harmful effects, considering and complying with regulatory and legislative requirements.

7.2 *Purpose*—Ensuring that exhaust smokes, drained out chemicals, solid wastes do not pollute the environment; protect the people from health hazards.

7.3 *Materials*—Flip charts, marker pens, adhesive tape or board pins, paper, pen, pencil, and eraser.

7.3.1 *Inputs*—Standard ISO 14001, technological processes, waste analysis reports, documents on environmental regulations and legislations, etc.

7.4 *Team composition*—Management representative (EMS; ISO 14001), head of environment management cell, two chemical process experts from the production department, and two divisional managers. One expert from the pollution control board was co-opted as a special invitee.

7.5 *Tools*—Group discussion

7.6 *Physical setting*—Chairs and tables arranged in a circle

7.7 *Procedure*—The management representative discussed some salient points from the records of discussions held on environmental management issues. He also discussed the new processes introduced to manufacture the new chemicals included in the product range vis-à-vis the manufacturing process adopted, and need of waste analysis. He also circulated the environmental policies of some other chemical manufacturers as guidelines. Then the group held a focused discussion regarding the existing and new processes used to produce the chemicals. The policy was drafted in four sessions each of 1–1.5-hour duration.

7.8 *Outcome*—The Environmental Policy (Box 12.3).

7.9 *After-activity reviews*—The draft policy was submitted to another committee formed by the chief executive officer to review.

7.10 *Approval seeking*—The chief executive officer approved the policy.

7.11 *Documentation*—The management representative (also member secretary) allotted document number, issue number and date, revision number and

> ## Box 12.3 Environmental Policy
> ## Belur Chemicals Limited
>
> We are engaged in the manufacture of basic chemicals required by industries and we have production plants, plant and equipment maintenance departments, and quality control department, supported by general and administrative offices.
>
> In our works an environmental management cell observes, monitors, and liaises with internal and external agencies on environmental issues.
>
> We are committed to
>
> · Raise awareness of workforce regarding environment.
> · Keep environment clean by minimizing dust, fumes, smoke and wastes in any form generated in the processes and activities.
> · Use resources efficiently through good management practices and technological measures.
> · Comply with or surpass all applicable environmental regulations and legislations at all time and adhere to environmentally acceptable management of wastes in such a manner as to prevent pollution.
> · Review the policy, its objectives and targets, and the level of implementation, and to communicate the same to all interested parties including stakeholders.
>
> Sd.
>
> Date
>
> Chief Executive Officer
>
> Belur Chemicals Limited

date. The ink-signed copies were filed in the master copies of documents. He made copies, and circulated to all managers and departments, maintaining records of despatch. He retained the master copy in environment cell.

Activity 8: Process Analysis Document for Training Programmes

8.1 *Organizational need*—The organization needed to develop its training documents in a systematic manner to meet specific requirements of its clients and in compliance with the instructions of corporate headquarters. The organization further wanted to develop the objectives in measurable terms for subsequent analysis.

8.2 *Purpose*—Adopting a process approach and preparing process analysis documents.

8.3 *Materials*—Flip charts, marker pens, adhesive tape or board pins, paper, pen, pencil, and eraser.

8.3.1 *Inputs*—Views of functional heads, course calendar of previous year, requests from clients, minutes of meeting of regional directors' conference, directives of corporate HQ, feedback report of previous courses, current syllabus, syllabi of other institute, etc.

8.4 *Team composition*—Management representative (MR-ISO 9001), coordinating manager, immediate past coordinating manager, and four programme directors.

8.5 *Tools*—Brainstorming session (Structured)

8.6 *Physical setting*—Chairs and tables arranged in a circle

8.7 *Procedure*—The team brainstormed to get ideas like (a) required outputs, (b) identifying activities and inputs for each activity, (c) analysis required, and (d) finally assignment of responsibilities. Then the team identified a list of outputs. The management representative (ISO 9001) played the nodal role as leader as he was the person responsible for establishing, implementing, and maintaining the system.

8.7.1 *The output*—Draft annual course calendar (ACC), obtaining approval of the draft calendar, deploying programme director (PD) and programme coordinator (PC), developing the syllabus, developing each programme, intimating clients, conducting the programmes, evaluating each programme, and sending the report to corporate headquarters.

8.7.2 *Activity and input*—Each output needs certain activities to be performed, and each activity needs certain specific inputs. For example, draft annual course calendar needed three distinct inputs: (a) views of functional heads, (b) course calendar of previous year (for reference), and (c) requests from clients.

8.7.3 *Analysis done*—To exercise control, each activity needs to be analysed separately.

8.7.4 *Responsibility*—Specific responsibility must be assigned to raise accountability.

8.8 *Outcome*—The outcome of this stupendous activity was the 'process analysis document' for the 'course conduction process' (Table 12.3).

8.9 *After-activity reviews*—The regional director and chief executive officer

TABLE 12.3   Process analysis document (PAD)

S. No.	Input	Activities	Output	Analysis done	Responsibility
1	• Views of functional heads • Course calendar of previous year • Requests from clients	Preparation of Draft Annual Course Calendar (ACC)	Draft ACC	Incorporation of all courses	HOS (Coord)
2	• Draft ACC • RD's Conference (minutes of meeting) • Views conveyed through MDO or HRD Officer • Directives of OFB	Preparation of ACC	ACC	Incorporation of all courses	HOS (Coord)
3	ACC	Sending to HQ for approval	Approved ACC	—	HOS (Coord)
4	Approved ACC	Defining course-wise PD and PC	ACC indicating PD and PC	—	HOS
5	• ACC indicating PD and PC • Views of PD and PC • Feedback reports of last courses • Current syllabus • Syllabi of other institutes	Preparation and review of syllabus	Syllabus	Customer requirement adequately addressed	HOS, PD
6	• Syllabus • Previous programme	Preparation and review of programme	Programme	Coverage of all topics	PD, PC
7a	Programme	Selection of internal and external faculty	Intimation letter to faculty members	Coverage of all topics	PD, PC
7b	Programme	Course conduction	Trained personnel	—	PD, PC
8	Feedback of trained personnel	Review and evaluation	Evaluated course programme	To be reviewed	HOS, PD, PC
9	Executed training course	Preparation of reports on executed training	Training report to HQ	—	HOS (Coord)

Note: PAD: Process Analyses Document, HOS: Head of Section, PD: Programme Director, PC: Programme Coordinator, Coord: Coordination.

reviewed the process analysis document and consulted the HRD division at the corporate headquarters.

8.10 *Approval seeking*—The regional director approved the document.

8.11 *Documentation*—The coordinating manager, being the custodian of all training-related documents, made copies of the process analysis document and circulated it to all programme directors and programme coordinators. He retained the ink-signed document in his master file.

Activity 9: Developing Quality Objective Document

9.1 *Organizational need*—The training institute (OFILIS) desired to initiate a systematic approach to strengthen the value and worth of the training programmes it was conducting, and thereby enhance image and loyalty of its regular organizational customers. It decided to strive to promote customer satisfaction. (This need was realized while developing the process analysis document.)

9.2 *Purpose*—To develop a consolidated document to undertake the analyses mentioned in the process analysis document (refer Activity 8).

9.3 *Materials*—Flip charts, marker pens, adhesive tape or board pins, paper, pen, pencil, and eraser.

9.3.1 *Inputs*—Process analysis document.

9.4 *Team composition*—Management representative (MR-ISO 9001), coordinating manager, immediate past coordinating manager, and four programme directors (same as Activity 8).

9.5 *Tools*—Group discussion.

9.6 *Physical setting*—Chairs and tables arranged in a circle.

9.7 *Procedure*—The team leader explained to the members the purpose of the activity and its need for the organization. They brainstormed to pinpoint the fundamental objectives to achieve the purpose. They discussed and finalized the objectives: (a) adhering to course calendar (PLAN), (b) improving quality of courses by enhancing yearly course grading (YCG), and (c) enhancing customer satisfaction level by PTIM. Second, the team identified the means of achieving each objective (refer to the second column in Table 12.4). In the third phase, they identified the indicators of each means. Thereafter, they tabulated the present status and target, periodicity of review, and quality objective monitoring document.

TABLE 12.4 Quality objective document (QOD)

S. No.	Quality Objective	Means of Achieving QO	Indicator	Present Status	Target	Periodicity of Review	QO Monitoring Document
1	Adhering to course calendar (PLAN)	· Faculty deployment · Resource allocation · Monitoring and measuring of actual with respect to plan	Per cent adherence with PLAN	100 per cent	100 per cent	Monthly	Monthly report
2	Improving quality of courses by enhancing yearly course (YCG)	· Monitoring average course grading (ACG)	Per cent of present to previous ACG	Introduced	Between 100 per cent and 110 per cent	Quarterly	ACG summary report by PD
3	Enhancing customer satisfaction level by post-training impact measurement (PTIM)	· Monitoring different courses · Enhancing quality of courses · Interaction with participants · Interaction with participants' supervisor · Follow-up with clients	Per cent	Introduced	5 per cent enhancement from the level to be measured from January 2004	Half-yearly (after conducting the course)	Customer satisfaction report by PD

9.8 *Outcome*—The outcome of this rational activity was the quality objective document (QOD) (Table 12.4).

9.9 *After-activity reviews*—The quality objective document was submitted to the regional director. He consulted the HRD division at corporate headquarters.

9.10 *Approval seeking*—The regional director approved the document.

9.11 *Documentation*—The coordinating manager, being the custodian of all training-related documents, made copies of the quality objective document and circulated it to all programme directors and programme coordinators. He retained the ink-signed document in his master file.

Activity 10: Improving Quality Culture in Eureka Hospital

10.1 *Organizational need*—The hospital (name changed) desired to further improve the quality of service, interaction, develop after-service contacts, etc. through organization-wide drive. The hospital actually wishes to cast a lasting image in the minds of customers (patients and their associates) served; use word of mouth, thereby convert potential customers to actual customers.

10.2 *Purpose*—To promote quality culture, achieve behavioural modification, and develop 'total quality people'.

10.3 *Materials*—Flip charts, marker pens, adhesive tape or board pins, paper, pen, pencil, and eraser.

10.3.1 *Electronic gadgets*—Voice recorder and/or video recorder.

10.4 *Team composition*—Medical superintendent, manager HR, two members from board of governors, and three customers who objectively and logically expressed their grievances and suggested improvement measures. The hospital authorities decided to co-opt some other members depending on the needs that emerged.

10.5 *Tools*

- Brainstorming session (Structured)
- Force field analysis (see Key Terms)

10.6 *Physical setting*—Chairs and tables arranged in a circle.

10.7 *Procedure*—At the outset of the meeting, the medical superintendent welcomed and introduced the invited members in an affirmative manner and expressed the need of their valuable opinions, then outlined the organizational needs and purpose of the brainstorming sessions. Many ideas, which affect the quality culture of any organization, were recorded at the idea-generation stage in the record sheet. After collecting the ideas, they were evaluated. The evaluated ideas were: 'happy-go-lucky' employee attitude, awards and prizes, competitive environment, complacent '*chalta hai*' attitude, conflicts between managers, cost consciousness, customer not demanding, customer quality awareness, demotivated employees, dormant strength of people, employees not challenging, export obligation, fund restriction, high morale, inter-union/inter-association conflict, lack of confidence, monopoly, mutual trust, no export demand, observing quality month, poor leadership, posters, banners, badges, quality image, satisfaction with present status, seminar, competitions, technology upgrading, Total Quality Movement (TQM) environment, and use of HRD mechanisms.

In the next stage, the team classified the ideas as 'helping factors' and 'hindering factors'.

Helping factors (driving forces)—Competitive environment, customer quality awareness, cost consciousness, export obligation, technology upgrading, quality image, TQM environment, high morale, dormant strength of people, awards and prizes, posters, banners, badges, observation of quality month or week, seminar and lecture programmes, mutual trust, HRD mechanisms, etc.

Hindering factors (restraining forces)—Customer not demanding, employees not challenging, monopoly, no export demand, 'happy-go lucky' attitude, complacent '*chalta hai*' attitude, fund restriction, inter-union/inter-association conflict, satisfaction with present status, conflicting managers, lack of confidence, etc.

After classifying the factors in two groups, the team discussed about suitably presenting them. The team collectively decided to present the findings using force field diagram (see Key Terms).

10.8 *Outcome*—Force field diagram (Figure 12.2) showing helping factors (driving forces) and hindering factors (restraining factors).

10.9 *After-activity reviews*—The outcome was not formally reviewed; rather, it was decided to put it into practice.

10.10 *Approval seeking*—The chief executive officer approved the outcome provisionally.

10.11 *Documentation*—The outcome was numbered (EH/QC/PROV) and documented in the company manual.

FIGURE 12.2   Force field diagram

CONCLUDING REMARKS

I have discussed ten activities and outcomes. In fact, each activity discussed was to achieve a particular outcome. Ad-hoc teams were formed to perform the activities, which were non-routine and non-recurring in nature. In each activity, I have first mentioned the organizational need and then the purpose. Then in succession, I have described materials and inputs, team composition, tools, and physical setting. Readers may note that the teams were composed strictly on the basis of the nature of tasks required to be accomplished. The outcomes are the actual requirements. Subsequently after-activity reviews, approval seeking, and documentation are no less important.

The activities include both the service sector (education and health) and the manufacturing sector (both private and public). For some activities, section 3 on material contains a sub-section on 'inputs', which must be carefully noted. Ad-hoc teams were constituted, considering the specific organizational needs. It is emphasized that selection of members is of immense importance; a wrongly selected member may lead to disaster. The utmost need of using collective wisdom was felt. When people could not perform the tasks individually, teams were formed. These have been communicated in all the activities discussed.

Activity 1 was a multi-phased one. To decide the direction and to collect more and more ideas, the number of members was large. The ideas were recorded and were input to the next phase. Readers will gain an insight on how to form a team and about the need for after-activity reviews, approval seeking, and documentation.

While selecting members, the level of the employee is not important; rather, what is extremely important is the member's background, knowledge, and skills.

KEY TERMS

Cause–effect diagram, alternatively known as 'fish bone diagram' or 'herring bone diagram' or 'Ishikawa diagram', shows the causes, grouped into major cause categories, responsible for the effect.

Controlled copy is the copy the recipient is given of updated versions of the documents, on withdrawal of the obsolete documents and, with authentication.

Critical press machines are those machines which do not have any substitute in case of any breakdown and queuing takes place till the machine repaired.

Document is information and its supporting medium (can be paper, magnetic, electronic or optical computer disc, photograph or master samples, or a combination thereof). Examples of training documents include training calendar, brochure, schedule of a management development program (MDP), faculty grading, etc.

Documentation is the system of analysing organizational requirements, generating, scrutinizing, approving, issuing documents, and maintaining records of issue; system includes periodic updating of documents.

Force field analysis is a diagrammatic representation of brainstormed weighed up points/ideas for and against a proposed action to be installed.

Nominal group technique is an organizational planning tool or technique used by a team to prioritize activities when it cannot achieve consensus through discussion.

Quality policy of a company articulates the overall intention of the company with regard to quality to anyone—insider or outsider. This policy represents the management philosophy that is renovated or revamped, covering its products and services as well as its employees, customers, suppliers and everyone the company deals with.

REFERENCES

Haldar, U.K. (1999), Environmental Management Systems, *Kristitapa* (Journal of Regional Training Institute, Ishapore, Ordnance Factory Board), Vol. 2, No. 1.

Haldar, U.K. (2004), Adapting Quality Management System in the Academia: A Success Story, 46th National Convention of Indian Institution of Industrial Engineering, Trivandrum. Theme: Quality Management in the twenty-first Century.

Haldar, U.K. (2007), *Total Quality Management Text and Cases*, Dhanpat Rai & Co., New Delhi.

OFILIS, 'Response Manual', submitted by OFILIS to the Institute of Directors, New Delhi, in 2005 as application for the Golden Peacock National Training Award, 2005.

APPENDICES

Understanding Followership

Developing leadership, and forming and working in teams, are usually focused upon topics. We generally ignore and fail to acknowledge contributions of followers while we speak much about leaders, leadership, and teamwork. Followers pursue course of actions in synchronization with the leader to achieve team goals. Enabling capacities, enthusiasm, intelligence, diligence, self-reliance, workability with other followers in pursuit of the team goal are all that are essential for the team to be effective and successful. Followers must recognize the authority and responsibility of the leader; at the same time they ought to know his/her limitations.

Robert E. Kelley grouped followers into four categories considering two dimensions—'critical thinking' (high and low) and 'participation' (passive and active).

Category	Dimensions		Follower Types
	Critical Thinking	Participation	
1	Low	Passive	Sheep
2	High	Passive	Alienated followers
3	Low	Active	Yes people
4	High	Active	Effective followers

The above table indicates that active followers having the capacity to think critically are effective followers. Followers with critical thinking ability, if passive, remain alienated as strangers. They need to be involved for team progress. Often, managers do not try to understand the capacities of followers to make the best use of them, and in such situations the followers continue to remain passive. As such, organizations fail to gainfully utilize them. Thus, human resource utilization to the fullest extent remains unachieved. Gradually, they fail to trust the leader. Thus, we need to know the truths associated with followership.

THREE TRUTHS OF FOLLOWERSHIP

Trust is the hot-button issue in business, particularly in teamwork. There is no debate on the fact that the success of an organization depends on leadership fostering strong connections between teams, their members, and among colleagues and subordinates. Companies are in urgent need of trusted leaders. The question we face is, how can managers meet that need? 'Being trustworthy' is the short, logical answer. But being trustworthy and building trust in teams in an organization is not one and the same thing. Being trustworthy is an inherent part of a person, whereas building trust requires developed talent and considerable skill. The following truths may generate food for thought to realize the importance of followers' roles and responsibilities:

- The sum of the contributions of all the followers (team members) is much more than that of the leader, though he/she foresees, directs, leads, energizes, and plays the pivotal role. According to Sengupta (2006), if a leader contributes one-third to the success of the team, followers are critical to the completion of the remaining two-thirds.
- The majority of organizational members, irrespective of designations, spend more time in following than leading. Team members and also the leader follow policies, systems, standing instructions, and many more things.
- Although people spend most of their time and work life in contributing as followers, there is little mention about followers' roles. Of course, leader–member exchange theory throws some light on this.

ROLES AND RESPONSIBILITIES OF FOLLOWERS

Followers, as supporters of the leader, are required to perform various types of roles and discharge responsibilities. The roles must be clear, and responsibilities must be objectively assigned to them. A team will never be able to function effectively if roles are ambiguous and responsibilities are undefined or overlapping. The following is a discussion of the roles and responsibilities of followers.

Roles

Followers play certain significant roles in the accomplishment of team goals. These are participation role, responsible role, transformational role, serving role, and moral role.

Participation role—Spontaneous and active involvement, and participation of followers with team activities is essential to achieve team goals. These are the keys to the success of teams leading to organizational excellence.

Responsible role—A sense of responsibility among followers greatly contributes to teamwork. Responsible followers do not always need to be led. They should be able to move in and out of leadership roles in demanding situations.

Transformation role—In the changing environment, transformation is essential. A transformation can never be successful only on the basis of the vision laid down by the leader. Transformation needs to be initiated at the follower's level. Until a team member is geared up to transform himself/herself spontaneously, there is little or no chance of real transformation.

Serving role—Serving the team as a member is the primary task of a follower. Followers must have integrity and service has to be true.

Moral role—It is the moral responsibility of followers to make concerted efforts to conform to the structured rules of working, bring any lapses to the notice of the leader, inform about unavailability of any resource, take the advice of the leader in case of any conflicts within the team, and so forth.

Developing followers is an organizational responsibility. Research has established the importance of followers' role for organizational successes.

Responsibilities

Followers need to understand the gravity of an organizational situation, appreciate the effect of the situation on the organizational performance, and the consequence of team performance to achieve the business goal. A responsible follower can analyse an organizational situation. Raising responsibilities of followers is no less important than developing leaders. Sengupta (2006) recommends some prerequisites for effective followership, which are as follows:

* Ability to understand what the leader wants out of him/her
* Being empathetic to the leader; ability to understand the problems and concerns of the leader
* Correcting the leader in a decent manner, and assertively if a follower observes any mistake made by the leader
* Being enthusiastic about work and surpassing the leader's expectations
* Ability to prevent exposure of the leader's shortcomings to outsiders
* Helping the leader to identify his/her wrong concept and rectifying
* Exercising self-control to prevent depression due to disagreement with the leader or other member, thereby preventing dissent
* Acting as moderator between the leader and other followers in demanding situations
* Learning the ability to communicate effectively with the leader and others
* Keeping the wheel of excellence of team performance moving, by putting in all-round efforts
* Reporting, discussing, proposing, suggesting assertively, without fear and without trampling on other people's interest, and with modesty
* Developing oneself while working in a team
* Identifying oneself with the team
* Participating with a high degree of willingness

- Seeking expansion of one's periphery of work; role enlargement and role enrichment
- Standing by the leader and team members in hard times

Followership can be analogous to astronomical phenomenon—as the earth revolves around the sun, followers must remain around the leader. A true follower does not keep himself/herself confined only to achieve team goals. He/She further develops to become a great leader in the future.

TRUSTING RELATIONSHIPS

The literature on organizational trust consistently asserts that trusting relationships play a significant role in a leader's ability to shape and influence team members and thus, the organization itself. Research findings also suggest that perceived trustworthiness between team members is essential for stability and longevity of teams. Furthermore, it has been emphasized that high levels of trust generally spark the creation of flatter organizations with greater shared leadership, which in turn produces increased participation, involvement, and productivity. Mutual trust and interpersonal confidence is a unifying force in organizations. Moreover, it is believed that followers who trust their leader are more likely to provide superior performance, display positive attitudes, and show greater organizational commitment. The more the leader exhibits trust-producing behaviours, the greater is members' trust in his/her leadership.

An object can be purchased and inventoried. But trust is a feeling about others and not an object, and it cannot be taken for granted forever. In order to sustain the trust of team members, to win them over, and make them followers on a long-term basis, a leader must be aware of their aspirations and abilities. To make the resistance minimal, the leader has to be responsive and empathetic. To develop and maintain trustworthiness, command, and promote good followership a leader must:

- be caring and genuinely concerned for team members,
- exchange personal information and happiness,
- be conscious while communicating and be aware of the consequences of actions,
- practice what is preached,
- never break a promise or renege on assurances given,
- be transparent, systematic, and truthful,
- share success to enthuse members,
- be highly accountable and own up to the failures of followers, and
- identify weaknesses and suggest remedial measures, and identify strengths for augmenting them.

Developing trusting relationships should not be merely a lip service. It needs some systematic approach for which we need to be familiar with an equation of trust.

Equation of Trust

Sengupta (2006) reinterprets the equation of trust given by Galford and Seibold (2003) for the leader–follower loop. Trust is a factor of the aspirations of followers, the abilities and action of the leader, alignment between the action of the leader and aspirations of the followers, articulation or expression or communication, and resistance. The equation of trust is

$$\text{Trust} = \frac{(A1 + A2 + A3) * (A4 + A5)}{R}$$

where   A1   =   Aspirations (of the followers)

A2   =   Abilities (of the leader)

A3   =   Actions (of the leader)

A4   =   Alignment (between the action of the leader and aspirations of the followers)

A5   =   Articulation

R   =   Resistance

The resistance may develop because of

- insincere statements and actions of the leader,
- fear or insecurity among followers originating from actions and aspirations of the leader,
- frustration of being under- or overutilized,
- hierarchical mindset of the leader,
- difference in what is preached and what is practised by the leader,

Communication styles of leaders, their behaviour, understanding members' aspirations and sentiments, and frustration of members are responsible for resistance. If the aspiration of the leader is high, he/she demands more from members. If the capabilities of some team members are limited, they cannot respond to the leader's tasks, and as such fear or insecurity develops among them that manifests in the form of resistance.

STRATEGIES TO PROMOTE FOLLOWERSHIP

It is needless to emphasize that team success is the result of effective and efficient leadership and fruitful interactions between the leader and the followers. If the leader does something that concerns them, they will certainly voice their concern. If the leader mentors followers with a 'follow me' approach, delivering an eloquent speech, they may not follow since that would be an imitation of the learning imperative. Leaders must mentor followers for specific and objective abilities or traits to create dynamic subordinates. These dynamic follower competencies help form a foundation from which followers' initiative can grow more naturally to leader initiative. The identified follower competencies help leaders to lay sharper focus on their mentoring efforts. This approach encourages followers to develop fully, based on their personalities, strengths and weaknesses, and situational factors.

An organization must initiate the following actions:

- Realize the significance of trust and develop interpersonal trust through trust-building workshops since trust is the key to developing followership.
- Recognize the valuable interactions and contributions of followers, their weaknesses and strengths, and adopt a leadership style conducive to the situation.
- Communicate the philosophy of leadership and followership, in sessions attended by both leaders and followers, clearly throughout the organization.
- Conduct training programmes on the 'concept and practice of effective followership' for all employees including leaders.
- Conduct management development programmes for managers, supervisors, and team leaders to raise the awareness of the need for followership, and educate on how to encourage effective followers.
- Develop a yardstick to measure or evaluate followership, and launch incentive schemes for exemplary followership.
- Reward and celebrate outstanding examples of effective followership and follower-orientated leadership.
- Acknowledge effective followership and incorporate an item on this in the performance appraisals of all employees.
- Conduct training programmes on assertiveness and assertive communication.

In the case of self-leadership or a self-managed team, an individual has to follow his/her own ideals and thoughts to become a good leader, value values, counter all that may jeopardize team progress. If the above steps are carefully and systematically introduced in an organization, it would surely promote followership, which in turn would contribute to successful team performance.

SUMMARY

While we talk about leadership, we generally ignore followership. But leaders work with followers without whose spontaneous involvement a team cannot progress. Followers are categorized according to their power of critical thinking and extent of participation in team progress. Trust is the hot-button issue in teamworking.

Followers are supporters to the leader who are required to perform a variety of roles and discharge responsibilities. They must have role clarity and objectively assigned responsibilities for effectiveness. Trust between members and the leader is a prime necessity. Developing trusting relationship needs a systematic approach. A leader must be cautious while communicating with followers. However, he/she has to understand members' aspirations and sentiments to prevent resistance. Leaders should ensure that followers can work without fear and anxiety.

Critical Thinking Questions

1. 'The nature of leadership can perhaps be best understood by turning the coin over and studying followership.' Critically evaluate this concept and present your viewpoint with proper justifications and examples.
2. Followers need to discharge certain responsibilities. As such, followers' responsibilities must be raised. Discuss who should be responsible to do that task and the arsenals he/she can use to perform the task.
3. Trust building is considered the single most essential activity to make followership effective and thus it must be measured. How can an organization measure trusting relationships objectively?
4. Suppose some followers are unable to perform to the extent expected. Consider Ginnett's Team Effectiveness Leadership Model (Chapter 10). Discuss how to use the model to identify the root cause(s). Discuss critically.
5. Consider the prerequisites for effective followership and critically discuss whether they contribute to improve the LMX (Chapter 7).
6. 'Fight with your boss if necessary; but do it in private, avoid embarrassing situations, and never reveal to others what was discussed.' How does this statement sound in light of the concept of followership and its different types? Elucidate critically.
7. A successful leader chooses to have smart people around, who does the tasks. Examine the statement in light of the followership theory, which believes that two-thirds of a team's contribution is that of the followers.
8. 'The glue that holds all relationships together—including the relationship between the leader and the led is trust, and trust is based on integrity' (Brian Tracy). Elaborate the concept of trust in light of the theory of followership.

REFERENCES

Cox, Rod (2009), Synopsis, *The Trusted Leader*, www.xpastor.org/articles/barfoot_leader_follower_trust.html (accessed on 15 May 2009).

Galford, Robert and Anne Seibold Drapeau (2003), The Trusted Leader, *Executive Excellence*, March 2003.

Sengupta, Debashish (2006), Rediscovering Followership, *Indian Management* (Journal of the All India Management Association), Vol. 45, No. 7, July 2006. www.govleaders.org/dynamic_followership.htm (accessed 15 May 2009).

Leader Achievers—Biographies of Organizational Leaders

We have studied many aspects of leaders and leadership in Part 1 of this book. In Part 2, we studied about teams and their various facets including research and training, and activities to meet organizational needs and outcomes.

Tom Peters, a management philosopher and consultant of McKinsey & Company, has defined leadership as 'frighteningly smart with tons of animal energy, blessed with monumental impatience, able to distil a vision for troops, able to recognize and resolve big issues, with a healthy disgust of bureaucracy, a permanent freak, honest, straightforward, rapidly decisive, future focussed, non-report or past oriented, rigorous in their own execution and follow-up, and highly driven'. Compassion and courage are missing from the definition.

Lord Rama, in the epic Ramayana, was a compassionate and courageous leader who held values supreme even under tremendous pressure and symbolized all the qualities of a leader.

Knowing leadership as defined by Tom Peter, and remembering Lord Rama, let us learn about the life and works of a few organizational leaders, some of whom may already be familiar to us.

N.R. NARAYANA MURTHY

Narayana Murthy of Infosys was born on 20 August 1946. He is the embodiment of transparency, moral integrity, dynamism, spirit, and honesty. He obtained a BE in electrical engineering in 1967 from the University of Mysore, followed by an M.Tech. in 1969 from the Indian Institute of Technology, Kanpur, and then began his career with Patni Computer Systems in Pune.

In 1981, Narayana Murthy founded Infosys in Mumbai with six other software professionals. In 1987, Infosys opened its first international office in the US. Following the liberalization of the Indian economy in the 1991, Infosys grew rapidly. In 1993, the company came up with its initial public offering (IPO). In 1995, Infosys set up development centres across cities in India and in 1996, it set up its first office in Europe in Milton Keynes, UK. In 1999, Infosys became the first Indian company to be listed on the National Association of Securities Dealers

Automated Quotations (NASDAQ). In 2006, Infosys had a turnover of more than US$2 billion and had an employee strength of over 50,000. In 2002, Infosys was ranked number one in the 'Best Employers in India 2002' survey conducted by Hewitt, and in the *Business World*'s survey of 'India's Most Respected Company'. The success of Infosys is built on the twin pillars of a strong business model and sound corporate governance. Infosys Technologies Limited, popularly known as Infy, reported a net profit of Rs 1302 crore (Rs 13.02 billion) for the quarter ended June 2008.

Narayana Murthy propounds faith and hope in the future, and believes life is all about hope. Contextually, an excerpt from his statement is reproduced below: 'In 1990, there was an offer to buy out Infosys by an Indian group for about a million dollars. We had had a marathon for nine years. Revenues were increasing significantly. There was so much friction for Indian businesses. We could not open offices overseas. An IPO was not a viable financing option. The then Controller of Capital Issues would not give you a proper premium. Travelling abroad was not easy. Licensing was an issue. Given all these, we were just wondering—maybe we should hang up our boots. Fortunately, we sat down and decided to continue. That is the time when we told ourselves we will be positive, we will be enthusiastic and we will work hard. I had actually told my colleagues that I was willing to buy them out—not that I had any money. Then they realized that if this guy has so much of confidence and faith, we should continue being a part of the group. It was basically that faith in the future; hope in the future that life is all about.' Thus, the marathon started in 1981 in a garage of Mumbai (then known as Bombay) continued.

After serving for 21 years as the company's chief executive officer, Murthy handed over the reins to co-founder Nandan M. Nilekani in March 2002. Now, he is the non-executive chairman and chief mentor of Infosys Technologies Limited. He is a living legend and an epitome of the fact that honesty is not at variance with business acumen. He set new standards in corporate governance and morality when he stepped down as the executive chairman of Infosys at the age of 60.

Along with the growth of Infosys, Narayana Murthy too has grown in stature. He has received many honours and awards:

2000 (June): *Asiaweek* magazine featured him in a list of Asia's 50 Most Powerful People.

2001: Named as one of the 25 most influential global executives by *Time*/CNN.

2003: Chosen as the World Entrepreneur of the Year by Ernst & Young.

2003: First recipient of the Indo-French Forum Medal (2003).

2004 and 2005: Topped the *Economic Times* Corporate Dossier list of India's most powerful CEOs for two consecutive years.

2005: *The Economist* ranked him eighth on the list of the 15 most admired global leaders.

Narayana Murthy's has many success mantras, some of which reflect his life's philosophy and the philosophy of Infosys. The value system of Infosys was and is like the British Constitution—'all unwritten but extremely well practised'. The value system is the true strength of Infosys. Unless the company can sell well, it cannot do anything, such as create jobs, pay good salaries, and satisfy investors. Right from the beginning, the company realized that it has to focus on selling better and better in the marketplace. In Chapter 1 of this book, you have learned about the universal inner structure of successful leaders. Narayana Murthy also believes that 'Truth is God. Our success at Infosys depends on our continual learning.' He says: 'Entrepreneurship is about running a marathon, not a 100 metre dash. Anyone must dream and plan to realize that.' In this context he says: 'We were huddled together in a small room in Bombay in the hope of creating a brighter future for ourselves, for the Indian society, and perhaps, we dreamed, even for the world.'

He emphasizes that 'Leadership is an action, not a word.' He advises building a climate of honesty, hard work, and excellence; building a social conscience and benchmarking oneself with the best in the world, and being honest and true to the profession and acting fearlessly. His vision encompasses that information technology can help alleviate many of the problems that rural India faces. Health care, education, environment conservation can be comprehensively brought to the villages.

In his opinion, working long hours over the long term is harmful to the person and to the organization. Mindset and imagination are more critical than other resource. Essentially, this translates to becoming a group of educated people. He adds, 'Beyond a certain level of comfort I think one's wealth should be seen as an opportunity to make a difference to society.' He advises: 'Always seek the truth; learn from the advances abroad, think how you can support institutions that have helped you reach where you are—your school.' In order to be successful, one must epitomize the qualities of leadership by example, simplicity, and perseverance. In a knowledge company whose core competencies include human intellect and learning, leaders have to walk the talk.

Narayana Murthy believes that things happen twenty-four hours a day. Allowing for little rest is not ultimately practical. So he advises to take a nap; things will happen while you're asleep, but you will have the energy to catch up when you wake up. A person must love the job but never fall in love with the company he/she is working in. People with high aspirations sometimes get frustrated. They should remember that in most situations, the pleasure comes from the journey, not the destination.

Narayana Murthy's dictum is that performance leads to recognition; recognition brings respect; respect enhances power; and humility and grace in one's moments of power enhances the dignity of an organization. Corporations have an important duty to contribute to society. No corporation can sustain its progress unless it makes a difference to its context. Nevertheless, these initiatives should come from the corporation itself rather than being foisted upon it by outside parties. Obviously, an organization must feel responsible to develop society.

One should always be trustworthy with one's dealings. In organizations, mutual trust is the essence behind all-round success. Such foundations create great organizations and take them to great heights.

Narayana Murthy advocates that a value system is the protocol for behaviour that enhances the trust, confidence and commitment of members of the community. It must be mentioned that the most important attribute of a progressive society is respect for others who have accomplished more than they themselves have; we need to learn from them.

He has great respect for people and belief in the power of talent. He says, 'Our core corporate assets walk out every evening. It is our duty to make sure that these assets return the next morning, mentally and physically enthusiastic and energetic.' People must aspire. Aspiration is the main fuel for progress. Aspirations transform a set of ordinary people into extraordinary achievers.

KUMAR MANGALAM BIRLA

Kumar Mangalam Birla was born on 14 June 1967. He is the chairman of the Aditya Birla Group. He spent his early life in Calcutta and Mumbai. He is a chartered accountant and did his master's in business administration from the London Business School. Kumar Mangalam took over as chairman in 1995, at the age of 28, after the sudden demise of his father and noted industrialist Aditya Birla, after whom the group is named. The Birla group is India's third largest business house. Major companies of the Aditya Birla Group in India are Grasim, Hindalco, UltraTech Cement, Aditya Birla Nuvo, and Idea Cellular. The Aditya Birla Group's joint ventures include Birla SunLife (financial services) and Birla NGK (insulators). The group also has a presence in various countries such as Thailand, Indonesia, Malaysia, the Philippines, Egypt, Canada, China, and Australia.

When Kumar Mangalam Birla assumed the position of chairman at the Aditya Birla Group, doubts were raised about his ability to handle a giant business house with interests spanning viscose, textiles, and garments on the one hand, and cement, aluminium, and fertilizers, on the other. But Kumar Mangalam proved the sceptics wrong. He brought in radical changes, changed business strategies, professionalized the entire group, and replaced/redesigned the internal work system of ABG. He reduced his group's dependence on the cyclic commodities sectors by entering consumer products. Kumar Mangalam has exhibited his leadership skills in driving the Aditya Birla Group. Apart from consolidating the group's position in existing businesses, Kumar Mangalam has also ventured into sunrise sectors like cellular telephony, asset management, software, and business process outsourcing (BPO).

Kumar Mangalam, in addition to his efforts in the Birla group, also holds several key positions on various regulatory and professional boards, including chairmanship of the advisory committee constituted by the Ministry of Company Affairs for 2006 and 2007, membership of the Prime Minister's Council on Trade and Industry, chairmanship of the board of trade reconstituted by the Minister of Commerce and Industry, and membership of the central board of directors of the Reserve Bank of India.

Kumar Mangalam implemented innovative, breakthrough management practices, built meritocracy and a learning organization, espoused highest corporate governance principles in his companies in India and overseas, established operations in twenty-five countries across the globe. Kumar Mangalam has nurtured tomorrow's leader today through his role as inspirational educationist, as chancellor of the Birla Institute of Technology and Science (BITS), Pilani, and as member of the London Business School's Asian Regional Advisory Board. He has instituted the Aditya Birla India Centre at the London Business School and stoked interest in Indian managerial success stories as case studies and in doing so weaved India Inc. into the texture of that world-renowned institution. In order to take education to the interiors, Kumar Mangalam has established more than forty fine schools. He has spearheaded changes without losing continuity, and has been global in vision but remained Indian at heart.

Kumar Mangalam opines that 'making talent' must be a strategic priority; solving the talent paradox is not an impossible task as it just requires new and innovative ways to hunt talent. He quotes John Gardener who says, 'There are those who perform great deeds and those that make it possible for others to perform great deeds. There are pathfinders and path preservers. There are those who nurture and who inspire. There are those whose excellence involves doing something well and those whose excellence lies in being the kind of people they are, and in their kindness or honesty or courage.' He says that the term 'talent' has a broad connotation. He views talent in terms of the capabilities of people needed for the agenda of a particular organization, and that talent entails having those skills that provide the edge and make a difference to the organization.

While delivering the J.R.D. Tata Memorial Award Lecture at the All India Management Association, New Delhi, Kumar Mangalam Birla, on 21 February 2009, addressed four issues of leadership: Why does the Aditya Birla Group need global leaders? What are the common competencies common to all global leaders? What does the Aditya Birla Group develop global leadership talents? What are the challenges that the Aditya Birla Group faced in creating a global leadership pool?

Kumar Mangalam Birla has been recognized by different forums and won several honours. The major ones among them include Business Leader of the Year

2003 by *The Economic Times,* Businessman of the Year 2003 by *Business India,* and the Ernst & Young Entrepreneur of the Year India in 2005. On 21 February 2009, the All India Management Association, New Delhi, conferred the J.R.D. Tata Corporate Leadership Award on Dr Kumar Mangalam Birla.

RATAN TATA

Ratan Naval Tata was born on 28 December 1937 in Bombay. He was honoured with the Padma Vibhushan award in 2000. He received a B.Sc. degree in architecture with structural engineering from Cornell University in 1962. Ratan Tata had a short stint with Jones and Emmons in Los Angeles, California, before he returned to India in late 1962. He joined the Tata Group and was assigned to various companies before being appointed director-in-charge of the National Radio and Electronics Company (NELCO) in 1971.

In 1981, Ratan Tata was appointed chairman of Tata Industries. He was assigned the challenging tasks of transforming the company into a group strategy think-tank and promoting new ventures in high-technology businesses. In 1991, Ratan Tata took over the chairmanship from J.R.D. Tata. Under him, Tata Consultancy Services went public and Tata Motors was listed on the New York Stock Exchange. In 1998, Tata Motors came up with Tata Indica, the first truly Indian car. The car was the brainchild of Ratan Tata. Currently, Ratan Tata is chairman of Tata Sons, the holding company of the Tata Group. He is also chairman of major Tata companies such as Tata Steel, Tata Motors, Tata Power, Tata Consultancy Services, Tata Tea, Tata Chemicals, Indian Hotels, and Tata Teleservices. He has taken the Tata Group to new heights and under his leadership the group's revenues have grown manifold. He cares for the sentiments of people working in the Tata group companies. About four years back, the company suffered a Rs 500 crore loss when Ratan Tata told executives to give generous increments and so people did not think that the company was a sinking ship.

Dr Ratan Tata is the president of the Indian Institute of Science and chairman of the Council of Management of the Tata Institute of Fundamental Research (TIFR). He is a member of the board of trustees of Cornell University and the University of Southern California and of the Foundation Board of Ohio State University. Additionally, he is a member of the Global Business Council on HIV/AIDS and the Programme Board of the Bill & Melinda Gates Foundation's India AIDS Initiative.

He is chairman of the Government of India's Investment Commission and a member of the Prime Minister's Council on Trade and Industry, the National Hydrogen Energy Board, and the National Manufacturing Competitiveness Council. Dr Ratan Tata also serves on the International Investment Council set up by the President of the Republic of South Africa and the UK Prime Minister's Business Council for Britain. He is a member of the International Advisory Council of Singapore's Economic Development Board, and of the international advisory boards of the Mitsubishi Corporation, the American International Group, JP Morgan Chase, and Rolls-Royce. He also serves on the boards of Fiat SpA and Alcoa. He is also the Asia-Pacific Advisory Committee member of the board of directors of New York Stock Exchange.

Ohio State University conferred an honorary doctorate in business administration on Ratan Tata; the Asian Institute of Technology, Bangkok, awarded an honorary doctorate in technology; University of Warwick bestowed an honorary doctorate in science; and the London School of Economics an honorary fellowship. The Government of India honoured Dr Ratan Tata with its second highest civilian award, the Padma Vibhushan, in 2008.

Azim Hashim Premji

Padma Bhushan Azim Hashim Premji, born on 24 July 1945, is a graduate in electrical engineering from Stanford University.

Premji is chairman of Wipro Technologies, one of the largest software companies in India. He is an icon among Indian businessmen and his success story is a source of inspiration to budding entrepreneurs. He has led Wipro since 1966, from a $2 million hydrogenated cooking fat company to Wipro Limited to a $5 billion revenue information technology, BPO, and R&D services organization with a presence in over fifty countries. He is popularly addressed as 'Premji'. Premji is a value-driven person with one basic idea—to build an organization that is deeply committed to values. He firmly believes that success in business should be the inevitable and eventual outcome. Accordingly, unflinching commitment to values continues to remain at the core of Wipro.

Premji strongly believes that ordinary people are capable of extraordinary things and that the key to this is creating highly charged teams. This indicates his belief in encouraging team building. He takes a personal interest in developing teams and leaders and invests significant time as a faculty in Wipro's leadership development programmes.

According to Premji, the Wipro brand's promise of 'Applying Thought' is the driving force for delivering value for customers, which is at the heart of business success. This has driven Wipro's pioneering efforts in quality, culminating in the 'Wipro Way', which integrates the methods and practices of Six Sigma, 'People Capability Maturity Model' (PCMM), 'Capability Maturity Model Integration (CMMi), and Lean amongst others. The Wipro Way also drives Wipro's focus on applying innovation for direct benefit customers, improving their time-to-market, enhancing their predictability and reliability, and cutting their costs.

Wipro is discharging its corporate social responsibility. Premji is strongly committed to the belief that business organizations have a social responsibility and that this must be discharged by conducting ethical and fair business by involvement with community issues and by building an ecologically sustainable business. Wipro is deeply involved in trying to improve the quality of school education through its 'Wipro Applying Thought in Schools' initiative, in local community causes through 'Wipro Cares', and is determinedly committed to a journey that weaves ecological sensitivity in every aspect of its business and organization.

Over the years, Azim Premji has received many honours and accolades, which he believes are recognition for each person who has contributed to Wipro. *Business Week* in July 2007 listed him amongst the top 30 entrepreneurs in world history, and also featured him on their cover with the sobriquet 'India's Tech King' (October 2003). The *Financial Times* included him in the global list of 25 people who are 'dramatically reshaping the way people live, work or think' and have done most to bring about significant and lasting social, political, or cultural changes (November 2004 and October 2005). In April 2004, *Time* listed him as one of the 100 most influential people in the world. In August 2003, *Fortune* named Premji as one of the 25 most powerful business leaders outside the US, and in March 2003, *Forbes* listed him as one of the ten people globally who have the most 'power to effect change'. The *Economic Times* adjudged Premji as Business Leader of the Year 2004.

In 2005, Premji became the first Indian recipient of the Faraday Medal. The Indian Institute of Technology, Roorkee, and the Manipal Academy of Higher Education have both conferred honorary doctorates on him. XLRI, Jamshedpur, has conferred the Sir Jehangir Ghandy Medal for Industrial and Social Peace. In 2000, the Visvesvaraya Technological University conferred the Sir M. Visvesvaraya Memorial Award on him. The Institute of Electronics and Telecommunication Engineers conferred an honorary fellowship on him. He is a non-executive director on the board of the Reserve Bank of India. He is also a member of the Prime Minister's Committee for Trade and Industry in India.

In the year 2001, Premji established the Azim Premji Foundation, a not-for-profit organization with a vision of significantly contributing to quality primary education for every child, in order to build a just, equitable, and humane society. Funds for this foundation have been personally contributed by Premji. The current programmes of the Azim Premji Foundation engage 2.5 million children in more than 17,000 schools across India. The *Economic Times* recognized the Azim Premji Foundation, in October 2006, as the Corporate Citizen of the Year.

In January 2005, the Government of India conferred upon him the Padma Bhushan.

DHIRUBHAI AMBANI

The renowned industrialist Dhirubhai Ambani was born on 28 December 1932 at Chorwad, Gujarat, into a Modh family. His father was a schoolteacher. Obviously, he did not inherit a business. He started his entrepreneurial career by selling 'bhajias' to pilgrims in Mount Girnar over the weekends. Isn't it astonishing? However, after doing his matriculation at the age of 16, Dhirubhai moved to Aden, Yemen. He worked there as a gas station attendant and as a clerk in an oil company. He returned to India in 1958 with Rs 50,000 and set up a textile trading company. With the able assistance of his two sons, Mukesh and Anil, Dhirubhai Ambani built India's largest private sector company, Reliance India Limited, from scratch. Over time, his business diversified into core specialization in petrochemicals with additional interests in telecommunications, information technology, energy, power, retail, textiles, infrastructure services, capital markets, and logistics.

He built India's largest private sector company and created an equity cult in the late 1970s and is regarded as an icon for enterprise in India. Reliance is the first Indian company to feature in the Forbes 500 list. He founded Reliance as a textile company and led its evolution as a global leader in the materials and energy value chain businesses. Dhirubhai Ambani epitomized the spirit of 'dare to dream and learn to excel'. The Reliance Group is a living testimony to his indomitable will, single-minded dedication, and an unrelenting commitment to his goals. Dhirubhai shaped India's equity culture, attracted millions of retail investors in a market till then dominated by financial institutions, and revolutionized capital markets. His credit lies in generating billions of rupees in wealth for those who put their trust in his companies. His efforts helped create an 'equity cult' in the Indian capital market. With innovative instruments like the convertible debenture, Reliance quickly became a favourite of the stock market in the 1980s.

It is his visionary leadership that led the Reliance Group to emerge as the largest business conglomerate in India, and carved out a distinct place for itself among the global corporate giants. The group's track record of consistent growth is exemplary and unparalleled in Indian industry, perhaps internationally too. Today, the group's turnover represents nearly 3 per cent of India's GDP. Presumably, Dhirubhai is perhaps the first Indian businessman who recognized the strategic significance of investors and discover the vast untapped potential of the capital markets and channellized it for the growth and development of industry. He created an unbreakable bond of implicit trust between him and the shareholders. They placed their savings in his care and he worked with unflinching sincerity to get them the best returns. He brought happiness and prosperity into the homes of millions of investors. He challenged conventional wisdom in several areas and utilized his unique vision to redefine the potential of the Indian corporate sector. Dhirubhai Ambani was among the most enterprising Indian entrepreneurs. His life journey is reminiscent of the rags-to-riches story. He actually rewrote Indian corporate history and built a truly global corporate group for which he will be remembered forever.

It is not true that he was only an industrialist. He was an exceptional human being and an outstanding leader. A man far ahead of his times, he exhibited a dauntless entrepreneurial spirit. He dared to dream on a scale unimaginable before in Indian industry. But he realized whatever he dreamt. His life and achievements prove that backed by confidence. His life and achievements prove that confidence, courage, sacrifice, high commitment, and conviction helped to translate his dream to reality and be an icon in the industrial scenario.

Dhirubhai Ambani in his passage emphasized limitless growth, dreaming bigger, higher ambitions, deeper commitment, working with determination and with perfection for success, pursuing goals even in the face of difficulties, and converting adversities into opportunities, creating a proper work environment for youth, extending them the support they need, making the best use of their infinite sources of energy, relying on relationships and trust as the foundation of growth, betting on people, beating rather than meeting deadlines, not giving up, and treating courage as conviction. Under his leadership, in 1992 Reliance became the first Indian company to raise money in the global markets, its high credit-taking in international markets limited only by India's sovereign rating.

Dhirubhai Ambani bagged several awards: the Federation of Indian Chambers of Commerce and Industry (FICCI) named him Indian Entrepreneur of the 20th Century; a poll conducted by the *Times of India* in 2000 voted him 'greatest creator of wealth in the century'; TNS–Mode survey identified his as 'India's Most Admired Chief Executive'; *Asia Week* identified him among Asia's 50 most powerful people.

Dhirubhai was gifted with the power to overcome roadblocks on his way, and the vision to change the destiny of nations, to alter the course of corporate history. He was an institution and empire builder. This great man died on 6 July 2002 in Mumbai. The legend called Dhirubhai Ambani will never die; his spirit will live on forever. He is survived by two noted industrialists, Mukesh Ambani and Anil Ambani.

JACK WELCH

Jack Welch was born in 1935 in Salem, Massachusetts, to John, an Irish American railroad conductor with Boston & Maine Railroad, and Grace, a housewife. Family background matters, but not always. Welch, the only son of the family, attended Salem High School and later the University of Massachusetts, graduating in 1957 with a B.Sc. degree in chemical engineering. Welch went on to receive his MS and Ph.D. at the University of Illinois in 1960.

Welch joined General Electric (GE) in 1960 as a junior engineer. He joined fresh from a Ph.D. programme at a salary of $10,500 annually and determined make it $30,000 by age 30. However, the promotions started coming, many of them raised his stature, and by the mid-1970s, Jack began to think that 'maybe I could run the place one day'. Jack had many odds against him. Many of his peers regarded him as the round peg in a square hole, too different from GE. In the words of Welch, 'I was brutally honest and outspoken. I was impatient and, to many, abrasive. My behaviour wasn't the norm, especially the frequent parties at local bars to celebrate victories, large or small.'

Welch was once counselled by Reuben Gutoff, a young executive two levels higher than Welch, when Welch was displeased with the $1000 raise offered after his first year, as well as the strict bureaucracy within GE. Welch planned to leave the company to work with International Minerals & Chemicals, Illinois. Gutoff identified Welch as too valuable a resource for the company. He took Welch and his first wife Carolyn out to dinner at the Yellow Aster in Pittsfield, and spent time trying to convince Welch to stay. Gutoff was hell-bent on keeping Welch at GE. Gutoff vowed to work to change the bureaucracy, to create a small-company environment. Welch was surprised to learn that Gutoff shared his frustration with the bureaucracy. Gutoff showed Welch that he really cared.

Jack Welch knew the key to hiring smart people. 'The smartest people in the world hire the smartest people in the world,' declared Welch. Under his watch, Welch and his handpicked team of 4E (energy, energize, edge, and execute) leaders transformed GE from a lumbering manufacturing behemoth into one of the world's most agile enterprises that had 'change in the blood'. Jack Welch and GE used the celebrated 4E model to measure leadership potential and enhance profitability at every level of the organization.

Jack Welch is one of the most admired, emulated and studied chief executive officers of the twentieth century. His visionary initiatives and concepts and adaptive management strategies earned him the title of the most effective CEO in history (Krames 2002). Michael D. Eisner, chairman and CEO, Walt Disney Company, said, 'Jack Welch gave team leadership new meaning as he took an industrial giant and turned it into an industrial colossus with a heart and a soul and a brain.' Welch grew to fame in the business world through his management success and skills during his many years at GE. He turned the struggling slow-moving giant of a company into a dynamic growth company revered by many. During his twenty years of leadership at GE, Welch increased the value of the company from $13 billion to several hundred billion.

Welch strived to eradicate inefficiencies by trimming inventories and disregarding the bureaucracy. You have seen that GE's bureaucratic style of management had almost led him to leave the company in the past when Gutoff counselled and convinced him to stay on. He also pushed the managers to become more productive. He shut down factories, reduced payrolls, and cut lacklustre old-line units. Welch's philosophy was that a company should be either number one or two in a particular industry, or else leave it completely. Although he was initially treated with contempt by those under him for his policies, they eventually grew to respect him. Welch's strategy was later adopted by other CEOs across the corporate world.

GE saw great growth and expansion under Welch's leadership. He streamlined operations, acquired new businesses, and ensured that each business under the GE umbrella was one of the best in its field. The company was able to expand dramatically during the twenty years of his leadership from 1981 to 2001. In GE's April 1995 employee survey, quality emerged as a concern of many employees. At that time, GE was running at three to four Sigma. Getting to Motorola's Six Sigma quality level means you have fewer than 3.4 defects per million operations in manufacturing or service process. Welch adopted the Six Sigma quality programme in late 1995. His management ideas and leadership skills are both admired by business commentators and imitated by business leaders worldwide.

Welch was named vice-president of GE in 1972. He moved up the ranks to become senior vice-president in 1977 and vice-chairman in 1979. Welch became GE's youngest chairman and CEO in 1981, succeeding Reginald H. Jones. In about a year, by 1982, Welch had disassembled much of the earlier management put together by Jones. In 1981 he made a speech in New York City called 'Growing Fast in a Slow-Growth Economy'. It is believed that the audience took the message to heart. In 1986, GE acquired NBC, which was located in Rockefeller Center; Welch subsequently took up an office in the GE Building at 30 Rockefeller Plaza. During the 1990s, Welch helped to modernize GE by shifting from manufacturing to financial services through numerous acquisitions.

Each year, Welch would fire the bottom 10 per cent of his managers. He earned a reputation for brutal candour in his meetings with executives. He would push his managers to perform, but he would reward those in the top 20 per cent with bonuses and stock options. He also expanded the stock options programme at GE from just top executives to nearly one-third of all employees. Welch is also known for dismantling the nine-layer management hierarchy and introducing a sense of informality in the company.

He earned the company massive revenues. In 1980, the year before Welch became CEO, GE recorded revenues of roughly $26.8 billion. In 2000, the year before he left, revenues had increased to nearly $130 billion. When Jack Welch left GE, the company had gone from a market value of $14 billion to over $410 billion at the end of 2004, making it the most valuable and largest company in the world. In 1999 he was named 'Manager of the Century' by *Fortune* magazine.

Welch had little time for bureaucracy and archaic business ways. If managers didn't change, they were replaced with someone who could. Managers were given free rein as long as they followed the GE ethic of constant change and striving to do better. He ran GE like a small dynamic business able to change as opportunities arose or when a business became unprofitable.

During his 20-years at GE, Welch's management skills became almost legendary. His no-nonsense leadership style gave him a reputation of being hard, even ruthless, but also fair when making business decisions. At the time of his retirement, Welch received a salary of $4 million a year, followed by his record retirement plan of $8 million a year.

After retiring as GE chairman in 2001, Welch wrote a best-selling memoir, *Jack, Straight from the Gut*, and currently consults with several Fortune 500 businesses.

STEVEN PAUL JOBS

Steven Paul Jobs was born on 24 February 1955 in San Francisco. He was adopted by Paul and Clara Jobs of Mountain View, Santa Clara County, California, who named him Steven Paul. Jobs attended Cupertino Junior High School and Homestead High School in Cupertino, California, and normally attended after-school lectures at the Hewlett-Packard Company in Palo Alto, California. He was soon hired there as a summer employee and worked with Steve Wozniak. In 1972, Jobs graduated from high school and enrolled in Reed College in Portland, Oregon. Although he dropped out after only one semester, he continued auditing classes at Reed, such as one in calligraphy. Later in a graduation ceremony, Jobs said: 'If I had never dropped in on that single course in college, the Mac would have never had multiple typefaces or proportionally spaced fonts.' In his early life, Jobs worked as a technician at Atari, a manufacturer of popular video games, with the primary intent of saving money for a spiritual retreat to India. Jobs then travelled to India with a Reed College friend in search of spiritual enlightenment. He came back a Buddhist with his head shaved and wearing traditional Indian clothing. Jobs grew up in the apricot orchards, which later became known as Silicon Valley, and still lives there with his wife and three children.

Steven Jobs was formerly CEO of Pixar Animation Studios. In 1976, Jobs and Stephen Wozniak, with funding from multi-millionaire A.C. 'Mike' Markkula, founded Apple, Inc. Jobs and Wozniak had been friends for several years, having met in 1971. Jobs is the younger of the two. Jobs managed to interest Wozniak in assembling a computer and selling it. Steven and Apple co-founder Steve Wozniak invented one of the first commercially successful personal computers in the late 1970s—affordable compared to other computers of the time. In the next decade, Jobs was among the first to foresee the commercial potential of the mouse-driven graphical user interface.

As Apple continued to expand, the company began looking for an experienced executive to help manage its expansion. In 1983, Jobs lured John Sculley away from Pepsi-Cola to serve as Apple's CEO, asking, 'Do you want to spend the rest of your life selling sugared water to children, or do you want a chance to change the world?' The following year, Apple set out to do just that, starting with a Super Bowl television commercial titled, '1984'. At Apple's annual shareholders meeting on 24 January 1984, an emotional Jobs introduced the Macintosh to a wildly enthusiastic audience; a key member of Apple Mackintosh, Andy Hertzfeld, described the scene as 'pandemonium'. The Macintosh became the first commercially successful small computer with a graphical user interface. Of course, the development of the Mac was started by an American human–computer interface expert Jef Raskin, and eventually taken over by Jobs.

Steven Jobs was a persuasive and charismatic director for Apple. Yet, some of his employees described him as an erratic and temperamental manager. An industry-wide sales slump towards the end of 1984 caused a deterioration in Jobs's working relationship with Sculley. In the year 1985 Jobs got entangled in a power struggle with the board of directors, in which he lost. It is also believed that at the end of May 1985, following an internal power struggle and an announcement of significant layoffs, Sculley relieved Jobs of his duties as head of the Macintosh division. In fact, he was forced to resign from Apple.

Jobs founded a computer platform development company specializing in the higher education and business markets NeXT, Inc. (later NeXT Computer, Inc. and NeXT Software, Inc.). The NeXT workstation was technologically advanced; however, it was largely dismissed by industry as cost-prohibitive. The NeXT workstation garnered strong support because of its technical strengths, chief among them its object-oriented software development system. Jobs marketed NeXT products to the scientific and academic fields because of the innovative, experimental new technologies it incorporated (such as the Mach kernel, the digital signal processor chip, and the built-in Ethernet port). Jobs described the unique product 'NeXT Cube' as an 'interpersonal' computer, which he believed was the next step after 'personal' computing. That is, if computers could allow people to communicate and collaborate in an easy way, it would solve a lot of problems with personal computing. During a time when email for most people was plain text, Jobs loved to demonstrate NeXT's email system, 'NeXTMail', as an example of his 'interpersonal' philosophy. NeXTMail was one of the first to support universally visible, clickable embedded graphics and audio within email. Jobs always loved to work for NeXT with aesthetic perfection, as evidenced by such things as the NeXTcube's magnesium case. The hardware division of NeXT had to put in considerable efforts into this. After having sold only 50,000 machines, NeXT transitioned fully to software development with the release of NeXTSTEP/Intel. Jobs's passion for continuous improvement and unending support to designers and the development group made this possible.

In 1986, Jobs acquired the computer graphics division of Lucasfilm Ltd, which was spun off as Pixar Animation Studios (PAS). He remained CEO and majority shareholder until its acquisition by the Walt Disney Company in 2006. Jobs is currently the Walt Disney Company's largest individual shareholder and a member of its board of directors. He is considered a leading figure in both the computer and entertainment industries.

In 1996, Apple announced that it would buy NeXT. The deal was finalized in late 1996. In 1997, Apple Computer, Inc. bought out NeXT, and thus Steve Jobs came back to the company, after an era of having co-founded it. He soon became Apple's interim CEO when the directors lost confidence in and ousted the then CEO Gil Amelio in a boardroom coup. In March 1998, in order to concentrate Apple's efforts on returning to profitability, Jobs immediately terminated a number of projects such as Newton, Cyberdog, and OpenDoc. In the coming months, many employees developed a fear of encountering Jobs while riding in the elevator, 'afraid that they might not have a job when the doors opened'. Jobs's summary executions were rare, but a handful of victims were enough to terrorize a whole company. Following the acquisition of NeXT, its technology found its way into Apple products, most notable being the NeXTSTEP. Under Jobs's guidance, the company increased sales significantly with the introduction of the iMac and other new products; since then, appealing designs and powerful branding have worked well for Apple. At the 2000 Macworld Expo, Jobs officially dropped the 'interim' modifier from his title at Apple and became permanent CEO. It is said that Jobs joked at the time that he would be using the title 'iCEO.'

As on date, the company has branched out, introduced and improved upon other digital appliances. The company has introduced the iPod portable music player, the iTunes digital music software, and the iTunes Store, and ventured into consumer electronics and music distribution. In 2007, Apple entered the cellular phone business with the introduction of the iPhone, a multi-touch display cellphone, iPod, and internet device. While stimulating innovation, Jobs also reminds his employees that 'real artists ship', by which he means that delivering working products on time is as important as innovation and attractive design.

Apple leads the industry in innovation with its award-winning Macintosh computers, OS X operating system, and consumer and professional applications software. Apple is also leading the digital music revolution, having sold almost 200 million iPods and over 6 billion songs from its iTunes online store.

Steve Jobs also co-founded PAS, which has created eight of the most successful and beloved animated films of all time: *Toy Story, A Bug's Life, Toy Story 2, Monsters, Inc., Finding Nemo, The Incredibles, Cars,* and *Ratatouille.* Pixar has won 20 Academy Awards and its films have grossed more than $4 billion at the worldwide box office to date. Pixar merged with the Walt Disney Company in 2006 and Steve Jobs now serves on Disney's board of directors.

The management style of Jobs has always been distinguishable from others. Jobs is both admired and criticized for his consummate skill at persuasion and salesmanship. Much has been made of Jobs's aggressive and demanding personality.

Fortune noted that he 'is considered one of Silicon Valley's leading egomaniacs'. Steven Paul Jobs has received many achievements and honour some of which are the following:

In 1985, he was awarded the National Medal of Technology from President Ronald Reagan. Jobs is among the first people to receive this honour.

In 1987, he bagged the Jefferson Award for Public Service in the category 'Greatest Public Service by an Individual 35 Years or Under'.

On 27 November 2007, Jobs was named the most powerful person in business by *Fortune* magazine.

On 5 December 2007, California Governor Arnold Schwarzenegger and First Lady Maria Shriver inducted Jobs into the California Hall of Fame, located at the California Museum for History, Women and the Arts.

CONCLUDING REMARKS

We know that wisdom is knowing what is to be done, skill is knowing how to do it, and virtue is doing that. From this standpoint, we can conclude that the organizational leaders discussed above are all wise, possess skills, and have virtue. They are all great personalities, capturing the minds of people. But, if you think deeply, you will find that their inner core was similar.

In the first chapter of this book you have read about the universal inner structure of successful leaders: knowledge of the job, of people, of self, and courage, will power, initiative, and, most importantly, selflessness. All leader achievers are selfless, philanthropic, altruistic, and discharge corporate social responsibility.

EXERCISES

1. An organizational leader possesses a variety of skills; in demanding situations he/she applies a particular skill or a skill set from his/her arsenal. Can you identify the skills used in a case of merger and acquisition?

2. A tale is told of a man in Paris during the upheaval in 1948. He saw a friend marching after a crowd towards the barricades. On warning him that these could not be held against the troops and that he had better keep way, he received this reply, 'I must follow them. I am their leader.' How do the business leaders mentioned in this chapter remind you of the above description of a great leader?

3. How do you think Narayana Murthy's life and achievements at Infosys prove that it is the leader's value and emotional maturity that constructs the culture of the workplace?

4. In the light of the statement below, describe the attributes of a transformational leader whom you like most and consider your role model.

'If you fail to honour your people,
They will fail to honour you;
It is said of a good leader that
When the work is done, the aim fulfilled,
The people will say, "We did this ourselves".'

REFERENCES

AIMA (2009), *AIMA News* (Newsletter of the All India Management Association), New Delhi, January–March 2009.

Birla, Kumar Mangalam (2008), Confronting the Great Talent Crunch, *Indian Management* (Journal of the All India Management Association), February 2008, Vol. 47, No. 2, pp. 22–24.

Krames, Jeffrey. A. (2005), *Jack Welch and the 4Es of Leadership*, Tata McGraw-Hill, New Delhi.

Krames, Jeffrey A. (2002), *The Jack Welch Lexicon of Leadership*, McGraw-Hill, New York.

Majumdar, Shyamal and Leslie Dmonte (2008), Down to Earth, *Indian Management* (Journal of the All India Management Association), Vol. 47, No. 12, December 2008, pp. 14–27.

Welch, Jack and John A. Byrne (2001), *Jack Straight from the Gut*, Warner Books, Inc. New York.

Web Resources

en.wikipedia.org/wiki/NeXT (accessed on 5 May 2009).

www.4to40.com/legends/index.asp?id=2008 (accessed on 5 May 2009).

www.apple.com/pr/bios/jobs.html (accessed on 5 May 2009).

www.iloveindia.com/indian-heroes/kumar-mangalam-birla.html (accessed on 25 December and 10 April 2009).

www.ril.com/html/aboutus/founder.html (accessed on 12 April 2009).

www.tata.com/aboutus/articles/inside.aspx?artid=uBZjT+/ooH8= (accessed on 12 April 2009).

www.wipro.com/aboutus/azim_profile.htm (accessed on 12 April 2009).

Index